What We Know about Emotional Intelligence

WHAT WE KNOW ABOUT EMOTIONAL INTELLIGENCE

How It Affects Learning, Work, Relationships, and Our Mental Health

Moshe Zeidner, Gerald Matthews, and Richard D. Roberts

A Bradford Book
The MIT Press
Cambridge, Massachusetts
London, England

152,4
Zei

MIT Press books may be purchased at special quantity discounts for business or sales promotional use. For information, please email special_sales@mitpress.mit.edu or write to Special Sales Department, The MIT Press, 55 Hayward Street, Cambridge, MA 02142.

This book was set in Times New Roman and Syntax on 3B2 by Asco Typesetters, Hong Kong and was printed and bound in the United States of America.

Library of Congress Cataloging-in-Publication Data

Zeidner, Moshe.
What we know about emotional intelligence : how it affects learning, work, relationships, and our mental health / Moshe Zeidner, Gerald Matthews, and Richard D. Roberts.
  p.   cm.
"A Bradford book."
Includes bibliographical references and index.
ISBN 978-0-262-01260-7 (hardcover : alk. paper)—ISBN 978-0-262-25501-1 (el)
1. Emotional intelligence. I. Matthews, Gerald. II. Roberts, Richard D. III. Title.
BF576.Z45   2009
152.4—dc22   2008038272

10 9 8 7 6 5 4 3 2 1

to Omer and Yair Zeidner, with admiration and love

to Diana Ciupka

to Cristina Aicher, Matthew D. Roberts, and Lionel R. Benevides

Contents

V EMOTIONAL INTELLIGENCE... REVISITED

Foreword

Sir Henry Cavendish (1731–1810) was a brilliant scientist; emotionally, however, he was a dud. Among other things, he was deathly afraid of meeting strangers. On one occasion at a meeting, he was introduced with fanfare to a visiting scientist. Dumbfounded, Cavendish stood with his head bowed; then, spying an opening in the crowd, he hastily fled to his carriage. Women, especially, posed a problem. Cavendish had his house constructed so that he would not meet any female servant; if by chance one should cross his path, she was dismissed immediately.

Cavendish illustrates one kind of emotional ineptitude—a person who feels deeply but inappropriately. Another kind is illustrated by the psychopath who is adroit at manipulating the emotions of others, and yet who is unable to experience emotions himself, whether it be empathy with the suffering of his victims or fear of punishment for causing their plight. This is not to imply that everyone who is unable to experience emotion is a psychopath. To take a fictional example with whom many people sympathize, Mr. Spock of the television series *Star Trek* lacks emotion; yet he is a valued colleague on the starship Enterprise. Of course, Mr. Spock is not entirely human: His father was a Vulcan, an inhabitant of another planetary system. For better or worse, our emotions, as much as our intelligence, are a sign of our humanity.

About 2,300 years ago Aristotle observed that emotions "may be felt both too much and too little, and in both cases not well; but to feel them at the right times, with reference to the right objects, towards the right people, with the right motive, and in the right way, is what is both intermediate and best, and this is characteristic of virtue" (*Nicomachean Ethics* 1106^{b}20). More than of virtue, this is a good description of *emotional intelligence*.

As the quote by Aristotle illustrates, emotional intelligence has long been recognized as an important human characteristic; only within the past two decades, however, has it become the subject of concerted scientific investigation. Also in that time, the topic has captured the popular imagination. The authors of this primer—Zeidner, Matthews, and Roberts—note that a search on Google yields more than 3 million hits under the heading "emotional intelligence," of which they estimate fewer than 1,000 are to scientific publications. The authors are rightly troubled by the way the popular literature has far outpaced scientific research. Also problematic, though in a more favorable way, is the sheer number of scientific publications. If a person were to read one scientific article a day, taking off only Sundays and holidays, it would require more than three years to cover the extant literature. And by the end of three years there would perhaps be another thousand articles to be read. Fortunately for anyone seriously interested in the topic, that need not be a concern. Zeidner, Roberts, and Matthews have proved themselves more than equal to the task. Each is an accomplished researcher in his own right, and together they provide an excellent summary of what is—and is not—known about emotional intelligence. How can emotional intelligence be measured? Is there more than one kind of emotional intelligence, just as there is more than one kind of emotional ineptitude? How is emotional intelligence related to cognitive intelligence (IQ)? What are the real-world consequences of emotional intelligence? Can emotional intelligence be taught? These and other questions are addressed in a manner that is authoritative, objective, and yet accessible to the interested reader.

But why should the reader be interested? Zeidner, Matthews, and Roberts speculate that one reason for the popular interest in emotional intelligence is the egalitarian ideal. Those who are poor in words and numbers (the traditional components of IQ) may still succeed emotionally. That, at least, is the hype behind workshops on emotional intelligence, which have become a growth industry. In this volume the reader will find a critical yet constructive review of the evidence behind the hype.

There is another, more subtle reason why the reader should be interested. Throughout Western history, a deep divide has existed between reason and emotion, action and passion. In the words of Blaise Pascal— the great seventeenth-century mathematician and sometime mystic—"the heart has its reasons, which reason does not know" (*Pensées* IV, p. 277). The concept of emotional intelligence bridges that divide, allowing intelligence to be viewed from the perspective of emotion and emotion from the perspective of intelligence, and our understanding of each is enriched in the process.

James R. Averill

Preface

In this book we aim to present the state of the art of an emerging science of emotional intelligence. In so doing, we examine the foundations of knowledge, research, assessment methods, applications, and (wherever possible) accepted standards upon which understanding of the construct has, and can be further, developed. The research presented in the various chapters of this book is grounded both in our own work and in the writings of scores of researchers tackling the issues of emotional intelligence, emotion, intelligence, and/or personality around the globe. We trust that you find such a synthesis amenable.

Over what is close to two decades, emotional intelligence—or EI, as you will frequently hear it referred to—has emerged as one of the most high-powered modern psychological constructs. In these two letters are embedded competence in perceiving and communicating emotions, understanding the emotions of self and others, and effectively regulating emotions. The EI concept has prospered partly because of a cultural "zeitgeist" that emphasizes the positive role of the emotions and the more empathic side of the human psyche. The relatively new discipline of "positive psychology" reinforces this concern by placing great importance on having a rich and fulfilling life. Conversely, far too many people misunderstand their own emotional reactions, fail to control emotional outbursts, or act stupidly under various pressures—with deleterious consequences for self, others, and society. A culture-driven concern with emotions is complemented by increasing efforts at a scientifically meaningful assessment of individual differences in "soft skills." Across various applied disciplines, covering the home, work, and school, the challenge is to develop reliable and valid tests especially of one of these skills—a person's emotional intelligence—and to develop interventions that may remediate those that are low in EI effectively enough to affect learning and broader social development.

With this societal thrust, almost since its inception into the scientific literature, emotional intelligence has received widespread public attention. This interest subsumes Daniel Goleman's (1995) book on the topic, which appeared on the *New York Times* Best-Sellers List, a *Time Magazine* (Gibbs 1996) article devoted to detailed exposition of the topic, and numerous mentions in mass media, virtually every day. There are besides a plethora of trade texts dealing with self-help and management practices, assessment, and other practical applications related to EI, "EQ," the "hot intelligences," and related concepts. Popular interest notwithstanding, scientific investigation of a clearly identified construct of emotional intelligence is sparse, though growing. Tests and measures of EI have proliferated over time, but many are of uncertain validity. A particular difficulty is that much EI research simply repackages knowledge familiar to psychologists working within the fields of personality, intelligence, and applied psychology. Moreover the media hype, vast number of trade texts, and Web sites devoted to the topic often re-couch findings from scientific fields to fit into the fad rather than deal with a near consensually defined construct that scientists are grappling to articulate.

The reach of EI into disparate domains appears as expansive as unconstrained definitions of the concept allow. Thus EI has commonly been offered as a panacea for problems and maladies in education, work, health, school, and personal relations. Do you have problems relating to people whenever you share a social encounter? Is the school in your district failing to meet state or national standards? Are you overwhelmed by stress and other hassles in your daily life? Are you having issues with your partner? Perhaps your problem is low emotional literacy. There is no shortage of coaches and consultants who will remedy your unfortunate deficiency, on very reasonable terms. Training EI at work or school may indeed offer a solution to many of society's problems, but interventions must be soundly based in psychological theory and careful definition and analysis of emotional competencies. The present book seeks to ask and answer the simple question: Is this happening in applied settings?

Yet another reason for the popularity of the EI concept is that it offers an optimistic outlook and future for those individuals who are not particularly successful in achieving high scores on intelligence and achievement tests. These same individuals can now aspire to succeed and progress up the social, corporate, and economic ladder based on their high "EQ." Similarly the EI construct gives hope for a more utopian, classless society. This vision for the future stands in contrast to research suggesting that there is a preordained "cognitive elite" (Herrnstein and Murray 1994).

According to this perspective, EI is within anyone's reach to learn and cultivate. Furthermore proponents of EI claim that individuals can enjoy happier and more fulfilled lives if they are aware of their own emotions and those of other people and are then able to regulate emotions effectively. Clearly, the concept appears to resonate with the emotional experiences of most people, who do believe that such a concept exists: When their heart speaks, they want to learn how to tune in, and they want to learn how to listen.

However, there are various obstacles to realizing the potential benefits of studying emotional intelligence. First, there is no agreed-upon definition or conceptualization of the concept. It is unclear whether EI is cognitive or noncognitive, whether it refers to explicit or implicit knowledge of emotion, and whether it refers to a basic aptitude or to some adaptation to a specific social and cultural milieu. Second, it is uncertain how EI may be best measured. For example, both objective tests and self-report questionnaires have been developed, but scores on different instruments fail to converge. Third, the practical utility of tests for EI is limited by these conceptual and psychometric deficiencies. There is as yet too little validity evidence for tests to be used with confidence in making real-world decisions, such as clinical diagnosis or high stake testing for academic admissions. Moreover intervention programs that seek to raise EI typically lack a clear theoretical and methodological basis, and often employ a ragbag of techniques, whose psychological effects are indeterminate.

Goals of This Book

The main goal of this book is to provide a state-of-the-art account of conceptualization, assessment, and application of emotional intelligence. In writing our lengthy 2002 tome—*Emotional Intelligence: Science and Myth* (MIT Press)—we were not entirely certain whether EI was merely a passing fad or a concept here to stay for the long haul. In the intervening years EI has become an established player in modern-day psychological research, appearing as one of the most widely discussed aspects of intelligence in the current literature. In view of the growing interest and burgeoning research on various aspects of EI, and the progress achieved by researchers working in the field, the time seems ripe for presenting an up-to-date "executive summary" of what we have learned. Such a summary should, and does, include discussion of theory, assessment, and applications of EI and key issues that remain unresolved in these areas and in still further domains.

This book aims at shedding light on the scientific status and validity of the construct of emotional intelligence, in particular. Whereas there are over 3 million hits when one "Googles" *emotional intelligence*, there are less than 1,000 scientific publications in peer-reviewed journals. These facts point to a disjunction between the popular treatment of EI and the scientific discourse, and critical discussion, surrounding the topic. This book examines emotional intelligence from the perspective especially of theory and practice in the areas of intelligence, personality, emotions, individual differences, and applied psychology.

The focus of our book is decidedly then on the scientific rather than folklore or anecdotal stories. It is necessary for a science of EI to (1) have an adequate methodology for assessment of the construct; (2) demonstrate its partial (or complete) independence from other, seemingly analogous, concepts; and (3) show how it can explain phenomena in a parsimonious way. Our approach throughout is to systematically address these issues. In addition to tackling concepts and definitions, we have recently been actively involved in attempting to determine current consensus and controversy among leading researchers in the field (Matthews et al. 2007), as well as analyzing data on multiple samples given prominent measures of EI, personality, and intelligence (e.g., Roberts, Schulze, et al. 2006). We trust that these models, insights, and data, woven into the present exposition, represent "cutting-edge" empirical thinking and research. We also trust that they help the reader to bring into sharp relief the prospects and limitations of the emotional intelligence concept.

Organization and Structure of This Book

The chapters are arranged to reflect five broad, but overlapping, categories that are described in the passages that follow.

In part I we discuss basic issues related to research on emotional intelligence, and provide a conceptual framework for reviewing the evidence surrounding emotion, ability, and other individual differences constructs. Chapter 1 provides a broad overview of the construct of emotional intelligence, summarizing "what's what" and "what's not" with respect to conceptualization of the construct. More specifically, this chapter delineates the historical and sociocultural backdrop for the emergence of EI; highlights reasons for the salience and recent widespread interest in the construct; and surveys current directions in mapping out the conceptual domain of EI.

Part II expands on a scientific framework for understanding the conceptualization and operationalization of the EI construct, first introduced in chapter 1. Chapter 2 also delineates key issues related to assessing and validating new scientific constructs, in general, and EI, in particular. The chapter summarizes criteria that the concept of EI should satisfy (e.g., reliability, meaningful test-criterion relations) and critically assesses the success of current measures in meeting established standards. Chapters 3 and 4, respectively, provide the conceptual framework for understanding the grand constructs that serve as building blocks for the hybrid concept of emotional intelligence—intelligence and personality. Specifically, chapter 3 reviews key issues, concepts, and controversies that over a century of research on intelligence have given us. A number of formal structural models of intelligence are presented, and the implications that emerge from these models for the concept of EI are discussed. Key ability-based assessments of EI are presented and analyzed, with directions for future research and test development also presented. Chapter 4 discusses ways of understanding personality traits and emotion states that might provide a basis for understanding EI. Based on a cognitive-adaptational framework, key dimensions of personality are viewed as adaptive specializations. The chapter also differentiates personality and ability models of EI and surveys current instruments that view EI within the framework of personality trait assessment.

Part III looks at the developmental facets of the construct and its role in social contexts and in stressful daily encounters; in short, how the new construct of EI may be integrated with the existing psychology of emotional functioning in real life. Chapter 5 employs the authors' investment model as a heuristic framework to understand factors contributing to the origins and development of emotional competence during childhood, including biology, primary socialization, and adaptive behaviors. The next two chapters focus on the adaptive benefits that might result from individual differences in emotion competencies in social contexts. Chapter 6 discusses the potential adaptive role of EI, as well as personality dispositions, in social situations. The chapter concludes with an analysis of the potential disutility of EI in certain social contexts. Chapter 7 focuses on emotional intelligence and personality dispositions in coping with stress. Various hypotheses regarding the causal mechanisms relating EI to adaptive coping are presented and available research evaluated.

Part IV is devoted to examining the utility of EI in various applied settings. Specifically, chapters 8 through 11 discuss the potential importance of EI in educational, occupational, and clinical settings, including evaluation of evidence where applications are purportedly based on EI models. More specifically, chapter 8 discusses current attempts to incorporate EI in the school curricula. The empirical data relating EI to school attainment are presented and attempts to cultivate and train EI in educational settings are considered. Current educational programs for affective education are critically evaluated, as are criteria for the development of EI intervention programs. Chapter 9 examines how EI may impact on organizational success. The empirical research on the association between EI and key outcomes at work (e.g., training, job performance, satisfaction) is reviewed. In chapter 10 we look at the potential role of EI in workplace behaviors that are decidedly toxic by their nature (e.g., aggression and stress). Chapter 11 discusses the nature and origin of clinical disorders related to dysfunction of negative emotions (e.g., anxiety, depression), and links EI to the extensively researched constructs of alexithymia, internalization, and externalization dysfunctions. It also looks at the potential for targeting therapeutic techniques toward EI diagnosis.

Part V identifies consensual issues and basic controversies in the field, pointing to priorities and directions for future research.

Given the widespread public interest in the topic and the extensive coverage of EI by the media, the primary target audience we had in mind in writing the current book is the general educated public. As such, we hope that a wide group of people will enjoy this book. We have included a glossary of terms in the back of the book to make some of the concepts more accessible to the reader, and we urge the reader to use the glossary without fear of favor or prejudice. However, we trust that special interest groups might also find this book useful, especially professionals and students in management, human resources, industrial relations, psychology, psychiatry, education, social work, and the health sciences. In the end, though, the interest showed by any reader to this book serves as a buffer, and welcome respite, from the sound of one hand clapping.

Acknowledgments

We are grateful to a number of colleagues and friends for their support throughout the writing of this book. We wish to thank James Averill, an internationally acclaimed "maven" in the area of emotions and wisdom of the heart, for graciously agreeing to write the foreword. Special thanks are due also to Tom Stone, our trusted editor at the MIT Press, for his guidance, patience, and encouragement throughout the extended writing process. Tom, we couldn't have done it without you!

During the writing of our respective chapters and the editing of this book, the University of Haifa, the Educational Testing Service (ETS), and the University of Cincinnati, provided the facilities and resources necessary to undertake and complete this work.

Richard D. Roberts would like to acknowledge senior staff and management at ETS for supporting the project at various points along its life cycle: Ida Lawrence (senior vice president, Research and Development), Patrick Kyllonen (director, Center for New Constructs); T. J. Elliott (vice president, Strategic Workforce Solutions), Marissa Farnum (associate vice president, New Product Development), and Cathy Wendler (director, Foundational and Validity Research).

In addition, over the several years of working on this book, the authors have additional institutions, supporting mechanisms, and senior individuals to thank:

Moshe Zeidner: Edmund T. Rolls (who sponsored a sabbatical year at the Department of Experimental Psychology, Oxford University).

Richard D. Roberts: Army Research Institute (whose time over the last few months finishing up aspects of this book was supported in part, by US Army Research Institute Contract W91WAW-07-C-0025 to the Educational Testing Service).

Co-authored books can be difficult to finish (let alone start) as anyone who has set out on this onerous, yet rewarding, task will testify. We are hugely indebted to Anthony Betancourt, Rachel Carmel, Muna Haddad, and "Wild" Bill Monagahan, for their work pulling together many different pre-production pieces. (Anthony—in particular—you went above and beyond the call of duty). Warm sentiments to the production team at the MIT Press for making the final leg of this process almost enjoyable. Many thanks are also extended to Moran Barak and Neta Ram for preparing the creative graphics for several of the chapters and to Navit Ogen for helping track down some elusive references.

We are grateful to many people across the globe for other forms of support throughout this extended project. First and foremost, it would be remiss not to acknowledge our respective partners—Esther (Eti) Zeidner, Cristina Aicher, and Diana Ciupka—each of whom have variously lost us for months as we: grappled with who should write what sections, stole time away from home to write pages, filled in a missing reference, or made a new figure or table. To each of you, many thanks for being so supportive in so many different ways. And to the following friends, family, students, and/or colleagues who have helped in so many different ways, a simple, but important thank you very, very much also: Camilla Aicher, Peter Cooper, Walter Emmerich, Amanda Emo, Angie Fellner, Greg Funke, Eugene Gonzales, Krishna Kumar, John D. Mayer, Carolyn MacCann, Heather Nadelman, Gerry Pallier, Juan Carlos Pérez-González, John Sabatini, Ralf Schulze, Sandip Sinahray, Namrata Tognatta, Michaela Turss, and Joel Warm.

This activity has been a challenging, thought provoking, and rewarding collaborative experience (and as it turns out, one that has kept the authors together one way or the other for most of the twenty-first century). We hope this volume will give readers a deeper understanding and appreciation of current emotional intelligence research and help in guiding future theory, research, and applications in this growing domain.

Moshe Zeidner
Richard D. Roberts
Gerry Matthews

INTRODUCING...EMOTIONAL INTELLIGENCE

1 Emotional Intelligence: Mapping out the Terrain

The advantage of the emotions is that they lead us astray, and the advantage of science is that it is not emotional.
—Oscar Wilde, 1891, *The Picture of Dorian Gray*

Emotional intelligence seems to be everywhere. Educators, executives, and life-style gurus have all bowed to the notion that what people need most in contemporary life is emotional awareness, heightened sensitivity, and street smarts. But what is "emotional intelligence"? And why has it assumed such prominence in the present culture?

To answer such questions, it is important to start with a working definition of emotional intelligence. For now, we will take this term to refer to a generic competence in perceiving emotions (both in oneself and in others). This competence also helps us regulate emotions and cope effectively with emotive situations (e.g., Goleman 1995a, b). Thus conceived, emotional intelligence appears important because many people fail to manage emotions successfully. We may be blind to our own emotional reactions. Or we may fail to control our emotional outbursts. Worse still, we may act foolishly under pressure.

From this standpoint the potential importance of emotional intelligence should become self-evident. Have you a problem in a personal relationship or in your marriage? Difficulties coping with work stress and assignments? Is your school climate of concern? Low emotional intelligence may be at play. Training emotional intelligence in schools, workplaces, and psychiatric clinics then offers a viable, and valuable, solution to perceived individual, community, national, and global needs. It is the quick fix panacea for manifest problems in personal relations, at work, and during the educational process.

Despite much recent enthusiasm in the media, trade texts, and even psychological handbooks, some caution and skepticism are requisite. Perhaps emotional intelligence is nothing more than a popular fad along the lines of crystal healing, sexual intelligence, feng shui, and other New Age excesses. Our stated goal in writing this book is to offer a state-of-the-art overview of "what's what and what's not" in the domain of emotional intelligence. We do so by examining the "knowns and unknowns" of "emotional intelligence" from a scientific angle. It is our intention to arm the reader with a cache of facts, figures, and anecdotes from which to evaluate the status of this newly minted construct.

Popular interest in emotional intelligence stems from a perspective that is cross-fertilized by academic studies. These studies seek to develop sophisticated theories of the psychological and biological concomitants, causes, and antecedents of emotionally intelligent behaviors. They also seek accurate measures of these character traits and behaviors. Further still, such studies are conducted to understand how emotional intelligence is related to valued social outcomes and functions. In this chapter we lay out some of the reasons why there has been so much "buzz" surrounding emotional intelligence, as well as its place within a cultural zeitgeist that is increasingly accepting and valuing the expression of human emotions. We also set forth a case for developing a rigorous science of emotional intelligence, touching on different visions proposed by leading authorities. Further we examine why applications of this new construct may be important. This section covers the potential of emotional intelligence research for improving mental health, prosocial behavior, educational outcomes, and occupational success. We conclude the chapter by listing key issues that we will discuss in subsequent chapters.

The Emergence of a New Intelligence

It is of pivotal importance to note, at the outset, that emotional intelligence is thought of as a type of *intelligence*. That is to say, individuals differ by some objective ability in dealing with emotion. It is believed that the ways in which the difference is manifest are complex and varied. Consider thus one of many principled lists of abilities we might compile:

1. Detecting a person's emotions by facial cue, voice pitch and rhythm, bodily posture both standing and sitting

2. Understanding the antecedents and consequences of emotions

3. Facilitating thought by evoking particular emotions

4. Regulating negative emotions such as anger and sadness

The concept of emotion connected to intelligence seems reasonable because we likely encounter emotional geniuses, emotional idiots, and the

Figure 1.1
Emotional stupidity in action during the 2006 FIFA World Cup

typical person of moderate emotional competence in our day-to-day activities. In short, the idea of an intelligence continuum is compelling. Unfortunately, it is often "emotional stupidity" in action that is witnessed in real time by billions across the globe, as highlighted by the example shown in figure 1.1. A contrasting, alternate position is how people typically deal with emotion by a qualitative style of behavior that is neither intrinsically good nor bad; that is, some people tend to be calm whereas others are more excitable. Calmness, however, is not necessarily better (or worse) than excitability. We will have more to say about this way of behaving later in the chapter. The concept of emotional intelligence currently being discussed implies a strict structure that interlinks emotional abilities with other aptitudes, including conventional mental ability. Thus, to understand what is meant by emotional intelligence, we must examine how "emotional" intelligence might be different from standard, consensually agreed-on forms of "cognitive" intelligence.

General Intelligence and Its Critics
The concept of emotional intelligence did not appear out of the blue. It is firmly rooted in past psychological thinking, research, and practice. The concept has come to prominence against a background of dissatisfaction

with conventional theories of intelligence. It has been nurtured beyond infancy by those who contend that a single IQ score does not do justice to all the potential that an individual may possess. To understand the historical underpinnings of emotional intelligence, we briefly discuss the concept of human intelligence and how it is currently viewed by experts.

Most people believe they know what intelligence is, possibly because they have had to take tests of this, or related attributes, over the course of their lives. The term typically refers to intellectual and academic capacities for abstract reasoning, analysis, and problem-solving. Indeed for more than a century psychologists have labored to devise ever more sophisticated tests of such qualities. The efforts have borne fruit to the extent that standardized IQ tests predict an individual's future academic and occupational success. Nobel laureates, college professors, and rocket scientists do in fact typically obtain higher scores on these types of tests than most people. A key assumption is that there is a unitary general intelligence. That is, although people differ somewhat in their aptitudes for particular kinds of thinking—such as verbal or mathematical reasoning—there is an overarching general cognitive ability that contributes to a wide range of intelligent behaviors.

This scientific model of intelligence, which is based on rigorous theory, measurement, and application, undoubtedly captures the essence of what it means to be an intelligent person. Still many psychologists have challenged the notion that intelligence is nothing more than abstract problem-solving ability. Doubts about conventional intelligence go back to the beginnings of the field in the twentieth century. Pioneers of intelligence testing, such as Alfred Binet (see the sidebar on the next page), were aware that general intelligence might not be the only factor important for social functioning (Landy 2005).

Emotional intelligence may be viewed as a subset of the "social intelligence" domain. Landy (2006) traces the term to the educator John Dewey (1909), whom he quotes as follows: "Ultimate moral motives and forces are nothing more or less than social *intelligence* [italics in the original]—the power of observing and comprehending social situations—and *social power* [italics in the original]—trained capacities of control—at work in the service of social interests and aims" (p. 43). Dewey's concern was the school curriculum. Subsequently the psychologist Edward L. Thorndike described social intelligence as an ability distinct from abstract intelligence, defining it as "the ability to manage and understand men and women, boys and girls, to act wisely in human relations" (1920, p. 228). Thorndike never attempted to develop a test for social intelligence, believ-

Alfred Binet (1857–1911)	Brief biography of Alfred Binet, one of the pioneers of intelligence testing
	How did Alfred Binet create the first intelligence test? Fortunately for the millions of children with learning disorders, Binet had spent "quality time" with his daughters. He asked them questions and queried how they solved them. This led to an understanding of their individual differences, and more important, that not all thought processes follow the same course. Binet was thus able to argue against the prevailing view that "lack" of intellect in certain fields was an "illness." His discovery of different kinds of memory led to a government appointment to develop tests intended to identify areas of weakness in school children. In association with Theophile Simon, Binet identified developmental achievement levels expected of normal children. The *mental age* criteria that were the basis of these tests remain a benchmark in assisting children exhibiting poor performance in specific areas. Unfortunately, Binet died only five years after the first use of his test, and the necessary revisions and refinements were left largely to others. The antecedents in Binet's career show how some decisions can lead to change that is for the better. His first degree was in law, after which he worked with Jean-Martin Charcot in hypnosis. He also studied phrenology and is reported to have great sympathy with the physiognomists to boot.

ing that it should be observed in real-life behavior. In the decades that followed, researchers sporadically tried to develop and validate standardized tests for social intelligence. These measures included, for example, tests of the respondent's ability to recognize emotive gestures and facial expressions, measures that bear more than passing resemblance to some contemporary indicators of emotional intelligence.

With behavioral, and later cognitive, models serving as major scientific movements, the status of emotions were relegated to a supporting role in many psychological theories. These accounts variously framed the accepted subject matter of intelligence research as that dealing with behaviors or cognitive thought. In recent years, however, the notion of a unitary, general intelligence has come under attack. For example, Howard Gardner (1983, 1999) has proposed that there are multiple intelligences in addition to abstract reasoning, such as musical and kinesthetic intelligence. Gardner also refers to two types of ability that resemble emotional intelligence, and most likely were a major factor in its development: inter-personal intelligence (understanding the feelings and intentions of others) and intrapersonal intelligence (awareness and discrimination of one's feelings).

Assuming Gardner to be correct, we can no longer refer to people as being more or less intelligent in some general sense. Instead, people typically show more complex patterns of higher functioning for some activities, and lower for others. At the extreme Gardner describes cases of so-called savants who may be subnormal in terms of their intelligence test score but capable of remarkable artistic accomplishments. Movies such as *Forrest Gump* seem to encapsulate this idea as it pertains to the intra- (and inter-) personal realm. Thus the lead character possesses subnormal intellectual talents yet is capable of remarkable life-affirming emotional connections with others. Such fictional accounts are not without precedent, sometimes on the flip side. For example, some individuals with autism or Asperger's syndrome do obtain high IQ scores but fail to understand or connect with people around them.

Origins of the Concept of Emotional Intelligence

The term emotional intelligence—which we will abbreviate to EI—has been attributed to various sources. Literary accounts of Jane Austen's *Pride and Prejudice* refer to various characters possessing this quality (Van Ghent 1953, p. 106–107; see figure 1.2). On Wikipedia (http://en .wikipedia.org 2007), reference is made to the Dutch science fiction author Carl Lans who published two novels in the 1960s elaborating the concept, including use of the phrase "emotional quotient." In scientific psychology, the first reference appears to come from the German psycho-analyst Barbara Leuner. Writing in 1966, she suggested that the halluci-nogenic drug LSD might help women with low emotional intelligence. Leuner believed this condition resulted from early separation from their mothers and led to these women having more emotional problems than their counterparts. (Thankfully perhaps, the use of hallucinogens married with psychotherapy to improve EI has not survived the 1960s.) Wayne Payne (1986) was the first author to use the term in an English language source, arguing that emotional awareness was an important component to develop in children. The first systematic research on EI was conducted by two psychologists whose work is featured prominently in the current volume: Jack Mayer and Peter Salovey (e.g., 1993). Yet the current popularity of EI reflects the impact of a single book, Daniel Goleman's (1995a) *Emotional Intelligence*, an international best seller (Gibbs 1995).

Figure 1.2
Author Jane Austen, to whom the literary critic Dorothy Van Ghent, as early as 1953, attributes various aspects of emotional intelligence in the characters she penned

The Vision Thing: How Daniel Goleman Created Interest in a "New" Intelligence?
Having obtained a PhD from Harvard University, Daniel Goleman became a journalist at the *New York Times*. During his twelve years there he worked on various stories relating to the brain and emotion. After reading a scientific article by Mayer and Salovey, he was inspired to write a book that would become one of the best-selling psychological texts ever: *Emotional Intelligence: Why It Can Matter More Than IQ*. In the book Goleman (1995a) sets out a comprehensive account of EI and its relevance to society. His central thesis is that emotional illiteracy is responsible for many social evils including mental illness, crime, and educational failure. Furthermore people at work often fall short of their potential through failing to manage their emotions appropriately. Job satisfaction and productivity are threatened by unnecessary conflicts with coworkers,

failure to assert one's legitimate needs, and failure to communicate one's feelings to others. Goleman pushes the intelligence envelope in various respects throughout his writings. Some of the ways in which his thesis conflicts with conventional psychology are as follows:

Definition of intelligence   Goleman includes qualities such as optimism, self-control, and moral character as part of intelligence. Normally such qualities are seen as reflecting components of personality, not ability.

Stability of intelligence   Typically cognitive intelligence has been viewed as fairly stable over time. By contrast, Goleman emphasizes that emotional intelligence can be learned and increased, seemingly at any time, over one's life span.

Intelligence in everyday life   In order to enjoy a successful life Goleman (1995a, 1998) claims that "EQ" is more important than IQ. These success factors include such disparate indicators as being promoted at work and maintaining secure and fruitful relationships with others. Indeed a subtext of Goleman's (1995a) book is that IQ is much overrated; as one of the chapter headings reads, "Smart is dumb."

Intelligence with a moral dimension   Conventionally intelligence refers to a set of capabilities and skills that are equally at the service of the philanthropist and the evil genius. Goleman (1995a), however, relates EI to moral character: "emotional literacy goes hand in hand with education for character, for moral development, and for citizenship" (p. 286; see chapter 5 of this volume for a contrarian view).

So what exactly did Goleman (1995a) mean by "emotional intelligence"? His first book set out a laundry list of desirable qualities, including self-confidence, sensitivity, self-awareness, self-control, empathy, optimism, and social skills. Indeed the present authors (Matthews, Zeidner, et al. 2002) criticized Goleman for listing almost every positive quality that was not actually cognitive intelligence. Subsequently Goleman (2001) sought to put the traits that focally define EI on a more systematic basis. This basic schema is reproduced in table 1.1.

Goleman's model suggests two key divisions separating different aspects of EI. First are distinguished those elements of EI that refer to personal competencies (e.g., self-awareness) from those that relate to social competencies (e.g., empathy). This distinction corresponds to Gardner's (1983) intrapersonal and interpersonal competencies. Second are distinguished facets of EI that relate to awareness from those that concern the management and regulation of emotion. For example, recognizing that someone

Table 1.1
Goleman's (2001) 2 by 2 model of emotional competencies, with examples of each of four types of competency

	Self (personal competence)	Other (social competence)
Recognition	Self-awareness • Emotional self-awareness • Accurate self-assessment • Self-confidence	Social awareness • Empathy • Service orientation • Organizational awareness
Regulation	Self-management • Self-control • Trustworthiness • Conscientiousness	Relationship management • Communication • Conflict management • Teamwork and collaboration

is unhappy is different from being able to cheer the person up. And yet both "reading" emotions and changing emotions constructively relate to the overall facility of EI. Combining the division of "self" compared to "others" and "recognition" compared to "regulation" yields the 2 by 2 classification for emotional competencies given in table 1.1. Each of the various attributes of EI can be classified as belonging to one of the four cells of the table.

Goleman (2001) argues that the qualities listed are *emotional competencies*. As such, they may be defined as learned capabilities based on emotional intelligence that result in outstanding performance at work or in other domains of life (see also Goleman 1998). Leaving aside the circularity of defining emotional competence in terms of emotional intelligence, the definition here emphasizes the dependence of emotional intelligence on learning. By contrast, psychological theories of intelligence have typically defined mental ability in terms of *aptitude*, that is, a preexisting capacity to acquire specific mental skills through learning. Thus IQ test scores are normally seen as indicators of the person's potential for acquiring academic knowledge and not the knowledge itself (Jensen 1998).

In contrast, Goleman (1998) sees emotional intelligence as a set of learned skills that may translate directly into success in various social domains, such as the workplace. For example, "the empathy competence" helps team leaders to understand the feelings of team members, leading to greater team effectiveness. This same competence helps the salesperson to close more sales by being better able to "read" the customer's emotional reactions to a given product. Conversely, emotionally unintelligent behaviors may be highly damaging to organizations. While ostensibly such an argument may be persuasive, more often it is the obverse: as Hogan and Stokes (2006) pithily note, "the primary reason employees leave a company is poor management—people don't quit organizations, they quit managers" (p. 269).

Emotion and the Culture Wars

Despite, or perhaps because of, its lack of psychological orthodoxy, *Emotional Intelligence* struck a powerful chord with various professional groups and the general public. Leaving aside the issue of whether Goleman's revision of intelligence is correct, there are several sociological and cultural reasons for the success of the EI concept. Historically, as several writers (e.g., Mayer, Salovey, et al. 2000a) have noted, Western culture has embraced conflicting attitudes toward emotions, especially strong, passionate emotion (as a case in point, see the conflict and confluence between emotions and intelligence described by various luminaries in table 1.2). The dangers of furious anger and erotic passion are always clear, however, and as Ben Ze'ev (1997) points out, the spontaneous nature of these emotional reactions are perceived as antithetical to moral responsibility.

At times the intellect has ruled the passions, as exemplified by the classical virtue of temperance, and the Stoic philosophy that judgment should be unclouded by emotion. Other cultural trends have placed more value on the heart than on the head, including romantic philosophy and the 1960s counterculture. There may be a contemporary zeitgeist that favors free emotional expression, arising as a counterpoint to technocratic Western society's increasing emphasis on formal academic qualifications, standardized testing, and reliance on hard statistical data in policy-making. Take the enthusiasm for remedies from "alternative medicine," such as homeopathy, despite the lack of any scientific data supporting their medical effectiveness. Such a zeitgeist is entirely in tune with Goleman's view that "the wisdom of the heart" has been unduly neglected (see figure 1.3 for our take on this issue).

Goleman's vision also downgrades cognitive or academic intelligence. Another best-seller of the 1990s, Herrnstein and Murray's (1994) *The Bell Curve,* offers what appears, to many, a dark vision of IQ as destiny. They argue that because IQ is stable and strongly influenced by genetics, society is arranged by strata that are defined by intelligence, with a "cognitive elite" at the top. Those of low IQ have little choice but to accept

Table 1.2
Conflict and confluence of intelligence and emotions as exemplified by a selection of quotes from famous luminaries

Artists
The artist is a receptacle for emotions that come from all over the place: from the sky, from the earth, from a scrap of paper, from a passing shape, from a spider's web.—Pablo Picasso, sculptor and painter, 1881–1973
Let's not forget that the little emotions are the great captains of our lives and we obey them without realizing it.—Vincent Van Gogh, painter, 1853–1890

Philosophers
Man becomes man only by his intelligence, but he is man only by his heart—Henri Frédéric Amiel, philosopher, 1821–1881
The degree of one's emotions varies inversely with one's knowledge of the facts: the less you know the hotter you get.—Bertrand Russell, philosopher, 1872–1970

Scientists
Intellectuals solve problems; geniuses prevent them.—Albert Einstein, physicist and philosopher, 1879–1955
We should take care not to make the intellect our god; it has, of course, powerful muscles, but no personality.—Albert Einstein, physicist and philosopher, 1879–1955
The fairest thing we can experience is the mysterious. It is the fundamental emotion which stands at the cradle of true art and true science. He who know it not and can no longer wonder, no longer feel amazement, is as good as dead, a snuffed-out candle.—Albert Einstein, physicist and philosopher, 1879–1955
What a distressing contrast there is between the radiant intelligence of the child and the feeble mentality of the average adult.—Sigmund Freud, psychiatrist and philosopher, 1856–1939
Where we have strong emotions, we're liable to fool ourselves.—Carl Sagan, astronomer, 1934–1996

Writers
There can be no knowledge without emotion. We may be aware of a truth, yet until we have felt its force, it is not ours. To the cognition of the brain must be added the experience of the soul.—Arnold Bennett, novelist, 1867–1931
Character is higher than intellect. A great soul will be strong to live as well as think.—Ralph Waldo Emerson, poet, 1803–1882
There is no human being who having both passions and thoughts does not think in consequence of his passions—does not find images rising in his mind which soothe the passion with hope or sting it will dread.—George Eliot, novelist, 1819–1880
One is certain of nothing but the truth of one's own emotions.—E. M. [Edward Morgan] Forster, novelist and essayist, 1879–1970

Table 1.2
(continued)

The course of every intellectual, if he pursues his journey long and unflinchingly enough, ends in the obvious, from which the non-intellectuals have never stirred.—Aldous Huxley, novelist, 1894–1963
The sign of an intelligent people is their ability to control emotions by the application of reason.—Marya Mannes, writer and critic, 1904–1990
Glamour [is] the power to rearrange people's emotions, which, in effect, is the power to control one's environment.—Arthur Miller, author, 1915–2005
Emotion turning back on itself, and not leading on to thought or action, is the element of madness.—John Sterling, poet, 1806–1844

Figure 1.3
A caricature of Goleman's (1995a, 1998) vision for the future, where the heart is the ruler of human intellect and interaction.

poor educational prospects, menial jobs, and a relatively unrewarding economic life.

Against this backdrop, many critics then argued that consideration needs to be given to alternative life-success factors. For example, Epstein (1998) argues that people are resentful of the excessive importance attached to IQ and scholastic attainment. Real-life experience and "street smarts (over "book smarts") should be venerated as well. Although part of this argument is a reaction to the messages contained in *The Bell Curve,* another is part of a perceived stereotype associated with "academic-types." As the British literary critic Terry Eagleton (*New Statesman,* September 13, 2004) notes:

Intellectuals are weird, creepy creatures, akin to aliens in their clinical detachment from the everyday human world. Yet you can also see them as just the opposite. If they are feared as sinisterly cerebral, they are also pitied as bumbling figures who wear their underpants back to front, harmless eccentrics who know the price of everything and the value of nothing.

With such boundaries drawn, authors that denigrate academic ability are likely to find a receptive audience. Indeed the zeitgeist, at least as expressed through various media outlets, seems to include a remarkable hostility to studious children and adults alike. Witness, for example, the success of the *Revenge of the Nerds* movie franchise, with sales of a recent special edition doing remarkably well. Part of its continued appeal is undoubtedly related to Eagleton's tacit critique. It is within such a fertile climate, that Goleman's best-selling trade text was cultivated. Furthermore Goleman emphasizes that emotional intelligence differs from IQ in being malleable and trainable; it serves as a democratic form of intelligence that virtually anyone can acquire.

Positive Psychology: Toward an Emotion-Friendly Culture
In academic circles the more emotion-friendly zeitgeist is also expressed by the increasing movement toward a "positive psychology" that explores the sources of happiness, satisfaction, optimism, and well-being (e.g., Fredrickson and Losasda 2005; Seligman and Csikzentmihalyi 2000). One of the key figures in this movement, Martin Seligman, sees psychology as historically fixated on people's problems, which in turn has led to an overemphasis on treating various forms of mental illness. However, personal fulfillment requires more than the absence of pathology. Seligman and Csikszentmihalyi (2000) argue that people need positive emotional experiences, autonomy, and self-determination in pursing personally important goals. Also requisite is connection to community and positive social interactions. A mission statement on the Web site for Seligman's Positive Psychology Center (http://www.ppc.sas.upenn.edu) describes three pillars for the movement:

Positive Psychology has three central concerns: positive experiences, positive individual traits, and positive institutions. Understanding positive emotions entails the study of contentment with the past, happiness in the present, and hope for the future. Understanding positive individual traits consists of the study of the strengths and virtues: the capacity for love and work, courage, compassion, resilience, creativity, curiosity, integrity, self-knowledge, moderation, self-control, and wisdom. Understanding positive institutions entails the study of the strengths that foster better communities, such as justice, responsibility, civility, parenting, nurturance, work ethic, leadership, teamwork, purpose, and tolerance.

These sentiments echo Goleman's (1995a) hope for improving the human condition by raising emotional intelligence. Like Goleman, by their positive psychology, Seligman and Csikszentmihalyi focus on improving the quality of life through educational and workplace interventions, and through fostering communities that encourage civic engagement. They also emphasize the need for scientific research that supports these goals. They point out that earlier attempts to develop a "positive psychology" of personal growth and self-actualization (notably the humanistic psychology of Carl Rogers and Abraham Maslow) lacked empirical rigor. Afterward humanistic psychology spawned excessive enthusiasm for invalid self-help programs responsible for New Age excesses such as crystal healing.

Indeed it is difficult to take issue with the aims of positive psychology. The movement has done the field of psychology a service by directing research toward important neglected topics. However, some concerns have been voiced by critics of positive psychology. For example, Richard Lazarus (2003) points out that positive psychology artificially separates positive and negative experiences. The meaningful events of people's lives typically interweave both types of emotion. In short, the good side of life cannot be appreciated or understood without reference to its downside. There is virtue in being resilient in the face of adversity, and learning from one's failures.

Lazarus (2003) also sees disquieting parallels between positive psychology and a long tradition of popular self-help books trumpeting the virtues of positive thinking. Although Seligman (e.g., Seligman and Csikszentmihalyi 2000) has distanced himself from this position, there is a danger of positive psychology degenerating into "happyology," addressing a naïve belief that the only important thing to life is being happy. A search on amazon.com in early 2008 revealed 48 titles containing "positive psychology," virtually all of which were self-help books. There is a wider positive psychology movement that feeds off the scientific program of Seligman and colleagues but does not necessarily exercise due scientific caution and rigor. We imagine that researchers on positive psychology would wish to separate their work from this self-help movement.

There may be a message here for EI researchers. Proponents of EI (e.g., Goleman 2001) see self-confident and happy workers as being more productive, but as we will see in chapter 9, the empirical evidence is more nuanced. Dissatisfaction with prevailing conditions at home, work, and school can be a powerful motivator toward achievement. Conversely, happiness can breed complacency. A related issue is whether positive moods interfere with realistic perceptions. Optimism can lead people to neglect danger signs, as when someone fails to see a doctor about a potential health problem. A review of the issue recognizes that self-deceptive beliefs can lull people into an illusory contentment, but positive emotions are beneficial if they are integrated with realism and active engagement with life (Schneider 2001). Proponents of emotional intelligence are unlikely to dissent. Yet there remains a danger that research on emotional intelligence cannot in practice distinguish between illusory and authentic self-fulfillment.

Rationality Bites Back

As we have noted, historically, positive emotions have sometimes been viewed with no less suspicion than negative emotions for promoting irrationality, impulsiveness, and mindless hedonism. At the present time something of a backlash against the values of the positive psychology movement may be discerned. A case in point is self-esteem. In the 1970s and 1980s the United States saw a wave of enthusiasm for self-esteem training in children as an educational tool for increasing school achievement. California even created a task force for this purpose. However, social commentators (e.g., Stout 2000; Twenge 2006) have increasingly seen this effort as doing more harm than good. A curriculum that places feeling good about oneself as the top priority, regardless of actual behavior or accomplishment, simply fosters a false sense of entitlement. Children might come to believe that whatever school work they do merits praise regardless of its quality. Stout (2000) believes that the self-esteem curriculum promotes a narcissistic sense of inflated personal worth, and emotivity, in the sense that feelings rather than rational analysis are seen as the key to success in life. The term "trophy generation" has been coined to reflect the trend in competitive sports—as well as many other aspects of life—where "no one loses" and everyone gets a "Thanks for participating" trophy. The emphasis is on a heightened sense of entitlement, of comfort, and of rights and privileges. Twenge (2006) claims that today's young adults—called the "Me Generation"—are characterized by excessive individualism and narcissism that feeds into social disconnection and depression. Her thesis is supported by several studies tracking changes in these personal qualities over the latter part of the twentieth century (e.g., Twenge and Im 2007).

As we will see in chapter 6, the doubts of educators about the value of self-esteem are supported by research. Baumeister et al. (2005) review extensive studies suggesting that although raising self-esteem improves positive emotions, it does little else. For example, high self-esteem appears a consequence rather than a cause of academic achievement. Baumeister et al. also points out a "dark side" to high self-esteem, which can promote narcissism and aggression toward others. Paulhus (1998) describes a character trait of self-enhancement, a sometimes unrealistically positive view of the self that raises both self-esteem and narcissism but can provoke negative reaction from others. Arrogance is not always popular. As we will see, questionnaires assessing emotional intelligence typically contain a self-esteem component (e.g., Bar-On 2000). But is this self-esteem rooted in a realistic understanding of one's emotional competencies, or is it more narcissistic in nature?

We noted earlier that Western culture is ambivalent about emotions. The same applies to the intellect. Research does not show any downside to academic intelligence; if anything, on average, high IQ individuals are a little better adjusted than those lower in IQ (Zeidner and Matthews 2000). Yet there is a persistent stereotype, played to the full by Goleman (1995a) and other EI researchers, to the effect that academic intelligence is incompatible with common sense and real-life competence. To quote George Orwell, "there are certain things one has to be an intellectual to believe, since no ordinary man could be so stupid." Of course, there may be a conflation here of the crustier variant of the college professor with high IQ, a type found in all walks of life. As we have mentioned already, part of the popular appeal of EI is that it resonates with an anti-intellectual sentiment.

During our writing a skirmish in the culture wars surrounded a purportedly honest and accurate memoir of drug addiction, James Frey's *A Million Little Pieces*. Confronted by evidence from police reports and court records that the book falsely records key elements of Frey's life, the author's response appears illuminating. According to various reports (e.g., Associated Press, January 12, 2006) Frey "acknowledged he had embellished parts of the book but said that was common for memoirs and defended 'the essential truth' of 'A Million Little Pieces.'" The book is "about drug addiction and alcoholism," he said. "*The emotional truth is there*" [our italics]. Whatever the facts of this case, the author's response represents a contemporary view, that "emotional truth" and personal authenticity may be more important than the literal or factual truth revealed by objective evidence and intellectual analysis.

On the value of the intellect, however, there are also signs of a cultural backlash. The title of Charles Sykes's (1995) book conveys this concern: *Dumbing down Our Kids: Why America's Children Feel Good about Them-*

selves but Can't Read, Write, or Add. As with popular works on EI, there is an obvious element of hyperbole, but there are evidently popular worries, whether or not well-founded. The sociologist Frank Furedi (2006) has written on the declining status of the intellectual in contemporary culture. He argues that truth and objectivity are increasingly denigrated by a postmodernism relativism that promotes social inclusion above all else. In a complementary book Furedi (2004) made a case that Anglo-American countries are orienting toward a "therapy culture" that frames everyday life in terms of emotions, and especially vulnerability and "victimhood." Not everyone believes that emotions are undervalued.

It is not our intention to endorse or reject any of the cultural views on the respective roles of emotion and the intellect to which we have referred. Our central point is simply this. To a perhaps unprecedented degree, Western culture is perplexed by emotions. Indeed Furedi (2006) points to a modern dilemma associated with complexity: it seems no one person can understand the culture in its entirety, leading to increased specialization of knowledge. Perhaps our understandings of emotions are becoming similarly fragmented. These dissonant views form a dangerous backdrop to the emergence of emotional intelligence. It is dangerous because scientists are likely no less susceptible to cultural pressures and biases than anyone else. The vulnerability of thinking to cultural tides and currents makes a rigorous and skeptical analysis of emotional intelligence complicated but essential.

Toward a Science of Emotional Intelligence

Why Science?

Our message thus far is that emotional intelligence is difficult to research. The concept is so wide-ranging that it is unclear what human qualities are central to it. Social-emotional abilities cannot be expressed in conventional psychological tests, even those that purport to measure emotional competencies. Both popular and professional notions of emotional intelligence can be powerfully shaped by the conflicting currents of thought about the value of emotion held within contemporary Western culture.

Beyond a concern with objective truth, there are several reasons why a scientific understanding of emotional intelligence is necessary. In the passages that follow, we discuss these reasons in some depth.

Targeting the Exceptional   If we want to foster emotional intelligence and brilliance in order to profit from the wisdom of the emotionally gifted, we need to know who they are. Equally we need to be able to identify the emotionally impoverished in order to develop meaningful interventions. Just as good IQ tests are needed to identify cognitively gifted (as well as challenged) individuals, standardized EI tests are required to identify those individuals who may need emotional enrichment, as well as support and training in dealing with emotion-laden situations.

Understanding Abnormality and Deviance   One of Goleman's (1995a) themes is that low EI leads to various mental problems, including emotional disorders and antisocial behaviors. British Conservative Party leader David Cameron recently attracted some ridicule in the press for suggesting that "hoodies" (young thugs) need love and hugs rather than jail time. Evidently an enthusiast for cryptopositive psychology, Cameron was also quoted as saying "Improving our society's sense of well-being is, I believe, the central political challenge of our time" (AP, July 20, 2006). But is it true that interventions geared toward increasing subjective well-being and positive emotional support will contribute to solving societal problems such as violent crime? As our picture (figure 1.4) suggests, at least one "hoodie" was unimpressed with the idea. We need a scientific account of the role of EI in abnormality and deviant behavior to inform us whether raising EI will improve individual and societal well-being.

Mapping the Natural Ecology of Emotional Intelligence   It is unlikely that emotional intelligence is distributed randomly across human social groups. For example, both popular stereotypes and rigorous personality research (Costa et al. 2001) suggest that women are more likely to possess "agreeable" characteristics. In turn, components comprising agreeableness such as empathy, awareness of the feelings of others, and coping with stress through "tending and befriending" are thought by some to be central to emotional intelligence. Valid measurement of EI is necessary to test whether there are such gender differences and other types of group differences, including age, social class, and cross-cultural differences. It is also important to understand how emotional intelligence might be distributed across different occupational groups. Are social workers really more emotionally intelligent than computer programmers? And does having high EI benefit (or hinder), for example, those involved in law and order?

Discovering the Sources of Emotional Intelligence   Assuming emotional intelligence exists, what determines the affective intelligence of an indi-

Figure 1.4
A "hoodie" responds to politician David Cameron's suggestion that young criminals need
more love

vidual? If EI is like most other human characteristics, we may assume
that it reflects both genes and the social environment in which the child
develops. The individual's DNA interacts with external stimulation in
building the brain, including those brain structures that influence emotion. Perhaps emotional intelligence can be linked to the neurology of
structures in the frontal lobes of the brain, which are known to be important for regulating and controlling emotion (Bechara et al. 2000). Already recent research suggests that both frontal and temporal lobes
support emotionally intelligent reasoning (Reis et al. 2007). In addition
the quality of interactions with caregivers and peers, which the child experiences, is known to affect emotional development. For example, mal-
treatment and deprivation are known to have various serious adverse
effects (Smith and Walden 1999). Perhaps emotional intelligence reflects
the extent to which the child is exposed to good role models for expressing and managing emotion.

Understanding Emotional Intelligence as a Process   It is often said that the concept of "intelligence" is poorly formulated and largely misunderstood. Simply enumerating a person's IQ fails to inform us of how intelligence plays out as an ongoing process in real-life contexts (Sternberg 1985). Similarly we need a scientific account of how emotional intelligence is expressed in handling the problems and challenges of life. We need, for example, to know how it helps the person *adapt* to threats and opportunities. This process view is especially important if emotional intelligence, as claimed, is more malleable than IQ. In the absence of understanding processes, interventions are likely to be futile at best, perhaps even dangerous.

Debunking Myths   We have demonstrated that some of the claims made about emotional intelligence are grandiose. Moreover popular culture is vulnerable to fads and enthusiasms that have little relation to reality. It is essential to develop a rigorous science that allows for a skeptical examination of popular beliefs about emotional intelligence. If myths are debunked, scientific progress becomes "easier" to foster.

The Three Pillars Supporting a Science of Emotional Intelligence

Having made a case as to why a scientific account of emotional intelligence is important, it is imperative now to suggest what shape such a program of inquiry might take. Matthews, Zeidner, et al. (2002) list three essential pillars for a scientific treatment of emotional intelligence (see figure 1.5). In what follows, we delineate these pillars as there are germane to many of the arguments made throughout the current book.

Scientifically Justifiable Measurement   As an essential condition, any new construct must be open to reliable and valid measurement. In the case of EI, measurement is pivotal because of uncertainties over what "emotional intelligence" actually is. Anyone can write a laundry list of desirable personal qualities (and many have done so). To show, however, that the list of qualities has some unique common element that can be meaningfully labeled "emotional intelligence" is another matter. For the fledgling construct of EI to take wing, it must be measured as a distinct personal quality that promotes effective social functioning. Without measurement, accounts of EI are little more than verbiage; armchair discourse (or better still, cocktail hour conversation) whose validity cannot be determined.

   Measurement places the study of emotional intelligence in the field of *individual differences*, or differential psychology, because it allows the sci-

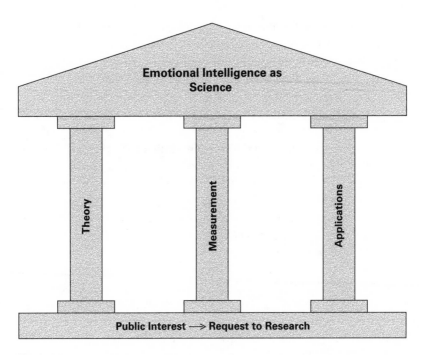

Figure 1.5
The three pillars of a science of emotional intelligence

entific researcher to evaluate individuals as being more or less emotionally intelligent. Standard differential psychology recognizes that ability, or superior performance in some domain, is fundamentally distinct from personality. The latter refers to styles of behavior that differ from one another qualitatively but are not "correct" or "incorrect." Thus an important goal for research is to show how tests for EI fit into this larger scheme of individual differences. Also pivotal in such a framework is to differentiate emotional intelligence from personality and conventional intelligence.

Compelling Theory We also need a theory of what it means to be emotionally intelligent, a theory that identifies the key psychological processes involved. Suppose that we have a test that succeeds in picking out those people that have a talent for understanding and dealing with emotions. What is special about the way that these emotionally gifted individuals process emotional information? What is special about how they respond to emotive situations? And what features of emotional processing contribute to emotional illiteracy?

Various psychological theories may help us in seeking the sources of emotional intelligence. One possibility—highlighted by Goleman (1995a)—is that EI is engrained in the neurons of the brain. Neuroscientists have been especially interested in areas of the frontal lobes of the brain that seem to control the infusion of emotion into decision-making. Damage to these areas causes emotionally unintelligent behaviors such as violent mood swings, reckless impulsivity, and poor decision-making. Alternatively, we may look to the software (rather than the hardware) of the brain, in terms of the mental models that people build of their place in the social world around them. There is an important cognitive-psychological tradition of linking emotion to personal beliefs and evaluations and emotional dysfunction to excessively negative cognitions. Perhaps EI resides in building mental models that promote productive social engagement with others.

We should note, however, that a subtext of much writing on EI is that emotions have a mental life independent of thought and cognition (which may or may not be true). We will not say much more about theory at this point, but we will return to these issues in later chapters. A related issue is whether the attributes of EI are truly adaptive. Do they truly promote success in real life? Is it really important to have high self-esteem, empathy for others, and accurate perceptions of emotions? Perhaps only a psychologist would be introspective enough to ask these questions, but it is important to demonstrate evidence for their utility in life.

Meaningful Applications   In addition the practical value of EI must be demonstrated, and across diverse fields. These fields might include education (see chapter 8), organizational psychology (see chapters 9 and 10), and mental health (see chapter 11). We are not painting on a blank canvas here. Applied psychologists have contributed much in developing practical interventions already. In many cases interventions are based on theory and supported by evidence. So it needs to be shown that emotional intelligence offers something new, that it adds to and augments current practice. Applied research has in fact tended to proceed at one remove from laboratory-based research that is more focused on measurement issues. We will argue that although basic and applied research could be seen as separate strands of research, they would both benefit from greater integration. The practitioner, of course, focuses on remedial measures against some specific problem, such as children with behavior problems, ineffective leadership at work, or severe depression requiring clinical treatment.

We will shortly look again at the potential of emotional intelligence in applied settings.

Visions in Conflict: Alternate Models of Emotional Intelligence

In this section we provide a quick tour of the state-of-the-art in scientific research on EI. We aim simply to summarize the different approaches researchers have taken in their search for the essence of emotional intelligence. At this point our survey will be fairly uncritical. Subsequently we will look at some of the challenges faced by this program of research.

A basic difficulty has been that different psychologists have disparate visions of what a science of emotional intelligence should look like. Indeed it may be that different research teams are investigating entirely different personal qualities. We have already introduced Jack Mayer and Peter Salovey as two of the founders of the scientific study of emotional intelligence. In several articles (e.g., Mayer, Salovey, et al. 2000a, b) they aim to discriminate among some of the different scientific conceptions of emotional intelligence. Other authors (e.g., Perez et al. 2005) have been concerned especially with the relationship between EI and personality theory. These analyses give us three conflicting ways of understanding emotional intelligence, which we discuss below.

Ability Models Mayer, Salovey, et al. (2000b) favor defining emotional intelligence as an ability resembling other standard intelligences. That is, high EI persons are objectively superior to those of lower EI in performing certain activities associated with emotions. In their four-branch model (see chapter 3) Mayer and colleagues differentiate four essential components of EI: identifying emotions, assimilating emotions into thought, understanding emotions, and managing the emotions of oneself and others. This ability model is relatively narrow in scope; much of what Goleman (1995a) describes as EI is not relevant to the Mayer, Salovey, et al. (2000b) conception. Mayer, Salovey et al. (2000a, b) claim that EI relates specifically to interactions between emotions and cognitions; using emotion to enhancing thinking and using thought to regulate emotion. A third psychological domain—motivation—falls outside their definition, although other authors have attributed motivational components to EI, such as persistence in adversity and motivations to support and connect with other people (e.g., Goleman 1995a).

Besides the four-branch model, other ability-based definitions are possible. For example, Scherer (2007) cites competencies in appraisal (accurate perceptions of emotive events) and communication (effective listening and speech) as possible bases for emotional intelligence. There is also research concerned specifically with accurate perception of emotions, a faculty that is relatively straightforward to measure using objective techniques (e.g., Davies et al. 1998; Roberts, Schulze, et al. 2005, 2006). Further still, Lane (2000) has suggested that awareness and verbal expression of emotion may be critical for human survival; EI may relate to the sophistication with which the person can articulate emotional experience.

Abilities are best measured through objective tests akin to IQ tests. These tasks present the respondent with problems that can be scored on a right-or-wrong basis. The difficulty is that it is hard to write test items relating to emotional functioning that can be objectively scored. The correct way to handle an aggressive coworker or comfort an upset family member may depend on circumstances and the particular individuals concerned. Nonetheless, Mayer and colleagues have published two widely used tests for EI, the Multi-factor Emotional Intelligence Scale (MEIS), and its successor, the Mayer-Salovey-Caruso Emotional Intelligence Test (MSCEIT). We examine these tests in depth in chapter 3.

Mixed Models   A broader conception of emotional intelligence incorporates both abilities and qualities such as personality and motivational traits that assist the person in using EI in real life. For example, a person with a warm, sympathetic personality may find it easier to deploy skills for managing the emotions of others. Goleman's (1995a) account of EI, which includes qualities such as optimism, empathy, and good character, is a mixed model. More scientific approaches aim to list the specific abilities and traits that contribute to real-world adaptation (e.g., Bar-On 2000). As we will see in chapter 4, mixed models embrace a multitude of qualities. Questionnaires have also been used to assess more narrowly defined personal characteristics relevant to EI, including regulation of moods (Salovey et al. 1995) and "alexithymia," which is a deficiency in the ability to understand and verbalize one's own feelings (Taylor and Bagby 2004).

Researchers in the mixed model tradition have typically used questionnaires to assess emotional intelligence (e.g., Schutte et al. 1998). The approach is based on the often unstated assumption that people have sufficient insight into their own emotions and real-life functioning for self-reports to be valid. This assumption, as we will see in chapter 4, is questionable. Another difficulty is that questionnaire assessments tend to overlap with standard personality traits such as extraversion and emotional stability. Nevertheless, questionnaires for EI have become widely used in research. In principle, they provide a straightforward and economical means for measuring individual differences in emotional functioning.

Trait Emotional Intelligence The difficulties of trying to assess abilities by self-report, exemplified by mixed model research, has led some researchers (e.g., Perez et al. 2005; Tett et al. 2005) toward a radical re-conceptualization of emotional intelligence. The idea is that emotional abilities and competencies may be dauntingly difficult to measure systematically, certainly by questionnaire. However, there may be personality traits that relate directly to emotional functioning (e.g., assertiveness, empathy). Trait emotional intelligence represents an overarching personality factor that represents the person's emotional self-confidence (Petrides et al. 2007). Like conventional personality traits, trait EI represents a qualitatively style of behavior and experience that is adaptive in some contexts but not in others.

A focal research challenge is then to integrate trait EI and its facets into standard personality research. Does work on trait EI add new facets to existing personality models? Or does it just describe existing traits from a different perspective? We will also address these issues in chapter 4.

Loose Ends Some important conceptual issues not entirely accommodated within the different EI models that we have described thus far appear worthy of mention. One issue is the extent to which EI is primarily a *social* intelligence. There is a long tradition of researchers who have attempted to develop objective tests for social abilities (e.g., understanding and coping with the behaviors of others) with rather mixed results (Kihlstrom and Cantor 2000; Matthews, Zeidner, et al. 2002). As we noted earlier, Gardner (1983) differentiates intrapersonal from interpersonal intelligence. Although some authors, including Goleman (2001), have recognized that self-related can be distinguished from other-related aspects of EI, it remains unclear to what extent EI is expressed only through interaction with others. We should bear in mind that emotions have important social functions, in communicating personal status and needs to others (Oatley and Johnson-Laird 1995).

A second issue is the extent to which emotional intelligence is conscious or unconscious. Psychology makes a pivotal distinction between processes that are explicit or implicit. On the one hand, explicit processes are accessible to consciousness; the person can describe them verbally. Implicit processes, on the other hand, are unconscious and resistant to articulation. For example, describing the parts of a bicycle (wheels, handlebars, etc.) requires explicit memory, whereas actually riding a bike requires implicit memory; it is difficult to verbalize the motor skills involved. There may indeed be separate brain systems for implicit and explicit processing (Rolls 1999). Similarly, describing how one would deal with an emotionally challenging situation is an explicit activity, but actually interacting with someone who is emotionally upset also involves implicit processing. Responses to another's body language and other social signals may be unconscious (Bargh and Williams 2006), as is our own nonverbal behavior. One of our themes in this book is that the focus of research on explicit EI may lead to neglect of important implicit competencies and skills.

A third issue we might call the "de-contextualization" of emotional intelligence. Can we ever really separate emotional competence from the contexts and situations to which it applies? Similar concerns about cognitive intelligence have generated the controversial suggestion that practical intelligence geared to real-life problems should be separated from abstract, academic intelligence (Wagner 2000). The way we process emotions is highly context-dependent. Although there are universal facial expressions of emotion, we use contextual knowledge to decode emotion expressions. For example, we know from experience which of our friends tend to exaggerate their emotions. We also have no difficulty laughing when a comedian puts on a tragic expression. A test of how quickly the person recognizes standard emotion expressions may not capture the real-life richness and context-dependence of our understanding of facial emotions.

A particular instance of context is culture. A display of emotion that is acceptable in one culture may be deeply offensive in another. Research on EI has tended to shy away from cross-cultural analyses, but it is likely that emotionally intelligent behavior is culturally dependent. At the extreme we might wonder whether emotional intelligence refers not to any basic universal human ability but to the extent of the person's learning of their culture's rules for handling emotion. Most Westerners would instantly lose 20 emotional intelligence points as soon as they arrive at Narita airport in Japan. Alternatively, a foreigner's speed of adaptation to novel cultural norms may be an index of EI. Indeed it appears on such a premise that the eminently popular film *Lost in Translation* was based.

Applied Research

It is a well-tried tactic in psychology to begin with a test and then explore what the results tells us about the person tested. However, applied psychologists typically begin, not with a test, but with a problem. Applied research focuses on solving problems, and assessment is considered useful only in so far as it supports solutions. Goleman's (1995a) book was rich in problems—ironically so, given the interest of positive psychologists in emotional intelligence. If the book is in fact to be believed, our civilization is experiencing an emotional decline and fall, as reflected in an "age of melancholy" (p. 240), a "modern epidemic of depression (p. 240), and "poisoning the very experience of childhood" (p. 233). The solution, according to Goleman, is a concerted effort to train emotional intelligence in schools and the workplace.

Emotional problems in childhood are usually divided into "externalizing"—acting out in often antisocial ways—and "internalizing" problems such as anxiety and depression. The emotionally intelligent educator is concerned with both. As we will see in chapter 8, programs for social and emotional learning (SEL) aim to educate children in emotional competence, to improve their well-being (less internalizing), to make them more responsible citizens (less externalizing), and to enhance classroom learning. Advocates of SEL encourage schools to find room in the curriculum for training in skills such as constructive conflict resolution, avoiding drug and alcohol use, and relating to their peers. There is evidence for the effectiveness of such programs. However, training programs for social skills existed long before the notion of emotional intelligence. So it seems reasonable to ask whether research on EI has really added anything to such programs or whether it is just a convenient banner under which to raise awareness of the issues.

There is also growing interest in emotional intelligence at work, in terms of improving both worker well-being and company productivity. As in education these applications rest in part on truisms, for example, that it is important that employees are able to work constructively with others. It is difficult to argue against the notion that it is useful to train skills such as teamwork, conflict resolution, and leadership. However, as with education it is unclear how much "added value" can be attached to emotional intelligence. There has even been backlash against the idea that EI is the panacea for all organizational problems (e.g., Landy 2005). For example, a leading applied psychologist, Kevin Murphy, has described emotional intelligence as one of the big ten misses of industrial and organizational psychology over the last decade (see Murphy 2006a, b). According to Murphy (see Murphy and Sideman 2006; Murphy 2006a), whereas the version of EI managers prefer is a mess, the version scientists can live with doesn't predict that much. Murphy's caustic comments aside, it is perhaps unfortunate that EI was ushered into industrial-organizational psychology with such a fanfare of hyperbole. The more sober advocates of EI (e.g., Jordan et al. 2007) rightly call for careful evidence-based research to realize the promise of increasing emotional competence at work.

A final area of application is in promoting mental health and well-being. Both ordinary unhappiness and clinical disorders may follow from poor understanding and management of one's own emotions. In everyday life, misunderstanding others' feelings, lashing out impulsively in challenging situations, and failing to engage positively with others may all lead to stress and avoidable unhappiness. These symptoms of emotional illiteracy have been addressed in studies of how people cope with stress, how they negotiate intimate relationships and marriage, and how lack of self-control may lead to deviant behaviors such as substance abuse and crime. Clinical psychology has for many years recognized that unrealistic beliefs about oneself contribute to emotional dysfunction. But a closer focus on how people understand and regulate their emotional states may bring therapeutic benefits. A particularly dramatic example of low EI may be provided by autism and related developmental disorders. The autistic child appears to be unable to understand other people or form emotional connections with them, leading to social withdrawal and abnormality. Again, a science of EI may provide important clinical benefits (Vachon and Bagby 2007).

Concluding Comments: Atlantis Is to Myth as Emotional Intelligence Is to ...?

In 1665 the Jesuit polymath Athanasius Kircher published his book *Mundus Subterraneus* in Amsterdam. Among many wonders and mysteries (including a toad sealed within a stone and a Swiss dragon) is a map showing the continent of Atlantis placed squarely between Spain and the Americas (see figure 1.6). Of course, the continent is mythical, but the map poses the challenge of research on emotional intelligence. We know there may well be uncharted terrain—and perhaps whole continents—to be mapped, but we do not know exactly where to look or where the new land is to be located on existing world maps. That is, we have quite good "maps" of personality and ability already, but it is unclear where emo-

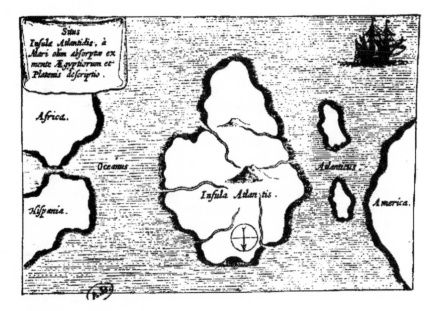

Figure 1.6
Map of Atlantis, from *Mundus Subterraneus* published by Athanasius Kircher in 1665. Is emotional intelligence is akin to Atlantis or a scientifically verifiable construct?

tional intelligence should be placed within this existing sphere. Like early explorers in search of new continents, researchers on EI are at risk of several distinct errors:

1. Emotional intelligence may be entirely mythical, like Atlantis.

2. Emotional intelligence may exist, but be of relatively minor importance—a small island rather than a major landmass.

3. What is labeled as emotional intelligence may in fact be known and charted terrain—like marking Ireland as Atlantis on the map.

4. Different researchers may attach the name emotional intelligence to many different constructs; rather as historians have variously identified Atlantis with Santorini, the Azores, the Bahamas, and numerous other islands.

Alternatively, it may be that emotional intelligence truly represents a large swathe of new psychological terrain, and its exploration will add much to our understanding of individual differences in emotion. Another, more subtle possibility is that work on emotional intelligence will discover little new terrain but will add importantly to our understanding of existing constructs, like mapping the universe with radio waves rather than visible light.

We have seen how scientific conceptions of EI differ from one another, sometimes radically. These uncertainties in definition carry over into difficulties in measurement. Tests for EI may not measure any true ability at all. Alternatively, they may simply re-package existing personality and ability scales, or they may measure some trivial competence that is weakly related (or worse still unrelated) to real life. Careful scientific research is needed to discern whether emotional abilities, competencies, and personality traits lie beyond our current charts of human intelligences and dispositions. Without such a scientific effort, we can have no clear notion of how people differ in their regulation of emotion. Nor can we hope to help practitioners in workplaces, schools, and psychiatric clinics.

In our previous book (Matthews, Zeidner, et al. 2002) we concluded that there is no evidence for the extreme claims made for the importance of EI in the popular literature on the subject. It is simply false to say that studies show that EQ is more predictive of real-life success than IQ, for example. We also argued that there is little support for Goleman's (1995a) position that training EI will serve as a panacea for the problems of the world. The evidence we will review in later chapters of the present book will support a similarly cautious appraisal of the potential value of emotional intelligence.

At the same time it is important to evaluate what new knowledge studies of emotional intelligence may add to our understanding of emotional competence. One vision is that of Mayer, Salovey, et al. (2000a, b), a vision perhaps shared by other researchers that are relatively optimistic about the scientific status and impact of emotional intelligence (e.g., Jordan et al. 2007). In their conception, EI meets criteria for a standard intelligence; it represents a true ability with far-reaching implications for real life. As we will see in chapter 3, they argue that their test assesses a major quality of the person, distinct from standard personality and intelligence measures. To evaluate such a claim, we will look at the measurement properties of their tests, and research that examines whether EI test scores are actually predictive of real-life emotional and social competence (chapter 6). Another vision is of EI as being more akin to personality, and so measurable by questionnaire. We will consider "mixed" and "trait" models of EI in chapter 4, and evaluate whether the increasingly popular questionnaires for EI measure anything different from standard personality traits.

While much of this book will be geared toward evaluating existing research, we will also suggest an alternative vision of emotional intelligence; one that is in some ways at odds with that of proponents of EI, as currently defined. Our position is that there may be no common element to the various constructs and accompanying measures labeled as emotional intelligence. Current research may instead relate to a potpourri of often unrelated personal characteristics. We will try to sift what is new and important in this research from what adds little to existing understanding. Some constructs may be discarded altogether, some may be seen as no more than existing constructs repackaged, and some may be genuinely new and interesting. There may be both new personality traits and new abilities in the latter category. We will propose too that much work on emotional intelligence neglects the psychological theory of emotion. We will explore how emotional competencies and temperaments develop in childhood (chapter 5), how emotion infuses our social relationships (chapter 6), and how people differ in their coping with stress (chapter 7). By the end of the book we will have set out systematically the diversity of personal qualities labeled—aptly or not—as emotional intelligence, and their psychological significance. We will also have assessed the practical relevance of emotional intelligence in various fields (chapters 7 to 11).

Summary Points: Chapter 1

• Emotional intelligence may be defined as a generic competence in perceiving emotions (both in oneself and in others), in regulating emotions, and in coping effectively with emotive situations.

• Viewed as a form of intelligence, emotional intelligence has a rich history, including links to social, practical, interpersonal, and intrapersonal intelligences. That history suggests difficulties with measurement and theory that, while not insurmountable, pose challenges for the concept virtually from its inception.

• Emotional intelligence also has close links to the positive psychology movement, which has placed increasing emphasis on the importance of happiness and well-being. Recent trends suggest something of a backlash against this movement; negative emotions, for example, have an important role in adaptive functioning.

• A scientific understanding of emotional intelligence is needed in order to (1) target the exceptional, (2) understand abnormality and deviance, (3) comprehend group differences, (4) uncover underlying processes, and (5) debunk myths and fads that are associated with popularization of the concept.

• The three pillars that are needed to establish a science of emotional intelligence are sound measurement, compelling theory, and successful application. We will use these pillars to evaluate the success (or otherwise) of various approaches to emotional intelligence covered in the remainder of this book.

II   EMOTIONAL INTELLIGENCE: A NEW CONSTRUCT?

2 Measure for Emotional Intelligence Measures

Great theories are expansive; failures mire us in dogmatism and tunnel vision.
—Stephen J. Gould, *Eight Little Piggies: Reflections on Natural History*, p. 165

In science a fundamental consideration when introducing a new concept to the field is the establishment of a set of conditions, operations, and/or procedures for the measurement of the phenomenon in question. Our understanding of everything, from the smallest microbe to the wonders of the universe, is constrained largely by our finding ways to measure these entities. Indeed with new measurements often come new findings. The recent discovery of OGLE-2005-BLG-390Lb, a distant planet not unlike earth, was the result of micro-lensing, a new measurement technique based on an extension of Einstein's theories on gravity, space, and time (see figure 2.1). Conversely, faulty measurement instruments can lead us astray. Astronomers of the nineteenth century believed they could see canals on Mars—an illusion fostered by telescopes of poor quality.

Psychology is no different. Measurement is a necessary condition for establishing scientific theories of learning rate and intelligence level. It is also important in understanding a person's motivation, reading skill, or capacity to understand another individual. History has taught us that progress in understanding scientific concepts is a function of finding ways of measuring them. If the study of emotional intelligence is ever to be taken seriously, especially as a scientific enterprise, the same holds true of it. The present chapter examines the measurement techniques and tools available to the researcher working with emotional intelligence. These psychological methods hold the potential to unravel the mysteries of emotional intelligence.

In chapter 1 we outlined some major conceptualizations of emotional intelligence (EI) and their chief protagonists. As we noted briefly in those passages, each of these luminaries has developed instruments for the

Figure 2.1
Artist's conception of the newly discovered planet OGLE-2005-BLG-390Lb

assessment of emotional intelligence. A significant portion of the present chapter is devoted to discussing these measures. An eye is simultaneously cast on how they meet established scientific standards. To fully appreciate these instruments, some further discussion of the conceptual background in which they emerged is also necessary. A major aim then, of the present chapter, is to provide descriptions and critical commentary of several different EI models reflecting the close relationship between theory and measurement.

Psychological Assessment: A Brief Primer

Someone told me that each equation I included in the book would halve the sales.
—Stephen Hawking

Before proceeding further, we make the assumption that the current reader is relatively unfamiliar with some of the more technical aspects of psychological measurement. The term "psychological assessment" is often used to describe this field of study. Thus a brief primer on this topic would seem appropriate. To this end we have also compiled a glossary of key terms, which the reader might wish to consult if a term appears problematic or if we have inadvertently lapsed into jargon. These user-friendly definitions can be found at the end of the book.

Our discussion of psychological measurements may not be for everyone, though we do recommend that you read them. For example, you might claim a certain degree of numerophobia. We deal with this by keeping the discussion largely at a conceptual level. Or you might have learned about psychological assessment, psychometrics, or educational statistics in an undergraduate course and consider such a discussion superfluous. Even then, a review of these passages is likely appropriate because psychological assessment is a field that changes from time to time as knowledge about procedures improves with technological and conceptual innovations. Most important, we acknowledge that in the rush to measure emotional intelligence, conformity to these standards is not always as it should be. Indeed these standards have sometimes been ignored, even by chief proponents of various emotional intelligence models and measures. Thus it is vital to have a basic understanding of what these standards imply.

Standards for Developing Scientifically Sound Psychological Tests
The discipline of psychometrics provides *relatively* uncontroversial principles for determining what constitutes sound measurement. Almost all major organizations concerned with educational and psychological testing have endorsed a set of standards for determining the efficacy of a given measure (see *Standards for Educational and Psychological Testing*; AERA/APA/NCME 1999). These standards address many different components. For example, how test development should be documented and how the corpus of research should confirm the status of the instrument. Standards also provide guidelines for how items should be constructed so as to not be biased toward a particular subgroup. They even address how scoring rubrics need to be devised and made publicly accessible, and the various ethical considerations related to reporting. Most important, five major criteria are used to determine whether a test meets best practices:

1. Reliability
2. Content validity
3. Predictive validity
4. Consequential validity
5. Construct validity

Modern-day accounts embrace construct validity as the all-encompassing, unifying concept for all types of validity evidence (i.e., criteria 2 through 4). Within this perspective all forms of validity evidence are merely supporting players in the cumulative, never-ending quest for construct validation (i.e., determining if a test score represents the hypothetical entity that it was designed to represent). Extending this notion to the special case of EI, its chief proponents might make a reasonable claim in its defense. Put simply, the quest for construct validity has only begun, and there are bound to be some ideas that do not move the field forward. Thus the construct is too new to dismiss any of its measures out of hand. Equally, however, preliminary evidence for construct validity would appear requisite to push the science of EI further afield.

But we digress. Let us consider the five criteria detailed above a little more closely, in the order we introduced them in the preceding passage.

Reliability   For a test to measure a scientifically meaningful construct, people must differ reliably across its dimensions. In particular, should a person taking an EI test obtain a below-average score on one occasion, then that same person should get a below-average score when given the same test again (some time in the future). This is termed the test-retest reliability of a measure. If performance is inconsistent, especially across all individuals tested, then what is being measured is unstable. Consequently it is also of questionable value.

Another important form of reliability involves determining the extent to which responses that people give on items, within the same test, correlate with other items of this test (i.e., internal consistency reliability). For example, if each item in a test of happiness is measuring happiness (rather than another emotion), then responses to each item should relate in a meaningful way with responses to all the other items of this test. If the relationship is low, it just might be that it is not happiness we are assessing but rather some other concept. Or it could be happiness plus something unrelated or a different aspect of happiness altogether.

Content Validity   A psychometrically valid test must cover a representative sample of the domain that it was designed to assess. The issue here is one of *conceptualization*; deciding what qualities should be assessed as components of the measure. Equally we need to decide on the qualities that should be excluded. For example, if a test is to serve as a measure of emotion perception, then its developers need to ensure that major aspects of emotion perception are covered by the test items. Based on existing research, such a test should probably cover the perception of emotions in faces, music, voices, postures, abstract designs, human interaction, and colors. Moreover test developers should not focus exclusively on one type of perception (e.g., happiness) to the exclusion of other basic emotions (fear, anger, sadness, etc.). Determining the content validity of a test is a tricky exercise, often requiring expert panels to agree on the content comprising the assessment.

A related issue is that of face validity. Does the measure in question look as though it assesses the construct that we are interested in measuring? We know, for example, that there is a meaningful relation between reaction time and intelligence. We also know that reaction time is capable of being assessed by how fast you sort a deck of playing cards, say into suits (see Roberts et al. 1988; Roberts, Markham, et al. 2005). However, such a task has poor face validity. Imagine the public outcry if this assessment was used to measure a student's academic potential or a job candidate's suitability for a particular position. (There always are, of course, possible exceptions; this test might be face valid for those working in the gambling industry.)

Predictive Validity   Measures should predict important practical outcomes of life; if not, the test is of little use. In the special case of emotional intelligence, these might include how well people deal with stress or how effective they are at maintaining intimate relationships. It might also include how respected they are by their peers, how well they deal with others in emotional turmoil, and how easily they are able to gather social support during times of crisis, to name a few conditions. The importance of a test in predicting relevant criteria should not be underestimated. Without demonstration of this capacity, a test is rendered vacuous. In contemporary science, researching a concept for the sake of research is a noble enterprise but that augurs poorly for the researcher's future. Most funding agencies—to which scientific progress is often beholden—require demonstration of the societal relevance of a particular research program. As a taxpayer contributing to the scientific enterprises, in your home country, you may be sympathetic to this element of accountability.

Consequential Validity   In addition to these aspects of validity, which pertain to the usefulness of a test as a decision-making aid, researchers have begun to incorporate the notion of consequential validity. As the prominent measurement theoretician Samuel Messick (1988) once put it, this form of validity evidence "requires evaluation of the intended and unintended social consequences of test interpretation and use" (p. 39). Consequential validity evidence is a relatively new and somewhat controversial addition to the test standards. It is important to evaluate, however, because of the frequent misuse of test scores. It is also something few people have considered thus far when investigating the nature of emotional intelligence. In his trade text, Goleman (1998), for example, paints a rosy world if all follow his emotional intelligence mantra. However, it remains to be seen whether assessment of emotional intelligence might not result in similar unintended social consequences as have sometimes occurred with cognitive tests (e.g., sociocultural group bias).

Construct Validity   Construct validation is the process of determining whether a test (and its attendant score) actually measures what it is that it claims to measure. The demonstration of construct validity rests on the collection and establishment of a large corpus of well-conducted research using a number of diverse procedures. To successfully evaluate the construct validity of a test score, a variety of evidence from numerous sources should be accumulated. There should be a rigorous theory that explains this evidence and makes novel predictions. Because scientific theories are provisional and subject to revision, theorists often see construct validation as a process without end. No study represents an endpoint in this process. Rather, all studies should continue to add to construct validity evidence. Conversely, if research consistently fails to tie test scores to theoretically meaningful outcomes, the wider scientific community will probably reject the test.

Although construct validity is a lengthy and complex process, each procedure used to investigate the construct validity of test scores is designed to answer a crucial question. The main issue is this: Based on the current theoretical understanding of the construct that the test claims to measure, do we find the kinds of relationships with other criteria that the theory predicts? For example, we might propose, as a viable theory, the idea that intelligence scores increase from early childhood through to adolescence and adulthood (a finding that has consistently been demonstrated). Any new measure of intelligence should reflect this developmental trend.

Within this context an important construct validation technique involves determining whether there is evidence of convergent and discriminant validity. For example, tests in the traditional intelligence realm consistently show high correlations with tests of similar abilities (i.e., convergent validity evidence). They should also correlate weakly with other qualities, such as extraversion (i.e., discriminant validity evidence).

In the special case of emotional intelligence, these criteria are pivotal. It needs to be established that EI is a form of cognitive ability and that it is independent from well-established constructs like personality and intelligence. There is a tension, however, between these two criteria. The relationship between emotional intelligence and ability might turn out to be so strong that EI simply represents an old wine (i.e., intelligence) in a new bottle (i.e., emotional intelligence). Most conceptualizations of EI in fact suggest that it should share some overlap with both intelligence and personality constructs. However, these accounts fail to specify just how large the correlations between emotional intelligence and the existing constructs should be in order for EI to remain independent.

Thus, in any attempt to evaluate the distinctiveness of emotional intelligence, the magnitude of relationship between it and other relevant psychological variables must be ascertained. Intelligence is high on this list of "other variables," as is the assessment of emotional states. Researchers need also to determine how distinct emotional intelligence is from well-established personality dimensions, such as those encapsulated under the five factor model: neuroticism, extroversion, openness, agreeableness, and conscientiousness (see chapters 4 and 6). Throughout this book we will have cause to discuss psychometric issues and the extent of overlap between emotional intelligence and these personality dimensions, as has proved to be an important, and at times controversial, aspect of the research associated with emotional intelligence (Davies et al. 1998). We will also present data showing that for self-assessment of EI, at least, the amount of overlap between emotional intelligence instruments and personality measures can be extraordinarily high.

It is equally important to address convergent validity, and to demonstrate the close correspondence between alternative measures of emotional intelligence. Evidence is limited because of the relatively recent history of the vast majority of EI tests. Nevertheless, some relevant information is at hand, and the results are mixed. Thus, as we will demonstrate, relationships between EI and extant psychological constructs are sometimes very high. At other times, however, these are surprisingly low. Moreover in certain instances these relations are opposite in sign (i.e., negative when they should be positive, and vice versa) to that predicted by theories of emotion. The same holds true when certain classes of EI tests are related to measures of intelligence.

Statistical Techniques Used in Validation

The Pearson Correlation   Correlational data will feature largely in this book. In probability theory and statistics, correlation and its ensuing metric the correlation coefficient (denoted by r) indicate both the strength and direction of the relationship between two variables. Broadly speaking, this is a numeric measure of the strength of linear relationship between two variables, bounded by -1 (where two variables are perfectly inversely related) and 1 (where two variables are perfectly related). A correlation coefficient of zero indicates the two variables are completely independent (see figure 2.2 for a graphical representation of different correlations).

It can be difficult to attach meaning to coefficients of different magnitude, and to decide whether a correlation is large enough to be interesting in addressing a particular problem. Unlike many statistical metrics, the issue here is one of effect size rather than statistical significance. For instance, a trivially small correlation (e.g., $r = 0.09$) may attain significance if the sample size (i.e., having 10,000 respondents tested) is large enough.

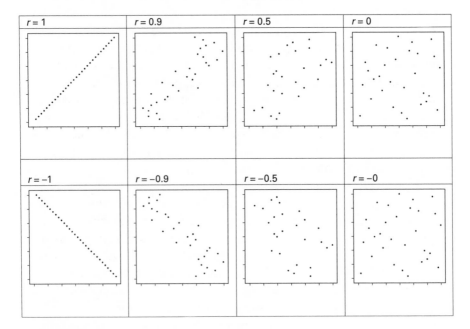

| $r = 1$ | $r = 0.9$ | $r = 0.5$ | $r = 0$ |
| $r = -1$ | $r = -0.9$ | $r = -0.5$ | $r = -0$ |

Figure 2.2
Correlations between pairs of variables, represented graphically, in what is known as a scatter plot, with the correlation coefficients r given at the top

Assigning verbal labels to coefficients of different size is more or less arbitrary (see Cohen 1988). It is necessary however, to establish a consistent standard. Thus we will interpret the strength of correlation between emotional intelligence and other measures as follows:

1. Nonexistent or trivial (absolute value of correlation between $r = 0.00 - 0.09$).

2. Small (absolute value of correlation between $r = 0.10 - 0.29$).

3. Moderate or medium (absolute value of $r = 0.30 - 0.49$).

4. Large (absolute value of $r = 0.50 - 0.69$).

5. Very large (absolute value of $r = 0.70 - 1.00$).

Provided that an emotional intelligence test has small to medium overlap with another test (and assuming that each of these tests is moderately reliable), we can be reasonably certain that the two tests are different but related. In such instances we might claim that the EI test has shown discriminant validity. A large correlation calls this property into question, while a very large correlation suggests considerable redundancy. Convergent validity evidence requires a very large correlation (e.g., as typically found when correlating very similar intelligence tests). A large correlation between two tests might suggest that further test refinement can bring about better convergence, but a correlation of less than 0.50 suggests that the prospects for attaining convergent validity are gloomy.

Clearly, judging whether a given emotional intelligence test has predictive power is a complex undertaking. The task becomes thornier when one wishes to know the extent that a result holds true over and above other tests to which an EI test relates. Generally, the poorer the discrimination between two tests (i.e., the more they share in common, evidenced through a large correlation), the less likely it is that each test's predictive power, for predicting scores on one test from scores on the other test, will be high. However, the small overlap between a measure of EI and an intelligence test may explain the apparent predictive power of the emotional intelligence test disappearing when that cognitive ability is controlled. Conversely, even with large to very large overlap, it is conceivable that the EI test will remain predictive with the second test controlled.

Correlation undoubtedly provides an important tool for assessing validity evidence. Beyond what we have discussed, the calculation of reliability parameters is also based on the general principles underlying the correlation coefficient. However, there are a range of additional statistical procedures, some fairly simple to conduct, others based on high-level mathematical models, that psychometricians have at their disposal to ascertain validity. By far and away, the simplest of these techniques involves assessing mean differences between groups. As we saw earlier, this is because construct validity evidence is often based on demonstration of group differences. More complex procedures are in abundance, including those based on classic test theory, Bayesian statistics, regression analysis, item response theory, mixture models, and exploratory and confirmatory factor analyses. Because of their importance we discuss some of the major approaches in the passages that follow (see, however, Crocker and Algina 1986 and Nunnally 1978 if you are interested in learning more about these topics).

Multivariate Techniques   A correlation coefficient is a *bivariate* statistic; that is, it tells us about the association between two variables only. At other times we want to analyze multiple variables simultaneously. We can give only a brief introduction to the multivariate statistics used for this purpose here, but we will briefly outline two families of statistics that are important in the psychometrics of EI: multiple regression and factor analysis. We should point out that use of multivariate statistics tends to be more contentious than basic statistics. Multivariate statistics often depend on a greater number of assumptions about the form of the data, such that researchers may need to make subjective judgments in running and interpreting these analyses. We present a highly simplified account here, which does not aim to do justice to the many analytical and interpretive controversies of multivariate statistics.

Multiple regression is an extension of standard correlation that evaluates how well we can predict a dependent or outcome variable from multiple predictors. In personality research we might predict job performance using a questionnaire with multiple scales, such as the Big Five dimensions previously mentioned. We could work out the five correlations relating performance to each of the Big Five separately. Multiple regression takes the analysis further, by telling us how well the five scales *jointly* predict performance; we may be able to improve prediction by using all five scales together.

The technique is based on constructing a regression equation that relates the outcome variable to a weighted sum of the predictor variables. If we use standardized variables, then the weight (or "regression coefficient") for each predictor varies between -1 and $+1$ (similar to the correlation coefficient). For example, we might have an equation for predicting job performance from the Big Five thus:

Job performance $= 0.4$ (Extraversion) $- 0.1$ (Neuroticism)

$+ 0.4$ (Conscientiousness) $+ 0.1$ (Agreeableness)

$- 0.1$ (Openness)

The weights in the equation indicate (crudely) the relevance of the individual predictors. In the example, perhaps the job is a sales job, where extraversion (E) and conscientiousness (C) are important for success. Clearly, these predictors have higher weights, and neuroticism (N), agreeableness (A), and openness (O) are of lesser importance.

We can obtain several useful pieces of information from a regression analysis. We can calculate a multiple regression coefficient (R) that tells us how well we can predict the outcome variable from all the predictors taken together. Unlike, the bivariate r, R varies between 0 and $+1$, although its interpretation is otherwise similar. The square of R is often interpreted as the proportion of the variance in the outcome that can be predicted. The regression equation can also be used in practical settings to estimate the likely outcome for an individual; such as the anticipated performance of a job applicant who has completed a personality questionnaire. A company could then use predicted job performance, along with other relevant information, as a basis for hiring applicants.

We can also test whether each individual predictor adds significantly to R, which can help us simplify the equation by stripping out variables that do not contribute to improved prediction. By extension, we can test whether *sets* of variables add significantly to predicting variation in the outcome, which gives us a further test for the discriminant validity of measures of EI (also called incremental validity).

For example, suppose that we measure personality, job performance, and a set of questionnaires for EI in a sample of employees. We might first construct a regression equation that relates job performance to the Big Five personality factors, as above. Then we can add the EI measures to the regression equation, and test whether, as a set, they add significantly to the variance in job performance accounted for. If the test is significant—meaning EI improves our prediction of job performance— we can say that the EI measures have discriminant and incremental validity in relation to the Big Five. That is, even if there is some overlap or correlation between EI and the Big Five, the EI measures pick up some meaningful personal qualities that are *not* covered by the conventional personality measure. Conversely, if tests of this kind fail to provide discriminant evidence, we may question whether assessing EI tells us anything of value or practical utility about the test takers.

Factor analysis is also concerned with the interrelationships of variables. That is to say, the analysis aims to simplify data by grouping together sets of variables as manifestations of a common underlying (or "latent") factor. Loosely speaking, factor analysis identifies groups of variables that correlate with one another. For example, if, in personality research, we had scales for anxiety, depression, anger, and stress, factor analysis might tell us that these measures "belong together" as expressions of a common factor of negative emotionality (neuroticism in the Big Five). Factor analysis is most useful for discriminating different dimensions within a domain. For example, in personality research (e.g., Goldberg 1993) factor analysis has shown that people's self-descriptions cluster into five separate groups of personality traits (the five factor model). Similarly, in EI research, the four-branch model of Mayer et al. (2003) is supported by factor analytic data showing that ability-based tests for EI relate to four separate dimensions (emotion perception, assimilation, understanding, and management). The dimensions may be required to be independent ("orthogonal rotation"), or allowed to correlate ("oblique rotation"). In ability research, dimensions are typically correlated because different "primary" abilities such as verbal and math abilities also relate to a general, overarching intelligence factor (see chapter 3).

Factor analysis is really a family of related techniques. An important distinction is that between *exploratory* and *confirmatory* factor analysis. Exploratory factor analysis seeks to map the factors in a domain without any preconceived notion of what those factors might be; it may be hard to choose between alternate factor solutions in this case. Confirmatory factor analysis starts with a hypothetical model, and tests the goodness of fit of the model to the data. This technique can decisively reject possible models, so it can be more powerful than exploratory approaches. For example, the researcher might test a model in which tests for EI and cognitive ability related to a single general intelligence factor against a model in which the tests related to two separate emotional and cognitive factors. Confirmatory factor analysis is an application of a more general approach to multivariate analysis known as structural equation modeling (e.g., Bentler 1980). The researcher may build and test fairly elaborate models of how latent psychological constructs (e.g., cognitive and emotional intelligence) relate to one another and to measured test scores.

The Many Varieties of Psychological Tests

It is difficult to get a precise estimate on the number of tests developed for psychology, education, and business, but these certainly number in the tens of thousands. Various sources, such as the *Mental Measurements Yearbook* or *Tests in Print,* review the better known among these measures. Often, with each passing dissertation, the rise (and fall) of new psychological constructs, or the advent of a new Internet site devoted to human resources or a consultancy service, there appears a new test. The tests range from the commercial to the entertaining (e.g., www.queendom .com). And at any given moment they are being used to make a range of personally relevant decisions that can be construed as being high, medium, low, or indeterminate stakes, dependent on the value attached to them by an organization, an application, or the test-user. For example, these tests might be used (with the stakes constrained by the preceding factors) to:

1. determine whether an individual can enter the college of their choice;

2. ascertain whether an individual may move into a higher position on the corporate ladder;

3. give the individual a certain level of self-insight or;

4. assist in choosing a dating partner on the basis of a compatibility metric (e.g., the service provided by eHarmony.com).

For those armed with a working knowledge of what reliability and validity are, it should be clear that not all these tests meet the required standards. Indeed it may be for fear that experts will find the measure problematic that a company is unwilling to put a favored commercial test into the scientific literature. This may also be why a large number of tests developed as part of dissertations are never published. Even so, large testing companies and experienced academics, generally working with an extensive background in psychometrics, are capable of providing construct validity evidence for their measures. Hence the number of reputable tests number in the thousands. Fortunately, there are ways of classifying the host of measures. It is to a discussion of this topic that we now turn.

Classifying Psychological Tests

Psychologists have devised different ways to measure phenomena of interest. Because there are so many tests available for use in psychology, education, and business, various commentators have proposed ways of

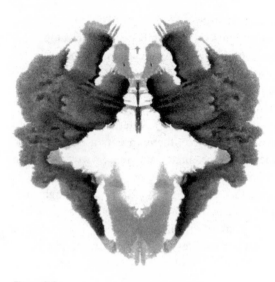

Figure 2.3
A sample item from the Rorschach Inkblot Test

classifying them. Some of the taxonomies will help give the reader a flavor for the nature of psychological tests. For example, tests have been classified as measuring either typical or maximum performance (Cronbach 1990). The former attempts to measure what a person will do, over the long run and all things being equal. Projective measures, such as the Rorschach inkblots (see figure 2.3), self-reports, peer reports, and supervisor reports, are generally considered typical performance measures. By contrast, maximal performance refers to what a person can do. Tests that have a "correct" solution (e.g., intelligence, achievement, and aptitude tests; most of the pesky tests you needed to do either in college or before you got a job) are the prominent maximum performance measures. Measures of response time to both simple and complex stimuli are also common instruments falling under this heading.

Because the system of psychological test classification is imperfect (i.e., there are tests that do not fall so readily within it), other systems have been proposed. For example, there is a growing trend to distinguish between cognitive (i.e., tests of complex thought processes) and noncognitive (i.e., all other personal qualities) assessment. Practitioners often prefer classifications based on the general purpose to which a test was designed. Tests are generally designed to assess a construct, such as personality type, interests, neuropsychological function, or intelligence. And whatever high-level system is adopted, aspects associated with test presentation remain yet another salient dimension for classification. The reader is doubtless familiar, for example, with the distinction between multiple-choice, open-ended, or short answer response options. Then there is the issue of who gives the test and to whom. Many tests are designed only to be given one-on-one by trained practitioners. Others may be administered to a group, generally under standardized conditions, with the credentials of the test administrator dependent on the intended purpose of the assessment (e.g., whether it is to be used for high or low stakes). Test medium represents still another dimension for classification. Tests can be given as paper and pencil, via computer, or over the Web (sometimes referred to as Internet based testing).

Self-report Assessment: A Worked Example Despite the multitude of options that are available for developing a test, it is worth noting that the assessment of EI has, by and large, focused on two broad approaches. The first is self-report assessment. Table 2.1 includes a set of questions, along with a response scale conforming to this convention, which we use only for illustrative purposes. You have simply to answer these items as honestly as you can. As with the vast majority of self-report measures, this test can easily be given to large groups of people concurrently. The test medium can be paper and pencil, computer, or an Internet platform. A trained test administer does not need to be present, although in validation studies this is always preferable. You could, for example, simply check all the response options corresponding to "Never" in the scale because you find it boring. Having someone monitor your performance often stops this practice from happening. The assessment also can be completed in a relatively short amount of time. Because generally this type of test is self-paced, there are differences in how fast people complete the items.

At this point we ask you to go ahead and answer the questions as openly and honestly as you can. We are going to use the test to illustrate a number of features that we have commented on previously, including those related to reliability and validity evidence. The exercise is also intended to cover new territory. This includes issues related to scoring (a scoring key is available in the sidebar); once you have completed the questionnaire, go to this and score it). As a working example this test should also serve to impress on the reader some of the nuances that the test developer must be aware of. In addition it reveals just how difficult it is to construct a questionnaire that meets the best available scientific standards as we have previously discussed.

Table 2.1
Items of a prototypical self-report measure of emotional intelligence

1. I can tell when someone is in a bad mood.	Never	Sometimes	Often	Always
2. I can read a good mood in another person's face.	Never	Sometimes	Often	Always
3. I can tell when someone is enthusiastic about something.	Never	Sometimes	Often	Always
4. I have problems identifying if someone is anxious about something.	Never	Sometimes	Often	Always
5. I can tell if a person is sad by the tone of their voice.	Never	Sometimes	Often	Always
6. I try to raise my level of enthusiasm to get the job done.	Never	Sometimes	Often	Always
7. I know how to get someone into a good mood.	Never	Sometimes	Often	Always
8. I have no idea how to create a happy environment at my work.	Never	Sometimes	Often	Always
9. I use laughter and smiles to make other people comfortable in uneasy situations.	Never	Sometimes	Often	Always
10. When I am feeling bad, I have no idea how to change the situation.	Never	Sometimes	Often	Always

Now that you have performed the test and have a set of scores, here are some things to consider. First, notice that there are a series of questions measuring the two subscales comprising this test, not just one or two. The reason for the range of questions relates to both reliability and validity. A self-reported test with just one or two questions turns out to have low reliability; it also has poor content validity because it can only sample a very limited number of items from the content domain. In fact, if our test were a true operational test, it would be two to three times longer and cover broader content. Second, you may notice that this test is somewhat incomplete; it measures emotion perception and emotional management, but there are no questions asking about how you understand emotions, for example. We have omitted measures of this, and other, components, because the test would obviously take much longer to complete. But for illustrative purposes it serves a dual role. It shows, for example, that if our theory is not quite right, we may miss out on important components of the concept that we are trying to assess.

Scoring key and score report for the emotional intelligence self-report items given in table 2.1

Scoring key	Never	Sometimes	Often	Always
Emotion perception				
1. I can tell when someone is in a bad mood.	1	2	3	4
2. I can read a good mood in another person's face.	1	2	3	4
3. I can tell when someone is enthusiastic about something.	1	2	3	4
4. I have problems identifying if someone is anxious about something.	4	3	2	1
5. I can tell if a person is sad from the tone of their voice.	1	2	3	4
Managing emotions				
6. I try to raise my level of enthusiasm to get the job done.	1	2	3	4
7. I know how to get someone into a good mood.	1	2	3	4
8. I have no idea how to create a happy environment at my work.	4	3	2	1
9. I use laughter and smiles to make other people comfortable in uneasy situations.	1	2	3	4
10. When I am feeling bad, I have no idea how to change the situation.	4	3	2	1

Note: Use the scoring key provided in this table to award points for your responses in table 2.1. Then sum up your responses for each of the two subscales: emotion perception (items 1 to 5) and emotion management (items 6 to 10). For example, if you answered "sometimes" for all 5 emotion perception questions in table 2.1, you would receive a score of 11.

Below is your score report. It tells you how to interpret the summed scores you have just calculated. To avoid attaching unwanted significance to the test, the capsule descriptions (while capturing aspects of the meaning of the constructs) are highly contrived and intended to flatter and/or amuse.

Emotion perception: The ability to identify the perception of emotions in the self and other people.

Low (1–6): You have some problems perceiving the emotional signals that people give out. You are also slightly out of touch with your own emotions. But don't distress. You are in good company. Many of the world's best academics score similarly to you. Aside from professorial duties, you might be best off taking a job in Antarctica or writing blogs on the Internet.

Medium (7–14): Like all people scoring in the middle of a distribution, the glass is both half-full and half-empty. There is nothing to worry about, neither is there anything to proclaim proudly to your friends. In the world of perceiving emotion, you are, sad to say, just like all the rest of us, sometimes good, and sometimes bad.

High (15–20): You can read people like a book, and you are not too bad with identifying your own emotions either. Jobs to consider: working as a customs agent, anything to do with the service industry, or the many helping professions. If you got 19 or more, think about a major career switch, the life of a Texas Holdem champion looms as a distinct possibility.

Managing emotions: The ability to manage your own, and other people's emotions.

Low (1–6): You have problems managing your emotions or those of other people. There are a long list of very successful folks, though, who have done wonders with a similar temperament. The tennis star John McEnroe (before he became a late night TV show host) springs to mind, so too a plethora of celebrities, including Tom Cruise, Russell Crowe, and Charlie Sheen. Don't forget too, the irascible Basil Fawlty.

Medium (7–14): It's likely that you can manage your own emotions pretty well and so too the emotions of other people. But let's face it. With all the other things one has to manage—finances, time, life—you have to make a decision where to excel. Trying to manage emotions is not as high on this laundry list and rightly so.

High (15–20): You can manage your own emotions and those of other people exceedingly well. With a little bit of luck you might end up the CEO of a large franchise, a kindergarten teacher, or the winner of a Nobel Peace Prize. But a word of warning if you scored too high (19–20). Niccolò Machiavelli encapsulated this dimension particularly well in *The Prince*; too much emotion management, particularly of others, can be a dangerous thing!

Third, some questions are reverse-keyed. That is, you have to answer in the opposite direction to questions that are positively-keyed to get a high numerical score. This technique is designed to reduce acquiescence and other response styles, a topic we will return to shortly. Fourth, it would be very easy to fake this test, if you knew in advance what it was measuring. Indeed, doubtless taking it again, if you wanted to impress a friend or loved one, you might give responses that elevate your score. Fifth, the numeric scores are based on the assumption that these components all sum together to represent the constructs of interest. But if the test is not reliable, this assumption may be incorrect. Sixth, you may feel the score you get is very accurate, or decidedly wrong. An inaccurate score may be because you were feeling tired, anxious, ill, or a host of other factors that introduced a major source of error. It might also be because you lack full insight into these aspects of your behavior. Finally, without the ensuing report, you might find the task of completing the questions to have been relatively pointless.

This exercise also should have raised a number of higher level questions that you might like to keep in mind as we review the various tests of emotional intelligence. For example, those of you who have taken a personality test, like the Myers-Briggs Type Indicator, might have found some of the questions bear a great deal of resemblance to assessments of this ilk. Moreover, if you have taken an intelligence test, you might lament this is decidedly different, perhaps too much so. You might also have contemplated that no two people's responses would be exactly the same. These might vary considerably depending on your gender or the country you live in. And the list of possible reasons for these differences is seemingly endless. The source of differences might result from whether you dwell in the city or the country, have had a good upbringing or not, are old or young, and so forth. These are all good issues to explore, and they feed into the validity of the measure.

Before moving on and giving you a similar first-hand experience of some performance items that might comprise a test of EI, a word of warning. You should not place great stock in the test you have just completed for a number of reasons. For one, these are but a selection of items from a full form that is currently being developed and used in research. As mentioned previously, it misses out on a number of important subcomponents. Moreover even the full form has limited construct validity evidence; there simply is not a corpus of research behind it.

The score report also was written so as to not be taken seriously and for good reason. Proper score reports require a large normative database to provide statistically meaningful results, including cut-scores (i.e., numeric ranges where low, intermediate, and high scores can be aligned to the population mean). The text related to your score should be supported by available scientific and clinical knowledge, with important caveats. For example, if this test had suitable validity evidence, too low (or sometimes too high) scores might require that you get a professional to administer related tests. At this point, coupled with clinical judgment, a professional might also recommend possible interventions if these ancillary tests yield converging information. By providing you with light-hearted feedback, we are intentionally preventing the test from possibly being misused (i.e., protecting its consequential validity). Most important, we are cautious about the status of self-report measures of emotional intelligence. But that is another story for a later day. Delay of gratification is, after all, a supposed important characteristic of the emotionally intelligent.

Performance-Based Assessment: A Worked Example   An alternative to asking people to self-evaluate with respect to their ability to perceive, understand, manage, or otherwise process emotions is to develop tests that assess actual performance in these domains. The sidebar on the next page contains a selection of prototypical measures falling under this category (i.e., performance-based assessment). These are all sample items, and they are drawn from a number of different sources conforming to this convention. Unlike the self-report example, we do not provide a score report for this set of items. Our intention here is different. We wish to highlight, in particular, not only the ostensibly different processes needed to solve test items of this type but also the nature of scoring performance assessments of emotional processes. As it turns out, this is a nontrivial task requiring some explanation.

Working through the various sample items given in the sidebar, you may immediately notice some important differences from the self-report items given previously. For example, likely you had to devote significantly more cognitive resources to complete the task. If you need any convincing of this, try performing both sets of tasks again, while holding a conversation with another person. Whereas the former may be doable, the latter is virtually impossible. This is exactly what one might come to expect of a task assessing a form of intelligence. Moreover you might find it particularly difficult to fake your responses on this task, for as we will demonstrate, the scoring here is complex. Each item also is relatively time-consuming to complete. In addition you might wish that you had a

---

Prototypical item types conforming to the assessment of emotional intelligence using performance-based approaches

Type A: Emotion perception of faces   Your task is to examine the picture, and then determine how much each of the listed emotions is represented in it. (Note that the picture is of one of the authors of the current book. Guess which one?)

	Definitely not present				Definitely present
Anger	1	2	3	4	5
Sadness	1	2	3	4	5
Happiness	1	2	3	4	5
Disgust	1	2	3	4	5
Fear	1	2	3	4	5
Surprise	1	2	3	4	5

---

trained administrator present to answer certain questions related to the tasks at hand.

There are nevertheless similarities between these performance-based prototypes and the self-report sample items that are worth mentioning. Both could, for example, be given by paper and pencil or over the Internet. You might even imagine noteworthy differences between people taking this test form, similar to the differences observed for the questionnaire. Moreover, although we do not provide you with a set of scores and response feedback, the big question we encounter is the same as for the questionnaire assessment: How exactly would you score these items? There appear to be no correct responses to any of these items.

Type B: Understanding emotions   Read the scenario and then answer the question to the best of your ability (adapted from the PhD thesis of Carolyn MacCann 2006).

If the current situation continues, Denise's employer will probably be able to move her job to a location much closer to her home, which is something she really wants.
Denise is most likely to feel?
[A] Distress
[B] Joy
[C] Surprise
[D] Hope
[E] Fear

Type C: Emotion management   Read the scenario and then rate possible responses for their effectiveness (adapted from the PhD thesis of Carolyn MacCann 2006).

Gerry has had several short-term jobs in the same industry, but is excited about starting a job in a different industry. His father casually remarks that he will probably last six months.
Rate the effectiveness of the following action that Gerry might take on the scale below:

	Ineffective				Effective
Tell his father he is completely wrong.	1	2	3	4	5
Prove him wrong by working hard to succeed at the new job.	1	2	3	4	5
Think of the positives of the new job.	1	2	3	4	5
Ignore his father's comments.	1	2	3	4	5

While there is considerable difficulty in determining how best to score responses to stimuli involving emotional content, the solutions offered have been ingenious. Proponents of EI measures have promoted three alternative scoring procedures, which are thought to discriminate right from wrong answers (Mayer, Caruso, et al. 2000). Below we discuss these approaches to scoring, along with arguments that might be used to either justify or else question these metrics.

1. *Consensual scoring* In this approach, an examinee receives credit for endorsing responses that the population of all test takers endorses. Thus, if the population of people taking the test agrees that happiness is definitely present in the face depicted in the sidebar, then that becomes the correct response. This approach assumes that observations obtained from a large, representative sample of people can be "pooled" and then jointly used to provide reliable indicators of EI. This approach adopts a commonly accepted dictum from sociology. That is, there are no right or wrong emotions that people feel, but rather correct or incorrect perception of peoples' emotions.

This approach assumes that EI reflects how emotions are perceived, and subsequently expressed, by the vast majority of individuals. For example, if the majority of people who see a particular film perceive it as sad, the emotionally intelligent response—and the one that would confer most benefits in dealing with others' emotions—is to view it as sad. This scoring ignores the expert view. For example, it does not matter that a film critic finds a film to be happy. What counts is the extent that the individual matches the majority opinion. If you will, the People's Choice Awards matter more than the views of Roger Ebert and Richard Roeper. This principle is in direct contrast to traditional measures of cognitive intelligence, where an objective measure of truth is considered, and is an important point at which EI diverges from other forms of intelligence.

The basis for consensus scoring is the view that the pooled response of large normative samples is accurate (Legree 1995). The idea seems to be that, if we ask respondents about typical emotional encounters, the group as a whole has sufficient expertise for the modal response to be correct. It is argued too that both evolution and culture tend to select emotionally correct responses, through natural selection, or some cultural analogue (Mayer, Caruso, et al. 2000). However, there are serious concerns about bias in consensus judgment. For example, there is a traditional British belief that a "stiff upper lip" is the best response to emotional problems. However, research on emotional disclosure (see Pennebaker 1997) suggests that this belief is incorrect (although it might prove to be consensual among Britons of a certain age). Similarly cultural consensus taken at different historical times might link emotional problems to evil spirits, to excess black bile, to the Oedipus complex; the list is quite vast. It would be foolhardy to suppose that current Western culture has a perfect clarity of emotional vision that was denied to our ancestors.

There are also concerns about the validity of consensus judgments that cut across gender and cultural boundaries. In some respects consensus scoring addresses the problem of cross-cultural differences in appropriate emotional behaviors, in that responses can be judged against the consensus for the respondent's culture. For example, cultures differ dramatically in the extent to which grief is expressed openly. The Kagwahiv people of Brazil traditionally suppressed mourning to the extent of disposing of the dead person's possessions and destroying his or her house (Kracke 1988). Muting of grief was motivated by a fear of ghosts and by a mood-regulative goal of avoiding sorrow evoked by memories of the dead person. Such behaviors would likely be perceived as cold-hearted by cultures in which the grief of mourning is more prolonged. People around the world increasingly live in multicultural societies with a variety of social norms for expressing and managing emotion, such that the normative values applied vary from setting to setting.

A final problem with consensus scoring is that is likely to be more effective in assessing "emotional stupidity" than emotional intelligence. Consensus is likely to be more accurate for questions that test whether a person would avoid a grossly incorrect response (e.g., spitting at one's friend) than questions that test the more delicate problems of everyday social interaction. In intelligence testing, it is usual to select items with a graduated series of difficulties, so the test discriminates between individuals equally well at all levels of intelligence. Item analyses may be conducted to ensure that the probability of correct response increases with overall test score. The issue of sampling items so that EI is reliably assessed across its full range seems to have been entirely ignored in the literature, although it is a major concern of intelligence test research (see Nunnally 1978). Consensus scoring is likely to lead to special problems at the top end of the scale, especially in distinguishing the "emotional genius" from the normally functioning, emotionally intelligent person. If a test item asks about an especially difficult emotional encounter, by definition, only a relatively small percentage of exceptionally gifted persons will answer correctly, meaning that the consensual answer will certainly be incorrect. For example, on a difficult four-choice question, if only 10 percent of respondents answer correctly, at least 30 percent will check the most popular, incorrect choice. Consensual scoring will then penalize the "correct" responders because their response differs from the typical answer. In consequence their EI score will be artificially reduced.

2. *Expert scoring* Experts in the field of emotions (psychologists, psychiatrists, philosophers, etc.) examine the stimuli (e.g., the prose passage) and then use their best judgment to determine the emotion expressed in that stimulus. Presumably, the expert brings professional savoir faire (along with a history of behavioral knowledge) to bear on judgments about emotional meanings. The test taker receives credit for ratings that correspond to those of the experts employed, which is an attempt at an objective criteria for truth, as employed in cognitive tests of ability.

The rationale for expert scoring is that psychologists versed in emotional intelligence can set those standards. However, some forms of emotional intelligence tests appear to be more open to this measurement procedure than others. For example, Mayer, Salovey, et al. (e.g., 2000a, b) propose branches of emotional intelligence, spanning a continuum of abstraction that one may get a flavor of by comparing the test items given in the sidebar. These range from basic skills of perception and appraisal of emotion to higher level synthetic skills for emotion management that integrate lower level skills. It seems plausible that lower level skills might be assessed objectively. For instance, the extensive research literature on facial expression as a universal indicator of emotion (e.g., Ekman 1999) might support objectively scored tests of identification of facial emotion because an expert can unequivocally identify the emotion expressed by a face.

However, expert scoring of more abstract, higher level qualities, such as managing the emotions of oneself and others, seems more problematic. Certain emotional reactions may be assessed, according to logically consistent criteria, only by reference to personal and societal standards. For example, the "emotionally intelligent" response to being insulted or mocked by a coworker depends on contextual factors such as personal and cultural norms for behavior, the individual's position in the status hierarchy, and the presence of other individuals (see Roberts et al. 2001). In different circumstances it might be appropriate to make a joke of the situation, to ignore the insult, or to confront the other person. Furthermore there are multiple criteria for deciding whether the response is effective, which may conflict (e.g., maintaining good relationships with others vs. advancing in one's career vs. maintaining self-esteem).

Figure 2.4
Super EQ makes for riveting fiction, but is unlikely to be realized in any one individual

Experts may indeed have more knowledge than "lay" persons, but even this expertise is limited. First, research on emotion typically reveals statistical rather than directly contingent, relationships. For example, being insulted most typically leads to anger. Second, there are multiple domains of expertise leading to conflicting viewpoints. A psychologist's expert judgment might differ from that of experts in other relevant fields. For example, the solutions to a child's emotional problems proposed by a cognitive therapist, an evolutionary psychologist, a psychoanalyst, a social worker, a high school teacher, and a gender studies professor would likely differ drastically. Our take on this issue is illustrated in another way in figure 2.4; the idea of an emotional intelligence superbeing is likely to lay only in the realm of fictitious characters such as the one depicted.

3. *Target scoring*   A judge (i.e., the test taker) assesses what a target (artist, photographer, musician, etc.) is portraying at the time they were engaged in some emotional activity (e.g., writing the passage of prose, taking the picture). A series of emotion rating scales are then used to match the emotions conveyed by the stimuli to those reported by the target. It is commonly held that the target has more information than is available to the outside observer (Mayer and Geher 1996) and is used as the criterion for scoring judges' responses. Criticisms of this scoring approach abound (e.g., the technique requires that the target has insight into processes that might operate unconsciously) such that it has rarely been used in scientific studies.

Table 2.2
Differences between performance-based and self-report measures of EI

Self-reported EI	Performance-based EI
Typical performance	Maximal performance
Internal appraisal of performance	External appraisal of performance
Response bias may be great	Response bias minimal (or nonexistent)
Administration time short, testing easy	Administration time long, testing complicated
Personality-like	Ability-like

Self-report versus Performance Assessment   Clearly, there are major differences between the self-report and performance measures that are implicated throughout the preceding discussion. These differences suggest certain strengths and weaknesses within each of these respective approaches, which we summarize in table 2.2. Below we discuss these qualities further and make a series of comments that we will reinforce in our review of specific EI measures.

1. *Typical versus maximal performance*   Performance tests have been developed to assess actual EI level. Self-report measures, by contrast, can only assess an individual's perceived level of EI, no matter how well they are marketed by test publishers as the "real thing." In short, using the terminology introduced earlier, performance tests are indicative of maximal attainment, whereas self-report measures assess typical attributes.

2. *Internal versus external appraisal*   Self-report measures require people to have insight into their own level of EI. Unfortunately, people may not have an accurate understanding of their intelligence level in any given domain. If you need any convincing, try asking someone to rate the following statement: "I am an extremely intelligent person." Doubtless, you will get responses that range from the modest to the absurd in terms of what you observe in the daily lives of that person. Indeed past research has found only modest correlations between self-rated and actual ability measures (e.g., see Paulhus et al. 1998). Similarly Ciarrochi et al. (2001) found that self-reported emotion perception is unrelated to how people actually perform in recognizing emotions. These problems are not relevant to performance tests; you are what you get on the test (assuming the test is both reliable and valid).

3. *Response bias*   A major difficulty with self-report measures is that people can distort their responses in order to appear better (or worse) than they actually are, consciously or unconsciously. Performance-based

tests are free of such bias. Indeed the self-perceptions assessed by questionnaire may not be particularly accurate or even available to conscious interpretation. They are also vulnerable to the entire gamut of response sets and social desirability factors afflicting self-report measures, as well as deception and impression management (see Furnham 1986).

Two types of problems may arise. First, especially in practical situations, people may deliberately lie. An applicant for a job requiring counseling skills may be reluctant to admit to lack of empathy or interpersonal skills. Ironically the more the public acceptance of EI, the greater the motivation to "fake" high EI is likely to be. Second, response bias may reflect not deliberate deception, but lack of awareness of one's own shortcomings. Paulhus and John (1998) identify two self-deceptive tendencies toward self-enhancement, which they link to power and approval motives, respectively. The first self-favoring tendency is an egoistic bias toward exaggerating one's social and intellectual status. The person has unrealistically positive self-perceptions with respect to qualities such as dominance, courage, and ability. The second tendency is a moralistic bias, associated with overestimation of traits such as agreeableness and dutifulness, and denial of socially unacceptable behaviors.

To combat these types of problems, self-report measures can include scales that measure the amount people are distorting or are otherwise open to socially desirable responding (e.g., Bar-On 1997). To counteract this criticism in other fields where self-reports are used, researchers have also compared self-assessed responses to reports provided by a respondent's peers (e.g., see Costa and McCrae 1992a). As we will see shortly, validation studies of this type have yet to be systematically conducted by researchers employing self-report EI assessment. And on the rare occasion where they have, the results turn out to be relatively disappointing.

4. *Practical considerations* Performance measures are generally time-consuming to complete and more difficult to score than are self-report measures. They also require more detailed instructions and greater training for the test giver to administer the test competently. These various disparities occur because self-report measures allow people to summarize their level of EI in a few, brief concise statements (e.g., "I am in touch with my emotions"). Performance measures, on the other hand, require a substantial number of observations before EI level can be ascertained with any degree of accuracy. It takes, for example, about 2 to 3 minutes to complete an emotion perception questionnaire, whereas it takes about 15 minutes to complete a performance measure assessing the same construct.

Concluding Comments on Measurement of Emotional Intelligence

The preceding, rather lengthy, foray into psychological assessment will have armed the reader with a set of critical tools to evaluate the tests reviewed in the chapters that follow. Central to sound measurement is the establishment of a test's reliability and construct validity evidence. By including a sample of assessment types, we also trust that a context has been established for the remainder of the book.

For the chapters that follow we will assume that EI is a viable scientific construct. We will therefore assume that measurement is possible through a set of prespecified operations, delineated in chapters 3 and 4 to follow. We also take the view that by critically appraising instruments designed to assess EI, we can move closer to providing a model of EI that will satisfy best scientific standards.

These later chapters are not for the fainthearted. Because psychological assessment is both a relatively benign scientific exercise and a rewarding commercial enterprise, the ensuing critical commentary is bound to engender controversy. In particular, we argue that some of EI is repackaged measures of other psychological processes and stamped with the "emotional intelligence" label. Of course, while this is not a bad marketing technique, it is an approach generally discouraged in science. Imagine the problems biologists would have if the exact same species were classified with four or five different names, and these were each studied as though separate species. Imagine too the confusion that would result if biologists used the same name for different species: Another problem for assessments of EI is that different tests actually measure very different personal qualities. So such tests cause *more* confusion than clarity and are damaging to the field. Arguably, they may even be harmful to the individual, especially if followed-up with extravagant claims. Such an instrument might even have been the one that you took that piqued your curiosity enough to purchase this book, and you might feel a certain degree of remorse or regret for having been seduced by its messages.

It is worth noting, however, the extent to which the various definitions and assessments of emotional intelligence enjoy a symbiotic relationship. In those instances where the term EI reflects broad-based emotional dispositions, the preferred methodology is that of the self-report protocol (see chapter 4). By contrast, in those instances where EI assumes the status of a type of intelligence, the move has been toward the development and implementation of objective, performance-based indexes (see chapter 3). Importantly, these two approaches provide a natural demarcation of the study of emotional intelligence (i.e., self-reported vs. performance-based EI). They also decisively frame the subject matter of chapters 3 and 4, to which topics we now turn.

Summary Points: Chapter 2

• Psychological tests can be evaluated against a range of criteria established by the scientific community, although particularly important is the reliability and validity evidence supporting the test.

• There are many forms of validity evidence, including content, predictive, consequential, and construct validity evidence. In contemporary accounts, construct validity is viewed as embracing all others, and this includes ascertaining whether a test is related to measures of similar constructs (convergent validity evidence) and unrelated to those that, according to theory, it should not share associations with (discriminant validity evidence).

• A variety of statistical techniques are available to the scientist to assess the veracity of claims associated with emotional intelligence assessments. These include correlation, regression, and factor analyses. A cursory understanding of these tools will arm the reader with the requisite critical skills to profit from the material we present in the later chapters of this book.

• The psychological tests in existence number in the tens of thousands. Various taxonomies exist for classifying these tests, including whether they are related to typical or maximum performance, use rating scales or veridical scoring keys, reflect preferences or abilities and aptitudes, are given on a one-to-one basis or in groups, and/or can be administered via paper and pencil or over the Internet. Available emotional intelligence tests may be classified with these systems.

• The two different approaches used to operationalize emotional intelligence are (1) self-report and (2) performance based. In the former, emotional intelligence is thought to be related to self-judgments of one's emotional life. In the latter, emotional intelligence is thought to be objectively verifiable with items that resemble intelligence tests. The two distinctive approaches have yielded separate theories, divergent research traditions, and different solutions to practical problems that we discuss in this and subsequent chapters.

3 The Intelligence in Emotional Intelligence

It is better to be unborn than untaught: for ignorance is the root of misfortune.
—Plato

The most successful applications of psychology to human society are predominantly in the development of reliable and valid assessments of intellectual functioning. Cognitive tests are widely used by clinicians, educators, human resource professionals, policy makers, and the like, to make decisions (of the type outlined in chapter 2) that affect many individuals and stakeholders. Many commentators (e.g., Anastasi and Urbina 1997; Cronbach 1990; Jensen 1998), in their capacity as researchers working within the field of intelligence (or human cognitive abilities, as it is referred to sometimes), have contributed to these accomplishments.

Traditional approaches to the assessment of cognitive abilities (and related research on intelligence, achievement, and aptitudes) are of a near formulaic nature. Generally, they require the solution to an abstract problem (e.g., rotating an object in three-dimensional space) or some factual item that is important to the dominant culture (e.g., knowing the meaning of words or recalling some important piece of information). Responses to such tests are scored as either right or wrong, with fast performance generally rewarded, all other things being equal. Thus assessed, cognitive ability provides one of the single best predictors of a wide range of meaningful, real-life criteria.

Beyond many individual studies, meta-analyses (a statistical technique that aggregates then summarizes the findings from a large pool of related studies) support the preceding assertions (Schmidt and Hunter 1998). Consistently this research suggests that cognitive ability measures predict job and academic performance better than any other measured concept of psychological, sociological, or demographic significance (Roberts, Markham, et al. 2005). However, while noteworthy, these relationships are actually constrained by modest limits. For example, even when cognitive tests are combined with other, well-established, psychological measures (e.g., personality, biographical data) and statistical corrections are made for a range of artifacts, validity coefficients for the prediction of real-life criteria seldom exceed 0.60 (Bowman et al. 2001; Jensen 1998). Moreover these cognitive ability constructs have often been criticized for being culturally insensitive, ecologically questionable, and largely contrived (i.e., life is seldom like a multiple-choice question). Findings from meta-analyses, along with attendant criticisms of cognitive tests, have spurred researchers to explore new psychological domains. Collectively it is hoped that such research will raise levels of prediction while simultaneously addressing critical concerns.

As may be apparent from chapter 2, emotional intelligence (EI) represents an important psychological phenomenon that has so far been given short shrift by scientists working within the intelligence tradition. From this perspective, emotional intelligence represents a form of ability that processes and benefits from the emotional system (Matthews, Zeidner, et al. 2002; Mayer et al. 1999; Roberts, Schulze, et al. 2006). Of note, EI comprises an entire family of constructs that may be juxtaposed to concepts that derive from traditional approaches to the measurement of cognitive intelligence. In turn, each emotional intelligence construct adds incremental validity (over and above cognitive abilities, as typically measured) to the prediction of real-life outcome variables. These valued outcomes include physical health, happiness, academic performance, perceived quality of life, job satisfaction, and psychological well-being, to name a few.

In this chapter we begin by providing an overview of intelligence models and their accompanying theoretical frameworks. We then move to discuss models of emotional intelligence that might be thought of as components and/or extensions of existing intelligence theories. Because assessment is an important aspect of ability models, this chapter reviews a number of different instruments that might be thought of as emotional intelligence measures. Because the veracity of these measures is a function of their reliability and validity, we then evaluate the instruments discussed in this chapter using the principles outlined in chapter 2.

Models of Human Intellectual Abilities

As a human being, one has been endowed with just enough intelligence to be able to see clearly how utterly inadequate that intelligence is when confronted with what exists.
—Albert Einstein

Scientific understanding of human abilities has gained much from the research of John Bissell Carroll (1993) who summarized and integrated
over 400 studies conducted within the factor analytic tradition over
a hundred year span. Carroll's re-analysis of each data set led him to a
model having three levels (or strata). On the first stratum lay numerous,
narrowly defined primary mental abilities. On the second stratum are a
variety of broad cognitive abilities also identified by Cattell, Horn, and
associates in their theory of fluid and crystallized intelligence (see below).
Finally, on the third stratum is a single, general intelligence factor.

This model may be better understood by reference to table 3.1 and figure 3.1. The table provides definitions of the major components of the
theory, as well as sample tests. Note the large number (66) of strata I concepts represented in figure 3.1; researchers continue to uncover more such
factors tied to olfaction and tactile perception. Generally, however, stratum I factors are of less importance than those of strata II and III. Figure
3.1 shows how each of the constructs is aligned with others. The scheme is
roughly equivalent to the periodic table in chemistry, and it similarly can
be consulted to ascertain the composition of a particular form of intelligence (see Flanagan et al. 2000). Note that general intelligence is comprised, to varying extent, of all the constructs measured by all of the
primary mental abilities. By contrast, fluid intelligence (a type of intelligence used especially to solve novel problems) is comprised of a much
more limited set, including especially reasoning concepts and attendant
measures.

The importance of Carroll's concepts extends to educational interventions, public policy on testing, and sociological issues. Carroll's model is
proving influential in the development too of intelligence and achievement tests. Revisions to well-known measures such as the Stanford-Binet,
Wechsler, and Woodcock-Johnson have been made with this framework
as a catalyst. Carroll's model is also likely to guide theory and research
on cognitive abilities for some time.

The uniqueness of Carroll's model is that virtually all models of cognitive abilities may be subsumed under its broad umbrella. In the passages
that follow we introduce each of these models, and we will refer to them
from time to time throughout the book. Before leaving Carroll, it is
perhaps appropriate to note that he did make suggestive comments of
direct relevance to the concept of emotional intelligence. In particular,
Carroll (1993) notes that in some data sets there is evidence for a domain
of behavioral knowledge that is relatively independent from stratum
II constructs. This domain includes assessment of a range of abilities
that appear relevant in the decoding and processing of social-emotional

Table 3.1
Definitions of major intelligence constructs, along with sample tests and items

Construct	Definition	Sample test and measure
Stratum III		
General intelligence (g)	A factor found at the highest order that determines the level of mastery in performing induction, reasoning, visualization, and language comprehension tasks	In principle, all tests listed below serve to measure this construct to varying degree
Stratum II		
Fluid intelligence (G_f)	A broad organization of ability concerned with basic processes that depend only minimally on learning and acculturation	*Induction*: What are the next 2 letters in this sequence: F F C H H E J J G L L ? *Arithmetic reasoning*: If 10 programmers are needed to finish a job in 6 days, how many programmers would be needed to finish the job in 1 day?
Crystallized intelligence (G_c)	A broad organization of ability that reflects the influences of formal learning and acculturation (including education)	*Vocabulary*: What is the meaning of the word, "obfuscate"? *General knowledge*: The author of the book *The Life and Opinions of Tristram Shandy* was?
Broad visualization (G_v)	A broad organization of ability involved in any task that requires the perception of visual forms	*Form boards*: Complete the shape at the top with the shapes from the bottom. Problem No.1
Broad auditory perception (G_a)	A broad organization of ability involved in any task or performance that requires the perception of, or discrimination of, auditory pattern of sounds or speech	*Auditory closure*: Words are presented orally, but with some sounds omitted. The task is to complete the word (*stimuli*: bo/le [bottle]).

Table 3.1
(continued)

Construct	Definition	Sample test and measure
Short-term acquisition and retrieval (SAR)	A broad organization of ability involved in any task where retention of material is over a short period of time	*Digit span*: The test administrator presents a series of digits with a one-second delay between each. The participant recalls the digit string (*stimuli*: 2 4 6 7 5 9). Note, this test is also given "backward," wherein, for the example, the correct answer is 9 5 7 6 4 2.
Tertiary storage and retrieval (TSR)	A broad organization of ability involved in any task involving retention of material learned in the distant past	*Ideational fluency*: In two minutes list the members of a broadly defined class, with the score being the number of things listed (e.g., "fluids that burn").
Broad processing speed (G_s)	A broad organization of ability in any task or performance that requires rapid cognitive processing of information	*Number comparison*: Indicate whether the two digit strings are the same or different (note, time, rather than accuracy, is the dependant variable): 367954381937—367954381937; 25698472365—25698479365
Broad decision speed (G_p)	A broad organization of ability in task or performance that requires rapid processing of very simple stimuli. The difference between it and G_s resides in the complexity of the stimuli.	*Choice Reaction Time*: Sort a deck of playing cards into colors, suits, or number. You will notice that your time varies considerably with the varied information contained in the stimuli, and that this is a good proxy for information processes measured by this constellation of tasks.

content. Carroll also suggests that the domains encapsulated by behavioral knowledge require more careful and systematic exploration than that accomplished up to the time of his writing.

Structural Models of Intelligence

In the following subsections we present a selection of prominent structural models of intelligence. They are all very closely related to the statistical technique of factor analysis, which we had recourse to discuss briefly in chapter 2. Note that because Carroll's model essentially combines salient features of all these structural theories, table 3.1 and figure 3.1 can be consulted frequently to understand the concepts discussed in these passages, for definitions or for sample tests.

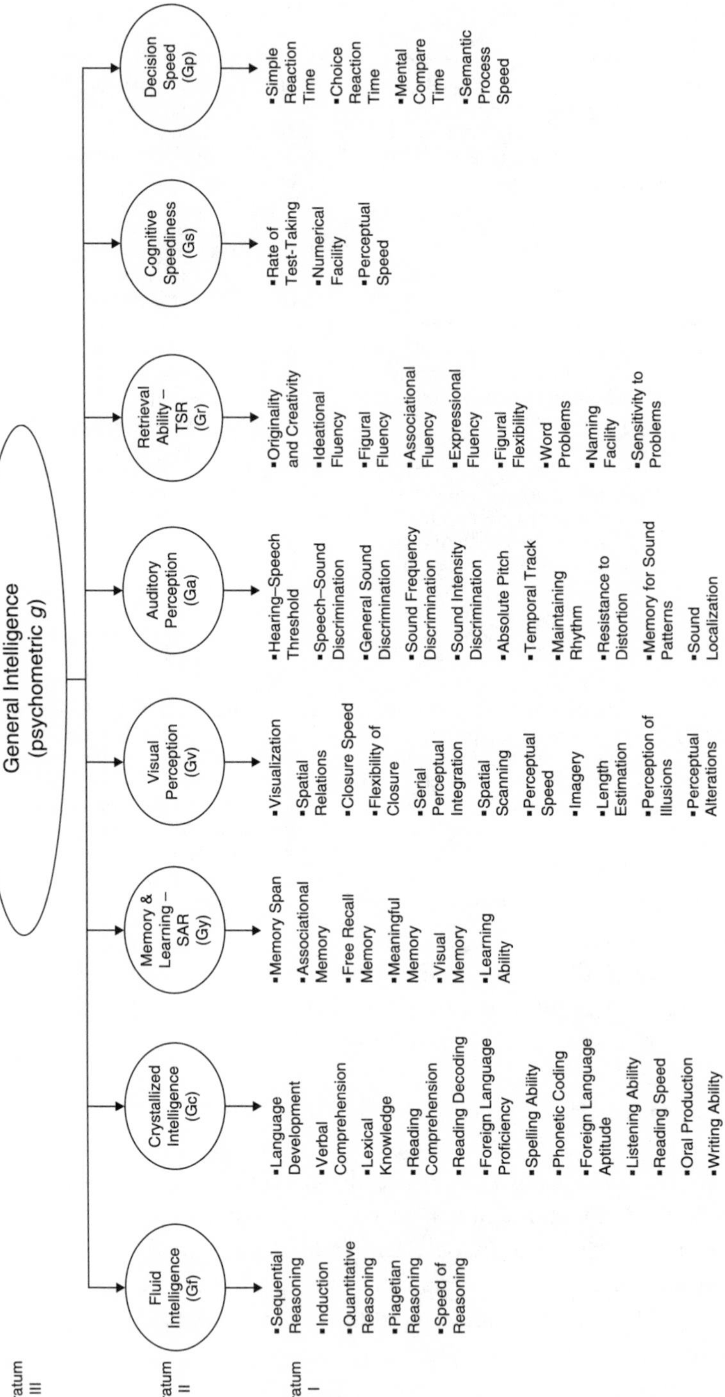

Figure 3.1
The structure of human cognitive abilities (adapted from Carroll 1993)

Theory of General Intelligence (g)   Perhaps the most famous theory of intelligence is that offered by Charles Spearman (1923; see the sidebar), who proposed that there are two factors underlying mental test performance: a general factor (which he called g) and specific factors (which he referred to as s). Specific factors are unique to performance on any cognitive test, whereas the general factor permeates performance on all intellectual tasks. As a consequence Spearman postulated that g alone is of psychological significance. Individual differences in g are the result of differences in the magnitude of mental energy invested in any given task. It is worth noting that a strict interpretation of Spearman's model of human intelligence renders the concept of EI quite problematic. By definition, EI requires the presence of at least one other intelligence (e.g., something we might call rational intelligence) for the qualifier (i.e., emotional) to have currency (Matthews, Zeidner, et al. 2002). The notion of a psychologically meaningful emotional intelligence is, if you will, clearly inconsistent with a general intelligence model.

Primary Mental Abilities   In a significant departure from Spearman's two-factor theory, Louis Thurstone (e.g., 1938; see the sidebar) proposed, and later provided supportive evidence for, primary mental abilities (PMAs), which collectively comprise intelligence. While originally finding thirteen such factors, Thurstone eventually settled on nine that he was both able to consistently validate and assign psychological labels. The primary mental abilities so derived include verbal comprehension, verbal fluency, number facility, spatial visualization, memory, inductive reasoning, deductive reasoning, practical problem solving, and perceptual speed. These factors are not ordered in any way and are thus of equal importance in understanding intelligent behavior. For this reason Thurstone's model is sometimes called an oligarchic theory. In such a model the concept of a primary mental ability, such as emotional perception, seems plausible. We will return to this possibility later in this chapter when we discuss each of the so-called branches of performance-based assessments of emotional intelligence.

Structure of Intellect (SOI) Model   While the number of factors in Thurstone's theory is large, Joy Paul Guilford (1967, 1988) took a more extreme view in positing that some 150 (and in some writings 180) factors comprise intelligence. Accordingly, for Guilford every mental task involves three aspects (also called facets): operation, content, and product. There are five kinds of operations in this model, five types of content,

Charles Edward
Spearman (1863–1945)

Brief biography of Charles Spearman, who proposed a two-factor theory of intelligence

Spearman's name is almost synonymous with the term *general intelligence* or g theory. While still a student (albeit a rather old one, Spearman was 48 when he received his PhD) in 1909, he published the two-factor theory of intelligence. Spearman speculated that all intellective functioning was underpinned by an overall mental ability accompanied by specific abilities for differing mental tasks. One of the great achievements of psychology evolved from Spearman's efforts to operationalize his theory—the statistical procedure we now know as "factor analysis" (see chapter 2). The procedure he developed (the method of tetrad differences) indicated to Spearman that his theory was indeed correct. Unfortunately, not everyone agreed with him. Objections ranged (and still do) from the simplistic nature of *g*, through to the relative stability of the mathematical procedures, and even to the existence of the general factor. Yet many eminent psychologists, such as Cyril Burt, concurred, and *g* became an established psychological construct. Spearman's *g* theory has its proponents to this day; books like *The Bell Curve* have at their core the idea that this theory is correct.

It took almost 30 years before Louis Thurstone developed, in 1930, the technique of multiple factor analysis. This procedure is based on the preservation of empirical evidence that seriously questions the nature and importance of *g*. Controversy still surrounds the question of whether intelligence is best conceived as a unitary entity (Spearman) or as a multi-faceted collection of abilities—"Horses for the course" as the saying goes. Perhaps Spearman's dogmatic determination in promoting and maintaining his position lay in his 15 years of military service as a British army officer in India?

Louis Leon Thurstone (1887–1955)

Brief biography of Louis Thurstone, who proposed a theory of primary mental abilities

Polymath and inventor turned psychometrician; that was Thurstone. He is considered by some the quintessential American psychometrician. This reflects not only his exceptional contributions to factor analysis (see chapter 2) but also his work in measurement theory and models of intelligence. Thurstone recognized the inadequacies of psychological measurement techniques and single-handedly devised methods to produce scales to which meaningful interval and ratio criteria could be applied. The ambiguities of "mental age" received his attention and led to the introduction of standardized IQ scores (mean *100*, standard deviation *15* is the norm for modern representations). Application of his new factor analytic techniques led Thurstone to postulate the notion of *Primary Mental Abilities*. This discovery led to inflamed debate over the nature of intelligence as it appeared to suggest the opposite to Spearman's general intelligence theory. The debate still continues with proponents of *g* pointing out that at the highest level of analysis a general factor emerges. Arguably, Thurstone's greatest contribution to psychology was the introduction of "simple structure" to factor analysis. Simple structure allows for meaningful *psychological* interpretation of factor analytic results, and thus insight into the potential processes involved in intellective endeavor.

Inventor? Well Thurstone began his career as an electrical engineer and was recruited by Thomas Edison as an assistant. Thurstone invented a method for making "talking pictures" and developed the flicker-free movie camera and projector. Furthermore he exhibited significant geometric ability by describing a method for trisecting angles. On top of all this, Thurstone was regarded as one of the first "greenies." He suggested techniques for extracting "pure energy" from river systems and Niagara Falls.

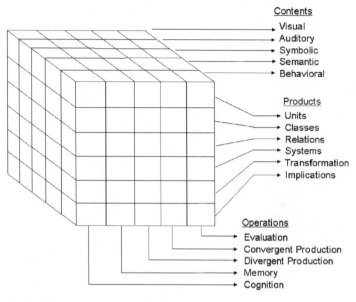

Contents
Visual
Auditory
Symbolic
Semantic
Behavioral

Products
Units
Classes
Relations
Systems
Transformation
Implications

Operations
Evaluation
Convergent Production
Divergent Production
Memory
Cognition

Figure 3.2
Guilford's structure of intellect (SOI) model

and six varieties of products. The structure of intellect has been symbol-
ized as a rectangular prism composed of 150 (i.e., $5 \times 5 \times 6$) smaller
prisms. Each dimension of this prism corresponds to one of the three
ingredients (i.e., operation, content, and product) with each of the 150
possible combinations of these three categories forming even smaller rectangular prisms. A graphical depiction of this model is given in figure 3.2.

An early appeal of this model was its ability to incorporate both creativity and social intelligence (what Guilford calls behavioral cognition;
see O'Sullivan et al. 1965) into its structure. Of note, these are psychological dimensions that few models of intelligence had included up to that
point in time. Unfortunately, Guilford's model has subsequently been
criticized on a number of grounds. Problems include his use of controversial statistical analyses, failure for independent researchers to recover his
factors, and questionable psychometric properties of many of the instruments he developed according to the model.

Fluid and Crystallized Intelligence (Gf-Gc) Theory   Various critical findings
bring into question each of the theories highlighted above. For example,
the number of primary mental abilities has shown to exceed nine, although equally the data attest that there are considerably less than 180.

Primary mental abilities tend to cluster together, suggesting a hierarchical arrangement of factors. For this reason contemporary focus has been given to hierarchical models of intelligence. In the most prominent of these frameworks—the theory of fluid (Gf) and crystallized (Gc) ability—there is considered to be enough structure among established primary mental abilities to define several distinct types of intelligence. Empirical evidence, from several lines of inquiry, supports the distinctions between factors of this theory (Cattell 1971; Roberts, Markham, et al. 2005). Data have also shown that these broad factors

1. involve different underlying cognitive processes,

2. share different predictive validities,

3. are differentially sensitive to intervention, and

4. appear to be subject to different sets of learning and genetic influences.

The most compelling evidence for the distinctions between these constructs comes from factor analytic and developmental research. The main distinguishing feature between Gf and Gc is the amount of formal education and acculturation that is present either in the content of, or operations required, in tests used to measure these abilities. It is well established that Gf depends to a much smaller extent on formal education experiences than does Gc. Moreover, while Gc remains constant or improves slightly over the course of an individual's life span, Gf generally declines as a function of age. Besides Gf and Gc, evidence suggests the existence of broad visualization (Gv), broad auditory function (Ga), short-term acquisition and retrieval (SAR), tertiary storage and retrieval (TSR), and broad speediness (Gs). (These correspond to each of the stratum II concepts defined in table 3.1; only Gp is missing, as that is thought to be related to elements of Gs.) In isolation, each construct represents a broad organization of ability that involves mental processes. And each factor is purported to have a neuropsychological counterpart.

Systems Theories of Intelligence

Two contemporary theorists, with a high public profile—Howard Gardner (1983) and Robert J. Sternberg (1985)—have proposed intelligence models that attempt to be fairly encompassing in dealing with both the internal and external world of the human being. Because such theories view intelligence as a complex system, they are often referred to as system models; a point of departure used to demarcate them from the structural models covered above. Such systems models, in expanding the subject matter of intelligence research, include concepts that structural models would not necessarily view as intelligence. Perhaps because of their breadth, EI researchers often embrace systems theory accounts of intelligence more strongly than they do structural theories. For example, one will find no mention in Goleman (1995a) of structural models of human cognitive abilities, although he cites Gardner (a systems modeler) to support scientific evidence for emotional intelligence quite frequently.

Multiple Intelligences Theory   Howard Gardner's (1983) theory of "multiple intelligences" derives from consideration of criteria such as domains where extraordinary degrees of talent/giftedness are exemplified, deficits in brain-damaged individuals have been isolated, or there may be evolutionary history and plausibility. Gardner originally posited seven independent types of intelligence. These include linguistic intelligence, spatial intelligence, logical-mathematical intelligence, musical intelligence, bodily kinesthetic intelligence, intrapersonal intelligence, and interpersonal intelligence.

The final two intelligences covered by Gardner concern the individual's attempts to understand their own, and other peoples, behaviors, motives, and/or emotions. Clearly, both of these constructs are relevant to emotional intelligence. Still Gardner's model has been subject to certain criticisms. These criticisms include an inability to operationalize each of these constructs in the form of reliable, fair, and valid assessments. Moreover the evolutionary history and plausibility of both intrapersonal and interpersonal intelligence have been contested (see Matthews, Zeidner, et al. 2002 for a detailed discussion).

Triarchic Theory   Robert J. Sternberg (1985) followed Gardner with a departure from traditional conceptualizations, on his part defining intelligence as "purposive adaptation to, and selection and shaping of, real-world environments relevant to one's life" (p. 45). By recourse to various analogies, Sternberg shows that academic intelligence, as assessed by standardized cognitive tests, is imperfectly related to the ability to function intelligently in everyday life. On this basis he goes "beyond IQ" to emphasize different aspects of intellectual functioning. While there are several important domains that he advocates in this extension, the most prominent construct may be practical intelligence (PI). According to Sternberg, PI is especially dependent on acquired tacit knowledge, which is (1) procedural rather than declarative, (2) informal rather than formal, and (3) generally learned without explicit instruction. In short, tacit knowledge is reflected in knowing what to do in a given situation, and getting on and doing it. It occurs without ever necessarily being taught what to do, how to do it, or even being able to articulate why you are doing it.

Practical, social, and emotional intelligence share a focus on acquired knowledge (declarative and procedural), flexible cognitive-retrieval mechanisms, and problem solving that does not lend itself to one correct solution. Recently Hedlund and Sternberg (2000) argued that the main distinguishing feature between each concept lies in the content of the knowledge, and the types of problems, emphasized. Thus, "unlike many approaches to understanding social and emotional intelligence, the tacit-knowledge approach limits the definition of practical intelligence to cognitive ability (such as knowledge acquisition) rather than encompassing an array of individual differences variables" (p. 157). Elsewhere we have suggested three categories of tacit knowledge that directly impinge on EI: managing self, managing others, and managing tasks (Matthews, Zeidner, et al. 2002).

Concluding Comments on Intelligence Theories

This brief foray into theories of intelligence suggests that the concept of EI has a richer history than many commentators often allow. Related concepts exist in virtually all contemporary intelligence models, or else there appear sufficient grounds to include EI within these frameworks. The possible exception is Spearman's theory, though notably even he entertained the possibility. Thus one of his students (Wedeck 1947) conducted research on something called the "personal ability." Our commentary also suggests that paramount to the development of EI models should be determining how constructs comprising it align with intelligence models (whether they be aligned with structural or systems approaches). This issue raises many questions. For example, is EI really a new form of ability or might it be subsumed with one (or more) of the already existing constructs? At what stratum might EI rightly be conceptualized? That is, should EI be seen as a narrowly defined primary ability, as a broad stratum II factor contributing to general intelligence, or a major top-level factor quite separate from conventional g? How does EI relate to related concepts such as tacit knowledge, practical, and social intelligence?

Measures of Emotional Intelligence in the Ability Model

As noted in chapter 1, one very prominent theoretical framework for EI is that proposed by Mayer, Salovey, and colleagues. A major assumption of this framework is that emotional intelligence is a cognitive ability, just like factors and concepts described thus far in this chapter. Indeed Mayer et al. (1999) assert that emotional intelligence meets standard measurement criteria to legitimately be considered a form of intelligence. Central to this ability conceptualization of EI are four constructs that resemble primary mental abilities, but that have variously been referred to as facets or branches. These constructs include emotional identification-perception, assimilating emotions (also known as emotional facilitation), understanding emotions, and emotional management. In the passages that follow we provide information on the processes thought to be captured by these branches.

The Four Branches of the Emotional Intelligence Ability Model

Emotion Perception-Identification   In the preceding definitional framework the most fundamental level of emotional intelligence includes perception, appraisal, and expression of emotions (Mayer, Caruso, et al. 2000). In other words, this aspect of EI involves the individual being aware both of their emotions and their thoughts concerning their emotions. It also requires the individual to be able to monitor emotions in themselves and others, and to differentiate among them, as well as being able to adequately express emotions.

Assimilating Emotion (or Emotional Facilitation)   Another component of emotional intelligence involves assimilating basic emotional experiences into mental life. The term assimilating emotion thus refers to using emotion to facilitate thoughts and actions (Mayer, Caruso, et al. 2000). The construct includes weighing emotions against one another and against other sensations and thoughts, and allowing emotions to direct attention (e.g., holding an emotional state in consciousness long enough to compare its correspondence to similar sensations in sound, color, and taste). From this perspective, marshaling one's emotions (in the service of a goal) appears essential for selective attention, self-monitoring, self-motivation, and so forth.

Understanding and Reasoning about Emotions   An aspect of emotional intelligence involves perceiving the lawfulness underlying specific emotions. For example, it would appear to include an individual's ability to understand that anger arises when justice is denied or an injustice is performed against one's own self or close ones. This process also involves the understanding of emotional problems, such as knowing what emotions are similar and what relation they convey.

Emotional Management, or the Regulation of Emotion in the Self and Others

Mayer, Caruso, et al. (2000) assert that the highest level in the hierarchy of emotional intelligence skills is the management and regulation of emotions. This facet of EI involves knowing how to calm down after feeling stressed, or alleviating the stress and emotion of others. This facet facilitates social adaptation and problem solving.

Instruments Designed to Assess Emotional Intelligence as a Type of Ability

Proponents of ability-based emotional intelligence have taken the correspondence of EI with intelligence seriously and attempted to develop objective measures of the construct. Almost all of these assessments have a similar format (and "feel") to the cognitive ability measures discussed above. While the correctness of responses elicited to stimuli comprising EI tests remains somewhat controversial, as pointed out already (see chapter 2), the approach to measure each of the branches seems scientifically plausible. Below we discuss these measures in some detail, and we will return to them throughout the book.

Instruments to assess EI (and related concepts) can be broadly grouped along two main dimensions. The first, given in table 3.2, involve extensive batteries that attempt to encapsulate all of the major components of EI. The second involve measures that assess specific components of EI rather than offering a global perspective. These are described in table 3.4, and later in these passages.

Omnibus Measures of Emotional Intelligence

In table 3.2 are listed a small set of omnibus measures of emotional intelligence that aim to assess various facets of EI as defined by a comprehensive factor model. Although omnibus assessments are challenging to build and require more extensive validity evidence than one-off measures, we believe that there is a need for more of these types of assessments.

Multifactor Emotional Intelligence Scale (MEIS)

The MEIS was designed to measure each of the four branches that are hypothesized to underlie EI (Mayer, Caruso, et al. 2000). Branch 1 consists of four tests that assess the perception and appraisal of emotion in stories, designs, music, and faces. Branch 2, by contrast, consists of two tasks that assess the ability to assimilate emotions into perceptual and cognitive processes. Branch 3 consists of four tests that assess the ability to reason about and understand emotions. Finally, Branch 4 consists of two tests that assess how skilled participants are at managing their own emotions and the emotions of others.

Table 3.2
Omnibus measures of emotional intelligence

Test name	Acronym	Source	Description
Multifactor Emotional Intelligence Scale	MEIS	Mayer et al. 1999	Contains 12 tasks related to emotional intelligence, 2–4 for each of the four branches. Sample tasks include emotional perception in (1) faces, (2) in designs, (3) in music, and (4) stories; emotional management in (5) oneself and (6) others.
Mayer-Salovey-Caruso Emotional Intelligence Test (version 2)	MSCEIT	Mayer et al. 2000	Contains 8 tasks related to emotional intelligence, two for each of the four branches. Tasks include (1) emotional perception in faces and (2) landscapes, (3) emotional synesthesia, (4) using emotions, (5) emotional blends, (6) emotional changes, (7) managing self, and (8) managing relationships.
Emotional Knowledge Test (also known as Perceiving and Labeling Emotion)	EKT (PLE)	Izard et al. 2001	Contains tasks appropriate for 5-year-olds. 18 item emotional recognition task, involving 9 cross-culturally validated facial expressions, in which child points to one of a triad that matches a description of the target emotion. The emotion-labeling task involves asking the child to produce the label for each emotion.

Interestingly, in terms of both face and content validity evidence, many of the branch measures (especially 2, 3, and 4) are composed of short vignettes, depicting real-life episodes that are specially selected to invoke emotional responses. For instance, the Relativity Test (branch 3) measures peoples' ability to estimate the feelings of two characters in conflict. One test item describes a car hitting a dog, and asks the participant to rate the dog owner's feelings and the driver's feelings. For example, participants must decide how likely it is that the dog's owner felt "ashamed about not being able to have better trained the dog."

Mayer-Salovey-Caruso Emotional Intelligence Test (MSCEIT)   Essentially the MSCEIT reflects refinements in the MEIS following empirical research in this domain. Pivotal to its construction would appear a desire to construct a performance-based measure that is administratively convenient. The authors (e.g., Mayer et al. 2003) have thus embarked on an ambitious enterprise to shorten the original MEIS, without sacrificing its psychometric properties.

At the time of writing, the MSCEIT had gone through its second revision. In the initial revamp the MSCEIT (version 1.1), like the MEIS, contained twelve subscales, most of which were common to both instruments. One test—Analogies—however, was added to branch 3, while another test—Music—was removed from branch 1, likely because this test was the most difficult to administer in group settings. MSCEIT (version 2) was at the time of writing, the operational measure advocated by Mayer and colleagues. It appears to represent a much more significant departure from the original MEIS, with two subtests only within a given branch, including some that have not appeared as performance-based tests in the past. The components of each area are also regarded as correlating with one another, forming two larger areas of experiential (perceiving and assimilating) and strategic (understanding and managing) EI. There is also an overall or general emotional intelligence composite. To give the reader a better understanding of this instrument, and especially its higher order structure and task composition, we reproduce its main components in table 3.3.

Measures of Emotional Adaptation   The four-branch model described above emphasizes mental processing, conscious thought, and correct answers to questions concerning emotions. Some theorists place greater emphasis on emotionally intelligent responses as a product of automatic mental processes. By contrast, Izard et al. (2001) argues that much emotional responding depends on automatically generated, socially selected, adaptive emotional responses that are thought to be influenced by an individual's temperament. Within this formulation Izard et al. (2001), for example, asks the astute reader to compare two equally thoughtful people, one of whom is often fearful and angry and the other of whom is often happy, joyful, and sociable. They remark: "emotion systems themselves generate these effects, sometimes without cognitive mediation and sometimes despite rational processes that would lead to other outcomes" (p. 255).

Certainly many emotional reactions evolve and/or are learned with minimal cognitive involvement. For that reason, Izard and colleagues argue, one should often think of emotional adaptiveness rather than emotional intelligence, per se. Similarly Parrott (2002) has distinguished two different approaches to the idea of emotional adaptation. One is a mechanical-like adaptive view of emotions. From this perspective, emergence of an emotion reflects an individual's (nonconscious) guess or assessment of what resources a given situation will call on, and preparing to respond accordingly. For example, if threatened, a fear response will

Table 3.3
Overview of the higher order model hypothesized for the MSCEIT

Level	Abilities and indicators			
General	Emotional intelligence (EI)			
Areas	"Experiential EI" is the ability to perceive, respond, and manipulate emotional information without necessarily understanding its meaning.		"Strategic EI" assesses ability to understand and manage emotions without necessarily experiencing the feelings of emotion.	
Branches	Ability to "perceive emotions" in faces and pictures	"Facilitating thought" by cognitive processing of emotions	"Understanding emotions" and how they blend and change over time	"Managing Emotions" by using feelings to create better outcomes
Tasks	• Faces: For each of four photographs of faces, participants must rate the presence of five emotions of from 1 (no emotion) to 5 (extreme emotion). • Pictures: For each of six pictures participants must rate the presence of five emotions from 1 to 5.	• Sensations: For each of five statements, participants are asked to make three judgments about the similarity of an emotion to a physical sensation from 1 (not alike) to 5 (alike). • Facilitation: For each of five scenarios, participants must rate the helpfulness of three different moods from 1 (not useful) to 5 (useful).	• Blends: Participants answer 12 multiple-choice questions assessing which combinations of emotions form complex emotions. • Changes: Participants answer 20 multiple-choice questions assessing which emotions are related to particular situations.	• Management: For each of five scenarios, participants rate the mood-management of actions on a 5-point scale from "very ineffective" to "very effective". • Relations: For each of five scenarios, participants must rate the effectiveness of three responses on a 5-point scale from "very ineffective" to "very effective".

Source: Mayer et al. (2002).

marshal resources and thereby prepare the individual for "a small and distinctive suite of action plans," such as fight or flight in response (Johnson-Laird and Oatley 1992, p. 206).

In the second, more open approach to adaptation (which plausibly Izard and colleagues adhere to), emotions also serve as abstract categories of responses that are malleable by context and open to strategic self-regulation. In this sense, an emotion may begin as a prepackaged suite of potential responses (as a strictly adaptive position would have it). An emotion in essence develops into a source of information (and potential response) that the individual must then choose from wisely or poorly in order for adaptive success (and intelligent performance) (Parrott 2002, pp. 351–55). For example, prepackaged fear responses, such as running away, may be replaced by more context-bound strategies. A hiker may learn that standing tall and backing away slowly is a more effective tactic for dealing with a threatening bear or snake than running. This strategy is not recommended in other contexts, such as confronting a charging elephant or swimming while bleeding with a white pointer shark.

Izard et al. (2001), and other (e.g., Zeidner et al. 2003) adaptive-focused approaches, take into account a child's preexisting emotional temperament and style more carefully than do the four-branch and specific models. At the same time Izard's operationalization of emotional adaptation is very similar to the emotional intelligence approaches described previously. For example, the Emotional Knowledge Test (EKT; see Izard et al. 2001) asks test takers to match an emotion such as sadness with a situation such as "your best friend moves away" as well as to identify emotions in faces. It provides an alternative model and measure within the scope of emotional intelligence (Mayer et al. 2008).

Specific Measures of Emotional Intelligence

As is evident from the preceding review, there are many specific mental abilities that appear as part of emotional intelligence; for example, the capacity to carry out accurate emotional perception. The MEIS and MSCEIT, in particular, have been developed to assess all four branches of EI, although in truth they are based on a number of well-established measures from the emotions literature. While these emotions measures have generally been treated in that literature as instruments to conduct experiments and address very clearly focused substantive issues via clearly articulated hypotheses, they can be (and indeed are currently being) reconceptualized as individual differences measures of emotional functioning. Table 3.4 catalogues a selection of such measures, which we briefly review in the passages that follow.

Table 3.4
Measures of specific emotional intelligence components

Test Name	Acronym	Further reading	Description
Emotion perception			
Diagnostic Analysis of Nonverbal Accuracy 2—Adult Facial Expressions	DANVA2-AF	Nowicki and Carton 1993	24 photographs of an equal number of happy, sad, angry and fearful facial expressions of high and low intensities, balanced also by gender. The participants' task is to indicate which of the four emotions is present in the faces. A youth form is also available.
Diagnostic Analysis of Nonverbal Accuracy 2—Adult Paralanguage	DANVA2-AP	Baum and Nowicki 1998	24 audio stimuli where two professional actors (one male, the other female) say a neutral sentence, "I am going out of the room now but I'll be back later" in one of four emotional states (happy, sad, angry or fearful) at high and low intensities. The participants' task is to indicate which of the four emotions is present in the voices. A youth form is also available.
Diagnostic Analysis of Nonverbal Accuracy 2 Posture Test	DANVA2-POS	Pitterman and Nowicki 2004	Measures an individual's ability to identify emotion in human standing and sitting postures. The stimuli are 2 men and 2 women portrayed standing and sitting, yielding 32 high- and low-intensity standing and sitting postures representing happiness, sadness, anger, and fear.
Japanese and Caucasian Brief Affect Recognition Test	JACBART	Matsumoto et al. 2000	An instrument consisting of 56 stimuli, presented in video format. Stimuli consist of Japanese or Caucasian faces portraying one of seven emotions: happiness, contempt, disgust, sadness, anger, surprise, and fear. Each stimulus is briefly presented (1/5 s) inside a backward and forward mask, which shows a neutral face.
Emotional Inspection Time	EIT	Austin 2005a	A computer administered IT task, in which a series of facial displays are displayed after a practice session at various durations (6–400 ms) inside a backward mask. Subjects are asked to discriminate between a happy or sad face and a neutral face. The task is scored as the number of correct identifications.

Vocal Expression Recognition Index	Vocal-I	Scherer 2007	A 30-item computer-administered, multiple-choice task that requires participants to make judgments about the emotion heard in a voice spoken in a foreign language. The phrases are uttered by actors so as to portray joy, sadness, fear, anger, and neutral.
Emotional facilitation			
Emotional Stroop Task	EST	Mogg et al. 1990	The task follows the classic Stroop paradigm in asking participants to select the color of a word (blue, green, yellow or red) presented on a screen. Some of the items are neutral words (e.g., gate), while others are threat words (e.g., death). Words were presented at a rate of 32 ms. Scores are calculated as the difference in response time for neutral and negative words (i.e., the extent to which negative emotional words hampers cognitive processing).
Appraisal, labeling, and understanding emotion			
Levels of Emotional Awareness Scale	LEAS	Lane et al. 1990	Participants are required to describe their anticipated feelings (and those of a second person) to each of 20 scenes. Four types of emotion are elicited: anger, fear, happiness, and sadness. Each scene is followed by two questions: "How would you feel?" and "How would the other person feel?" Corresponding to these questions, each person's answer receives two scores for each emotion described: self and other.
Emotional Accuracy Research Scale	EARS	Geher et al. 2001	Consists of 3 vignettes followed by 12 pairs of mood items, where test-takers must select one of the pair as representative of the person in the vignettes.
Managing emotions			
Emotional Management Performance Test	EMPT	Freudenthaler and Neubauer 2007	Vignette based test assessing managing own and managing others emotions.
Situational Judgment Test for Management	SJTM	MacCann 2006	A 40 item situational judgment test developed from critical incidents, where respondents are required to choose from multiple-choice options appropriate responses to emotionally charged scenarios.

Emotional Perception and Identification   Well before the concept of emotional intelligence arose, developmental psychologists, actors, emotions researchers, writers, cartoonists, and all those interested in nonverbal behavior (much of which communicates emotions) were studying individual differences in emotional perception (Buck 1984). This interest centered on the capacity to identify emotions in the face, voice, and other parts of the body as a human ability (Buck 1984). Tests were developed for measuring various components of emotion perception, including the accuracy of perceiving emotion in each sensory, input-output channel (e.g., see Nowicki and Duke 1994).

   Consequently a number of contemporary scales are designed to assess the ability to accurately perceive emotions in such stimuli. Among the most widely used of such measures are the Diagnostic Analysis of Nonverbal Accuracy Scales (DANVA) (Nowicki and Duke 1994), the Japanese and Caucasian Brief Affect Recognition Test (JACBART; Matsumoto et al. 2000), and Vocal-I (Scherer 2007); for some others, see table 3.4 (see also Elfenbein et al. 2006). In general, these scales present pictures of faces and of postures, gestures, or recordings of voice tones; the participant's task is to correctly identify the emotion expressed. For example, the DANVA-2 (an updated version of the original DANVA test) employs faces, postures, gestures, and voice tones that express one of four emotions (happiness, sadness, anger, and fear).

Use of Emotional Information in Thinking   Other specific-component models also appear to fall within the scope of EI. For example, many psychologists believe that emotions facilitate thought in diverse ways. Emotions may prioritize thinking (Mandler 1975), aid creativity (Averill and Thompson-Knowles 1991; Isen 2001), or allow people to be more realistic (Alloy and Abramson 1988). Moreover it has been suggested that a person who can accurately perceive emotions may be more adept at using that knowledge in artwork (Averill and Nunley 1992). Alternatively, persons who cannot prioritize what is important in their lives misspend their emotional reactions on petty details. If, for example, a person is constantly angered by their subordinate's nonessential errors in internal documents, then broader, more important concerns will not be addressed (Parrott 2002).

   Various attempts have been made to assess how well people's emotions enhance or facilitate their reasoning; usually these have appeared as part of larger batteries of EI tests (e.g., those comprising the MEIS and

MSCEIT). One freestanding measure is the Emotional Stroop test. On the Stroop, people first see neutral words printed in varying colors, and must say the colors without being distracted by the words. In the second test, negative/anxiety emotion words are employed; in the third, positive emotion words might be employed. It is common for people to be distracted and read the word rather than say the color. Higher EI (or better emotional adjustment) in this case, might be regarded as exhibiting less interference from the emotion words, although other interpretations are possible as well (e.g., Masia et al. 1999).

Reasoning with Emotions: Emotional Appraisal, Labeling, and Language Yet another specific component model concerns emotional reasoning and understanding. For example, appraisal researchers have developed decision rules for matching an internal state, or situation, to its emotion. Theorists have argued that accurate appraisal as well as awareness of somatic markers and feelings may be a hallmark of emotionally intelligent responding (MacCann, Matthews, et al. 2004; Parrott 2002). Thus, if a person has a racing heart, for instance, and wants to run away, and imagines bad things, then that individual will likely feel fear (Roseman 1984; see Scherer et al. 2001). If a person's appraisal process is awry, then the emotions exhibited will be way off.

Part of appraising a situation involves categorizing the emotion it gives rise to (e.g., Innes-Ker and Niedenthal 2002), and then labeling it. Labeling involves a good knowledge of the affective lexicon. This lexicon includes feeling words and where they came from (Clore et al. 1987). One method for measuring abilities in this area is through the Levels of Emotional Awareness Scale (LEAS; Lane et al. 1990). This scale presents twenty emotionally evocative situations involving the test taker ("you") and another person. Participants write both about how they and the other person would feel in the situation. Responses are scored according to whether the test taker appropriately includes emotional responses, and the degree of sophistication (complexity) of those responses, including, for example, the differentiation between their own and other's responses.

Emotion Management A final area of interest in individual differences concerns emotional self-control and self-management. This area came out of clinical findings that, for example, one's emotionality could become more positive by reframing perceptions of situations, as well as from the idea that work required considerable emotional control (Hochschild

1983). Acceptance of emotions may be modeled at an early age. Parents, who accept their children's expression of emotion rather than reject them, are more apt to have children who better control their emotions (Gottman et al. 1996). A great amount of research on emotional self-management and regulation has emerged in parallel with research in the emotional intelligence domain (Gross 1998). Denham and colleagues, for example, have used behavioral observations of children in order to assess their frustration tolerance, asking observers, for instance, to rate the degree of distress, crying, and tantrums in children (Denham et al. 2003). With the advent of emotional intelligence, researchers have also used the situational judgment paradigm to assess this construct (e.g., see the SJTM described in table 3.4).

Summary of Emotional Intelligence Measures
Emotional intelligence measures conforming to an ability model are clearly diverse. Yet they share something of a correspondence with the cognitive ability constructs outlined previously. For example, perceptual factors tied to audition and vision are part and parcel of Carroll's three-stratum model, as are constructs tied to speed of processing. Notably the ability perspective on EI includes perception measures (e.g., JACBART) as well as those measures where speed is critical (e.g., Emotional Stroop). What is uncertain is whether each of these EI constructs is sufficiently distinct from corresponding cognitive ability factors, an issue we return to frequently throughout the book.

While we have aligned each of the measures to various emotional intelligence branches, there is in reality a paucity of research showing that such a rigorous taxonomy exists. By contrast with intelligence models, there is no stratum-like theory of EI where branches are shown to have equal status as primary mental abilities. It is not entirely clear that emotion perception measures, in particular, correlate sufficiently highly among themselves to suggest a coherent domain (e.g., see Buck 1984; we also return to this topic later in this chapter). Nor do we know of the correspondence between many of the measures we have chosen to denote variously as putative measures of EI in table 3.4 and the branch tests comprising instruments such as the MEIS and MCEIT. Indeed no research has yet shown that even the MEIS and MSCEIT are measuring similar concepts (Matthews, Zeidner, et al. 2002). Each of these issues constitutes important future directions that researchers and theoreticians will need to pursue in order to imbue the field with greater scientific credibility.

Evaluating Emotional Intelligence Assessments That Conform to an Ability Model

Nor is the people's judgment always true: The most may err as grossly as the few.
—John Dryden

In the passages that follow we evaluate each of the measures given in tables 3.4 and 3.6, notably as an assessment of emotional intelligence. In principle, this exercise is relatively uncontroversial, as we have pointed out in chapter 2. In distilling key concepts from that chapter, we will evaluate each of the ability EI assessments that represent the criteria discussed in this chapter.

1. *To what extent are measures of emotional intelligence reliable?*   Recall from the principles illustrated in chapter 2 that two forms of reliability appear prominent in most testing applications. The first is test-retest reliability. Administering the same EI test twice, with a certain lapse of time between the two test sessions should allow the scores to correlate substantially enough to indicate that the measure is stable. The second is internal consistency reliability. The responses that people give, to individual items within a test (or subscale) assessing EI, should correlate meaningfully with other items from this test (or subscale).

2. *What evidence exists demonstrating a meaningful relationship between the content of emotional intelligence tests and the construct(s) intended to be measured?*   A psychometrically valid test must cover a representative sample of the domain that it was designed to assess. The issue here is one of conceptualization; deciding what qualities should be assessed as components of the measure. For example, a test designed to assess emotion perception should not focus on one type of emotion (e.g., happiness) to the detriment of other basic emotions (e.g., fear or anger). Equally, those qualities that should be excluded or minimized (e.g., personality) need to be ascertained.

3. *What evidence is there to support (or disconfirm) relationships between the construct(s) measured by an emotional intelligence test and the responses provided by the test taker?*   Of interest here, is whether there exist meaningful group differences among test takers, as might be postulated on the basis of theory. Equally, do studies ensure that a response to a test supposedly measuring EI is not an artifact of extraneous factors (e.g., social conformity, response bias, or faking)?

4. *What evidence is there for the internal structure of emotional intelligence tests?* Studies are required to determine whether the underlying theoretical structure of a given EI test is supported by real, empirical data. For example, the vast majority of the tests listed in table 3.4 postulate the existence of a single dimension. The statistical technique of factor analysis should support the presence (or otherwise) of this unitary trait. Other measures of EI, such as the MEIS and MSCEIT, hypothesize independent components whose arrangement is roughly hierarchical, and factor analysis should again support this trait.

5. *To what extent has construct validity evidence been accumulated for emotional intelligence tests?* This issue includes establishing convergent and discriminant evidence, test-criterion relationships, and documenting how validity generalizes across samples and situations. For example, a test for emotional intelligence should predict independent measures of emotionally intelligent behavior, such as effective communication with others, as established by some coherent theory of what it means to be emotionally intelligent.

Issues of consequential validity (i.e., demonstrating that the construct assessed by the test has meaningful societal consequences), fairness (i.e., showing that items are not biased against a particular subpopulation), and how to appropriately document test development are also critical components in evaluating an EI measure (Matthews, Emo, Roberts, et al. 2006; Roberts et al. 2007). Each of these various processes are ongoing and should feed back to guide theoretical refinements, test development, and future cycles of research. Each piece of evidence is also equally important to establish. Having briefly introduced the various ways that we will evaluate each measure, we now turn to an evaluation of studies where these features of various EI measure have been documented.

Emotional Intelligence Measures: Reliability
Many of the measures listed in tables 3.2 and 3.4 appear to possess adequate reliability. For example, Geher et al. (2001) report a reliability of 0.75 for the EARS; while two studies exploring the LEAS indicate that this too yields acceptable values (Ciarrochi, Caputi, et al. 2003 [0.89]; Lane et al. 1990 [0.81]). Similarly, in the original set of studies reporting the development of the JACBART, Matsumoto et al. (2000) report reliability coefficients ranging between 0.82 and 0.92. These findings appear robust across different laboratories, study designs, and populations (e.g.,

see Matsumoto et al. 2004 [0.82]; Roberts et al. 2006 [0.73]). However, the reliabilities of several tests of emotion perception, especially those involving sensory modalities other than vision, are more marginal. For instance, Roberts et al. (2006) found the Vocal-I to have an alpha of 0.45, while MacCann (2006) found this result for the Vocal-I to be even lower (i.e., 0.43).

With respect to omnibus measures of EI, available evidence accrued from a number of studies suggests that the internal consistency reliability of the MSCEIT, in particular, is acceptable (e.g., Brackett and Mayer 2003; Palmer et al. 2005; Zeidner, Shani-Zinovich, et al. 2005). Super-ordinate constructs such as general EI and experiential EI have especially high reliability coefficients (i.e., 0.90 or above). However, several subtests (e.g., Blends) and branches (e.g., Facilitation) of the MSCEIT have marginal (i.e., less than 0.60) reliabilities (e.g., see Barchard 2003; Barchard and Hakstian 2004; Bastian et al. 2005). This result also happens to hold true for its predecessor, the MEIS (Roberts et al. 2001).

Strategies for improving the reliability of EI tests, such as increasing the number of test items, have so far not been tried out systematically. The addition of items is likely necessary if subscale scores, in particular, are going to be used to make high stakes decisions (e.g., selecting an applicant for a job or using the information to design an educational or clinical intervention). There are also relatively few studies of the test-retest reliability of any measure. Moreover, although those that have been conducted are suggestive, they generally come from studies with fairly small sample sizes (e.g., Brackett and Mayer 2003). In sum, while reliability appears adequate for global constructs, the jury is out on whether subscales, and sometimes even measures designed to assess very specific subcomponents of EI, have high enough reliability coefficients for use in applied settings.

Emotional Intelligence Measures: Validity Evidence

In the quest to procure validity evidence for EI assessments, researchers have tended to focus on interpretable group differences, factor structure, convergent and discriminant validity evidence, and test-criterion relationships. In the passages that follow we discuss these validation strategies further, what we have learned thus far from available research, and any implications that these findings have for theory and research. Not all forms of validity evidence have been the subject of extant empirical research on EI, a point that should be abundantly clear after reading these sections.

Theoretically Interpretable Group Differences As is customary, in their attempting to acquire validity evidence, a major concern of researchers has been the identification of meaningful group differences. The impetus for this form of validity evidence comes from its successful implementation in both basic (especially individual differences) and applied research. Interpretable age differences, in particular, are tied to theoretical models of development and maturation in both intelligence and personality models, and also appear as important validity criteria for EI assessments (Mayer et al. 1999). Empirical evidence on this issue, however, is meager. In addition it should not be assumed that all EI constructs will necessarily show incremental gains over the person's life span (more especially if precedent is the driver of this validity argument). In the study of human abilities, for example, fluid intelligence has been shown to be subject to decline in the adult years (Horn and Hofer 1992). Similarly certain personality factors rise and fall as a function of age (e.g., McCrae et al. 1999).

Importantly, age is but one variable that constitutes a group difference approach to acquiring validity evidence. Other variables include gender, socioeconomic status, ethnicity, and whether a member of a clinical group or not (e.g., a patient who is emotionally dysfunctional). Of these, gender has been the subject of most serious empirical investigation by researchers, especially with respect to the MSCEIT (e.g., Brackett et al. 2006; Lyons and Schneider 2005) and to a lesser extent, the MEIS (Roberts et al. 2001). Here it is often hypothesized, and found, that females score higher on ability-based EI measures than do males.

Currently there is little validity evidence concerning ethnic or socioeconomic differences in emotional intelligence. Indeed a possible reason for the construct's pervasive appeal in wider society is its retort to the messages contained in the *Bell Curve* (Herrnstein and Murray 1994; see Matthews, Zeidner, et al. 2002). The claim is simple: EI is available to all, in near equal measure; a claim constantly reiterated in popular accounts (e.g., see Goleman 1995a). If true, ethnic or socioeconomic differences in EI should appear as weak to nonexistent. Because it represents a plausible way of addressing adverse impact for minority groups, studies of this kind are needed, but only if the study design is rigorous and data are reported in a sensitive manner. Furthermore researchers have not yet engaged with the difficult issue of the extent to which EI is culture bound, and how standardized tests such as the MSCEIT can accommodate cultural differences in norms for displaying and managing emotion. For example, the open expression of emotion that may be valued in Western societies (depending on context) may appear as crass in some Asian cultures.

Factor Structure   The issue here concerns the development of a taxonomic model for placing the subconstructs comprising each EI assessment. Also required is a demonstration that EI is relatively invariant across subpopulations, time, test administrators, and so forth. The importance of factorial stability should not be underestimated, especially if the constructs comprising a measure are to be imbued with scientific meaning or used to make practical decisions (e.g., see Carroll 1993). There are a growing number of research papers, articles, and thought pieces where this is a chief concern (e.g., Mayer et al. 2003, Palmer et al. 2005; Roberts et al. 2006).

The importance of this undertaking is clear, but the data attesting to the factorial validity of the measures listed in tables 3.4 and 3.6 are limited or otherwise equivocal. Indeed there is a paucity of published studies using either exploratory or confirmatory factor analytic techniques demonstrating that many of the measures purportedly assessing single components of EI do just that. The situation is slightly different for the more global assessments, where this has been a much more elevated concern, although the picture is far from clear. For example, some studies suggest that the MSCEIT has four recoverable factors as theory dictates (Mayer, Salovey, et al. 2003), but this has proved difficult to replicate. The problem appears largely with emotional facilitation (i.e., using emotions to facilitate thought) (e.g., see Palmer et al. 2005; Roberts et al. 2006), which often fails to emerge as an independent construct. Problems in factor structure also hold true for the MEIS (Ciarrochi, Caputi, et al. 2000; Roberts et al. 2001; Mayer et al. 1999). Missing from this program of research too are tests for factorial invariance in EI across different age, gender, social, and ethnic groups (i.e., the same test items define the same constructs regardless of what group is being analyzed). In the absence of this information the often found group differences should be treated with a certain degree of circumspection.

Convergent Validity Evidence   There seems to be a reasonable consensus on the appropriate variables with which to demonstrate convergent validity evidence for EI assessments. In particular, moderate relations should exist between EI and independent measures of cognitive abilities (general intelligence, fluid abilities, crystallized abilities, etc.). Of note, a good deal of the research has attempted to validate tests for EI against conventional ability measures.

Based on a rather large and growing corpus of research, it appears that EI tests correlate differentially with various aspects of intelligence. Studies, with a number of different measures, including the MEIS, MSCEIT, LEAS, and various developmental measures have thus shown moderate positive correlations with verbal, knowledge-based tests (i.e., crystallized intelligence). Especially strong are correlations between putative measures of emotional understanding and verbal ability measures (e.g., Bastian et al. 2005 [0.56]; Lumley et al. 2005 [0.57]; O'Connor and Little 2003 [0.51]). Correlations are also strong between managing emotions and verbal ability, with both facilitation and perception measures often being notably weaker correlates of acculturated knowledge. By contrast, many EI measures are relatively weakly related (i.e., 0.20 or less) to tests of reasoning ability (fluid intelligence; see Roberts, Schulze, et al., 2008). A notable exception is a study conducted with the JACBART, which did show higher correlations with Gf (Roberts et al. 2006) possibly because this has a speeded component (thereby replicating the oft-reported relation between fluid intelligence and measures of processing speed: see Roberts and Stankov 1999). Few studies have explored relations between EI and other intelligence constructs (e.g., visualization, broad auditory function, or clerical-perceptual speed). Clearly, such empirical research is needed.

In general, the evidence suggests that ability-based EI indexes emotional knowledge, which is related to crystallized intelligence. The magnitude of this correlation, while high, is not so high as to suggest that EI is simply verbal ability repackaged. Such a relationship also supports claims that EI is malleable, rather than innate (Goleman 1998).

It has been argued that if the meanings of the words *emotion* and *intelligence* are to be preserved, the term *emotional intelligence* should combine them in an effective manner (Mayer and Salovey 1997). In particular, it should combine the ideas that emotions can make thinking more intelligent and that one can think intelligently about emotions. If correct, this suggests that an equally important source of convergent validity evidence is a demonstration that EI assessments relate to standard measures from the emotions literature. However, to date, there has been little research linking EI, assessed as an ability, to objective indexes of emotion processing. To our present knowledge, indeed only one such published study has been conducted (Roberts et al. 2006), and here measures of emotion perception, assessed by the JACBART and Vocal-I, correlated near zero with MSCEIT emotion perception measures (but at the same time, these measures did correlate quite highly among themselves).

Discriminant Validity Evidence Demonstration that EI is differentiable from personality is widely agreed to be an important validation strategy, most especially because mixed and trait models of EI have been shown to be highly correlated with personality constructs (see chapter 4). Unlike many self-report measures of EI, however, ability scales show discriminant validity evidence with respect to the five factor personality traits—openness, conscientiousness, extraversion, agreeableness, and neuroticism—a finding that has now been consistently replicated across a series of studies (e.g., Brackett and Mayer 2003; Palmer et al. 2003; Roberts et al. 2001). All correlations are less than 0.40; with both the MEIS and MSCEIT showing highest correlation (around 0.30) with agreeableness, in particular.

Test-Criterion Relationships The test-criterion relationship is a contemporary term for what was once known as predictive validity. There is an ever-growing body of literature addressing this topic, much of which is dealt with, in depth, in various chapters of this book, and especially those that deal with applications. Suffice it to say, at this point, that there are some compelling relations between ability-based EI and a range of criteria, including well-being, school grades, job performance, citizenship, and the like. For example, in chapter 6 we discuss evidence that the MSCEIT predicts criteria related to higher quality social interactions (e.g., Lopes et al. 2004). However, some studies fail to provide strong support for criterion validity. For example, in chapter 7, we discuss how the MSCEIT is at best only weakly related to criteria for coping with stress (e.g., Burns et al. 2007; Matthews, Emo, Funke, et al. 2006). Another concern is that studies often fail to control for confounding of the MEIS and MSCEIT with conventional ability and, to a lesser degree, with personality. Brackett and Mayer (2003) found that only one out of six correlations between the MSCEIT and social-emotional criteria remained significant with personality and ability controlled. A final issue is that the theoretical basis for relating EI and its components to specific criteria is not always articulated well.

Emotional Intelligence Measures: The Need for Additional Validity Evidence
Currently there is no published account supporting the content validity of any EI assessment, though this clearly appears as an important aspect

of the current test standards. Consequential validity is another form of validity evidence that has received short shrift. This form of validity evidence "requires evaluation of the intended and unintended social consequences of test interpretation and use" (Messick 1988, p. 39). However, it remains to be seen whether such assessment of EI might not result in unintended social consequences as has occurred with various forms of cognitive testing. The issue is certainly one that should not be ignored and should be addressed in the near future.

Also of note is the absence of expert feedback for many ability-based EI assessments. Thus, while numeric information is often supplied with these tests, feedback given to the test taker is scant compared to intelligence and personality tests. Nor is it entirely clear what form this feedback might take given the paucity of carefully designed experimental and intervention studies of EI. Note that the nature of feedback is an important criterion covered in the AERA/APA/NCME Test Standards (1999). In addition cutoff points for identifying high or low EI individuals, or for diagnosing problems of a clinical nature, are lacking in current measures. These are not criticisms per se, but rather reflect important domains that future research and development should attempt to address in a systematic way.

Summary of Validity Evidence
The preceding evaluation suggests that there is still a good deal that needs to be done to accrue validity evidence for virtually all of the assessments covered in this chapter. In particular, we see the need for issues of test development to focus on the following:

1. *Improved reliability* While many measures have acceptable reliabilities for research applications, this is clearly too low for the purpose of making high stakes decisions. Internal consistency reliability can often be improved by simply making the test longer, and it appears incumbent on researchers interested in having EI measures be used in operational settings to address this concern.

2. *More studies documenting test-retest reliability* Our review uncovered very few studies directed at establishing the temporal stability of EI measures. This information needs to be documented if EI measures are to be used beyond research studies or low stakes applications.

3. *Factor structure of individual measures being ascertained* Currently it appears that the instruments assessing EI, one or two notable exceptions aside, have been developed without giving due consideration to their internal structure; research directed at this issue is sorely needed.

4. *Relations with related constructs being determined*   Our classification of existing instruments was based largely on conceptual correspondence. There is an urgent need to conduct studies showing moderate to high correlation between related EI components. Results thus far are somewhat troublesome, and it will be important to determine why this is the case. Also required would appear studies demonstrating that a new version of an EI instrument is highly correlated with the earlier version. This is a standard practice with intelligence tests, and one that is important in building a solid corpus of scientific findings.

5. *Expanding convergent and discriminant validity evidence*   This may be a trivial point, but it bears mentioning. Currently we know relatively little of the relations between emotional intelligence and many of the cognitive ability constructs comprising structural models that we described earlier (with the possible exception of *g*, fluid and crystallized intelligence). We also have imperfect knowledge concerning the relation between EI and concepts such as tacit knowledge, other emotions measures (e.g., biological markers), and a range of additional criteria related to emotional and social functioning.

Concluding Comments

Along with cumulative basic research on emotional intelligence, there is an emerging consensus among experts that, if properly defined, the ability-based concept of EI is scientifically plausible and practically meaningful. Theory development will be enhanced by better measures and better research on the adaptive functions of emotional intelligence. Most of all research is needed that places this construct in relation to established psychological constructs, especially including intelligence, emotions, and other key individual differences variables.

At the start of this chapter we suggested that intelligence testing constitutes one of the most important practical contributions that psychology has made to society. A similar consequence is doubtless hoped of ability models of emotional intelligence. By contrast with intelligence testing, the science of EI is relatively new. However, it is uncertain whether principled approaches such as those that have led to major advances in cognitive ability research are being followed by EI proponents. Already there are a sufficient number of instruments available that could be used to develop a taxonomy, and over time, also to ascertain how EI fits in relation to full-blown models of intelligence. Such work ultimately will feed back to improvements in the measurement instruments, as has been the case in the realm of the cognitive intelligences more generally, where iterations of the Wechsler and Stanford-Binet scales reflect advances in the knowledge acquired by basic researchers. One of the current difficulties is that the importance and scale of EI in the landscape of psychological constructs is hard to gauge. Are we looking at a major peak, a mountain range, or merely a foothill of crystallized intelligence? Fitting EI into multiple-level models of the kind developed by Carroll (1993) is essential to determine whether EI is no more than a novel primary mental ability or, in line with Gardner's (1983) multiple-intelligence model, a major, high-level factor of similar scope and importance to general cognitive ability.

Brody (2004) has pointed out that the MSCEIT assesses broad knowledge of how to deal with emotional situations but not the performance skills. For example, a psychology undergraduate could describe how to provide psychotherapy to an anxious client, but with good reason, undergraduates do not provide actual treatment. The ability approach thus far is sorely lacking direct performance-based assessment of social-emotional competencies—except primarily for emotion perception, which is relatively straightforward to assess objectively. Although it may be premature to suggest, a growing opportunity exists to employ more advanced psychometric models and innovative new measurement techniques than have been used yet (Roberts et al. 2007).

Summary Points: Chapter 3

• Intelligence assessment represents one of the most important practical applications that psychology has provided to society thus far. The promise of emotional intelligence is that it may supplement and extend on this domain, leading to improved prediction of many real-world criteria.

• Various structural models of intelligence have been proposed, ranging from those that emphasize the importance of a single, general component to those that posit the importance of several hundred equally important primary mental abilities. The three-stratum model of human cognitive abilities provides a synthesis of various intelligence theories, with a general intelligence at its apex, broad intelligences at an intermediate stage, and primary mental abilities below these constructs.

• The existence of emotional intelligence, as an additional type or component of intelligence inside available models, would seem scientifically plausible. (A possible exception is Spearman's *g* theory.) Indeed emotional intelligence may be a natural outgrowth of various systems theories of intelligence.

• Measures of emotional intelligence that subscribe to an ability model include those that are omnibus measures, such as the MSCEIT, as well as those that measure four specific components: emotional perception, emotional facilitation, emotional understanding, and emotional management.

• The reliability of emotional intelligence measures, as defined as a form of human ability, is adequate for research purposes. Clearly, there is a need for further test development, especially if these measures are ever to be used for high stakes assessment.

• Validity evidence for performance-based measures is beginning to accumulate. Thus assessed, certain measures of emotional intelligence appear to have reasonable structural validity, to be related to intelligence (but not so high as to make it redundant), to be only weakly related to personality factors, and to exhibit some important relations with external criteria. Not all such measures have been examined in sufficient detail, and further research should be coupled with more sophisticated, theory-driven test development.

4 The Personality in Emotional Intelligence

Man is the only creature that refuses to be what he is.
—Camus

We often gauge people by their emotions. We enjoy the company of some people because we are comfortable with the emotions they express. Others "rub us the wrong way," usually because of some misalignment between their emotion and ours. In the current chapter we examine the relationship between emotional intelligence (EI) and personality. Two core questions will guide our thinking. Do some people have personality traits that enhance their emotional competence? If so, is there any real difference between emotional intelligence and those facets of personality that relate to emotional functioning?

Usually psychologists think of personality traits as styles of behavior that are neither intrinsically good nor bad. If emotional intelligence relates to personality, should we then say that some personalities are superior to others? Our quote from Camus highlights a number of further twists. How much does emotional intelligence relate to basic temperament and how much to the person's self-directed efforts at character development? Perhaps emotional intelligence derives not from our basic cheerfulness or melancholy but from how effectively we have learned to channel our temperamental qualities toward personal and social success. In the world of emotions, it seems, there are many possibilities.

Consider the following five people: Which, if any, possesses superior emotional intelligence?

1. Enrique is the life and soul of the party. His infectious enthusiasm and ready conversation are sure to cheer up any social occasion. His outgoing nature and self-confidence win him many friends.

2. Nico is cool, calm, and collected. He manages to stay relaxed even in the most difficult of circumstances. His hardiness under stress makes him a great source of strength in times of crisis.

3. Cristina is one of the most reliable, dependable people around. She exercises good judgment and stays focused on her goals, even in trying situations. Her self-control and focus make her a natural leader at work.

4. Alicia is one of the nicest people one could hope to meet. She is always compassionate and caring, even toward strangers. Her many friends appreciate her empathy, her warmth, and her kindness.

5. Omar enjoys a vivid imagination and an inquiring mind. He has a gift for understanding both art and literature. In his work as a journalist he excels in conveying the emotions of people in the news in a few column inches.

We could probably make a case that each of these individuals has emotional skills, in rather different ways. The five have in fact been chosen to illustrate one of the leading theories of personality: the five factor model (FFM: Costa and McCrae 2000). It claims that the major features of personality are described by the "Big Five" traits: extraversion, neuroticism, conscientiousness, agreeableness, and openness. The five individuals exemplify the five traits, in order (note that Nico is *low* in neuroticism). Indeed each one of the traits has been linked to EI either conceptually (McCrae 2000) or empirically (e.g., Dawda and Hart 2000). The challenge here is to say whether each of the five is related to a common emotional ability or whether they exemplify five quite different personality traits.

There is some scope for confusion here, given that emotional intelligence is a form of "intelligence" and personality is generally seen as distinct from intelligence (Zeidner and Matthews 2000). An important distinction is that between "mixed" and "trait" models, introduced in chapter 1. The mixed-model perspective (e.g., Bar-On 2000) is that emotional intelligence comprises both abilities and aspects of personality but all the various facets of EI may be measured by questionnaire. This definition thus rests on the validity with which such abilities can be measured by questionnaire. Chapter 2 discussed reasons to be cautious of this approach; self-reports of abilities may not be valid. An alternative vision is that of EI as a distinctive personality trait, or set of traits, that expand the personality sphere to cover traits specifically related to emotional functioning and regulation (Petrides and Furnham 2003). If emotional intelligence is not a cognitive ability in the conventional sense, measurement by questionnaire may be acceptable.

Several challenges to the "trait emotional intelligence" position immediately arise. The first is whether EI can in fact be distinguished from traits such as extraversion, emotional stability (low neuroticism), conscientiousness, agreeableness, and openness. On the one hand, emotional intelligence may be not more than a mish-mash of existing personality factors. On the other hand, existing personality research may have neglected traits relating to emotional competence, such as insight into one's own and others' emotions, and effective regulation and control of emotions.

A second challenge concerns the assessment of EI as personality. Typically traits such as the Big Five are assessed using self-reports of the person's nature, feelings, and behaviors. Self-reports are open to various biases and distortions that make them suspect. Notwithstanding, there is sufficient validity evidence for the major personality traits to assert that questionnaires measure of them represent significant qualities of the person (Matthews et al. 2003). Measuring EI by self-report does, however, raise some special concerns. Typically we are asking for self-ratings of skills and competencies. As we will see, people may not be very good at making such self-assessments (Dunning et al. 2004). In addition rating one's own EI depends on insight and self-understanding; qualities that are themselves central to emotional intelligence. How can we expect an emotionally unintelligent person to meaningfully rate their own EI?

A third issue is whether the traits linked to EI really represent some true superiority in emotional functioning, as opposed to some qualitative style of emotional response. The personality sketches above were written to emphasize the positive features of certain traits. Perhaps if we got to know these people better, we would find that Enrique is an arrogant blowhard, and Nico is dangerously oblivious to real hazards. Cristina, by contrast, is a joyless workaholic, Alicia a doormat that everyone exploits, and Omar lacks all down-to-earth common sense. We will not presently dwell on this, but subsequently (see chapters 6 and 7) we will return to the issue of whether EI corresponds to adaptive features of personality or whether it has both an upside and a downside. Emotional intelligence might have more to do with how persons manage their temperamental qualities rather than temperament itself. Such self-regulation is difficult, however, to measure independently of general personality characteristics.

Understanding the enigmatic relationship between EI and personality requires us to focus on similar measurement issues to that covered in chapter 3 (i.e., principles laid out in chapter 2). It is known already that standard personality traits such as neuroticism and extraversion predict various emotional criteria, including mood and stress responses. If emotional intelligence provides any "added value" in understanding individual differences in emotional functioning, EI questionnaires must predict emotional criteria over and above existing personality traits. Demonstrating discriminant validity, as should be obvious from chapter 3, is a necessary but not sufficient condition. Even if measures of EI tell us about personal qualities that are poorly measured by standard personality inventories, we still need psychological theory to help us understand what it means to be "emotionally intelligent" according to the questionnaire.

In this chapter we first review what standard personality theory tells us about individual differences in emotional response. Next we survey questionnaire scales for EI that purport to assess qualities beyond standard personality traits. We begin with a look at pioneering attempts of this kind. Our review then explores newer work that is rather more cognizant of the difficulties of measuring emotional intelligence by self-report. Difficulties include the limitations intrinsic to self-report, excessive overlap with existing personality scales, and a lack of research driven by psychological theories of emotion. Our focus is especially on the validity of scales in relation to established personality measures. We will argue that the better scales show validity to the extent that they predict relevant indexes of social-emotional functioning, such as personal well-being, even with standard personality traits controlled. However, they tend to lack construct validity and especially, an underlying theory that would explain how EI influences well-being and social functioning.

Personality Traits: A Brief Outline

To understand how EI relates to personality, we must first say something about the nature of personality. Historically this has been a major and controversial field of inquiry, with roots in classical philosophy. In modern times Freud's psychoanalysis was influential, and understanding abnormalities and clinical disturbances in personality at the level of the individual remains important (Pervin 2005). Here, however, we focus on the scientific study of personality *traits*. These traits are defined as stable dispositions that influence emotional, cognitive, and behavioral function-

Table 4.1
Trait facets associated with the five domains of the five factor model of personality

Personality type	Personality traits
Neuroticism	Anxiety, angry hostility, depression, self-consciousness, impulsiveness, vulnerability
Extraversion	Warmth, gregariousness, assertiveness, activity, excitement-seeking, positive emotions
Openness	Fantasy, aesthetics, feelings, actions, ideas, values
Agreeableness	Trust, straightforwardness, altruism, compliance, modesty, tender-mindedness
Conscientiousness	Competence, order, dutifulness, achievement striving, self-discipline, deliberation

Source: Costa and McCrae (1992a, b).

ing across a range of different contexts or situations (Matthews et al. 2003). For example, an extraverted individual will tend to be cheerful, confident, and talkative at home, at work, and with friends. Note here though that the expression of personality traits, such as extraversion, depends critically also on external, situational factors. Not even an extravert is likely to make jokes at a funeral.

Table 4.1 illustrates a popular model of the major personality traits, the previously mentioned five factor model (FFM). The Big Five of extraversion, neuroticism, conscientiousness, agreeableness, and openness have been separately identified in many studies, and in adults these traits appear stable over time periods of many years (Costa and McCrae 2000). Various questionnaire measures of the FFM have good measurement properties, showing acceptable reliability and validity. Costa and McCrae (1992a, b) argue that these five factors are fundamental to understanding personality for the following reasons:

1. *Heritability* Personality traits are partially inherited, suggesting that personality reflects brain functioning, although social factors are also important.

2. *Consensual validation* Numerous researchers have identified the Big Five traits as central to personality.

3. *Cross-cultural invariance* It is claimed that the Big Five can be identified in all cultures (although culture does appear to affect personality structure; see de Raad 2000).

4. *Predictive utility* The five factors provide "added value" in that they predict not just superficial qualities of the person but additional criteria

such as attitudes to work and family, leisure and vocational interests, and objective performance on laboratory tasks.

Recent research has added much to both theoretical and practical understanding of personality. In a nutshell, the adult's personality traits result from a developmental process influenced by both genes and environment. The precursors of personality (sometimes called "temperament") become apparent early in childhood. Some children are especially active, some are easily upset, and some are particularly sociable. These emerging traits, in part, reflect individual differences in the brain systems that control these behaviors, differences that depend on how genes and the child's experiences with others interact to build the developing brain. As the child becomes older, cognitive representations of the self become increasingly important. For example, the active child may acquire a set of beliefs centered on themes of enjoying and valuing social activities. Thus the trait of extraversion in the adult is supported by a complex of biologically based predispositions together with socially shaped beliefs, preferences, and skills.

Assessment of personality traits is often practically useful. Clinical psychologists are concerned with the vulnerabilities to mental illness that personality may create. People with emotionally unstable or "neurotic" traits may be more likely to develop depression or an anxiety disorder following a life disturbance (Costa et al. 2005). Similarly educators may assess a child's personality to understand the roots of problems in the classroom. For instance, personality affects whether a child "acts out" behaviorally or becomes emotionally disturbed (Matthews, Zeidner, et al. 2006b). Personality assessment is widely used in industry to select those job applicants who are best-suited to a particular occupation (Barrick et al. 2001). Salespersons may need extraverted qualities, whereas police officers should be emotionally stable, for example.

Personality assessment is thus indubitably useful. There are limitations, however, in the questionnaire measures typically used. Personality influences, but does not determine, behavior. Whether a student is quiet or talkative in class, for example, depends not just on their level of extraversion-introversion, but other factors such as their interest in the subject material, their relationships with the teacher and other students, and their mood on any given occasion. Thus correlations between personality and behavioral criteria (e.g., academic or job proficiency) are often moderate in size (e.g., Barrick et al. 2001). Furthermore questionnaire assessment may not fully capture the major aspects of personality. An obvious problem is that people may be motivated to distort the image of their personality that they present to others (or even to themselves), so questionnaire responses are not fully accurate. Personality may be *implicit* as well as *explicit*. That is, people may show patterns of behavior of which they are unaware. For instance, a person may not believe him or herself to be racist but consistently avoids the company of ethnic minorities.

Personality and Emotion

We might expect some potential for confusion between personality and EI because personality traits exert a powerful influence on emotional functioning. As early as AD 150, it was recognized that some people have "sanguine" or cheerful personalities, whereas others tend to be "melancholic" or sad. The famous Greek physician Galen is often credited with one of the first theories of personality, suggesting some interesting features as we show in the sidebar on the next page.

Contemporary work recognizes extraversion–introversion and neuroticism as the two traits most relevant to emotion. Broadly speaking, extraverts are more prone to positive, happy emotional states than are introverts, although, as always, emotions are strongly influenced by the situation. In addition neurotic individuals experience more negative states such as anxiety and sadness than do emotionally stable persons. Biological models of personality (Corr 2004) attribute these links between personality and emotion to fundamental brain systems controlling the person's sensitivity to reward and punishment stimuli. Extraverts are more sensitive to rewards, or potential rewards, in the environment, and so become more easily happy than introverts. Similarly neurotic persons are especially sensitive to possible punishment, which impairs mood.

There is more to the link between personality and emotion than brain systems for reward and punishment. Personality also affects cognitive processes that may influence emotional state. Extraverts tend to appraise life events as challenging, and to use active, problem-focused coping strategies, ways of thinking about and handling events that may promote positive moods (e.g., Matthews et al. 2003). Similarly neurotic individuals are biased toward perceiving events as involving threat or loss. As a result they tend to use coping strategies such as self-criticism that may strengthen negative moods. Personality traits may also exert indirect effects on emotion that follow on from life events and encounters with others. Extraverts, for example, typically have more social engagement than introverts, and social activities are known to promote positive emotion (Watson and Clark 1988). Neuroticism, however, is linked

Galen of Pergamum (c. 130–200)	Brief biography of Galen, arguably the first great personality theorist
	Galen was physician to the roman emperor Marcus Aurelius. He remains most famous for his codification of Hippocrates's "four humors" as personality traits (a concept later adopted by Alfred Adler in his "Four Lifestyle Theory"). He taught the importance of maintaining balance between four bodily fluids (the so-called humors): blood, phlegm, yellow bile, and black bile. Each fluid was associated with a specific personality characteristic. Blood was associated with a sanguine personality, namely laughter, music, and a passionate disposition. Someone with a phlegmatic personality was sluggish and dull, while yellow bile represented an individual quick to anger or choleric. Lastly, black bile represented a melancholic or depressed personality. It was the job of the physician to restore harmony in those four humors by the use of cathartics, purgatives, and bloodletting. Galen's investigations were, however, far more wide ranging. He was the first to identify the brain–mind relation, the basic working structure of the eye and ear, as well as distinguishing differences between motor and sensory nerves (i.e., affective and effective impulses). He is believed to have practiced a number of complex surgical operations that were not used again for nearly two millennia, including brain and eye surgery. On a lighter note, Galen is also credited with investigating increased physiological activity among lovers.

to interpersonal conflicts and self-inflicted life problems (Magnus et al. 1993; Suls 2001), episodes that may elevate negative moods. Thus personality relates to emotional experience via multiple pathways. These include fundamental brain systems, modes of understanding and managing life events, and the consequences of different styles of social interaction with others.

Again, it must be emphasized that personality relates only to broad tendencies, since emotions are most immediately dependent on the nature of events and the person's appraisals of those events. Extraverts do not walk around in a state of permanent bliss. Nor are neurotic individuals doomed to a life of perpetual misery. However, personality does exert far-reaching influences on the physiological and psychological processes that control emotions.

Personality Traits and Emotional Competencies

The intimate association of personality and emotion sets a trap for researchers interested in emotional intelligence. It might seem that happy, calm states of mind should be seen as the hallmark of the person imbued with high emotional intelligence. However, such emotional tendencies may be no more than a consequence of biases in brain functioning or information-processing routines operating without insight or "intelligence." Some individuals—in part because of their DNA—are simply fortunate in being prone to pleasant moods. It follows that emotional states do not alone provide an index of emotional competence. Indeed someone like Abraham Lincoln, who was forced to struggle with a melancholy temperament all his life, might have a greater depth of understanding than a more sanguine individual for whom happiness and life satisfaction have come easily (we return to this issue in chapter 11). Hence it is essential to differentiate EI from personality traits associated with emotion. Re-labeling a cheerful temperament as "emotional intelligence" is an exercise in futility.

Although mood, in general, is not a marker for emotional intelligence, in some individuals positive moods may be an outcome of emotional competency. Thus we require research that is oriented toward the *processes* through which people adapt to life circumstances with differing degrees of success. Evidence is needed that emotional intelligence relates to individual differences in understanding and managing critical real-life situations and encounters that over time feed into greater success and happiness. We return to issues of coping and adaptation in chapter 7. For now we will simply note that cross-sectional studies showing that scales for EI correlate with measures of well-being are inadequate to demonstrate that emotional intelligence relates to specific adaptive processes. As a first step, though, it is essential that correlational studies provide *divergent evidence* for emotional intelligence with respect to personality traits, that is, that EI predicts mood and well-being, even when the influence of personality is statistically controlled.

Questionnaire Assessment of Emotional Intelligence

Testing intelligence through asking respondents to report on their own abilities seems to be an odd thing to do. As already noted, it is questionable whether people are able to accurately estimate their own emotional intelligence. It seems paradoxical to suppose that emotionally unintelligent people have sufficient insight and self-understanding to be aware of their own emotional shortcomings. There is also research evidence that suggests self-estimates of intelligence may not be accurate. Studies of conventional general intelligence show that people's self-ratings correlate at only about 0.2 to 0.3 with their intelligence as measured objectively (Chamorro-Premuzic et al. 2005).

A recent paper by Dunning et al. (2004) reviews evidence on self-assessments of educational attainment, workplace proficiencies, and health. Dunning and colleagues draw several conclusions that challenge the utility of these self-assessments. First, people's assessments of their own competencies are weakly correlated with objective measures, or ratings of the person made by other people. For example, a meta-analysis of studies comparing self-ratings with supervisor ratings of job performance showed a mean correlation of only 0.35 (Harris and Schaubroeck 1988). Disturbingly for emotional intelligence research, self-ratings of complex social skills appear to be especially inaccurate. Mabe and West (1982) report a meta-analysis showing correlations between self-report and objective performance of 0.04 for managerial competence and 0.17 for interpersonal skills.

Second, people are generally prone to overstate their competence in a variety of respects, including social skills, decision-making abilities, and maintaining health and safety. Dunning et al. (2004) cite a finding that 94 percent of college professors say their work is above average—a mathematical impossibility. According to these authors, Microsoft routinely adds 30 to 50 percent to the timeline for software development projects because software developers grossly underestimate how long it will take them to accomplish the tasks involved. These biases reflect a lack of needed information for estimating competence. They also suggest that individuals make errors in using the information available to them. In particular, it appears individuals place too much weight on positive feedback, and too little on feedback that suggests lack of competence.

Third, the least competent individuals are often those with the poorest grasp of their own (lack of) ability, an observation that Dunning et al. (2004) describe as the "double curse" of incompetence. For example, college students scoring in the bottom 25 percent on a course exam believed their performance as above average. Similar findings are reported for poorly performing debate teams, medical students, and hospital lab technicians.

The implications for self-assessments of emotional intelligence are clear. First, it is unlikely that such assessments are highly correlated with objective measures of competence. Indeed ratings of EI may be especially vulnerable to some of the factors that impede accurate self-judgment, such as the ill-defined nature of emotional competence, delayed or ambiguous feedback, and motivations to enhance one's beliefs in competence (Dunning et al. 2004). Second, most people likely overrate their own emotional competencies. Third, those individuals that are least emotionally intelligent may be those with the least awareness of their own deficiencies. Put another way, those people who congratulate themselves on their elevated emotional intelligence may instead be those that are lacking in the ability. In these circumstances development of questionnaire measures for EI takes some courage. We will next examine the work of some of the brave pioneers in this area.

A Case Study: The Bar-On EQ-i

One of the first systematic instruments purporting to assess emotional intelligence was Bar-On's (1997, 2004) EQ-i questionnaire. It is noteworthy because the author carried out an extensive program of development work in many countries across the world, and the questionnaire has been a popular choice for empirical research. Nevertheless, we have argued elsewhere that the EQ-i is a severely flawed instrument (Matthews, Zeidner, et al. 2002). It is instructive to look in more detail at the EQ-i and its limitations as an example of the difficulties that arise in trying to assess emotional intelligence via the questionnaire.

Introducing the measure, Bar-On (1997) describes how his experiences as a clinical psychologist led him to reflect on the most important personal factors that may determine well-being and life success. Bar-On (2004) states that in the early stages of the research he generated nearly 1,000 questionnaire items based on his clinical experience, as well as an analysis of key emotional and social competencies thought to impact personal effectiveness. Eventually these items were whittled down to the 133 items, representing 15 scales that comprise the current instrument. It was normed on 3,831 adults in North America in 1996, and has since been translated into over 30 languages.

Table 4.2 shows the factorial model proposed by Bar-On. Social and emotional competencies are assessed through 15 dimensions, grouped into 5 higher order composites. The first two composites are familiar throughout the EI literature as differentiating regulation of one's own emotions versus the emotions of others (see chapter 3). Unlike some authors (e.g., Mayer et al. 2000), Bar-On does not strongly differentiate perception and analysis of emotions from management of emotions. The remaining three composites—stress management, adaptability, and general mood—

Table 4.2
EQ-i composite scales and sub-scales, with brief descriptions

Composite/sub-scale	Brief description
Intrapersonal	
Emotional self-awareness	Recognize and understand one's feelings
Assertiveness	Express feelings, thoughts and beliefs, and defend one's rights in a nondestructive manner
Self-regard	Understand, accept, and respect oneself
Self-actualization	Realize one's potential capacities
Independence	Self-directed, self-controlled, and free of emotional dependency
Interpersonal	
Empathy	Aware and appreciative of the feelings of others
Interpersonal relationship	Establish and maintain satisfying relationships characterized by emotional closeness and mutual affection
Social responsibility	Cooperative and responsible member of one's social group
Adaptation	
Problem solving	Define problems and generate potentially effective solutions
Reality testing	Evaluate the correspondence between objective and subjective reality in realistic and "well-grounded" fashion
Flexibility	Adjust emotions, thoughts, and behaviors to changing conditions
Stress management	
Stress tolerance	Withstand adverse events, through positive, active coping
Impulse control	Resist or delay an impulse, drive, or temptation to act
General mood	
Happiness	Feel satisfied with life, and enjoy oneself and being with others
Optimism	Maintain a positive attitude, even in the face of adversity

feature more strongly in Bar-On's account than in competing models. These components reflect the author's concerns with functioning under the pressures and demands of everyday life. A so-called total EQ can also be calculated, analogous to an IQ.

The EQ-i meets some conventional psychometric criteria. The scales show acceptable internal consistencies, ranging from 0.70 to 0.89 (Bar-On 2004). Moreover these scales appear stable across a 6 month retest interval. The EQ-i shows convergent validity evidence to the extent that it correlates substantially with other questionnaire scales for emotional intelligence (Bar-On 2004).

There is also some evidence for test–criterion relations in studies of academic and work performance, and of well-being. Parker et al. (2004) found that some facets of the EQ-i correlated at about $r = 0.3$ with grade point average in a sample of first-year university students. However, correlations between first-year GPA and total EQ-i score were low or non-significant. Bar-On (2004) also claims that the EQ-i predicts performance in soldiers and executives, although, unfortunately, these studies have not been published in peer-reviewed outlets. Slaski and Cartwright (2002) found a small relation between EQ-i scores and managerial performance ($r = 0.22$). Similarly Bachman et al. (2000) reported that more successful account officers have higher EQ-i scores than less successful account officers. The EQ-i correlates rather more substantially with various questionnaire measures of well-being and mental health, and scores appear to be depressed in individuals with psychiatric problems (Bar-On 2004).

The Wheel Reinvented?   The EQ-i is seemingly a successful test that has been widely lauded (not least by the test author and his various colleagues). So, what could be wrong with this rosy picture? Next we will look at some criticisms of the questionnaire that may threaten its validity as a measure of emotional intelligence. It is important to note that these criticisms are not unique to the EQ-i; they may apply to many self-report measures of the construct.

Factor Structure   Taken individually, the scales of the EQ-i are internally consistent. However, the scales may not correspond well to true underlying traits of the person. Correlations between the 15 scales run as high as 0.80. With such high values, it becomes questionable whether the scales truly discriminate between distinct trait constructs. The usual method that psychologists use to address such questions is, as discussed in chapters 2 and 3, factor analysis. Bar-On (1997) reports an exploratory factor analysis that indicates 13 rather than 15 factors, but the analysis has a severe technical flaw. Bar-On used a factor analytic method that forces factors to be independent of one another. A part of the rationale for believing in a general factor of EI is that its different components are intercorrelated, so this method violates a basic assumption of the approach. Matthews, Zeidner, et al. (2002) re-analyzed Bar-On's (1997) own data, and showed that 70 percent of the variation in the EQ-i scales could be explained by just three factors, relating to self-reported positive mood, self-esteem, and stress resistance. The factors were allowed to correlate. When scale unreliability was taken into account, the three factors explained around 80 to 90 percent of the scale variance, implying that the 15 factors described by Bar-On do not exist as separate trait dimensions.

Bar-On (2000, 2004) reports a confirmatory factor analysis, after excluding some scales, which supports a 10 factor solution. Self-regard explained considerably more of the variance than any other factor. This finding implies that much of what the EQ-i measures is self-esteem, rather than any true ability. However, Bar-On fails to report essential statistics, including goodness of fit indexes or factor correlations, so it is difficult to evaluate the adequacy of the analysis. Rather oddly, Bar-On (2004) refers to the five scales omitted from the 10 factor solution as "facilitators" rather than actual components of EI, but the conceptual distinction here is not very clear (Matthews, Zeidner, et al. 2002). What makes this research rather frustrating to evaluate is that the bulk of it has not been subjected to review by scientific peers.

Lack of Convergent and Divergent Validity Evidence   As we emphasize in chapters 2 and 3, a measure should correlate highly with other variables that relate to the underlying construct (convergent evidence). Hence alternative measures of EI should correlate with another. Unfortunately, it appears that the EQ-i fails this test. Brackett and Mayer (2003) report a 0.21 correlation between their MSCEIT and Bar-On's (2000) EQ-i. Subsequently other studies have confirmed that ability-based and questionnaire-based assessments of EI are measuring essentially different constructs (Matthews et al. 2005). Because the MSCEIT has some claims to objective measurement of EI, the failure in convergent validity here is especially damaging for the EQ-i, and other questionnaire assessments. Similarly the EQ-i fails to correlate substantially with conventional intelligence tests (Derksen et al. 2002).

A test should also *not* correlate strongly with measures that assess distinct constructs. If, as Bar-On (2000) claims, the EQ-i assesses a type of ability, it should not correlate too highly with personality. However, several studies (e.g., Dawda and Hart 2000; Newsome et al. 2000) showed unacceptably high correlations (exceeding 0.7 in some cases) with standard personality traits. These studies reveal that so-called EQ is largely low neuroticism and extraversion, with some conscientiousness and agreeableness mixed in. A recent study using a short version of the EQ-i, the EQ-s (with "s" standing for short form), found a multiple correlation of 0.79 between EQ and the FFM (Grubb and McDaniel 2007), suggesting that EQ can be viewed as little else than an aggregation of the Big Five. This study also had respondents complete the EQ-i in a condition where they were asked to "fake good," that is, to try to present themselves in the best possible light. The instruction raised EQ by almost a full standard deviation, implying that the EQ-s is of little value for personnel selection.

Criterion Contamination A common problem in research using personality scales to predict well-being is that the personality scale used as a predictor includes items that relate to the criterion for well-being that is being predicted. This in turn leads to an artificially high correlation. For example, some scales for extraversion include items that refer to experiencing many positive moods. Correlations between such scales and criteria for positive mood will then be artificially inflated.

The EQ-i is flawed in just this way; it includes scales such as happiness and self-actualization that measure positive outcomes, rather than competencies that may lead to such outcomes. Indeed the first and largest factor in Bar-On's (1997) exploratory factor analysis was labeled "self-contentment" and covers "a broad range of items, all of which relate to contentment with oneself and one's life" (p. 104). If the questionnaire in substantial part measures contentment, then, of course, it will correlate with indices of well-being and lack of stress. However, the high correlations that purport to validate the questionnaire may simply be an artifact of overlap between the content of the EQ-i and the criterion measures. This concern is reinforced by Bar-On's (1997) own data, which show very large negative correlations between the EQ-i and criteria for psychopathology.

Status of the EQ-i The evidence we have reviewed provides a case study in the difficulties of assessing emotional and social competencies via self-report. In some ways the test development efforts seem well-founded. The facets of EI that the questionnaire aims to assess are among those commonly listed by researchers in the area (although the conceptual model is vague). Bar-On (1997) was assiduous in gathering normative data, and the EQ-i meets some reliability and validity criteria. Nevertheless, the empirical data show problems serious enough to threaten the validity of the EQ-i as an ability measure. It is unclear exactly what constructs are measured by the EQ-i (poor factor structure). Much of the reliable variance in the instrument reflects either (1) standard personality dimensions that are known to influence emotional response or (2) the well-being outcomes that the EQ-i is designed to predict. To a large degree the EQ-i is no more than a psychometrically maladroit mélange of established emotion constructs. A few studies (Brackett and Mayer 2003; van der Zee and Wabeke 2004) suggest that the EQ-i adds some modest incremental validity to the Big Five as predictors of outcome criteria, but its performance falls far short of the claims made by the test developers. Just as Dunning et al.'s (2004) critique of self-assessments of ability suggests, we cannot take self-reports of emotional intelligence at face value.

Take Two: The Schutte Self-Report Inventory

Another pioneer in the area of questionnaire development is Australian-based psychologist Nicola Schutte. The Schutte Self-Report Inventory (SSRI: Schutte et al. 1998) is founded on the Salovey and Mayer (1990) model for EI, which, as we saw in chapter 3, is one of the stronger conceptual frameworks for test development. The SSRI contains 33 items intended to assess appraisal, regulation, and utilization of emotion. Schutte et al. (1998) focus on the overall scale score as a measure of emotional intelligence, but they also reported an exploratory factor analysis that discriminated four subfactors of EI. Schutte and her group have reported a number of validation studies (e.g., Schutte et al. 1998; Schutte, Malouf, et al. 2001), and the SSRI has been a popular choice for independent research.

The SSRI turns out to show strengths and weaknesses similar to the EQ-i, with which it correlates. On the positive side, scores on the questionnaire are reliable and stable over time. The SSRI has also been shown to predict a variety of relevant criteria, including mood, well-being, and satisfaction with interpersonal and marital relations (e.g., Schutte et al. 1998; Schutte, Malouf, et al. 2001; Schutte et al. 2002). Like other EI instruments, the SSRI discriminates some deviant groups, such as adults with substance-use problems (Riley and Schutte 2003).

However, other findings recapitulate the shortcomings of the EQ-i. Again, Schutte et al.'s (1998) factor analysis is technically flawed through use of a statistical procedure that is inappropriate for factors that may correlate. Other researchers (e.g., Saklofske et al. 2003), using confirmatory methods, have obtained rather different factor solutions. Like the EQ-i, the SSRI is largely independent of objective intelligence tests. In this respect Zeidner, Shani-Zinovich, et al. (2005) obtained striking evidence against the convergent validity of the SSRI. A sample of academically gifted (high IQ) children scored more highly than controls on the MSCEIT, yet at the same time obtained *lower* SSRI scores. Concerns about criterion contamination may also be in order, as several of the SSRI items appear to signal a more optimistic outlook on life (e.g., "I expect good things to happen").

The SSRI is not so severely confounded with standard personality traits as is the EQ-i, but substantial correlations have been reported (i.e., up to 0.5 with extraversion; see Saklofske et al. 2003). The SSRI also correlates positively with conscientiousness and openness, and negatively with neuroticism (Brackett and Mayer 2003). Brackett and Mayer (2003) report a revealing factor analysis that links the SSRI to extraversion and positive well-being, and the EQ-i to low neuroticism. We might see the SSRI as infused with items referring to positive mood, and the EQ-i to items indicating the absence of stress symptoms. Schutte et al.'s various validation studies are remarkable for their neglect of the potentially confounding role of personality. For example, Schutte et al. (2002) found that high scorers on the SSRI showed greater response to a positive mood induction. This result corresponds exactly to findings from research on extraversion (e.g., Larsen and Ketelaar 1989). That is, "emotionally intelligent" persons in this study may simply be responding as extraverts are known to do.

As with the EQ-i, there is a little evidence that the SSRI strongly predicts criteria over and above the Big Five. Saklofske et al. (2003) found that the SSRI predicted some well-being indices with the Big Five personality factors controlled, although the additional variance explained was small (i.e., less than 5 percent). Other findings suggest only modest incremental validity. Brackett and Mayer (2003) found that the SSRI predicted only one of out six outcome criteria (high school rank) with the Big Five and verbal SAT score controlled statistically. Austin et al. (2005) examined predictors of various health-related outcomes in a subgroup of Scots (N ranged from 99 to 111). The SSRI was more strongly associated than the Big Five with social network size, but social network quality, life satisfaction, alcohol consumption, number of doctor consultations, and health status were more strongly related to personality. Thus, as with the EQ-i, the predictive utility of the SSRI appears notably limited.

EI Goes to Work: The Emotional Competence Inventory (ECI)

The third pioneering scale we review is concerned with the practical application of questionnaire assessments to measure EI in a work context. In his best-selling book, *Working with Emotional Intelligence*, Goleman (1998) proposed a model of EI with twenty-five competencies arrayed in five, higher order clusters, labeled as self-awareness, self-regulation, motivation, empathy, and social skills. Development of a measure to assess these competencies—the Emotional Competence Inventory (ECI)—

Table 4.3
Competencies comprising the various emotional intelligence models and measures developed by Goleman and colleagues

Goleman's (1998) model	ECI original version	ECI version 2.1	ECI version 2.2
Self-awareness	*Self-awareness*	*Self-awareness*	*Self-awareness*
Emotional self-awareness	Emotional self-awareness	Emotional self-awareness	Emotional self-awareness
Accurate self-assessment	Accurate self-assessment	Accurate self-assessment	Accurate self-assessment
Self-confidence	Conscientiousness	Self-confidence	Self-confidence
Self-regulation	*Self-management*	*Self-management*	*Self-management*
Self-control	Self-control	Self-control	Emotional self-control
Trustworthiness	Trustworthiness	Trustworthiness	Transparency
Conscientiousness	Self-confidence	Conscientiousness	
Adaptability	Adaptability	Adaptability	Adaptability
Innovation	Change catalyst		
Self-motivation			
Achievement orientation	Achievement orientation	Achievement orientation	Achievement
Commitment			
Initiative	Initiative	Initiative	Initiative
Optimism			Optimism
Empathy	*Social awareness*	*Social awareness*	*Social awareness*
Empathy	Empathy	Empathy	Empathy
Organizational awareness	Organizational awareness	Organizational awareness	Organizational awareness
Service orientation	Service orientation	Service orientation	Service orientation
Developing others	Developing others		
Leveraging diversity			

Table 4.3
(continued)

Goleman's (1998) model	ECI original version	ECI version 2.1	ECI version 2.2
Social skills	***Social skills***	***Social skills***	***Social skills***
Leadership	Leadership	Leadership	Inspirational leadership
Communication	Communication	Communication	
Influence	Influence	Influence	Influence
Change catalyst	Trustworthiness	Change catalyst	Change catalyst
Conflict management	Conflict management	Conflict management	Conflict management
Building bonds	Building bonds	Building bonds	
Collaboration and cooperation	Teamwork and collaboration	Teamwork and collaboration	Teamwork and collaboration
Team capabilities		Developing others	Developing others

produced a series of questionnaires, culminating in the latest revision, sometimes known as the ECI-2 (e.g., see Sala 2002). The development process, in fact, suggests major changes in the underlying model of EI from Goleman's original conception. Currently there are four higher order constructs reformulated as self-awareness, self-management, social awareness, and relationship management. To give the reader a flavor of the apparent indecisiveness associated with this assessment, we present the revised models underlying the ECI in table 4.3. Clearly, the ECI measures a different competence-based model than that described in *Working with Emotional Intelligence*.

The ECI is a multi-rater instrument that provides self, manager, direct report, and peer ratings on a series of behavioral indicators of emotional intelligence, based on the emotional competencies identified by Goleman (1998). This potential for "360" assessment is a strength for a business-human resources application. Goleman (2001) provides capsule descriptions for the first version of the ECI-2 (column 3 in table 4.3), which help give a flavor for the content of each scale. We distill the major aspects of these descriptions in table 4.4.

The ECI appears psychometrically weaker than the EQ-i and SSRI. The reliability of the self-report subscales reported by Boyatzis et al.

(2000) is marginal for high-stakes decision-making, ranging from 0.59 (trustworthiness) to 0.82 (conscientiousness). The situation, in a twist that almost defies precedence, appears worse for the latest version of the measure, for which internal consistency reliabilities range from 0.39 (conflict management) to 0.78 (developing others). There is also cause for concern in the test-retest reliability of the ECI (Sala 2002). This has been found to range from 0.05 (service orientation) to 0.82 (teamwork), with many values at the lower end. Indeed more than a few of the scales have test-retest reliabilities approaching zero, suggesting that it may not function much better than the proverbial lemon!

An actual evaluation of the validity evidence supporting (or otherwise) the ECI is difficult for three reasons. First, the use of multiple versions of the instrument means that findings may not generalize across each different instrument. Second, almost all of the empirical studies examining this measure emanate from working papers, unpublished manuscripts, graduate dissertations, or brief technical reports (see Boyatzis et al. 2000; Sala 2002). Thus we could find no analysis supporting the validity of the measure in the peer-reviewed scientific literature, although some technical papers are available on the Web (see, in particular, http://www.eiconsortium.org/research/research.htm).

As with other EI questionnaires, there is considerable potential for overlap with personality. For example, conscientiousness is a superfactor of the Big Five and emotional self-control appears related to emotional stability (low neuroticism). Similarly trustworthiness is a facet of agreeableness, while adaptability is a feature of openness. Unpublished studies confirm overlap between the ECI and traits of the Big Five (Sala 2002). In a still further disturbing twist, many of the ECI subscales correlate negatively with cognitive ability, as assessed by the Watson-Glaser Critical Thinking Test. If EI is a genuine intelligence it should show at least small positive correlations with other ability measures, so this finding calls into question the validity of the ECI. It also suggests that using the ECI for personnel selection might have the unintended consequence of selecting for low mental ability.

Sala (2002) reports several studies allegedly supporting the predictive validity of the ECI. ECI subscales are said to predict retention rates, salary level, and appraisal ratings from supervisors, for a wide array of jobs, including principals, call center agents, and people working in the finance sector. Two important observations need to be made concerning these findings. First, much is made of very weak correlations (e.g., $r = 0.20$) obtained with small samples (20 to 90 participants). Second, these rela-

Table 4.4
Capsule descriptions of the 20 competencies comprising the ECI (version 2)

Scale	Capsule description
Self-awareness cluster	
Emotional self-awareness	Recognizing one's feelings and how they influence performance
Accurate self-assessment	Awareness of abilities and limitations, learning from mistakes, seeking feedback, knowing where to improve, knowing when to work with people with complementary strengths
Self-confidence	Belief in the self and one's abilities; related to self-efficacy
Self-management cluster	
Emotional self-control	Manifested in absence of distress and disruptive feelings
Trustworthiness	Translates into letting people know one's values, principles, intentions, feelings, and acting in ways consistent with these actions
Conscientiousness	Being careful, self-disciplined, and scrupulous in attending to responsibilities
Adaptability	Openness to new information; can let go of old assumptions and adapt how one operates
Achievement orientation	Optimistically striving to continually improve performance
Initiative	Acting before being forced to by external events
Social awareness cluster	
Empathy	Astute awareness of others' emotions, concerns, and needs
Customer Service	Ability to identify client's often unstated needs and concerns; then matching them to one's own products and services
Organizational awareness	Ability to read the currents of emotions and political realities in groups
Social-skills cluster	
Influence	Entails handling and managing emotions in other people, and doing so persuasively
Communication	Effectiveness in give-and-take of emotional information, dealing with issues straightforwardly, listening well and sharing full disclosure of information, fostering open communication, being receptive to both good and bad news
Conflict management	Spotting troubles and taking steps to calm those involved
Leadership	A range of personal skills required to inspire people to work toward some common goal
Change catalyst	Being able to recognize the need for change, remove barriers, challenge the status quo, and enlist others in pursuit of new initiatives
Building bonds	Balancing own critical work with carefully chosen favors, and building accounts of goodwill with people who may become crucial resources down the line
Teamwork and collaboration	Teamwork depends on the collective EI of its members; the most productive teams are those that exhibit EI competencies at the team level, while collaboration is the ability to work cooperatively with peers
Developing others	Entails providing a supportive growth environment; teaching, mentoring, etc.

tions are not totally unexpected if the measure is serving as a proxy for personality factors. One of the most known findings in the scientific literature is that conscientiousness predicts job performance, over and above other psychological constructs (e.g., Barrick and Mount 1991). In the absence of studies where personality is also assessed, it is difficult to draw any firm conclusions regarding the predictive validity of the ECI.

In sum, it is difficult *not* to be cynical of this measure. Contributing to this feeling is the lack of publicly accessible data supplied by its creators and the constellation of old concepts packaged under its "new" label. Or to put it another way, as kindly as we can: we think it is imperative for the developers of the ECI to conduct more rigorous validity studies if the scale is ever to meet the standards deemed requisite of a sound scientific measure. Right now, we cannot decide about its validity, which is a sad state-of-affairs for an instrument that is being peddled in some professional quarters.

Questionnaires: The Second Wave

The questionnaires we have already reviewed represent a first pass at the problem of assessing emotional abilities via questionnaire, within the "mixed-model" framework. It is perhaps not surprising that problems would arise, notably the confounding of scores with standard personality traits. These difficulties have become fairly well known among researchers in the area, and there is an increasing concern with differentiation of emotional intelligence scales from personality. Next we look at some examples of this "second wave" of research. In fact there are far too many questionnaires developed in recent years to review them all: Perez et al. (2005) identified over fifty, and the number grows every year. We will focus on a few salient examples only in the passages that follow.

Trait Emotional Intelligence Questionnaire (TEIQue)   Petrides and Furnham (2000, 2001, 2003) start with the assumption that "trait EI," assessed by questionnaire, is fundamentally different from the abilities that may be revealed by objective tests such as the MSCEIT. Trait EI is seen as an aspect of personality concerning emotion-related dispositions and self-perceptions. Thus it is not required to correlate with objective tests of either conventional or emotional intelligence. It is a mistake to suppose that self-report questionnaires can be used to measure abilities and competencies.

The TEIque was initially developed from the EQ-i. A factor analytic study (Petrides and Furnham 2001) collected data from both the EQ-i and Costa and McCrae's (1992a) NEO-PI-R, which assesses a total of 30 facets of the "Big Five" traits. Some EQ-i scales were found to belong with one or other of the Big Five. However, an additional factor was defined by a subset of the EQ-i scales that seemed to be distinct from the Big Five, including, principally, assertiveness, emotional self-awareness, independence, emotion mastery, and self-regard. Petrides and Furnham correctly allowed factors to correlate; their "trait EI" factor correlated positively with extraversion and conscientiousness, and negatively with neuroticism. In effect, it appears that the EQ-i may be stripped down to reveal some variation in personality that constitutes rather more than the Big Five.

Subsequent studies (see Perez et al. 2005) refined this initial idea by including items adapted from various other instruments, among these the SSRI. The current version of the TEIque contains 144 items that may be scored for overall trait EI, and 15 subscales. The scales have acceptable alpha coefficients, and recent work suggests good cross-cultural generalization of the questionnaire. Furthermore some innovative validity studies have been reported. Notably, the authors do not insist that EI, as a trait, is necessarily adaptive in all circumstances, a point reinforced by the evidence. Petrides and Furnham (2003) showed that trait EI related to faster recognition of facial emotion and to greater reactivity to an experimental mood-induction. Like Schutte et al. (2002), they found that high trait EI individuals showed more mood elevation following a cheerful video. However, results also showed that trait EI related to greater mood deterioration following unpleasant videos. Petrides et al. (2004) showed that, in general, IQ was a better predictor of educational attainment than trait EI in British 11th-year pupils, as might be expected. However, an interaction between IQ and EI suggested that high trait EI might benefit low IQ pupils, perhaps because high EI helps pupils that are cognitively taxed to cope more successfully with the pressures of their academic struggles.

The TEIque appears to have a more coherent rationale than its predecessors, locating it squarely in the personality domain, rather than treating it as a notional ability. Its validation in experimental studies is especially important (see Petrides and Furnham 2003). Some of the same concerns already voiced remain. The factor analysis of Petrides and Furnham (2001) suggested that a leaner, meaner EI dimension, that did not just rehash existing personality variance, could be isolated. However, the TEIque retains aspects of self-reported emotional intelligence that relate strongly to the Big Five. Thus Petrides and Furnham (2003) found that

their trait EI correlated at −0.73 with neuroticism, and 0.69 with extraversion; correlations that are uncomfortably high.

The scale also continues to include EQ-i facets that are contaminated
with the outcome criteria they are intended to predict, notably happiness
and optimism. Although some of Petrides and Furnham's (e.g., 2001,
2003) studies show incremental validity for the TEIque over the Big
Five, concerns about possible criterion contamination remain. We see
the TEIque as an improvement over the EQ-i and SSRI, but more work
remains to be done in parsing out scales (and valid "EI" scores) that are
truly distinct from the Big Five personality factors and well-being criteria.

Survey of Emotional Intelligence (SEI) Tett and colleagues (2005) have
developed another promising multifactorial scale to assess trait emotional
intelligence. Their article begins with a critique of previous questionnaires, including overlap with personality and uncertainties over factor
structure. In search of an improved measure, Tett et al. (2005) developed
scales corresponding to ten facets of EI described by Salovey and Mayer
(1990). A factor analysis showed that there were three higher order factors, as shown in table 4.5 (included in this table also are sample items
for each of the ten primary scales). Two of the factors differentiated self-

Table 4.5
Three higher order EI factors identified by Tett et al. (2005)

Self-orientation	Other-orientation	Emotion sharing
Motivating emotions "I am highly self-motivated"	*Creative thinking* "Others think my ideas are daring"	*Nonverbal emotional expression* "Others would say that, emotionally, I am very easy to read"
Regulation of emotion in the self "I am clearly the master of my own emotions"	*Regulation of emotion in others* "I am generally very good at calming others down when they are upset"	*Empathy* "If I saw someone being harassed, I would get upset"
Recognition of emotion in the self "I know precisely what is bothering me when I am feeling down"	*Recognition of emotion in others* "I am good at reading the inner feelings of people even if I don't know them very well"	*Mood directed attention* "Getting upset allows me to see what is important in my life"
Intuition versus reason "In making big decisions, gut feelings are often better than reasoning through every detail"		

Note: The sample items are given in italics are listed at http://www.appliedpsychology.ws/
WEIS/SEIintro.htm.

and other-directed aspects of EI: self-orientation and other-orientation. The third factor, labeled "emotion sharing," was defined most strongly by empathy and nonverbal emotion expression.

Tett et al. (2005) also investigated the correlations of the SEI with personality scales, and tested its incremental validity with regard to personality, as a predictor of questionnaire measures of life satisfaction and "cross-cultural adaptability." (What this latter criterion means to the American psychology undergraduates tested is rather unclear.) The data suggest that some degree of separation between trait emotional intelligence and personality was achieved. About 50 percent of the reliable variance in the scales was explained by personality, although there was some variation in the extent to which the individual scales overlapped with personality dimensions. Five of the ten scales showed correlations in the 0.5 to 0.7 range with one or other of the Big Five, while the remaining scales seemed more distinctive. Regression analyses showed that the SEI added about 10 percent unique variance to the prediction of satisfaction, and about 15 percent to cross-cultural adaptability. The questionnaire developers were also more careful than most of their peers in addressing social desirability, and confirmed that the EI scales predicted the criteria with social desirability controlled statistically.

The SEI appears promising in that it assesses rather more variance distinct from standard personality traits than did the early EI scales. At the same time, doubts remain. At this early stage of questionnaire development, the evidence for criterion validity is limited to the additional questionnaires completed by the college student samples. It is also unclear how the Big Five and the EI factors may be put together into a common structural model for the trait domain. Should the three factors shown in table 4.5 be considered as primary personality traits? Or should some of the facets be assigned to the Big Five, and others assigned to an EI factor or factors? Again, we have a measure that has some promise for future research, but the research has yet to decisively separate EI from other, related constructs.

Not Quite Emotional Intelligence: Mood Regulation and the Trait Meta-Mood Scale (TMMS)

Before we finish our review of questionnaires for emotional intelligence, we look briefly at the subfield of *mood regulation*. This is a branch of emotion research that precedes research on emotional intelligence, concerned with how people actively manage their own moods (e.g., repair a negative mood or maintain a pleasant mood). People often regulate mood by choosing uplifting activities, such as enjoying leisure activities with friends (e.g., Thayer 1996). What has caught the attention of EI researchers is the *internal* regulation of mood. That is, changing mood via one's thought processes, such as positive thinking. Gross (1998; Gross and John 2003) describes two principal strategies of this kind. *Reappraisal* refers (typically) to attempts to see events in a more positive light, whereas *suppression* refers to attempts to inhibit the expression of feelings. Reappraisal tends to be a more adaptive strategy than suppression, although the latter may have its utility; at the poker table, for example. Gross (1998) also points out a multitude of individual difference factors that may relate to mood regulation, including emotional control, repression, rumination, impulsivity, and emotional intelligence.

Mood regulation can be—and generally is—studied without any reference to emotional intelligence. However, some of the questionnaires used in this field have been brought into the mainstream of EI research. A case in point is the Trait Meta-Mood Scale (TMMS; Salovey et al. 1995). The TMMS indexes the tendency to use particular strategies for working with moods. These strategies are paying attention to feelings (attention), discriminating clearly among feelings (clarity), and adaptive regulation of negative feelings (repair). The TMMS has generally sound psychometric properties, and it is more distinct from personality than EI questionnaires. The highest correlations with the Big Five reported by Warwick and Nettlebeck (2004) were 0.41, between repair and both extraversion and agreeableness, and -0.47 between clarity and neuroticism.

Salovey et al. (1995, 2002) suggest that individuals low in attention, clarity, and repair may be prone to "rumination" (i.e., the harmful process of brooding unproductively on problems and unpleasant feelings). Research has generally confirmed that mood regulation is related to well-being, as Salovey et al. (2002) suggest. The clarity subscale, in particular, has been found to be related to vulnerability to depression (Rude and McCarthy 2003) and to life satisfaction, even with neuroticism controlled (Extremera and Fernandez-Berrocal 2005; Palmer et al. 2002). Indeed the TMMS even relates to objective stress indexes. For instance, Salovey et al. (2002) show that attention and clarity relate to cortisol release during a stressful situation. Gohm and Clore (2002a) also find that clarity relates to well-being. They propose that clear thinking about one's emotions helps the person to plan effective coping actions, and facilitates positive reappraisal. By contrast, Warwick and Nettlebeck (2004) found that a correlation between the TMSS and task orientation (better prioritization of task-oriented behaviors) was mediated by personality. As in the case of EI, mood-regulation is partially, but not entirely, overlapping with standard personality traits.

Questionnaires for EI: The State of the Art

In this section we aim to synthesize what has been learned from a decade or so of research on questionnaire assessments of EI. We will keep coming back to the key issue of whether such questionnaires tell us any more about the person than we could learn from standard personality measures. First, we will address the psychometric issues; the extent to which research isolates dimensions of EI that are clearly distinct from personality. Second, we will examine whether EI scales are useful as predictors of meaningful personal qualities and life outcomes. To use Costa and McCrae's (1992b) phrase, do the scales have "added value" in telling us more about the person than is suggested by the superficial content of the questions? Third, we will examine the psychological meaning of the qualities assessed by the scales. Can we really say that a high scorer on the EQ-i or TEIQue is "emotionally intelligent," or can we find a better description of the underlying personal attribute being measured?

Psychometric Issues

In test development there are some comparatively easy issues to take care of, and some that are harder. In general, the EI scale developers have addressed the "easy stuff" fairly well, although the business-oriented ECI falls short of normal standards. The leading research questionnaires are made up of scales that are reliable, in the sense of being internally consistent and providing accurate measurement (of whatever it is they actually measure). Indeed most of the questionnaires have a substantial general factor, in that items tend to be positively correlated, so that overall "EI" may be reliably assessed. Test-retest correlations over extended periods of weeks or months also seem to be acceptably high, when determined (e.g., Tett et al. 2005). The questionnaires also typically have good "face validity" in that their items are recognizable as instances of the personal qualities linked to emotional intelligence by authors such as Salovey and Mayer (1990).

However, difficult questions remain. One issue is the structure of multiple facets or components of EI, the question addressed by factor analysis. How many separate (but correlated) aspects of EI should be measured?

The pioneers of the field committed some elementary errors, such as forcing correlated factors to be independent through inappropriate use of available statistical procedures. The factor structures of instruments such as the EQ-i and SSRI seem to be unstable across studies, suggesting that they do not distinguish different facets of emotional intelligence very effectively. Recent development efforts (Petrides and Furnham 2003; Tett et al. 2005) have approached the issue more systematically. However, in the absence of independent confirmation of the factor structures proposed by these and other authors, it remains to be seen what the key dimensions may be.

Test development has also been dogged by persistent criticisms that the scales fail to differentiate emotional intelligence from standard personality traits, including (but not limited to) the Big Five (Day 2004; Matthews, Zeidner, et al. 2002). The EQ-i, which correlates at up to 0.80 with existing measures of personality and psychopathology, is the worst offender in this regard, but the problem is common to all the tests we have reviewed. We agree with Petrides and Furnham (2003) that it is probably wise to define "trait EI" as a part of the personality domain, rather than as a true ability, referring most directly to the person's perceptions of their emotional and social functioning, perceptions that are unlikely to be entirely accurate. As our initial account of personality and emotion implies, individual differences in such self-perceptions often relate strongly to established personality traits, especially extraversion (related to positive affect) and neuroticism (related to negative affect). Much of the variance in many of the "emotional intelligence" dimensions measured by extant questionnaires simply reflects general personality.

Table 4.6 represents some of the stronger correspondences between the Big Five and components of trait EI established by the research we have covered. Many of these associations in fact were, with remarkable prescience, pointed out by McCrae (2000), in making a theoretical argument that many of the elements of trait EI were already part of the five factor model. De Raad (2005) also has shown that many of the qualities focal to EI can readily be categorized as belonging to one or other of the Big Five.

At the same time, especially in the case of newer tests (e.g., Tett et al. 2005) and specialized tests (e.g., Salovey et al. 1995), there is substantial variance in scores that is not fully explained by the five factor model of personality. It appears that traits related to mood regulation are among those most weakly correlated with the Big Five. For example, no Big Five factor has a correlation that is greater than 0.40 with mood-

Table 4.6
Correspondences between the five factor model and facets of trait emotional intelligence

Factor type	EI traits
Low N	Low negative affect
	Low neurotic psychopathology
	Well-being
	Stress resistance
	Adaptive self-regulation of emotions
E	Positive affect
	Well-being
	Optimism
	Social skills
	Adaptive regulation of others' emotions
C	Task motivation
	Perseverance
	Self-control
A	Empathy
	Interpersonal relationships
	Altruism
O	Creative thinking
	Aesthetic appreciation of emotion

Sources: Brackett and Mayer (2003), Petrides and Furnham, 2001, Saklofske et al. (2003), Tett et al. (2005).

redirected attention (Tett et al. 2005) and emotion appraisal and emotion utilization factors derived from the SSRI (Saklofske et al. 2003).

MacCann, Matthews, et al. (2004) propose that much of what is novel about EI may relate to *emotional self-concept*, namely positive beliefs about personal competence in internal regulation of emotions. One facet of the self-concept is simply self-regard. Some people believe—rightly or wrongly—that they are especially good at understanding and managing their emotions, whereas others lack confidence in their emotional competence. Emotional self-regard emerges most clearly in Petrides and Furnham's "trait EI" factor that combined assertiveness, emotional self-awareness, and other scales. Tett et al.'s self-orientation factor may be similar. A second potentially distinctive aspect of trait EI is *social self-concept*, referring to beliefs that one is good at communicating and regulating emotions during social interaction, as represented by Tett et al.'s (2005) other-orientation and emotion sharing factors. *Mood-regulation processes* may constitute a third, somewhat distinctive factor, as described in the previous paragraph. The TMMS scales refer to *processes* that regulate and change mood, that contrast with the *beliefs* that are at the core of emotional and social self-concepts.

Even the more distinctive aspects of self-rated EI are not independent of standard personality traits. Correlations approaching 0.40 are sufficient to link these emotional intelligence dimensions to the larger complexes of personal qualities represented by the Big Five. Indeed there is considerable empirical evidence linking neuroticism to negative self-appraisals (related to self-concept), to social anxiety (related to social self-concept), and to aspects of mood regulation such as metacognitive control of emotions and monitoring of moods (Matthews, Schwean, et al. 2000). There remains a pressing need for an overarching structural model that integrates what is new about "trait emotional intelligence" with existing personality models. The skeptical researcher may reasonably conclude that there is little about trait EI that cannot be brought into the five factor model, along the lines of table 4.6. At best then, recent research may have uncovered some primary traits that have been neglected in existing versions of the FFM.

Validity Evidence for Questionnaires
Superficially test developers have been successful in demonstrating that questionnaires predict outcome criteria related to social-emotional competence. In fact these criteria have been quite diverse. They include measures taken in the laboratory such as stress responses (Salovey et al. 2002), criteria for various forms of deviance and mental and physical health (e.g., Austin et al. 2005; Brackett and Mayer 2003; Schutte et al. 2001), and real-life educational and occupational attainment (e.g., Slaski and Cartwright 2002). Further detail on EI questionnaires as predictors of criteria for social adjustment, well-being, and mental health may be found in chapters 6, 7, and 11, respectively.

The effect sizes for these associations vary. Trait EI appears to be most strongly related to self-reports of well-being, satisfaction, and lack of psychopathology, whereas correlations between trait EI and real-world success criteria tend to be much smaller (Matthews, Zeidner, et al. 2002; Van Rooy and Viswesvaran 2004). Although cross-sectional studies provide concurrent validity evidence, few studies demonstrate that trait EI scales predict future social-emotion functioning. One exception is Parker, Hogan, et al. (2004) who show that a short EQ-i scale given to first-year university students in their first month of classes predicted their academic record at the end of the year (though the authors failed to assess whether personality factors have confounded these results).

One weakness of many validation studies is their complete reliance on self-reports. The majority of studies simply provide respondents with a questionnaire packet including EI and outcome measures to be completed during the same session. There is a place in personality research for correlating questionnaires with other questionnaires, but the limitations of this method are obvious. Only a handful of studies have used truly objective methods, such as Salovey et al.'s (2002) study of the TMMS and cortisol.

Studies investigating EI as a predictor of facial emotion processing provide a useful means for linking the construct to objective behavior. Petrides and Furnham (2003) had their subjects watch faces that "morphed" between different expressions. Higher scorers on the TEIQue were quicker to identify the morphed emotion. A weakness of this study is that it failed to differentiate perceptual sensitivity from readiness to respond; high scorers on the TEIQue may simply have been more "trigger-happy" in responding. A recent series of studies (Fellner et al. 2006, 2007) investigated the TEIQue, TMMS, and other questionnaires as predictors of various facial-processing tasks: learning to identify terrorists on the basis of an emotional cue, searching faces for a designated "target" emotion, and recognizing brief "micro-expressions" of emotion. The EI questionnaires were entirely nonpredictive of speed and accuracy measures on these tasks. By contrast, other measures including conventional intelligence, openness, mood, and coping predicted objective performance (depending somewhat on the particular task). Austin (2005a) tested seven subscales from the SSRI and EQ-i as predictors of a composite measure of performance on tasks requiring accurate identification of emotion. An "interpersonal" subscale derived from the SSRI correlated very weakly ($r = 0.21$) with emotion task performance; indeed finding one out of seven EI to performance correlations appears unimpressive. Generally, questionnaire scales of emotional intelligence are not robust predictors of objective performance measures.

A glaring weakness of most validation studies is their neglect of the overlap between personality and trait emotional intelligence (Day 2004; Matthews, Zeidner, et al. 2002). Many studies simply do not assess personality at all. Where researchers have attempted to control statistically for the trait EI by personality overlap, results have been rather mixed. Thus some EI scales add, modestly, to the predictive power of the five factor model in explaining variation in outcomes such as self-reported life satisfaction (e.g., Saklofske et al. 2003; Tett et al. 2005). Other studies (e.g., Barchard 2003; Brackett and Mayer 2003), however, provide little or no evidence for discriminant validity. It is encouraging that at least some studies provide evidence that EI adds to the predictive power of personality trait measures.

The status of trait EI must be tempered even further by three additional considerations. First, the additional variance explained by trait EI is often small. We can do a little better in prediction by using trait EI measures as well as the FFM, but not dramatically better. Second, if the novelty provided by trait EI scales resides in new primary personality traits, it is not surprising that we gain some predictive power. Multiple primary traits used together are often more predictive than second-level traits such as the Big Five (e.g., Costa and McCrae 1992a; Matthews 1997). The modest increments in prediction seen in trait EI studies are exactly what would be expected on this basis. Third, concerns remain about criterion contamination, and especially the tendency of many test developers to include items that relate directly to well-being outcome criteria such as positive mood and optimistic attitudes (e.g., Bar-On 1997). The second wave of test development has been more alert to this danger than the pioneers of the field were, but the problem stills tends to be brushed under the carpet. In sum, trait EI measures are modestly useful in improving the ability of the researcher to predict outcomes related to social-emotional functioning; with the word "modestly" key in this evaluation.

Building More Compelling Construct Validity Evidence

Granted that scales for emotional intelligence have meaningful test-criterion relations, the next issue is the development of a theory of the underlying, latent construct. What does it mean psychologically to be more or less emotionally intelligent? Such a question needs two answers. First, we must specify how high and low EI persons differ in the neurological or psychological processes that control emotional functioning. Personality studies suggest multiple processes may be involved, including the functioning of brain emotion systems, differing cognitive representations of events, and different styles of social interaction (Matthews, Derryberry, et al. 2000). Second, we must show that processing differences are adaptive, namely that the way individuals high in emotional intelligence process information leads to personal gains. For example, processes of accurate emotion perception might lead to benefits in social settings such as guessing the intentions of a competitor during a business negotiation, or recognizing the true feelings of an intimate partner. Such lines of reasoning are plausible but require research support. For example, Ciarrochi et al. (2002) showed that superior emotion perception was correlated with stronger negative emotional responses to daily hassles; there may be a downside to emotional awareness. We will return to the "dark side" of high EI in chapter 6.

Unfortunately, there has been rather little research devoted to these questions. For example, we may know that EI correlates with well-being, but not *why* the association is found (i.e., the mediating processes). Indeed, through their overlap with standard personality traits, questionnaires for EI are already picking up individual differences that are complex and multilayered. Existing research provides some clues: next, we survey three distinct types of construct that may (or may not) provide the foundation for what is unique about self-report EI. These positive qualities may also be balanced by a maladaptive, "dark side" to EI, as we will discuss in later chapters.

Abilities and Aptitudes

The pioneers of the self-report approach to EI (e.g., Bar-On 2000) assumed, seemingly uncritically, that questionnaires could directly assess aptitudes for handling emotional stimuli and situations. There may be circumstances in which self-reports of aptitude are of value (O'Sullivan 2007), but typically empirical studies have failed to validate self-reports of social-emotional abilities. Self-reports of empathy are unrelated to objective measures of person perception (Davis and Kraus 1997). Similarly, although reliable individual differences in emotion perception exist (Davies et al. 1998), self-report and objective emotion perception measures appear to be uncorrelated (Ciarrochi, Deane, et al. 2002). Like personality traits, scales for emotional intelligence may sometimes predict objective behavior, but there is little evidence to suggest that self-report EI picks up any general aptitude or competency.

Acquired Social and Mood-Regulative Skills

Emotional competence may depend on specific learned skills: both explicit (conscious) and implicit (unconscious). Skills might include social skills such as assertiveness and impulse control, as well as mood-regulation skills, such as deliberate positive thinking (Thayer 1996). Both types of skill may be assessed by emotional intelligence questionnaires. For example, a social skills dimension has been identified in the SSRI (Saklofske et al. 2003), and the TMMS plausibly focuses on mood-regulation skills. Again, we may expect that these self-ratings are subject to the same problems identified by Dunning et al. (2004). People with limited social skills may not be able to decode the feedback from others that would indicate that they are being tiresome or foolish. There is some evidence that people do better in reporting specific skills and knowledge than in giving broad self-appraisals (Ackerman et al. 2002).

Social anxiety is a case in point. It relates both to objective deficits in decoding of nonverbal cues, fluent communication, and self-presentation (Bruch 2002; Strahan 2003). However, it also includes underestimation of actual competence (Zeidner and Matthews 2005). Thus self-reports indicate an objective lack of social skill, but they are also distorted and exaggerated due to unrealistic negative influences. Use of self-reports to measure social-emotional skills appears to be fraught with difficulties, although EI scales may indeed relate in part to actual skill, and validity might be improved by careful questionnaire design.

Self-Concept

The construct of EI may also be grounded in core self-beliefs. The self is typically seen as an integrated psychological system that can be broken down into multiple components (Caprara and Cervone 2000). Generalized self-esteem is captured fairly well by standard personality traits, especially neuroticism (Judge et al. 2002). However, there may be some more specialized elements of self-knowledge that are closer to "emotional intelligence." These include beliefs about one's competence in handling the emotions of self and others, and relationship schemas (Baldwin and Ferguson 2001) that shape management of social encounters (see also chapter 6). Research is needed to explore in depth how persons high and low in EI differ in their self-representations. In fact self-knowledge is not fully conscious so that experimental techniques revealing "implicit" self-knowledge appear requisite (see chapter 6). Indeed there may be a whole new world of "unconscious emotional intelligence," supported by more constructive implicit social-emotional processes, waiting to be discovered.

Concluding Comments

The continuing saga of questionnaire assessment of emotional intelligence has at least two subplots. The first is a salutary tale of the difficulties of measuring abilities using self-report. Studies of self-assessments of abilities and competencies show that people are typically not very good at rating themselves. It is no surprise that self-ratings of EI are highly questionable. What self-reports often capture is familiar personality traits, including extraversion, agreeableness, conscientiousness, and emotional stability (low neuroticism). The most oft-used questionnaires assessing emotional intelligence—the EQ-i, SSRI, and TEIQue—predict a variety of criteria related to well-being, but they do so in large part because they tap personality traits that are known to relate to social-emotional functioning.

A second subplot is that work on EI may usefully expand our knowledge of personality, as recognized by the distinction of "trait EI" from true ability. There may well be traits for emotional self-regard, perceived social competence and mood regulation that are not fully captured by the Big Five. Studies showing (generally modest) incremental validity for EI scales support the view that they measure somewhat novel aspects of personality. We reiterate, though, that within multi-level models of personality, these additional traits may be seen as falling under the umbrella of one or more FFM traits.

The accomplishments of research on trait EI are limited by three areas of neglect. First, there is no overarching psychometric model that would provide a comprehensive structural description of the relationship between emotional intelligence traits and established personality dimensions. It is unclear what the key dimensions of trait EI should be, and how they are aligned with the Big Five. Second, few studies have related emotional intelligence to objective indicators of emotional functioning (as opposed to other questionnaire measures); those that have done so have not always provided evidence for validity. Third, scores on trait measures fail to demonstrate construct validity for various uses; researchers have mostly failed to probe the underlying neurological and psychological processes that control EI in action. Self-report scales provide only a distorted picture of emotional aptitudes, abilities, and/or skills, at best. They may, however, relate rather more directly to the person's self-concept, or rather that part of self-concept that is explicit and available to conscious awareness.

Summary Points: Chapter 4

• The five factor model represents a near consensual taxonomic model used contemporaneously by scientists attempting to understand personality processes. Its major components are extraversion, neuroticism, conscientiousness, agreeableness, and openness. The factors underlying the model have been shown consistently to be heritable, cross-culturally invariant, and to have predictive utility.

• Self-report or questionnaire approaches to emotional intelligence are many and varied, and include those that may be referred to as first-generation (i.e., EQ-i, SSRI, and ECI) and second-generation (e.g., TEI-Que, SEI) assessments.

• Validity evidence for the vast majority of first-generation assessments is mixed. Few if any of these measures have theoretically defensible factor structures, while test-criterion relations appear compromised by their overlap with the Big Five personality constructs, or criterion contamination.

• While second-generation measures appear more promising, their overlap with the Big Five factors of personality remains a cause for concern. Various attempts to recast these measurement paradigms as a new approach to personality assessment have met with some success. However, issues associated with faked, and possibly flawed, self-insight in self-report assessments render their use in applied settings as limited.

• There is an urgent need to build more compelling construct validity evidence for self-report assessments. Pivotal in this undertaking would appear to be the building of theories showing where these constructs are adaptive (or not) and the extent that they are explicit versus implicit.

III   EMOTIONAL INTELLIGENCE OBSERVED

Developing Emotional Intelligence: From Birth to Earth

From the moment of birth, when the stone-age baby confronts the twentieth-century mother, the baby is subjected to these forces of violence, called love, as its mother and father have been, and their parents and their parents before them. These forces are mainly concerned with destroying most of its potentialities. This enterprise is on the whole successful.
—R. D. Laing

Four-year-old Danny wiggled restlessly in his chair, awaiting the beginning of an "experiment" that his parents had brought him to at the Psychology Department of Stanford University. The experiment began with the following instructions: "There is a marshmallow placed in the middle of the table in front of you. Now, you have two choices: Either have the marshmallow; right now. Or, you can wait for a while until the man in the lab coat returns, and have two marshmallows instead." Once the adult with thick eye glasses left the room, Danny felt the urge to gobble down the marshmallow quite irresistible. In order to avoid making eye contact with the tempting marshmallow, Danny buried his head deep into his lap. Somehow Danny managed, during what seemed like an eternity, to distract himself long enough to earn two marshmallows. However, not all of the four-year olds partaking in this classic experiment, conducted by Walter Mischel in the late 1950s, were as successful as Danny in overcoming their desires. In fact about a third of the children yielded into temptation and consumed the marshmallow on the spot, then and there.

The child's ability to control impulsive behaviors and delay immediate gratification—variously referred to as "self-motivation" or "managing self" (Aronson 2000)—is regarded as a key component of emotional intelligence (EI). Moreover this competency appears to have more than the immediate short-term consequences of earning an extra marshmallow. A follow-up study, conducted over ten years after the experiment, showed that adolescents who had displayed greater self-control at age 4 appeared more verbally fluent, rational, able to concentrate, and more self-assured (Shoda et al. 1990). By contrast, adolescents who ate the marshmallow at age 4 were assessed as more likely to feel bad (especially about themselves) and to be short-tempered, resentful, and immobilized by stress.

But it does not stop there. When followed-up and assessed during their high school years, those who delayed gratification at age 4 showed greater academic motivation and eagerness to learn in high school. They were also better able to reason, organize, and express their ideas, and also had higher SAT scores compared to their more impulsive counterparts (Shoda et al. 1990). Consistent with the importance placed on this quality, a recent study by Duckworth and Seligman (2005) showed that a measure of self-discipline (based on self, parent, and teacher ratings) predicted final school grades. These researchers also found that self-discipline outdoes standardized measures of intelligence in predicting academic performance among eighth grade students. This study suggests that failure to exercise self-discipline may be one reason for students falling short of their academic potential.

Impulse control is one aspect of a broader process of self-regulation that is critical for emotional well-being and effective social interaction. Self-regulation broadly refers to the management of personal goals (i.e., setting goals, choosing strategies for attaining those goals, and coping with barriers to progress, including one's own emotional reactions). From an early age children face numerous self-regulative challenges:

How to handle potentially disruptive emotions Trisha has an important test at school. She feels anxious, even though she has studied hard. How does she overcome her anxiety in order to focus on the test?

How to best communicate feelings and needs Latetia wants a cookie but her mother will not always give her one. What display of emotion is most likely to succeed?

How to handle feelings of anger and aggression toward others Gautam's sister has broken his favorite toy. How should he express his anger about this happening?

How to help others in distress Kayla's best friend has skinned her knee in the playground. How can she comfort her, without getting too upset in the process?

Emotional intelligence is currently believed to play a major role in the development of interpersonal competencies and social skills, including the delay of immediate gratification and effective emotional communication. Accordingly early emotional competencies are viewed as being central to mental health. Indeed, if the life tasks of developing emotional competencies are not negotiated successfully, children are at risk for psychopathology, both concurrently and later on in life (Rubin and Clark 1983). Consequently understanding the origins of these competencies would appear of major importance in understanding normal emotional behavior, as well as developmental problems (Eisenberg, Cumberland, et al. 1998).

In this chapter we review what is known about the development of emotional competence. In particular, we examine how children learn to respond emotionally to environmental events. Also of interest is how they apply this knowledge to relationships with others so that they can strategically negotiate interpersonal exchanges and regulate emotional experiences. Our presentation of the material is based on an investment model for the development of emotional competencies that we have proposed (Zeidner et al. 2003). According to this model, emotional development depends on diverse processes. Components include biologically programmed modulation; use of behavioral strategies for self-control; and use of planned self-regulation, namely with conscious awareness. We begin with a general overview of the investment model and proceed then to discuss the developmental implications of each stage.

This chapter also marks a turning point in our exposition of emotional intelligence. Up until the present point, we have focused on EI as a quality of the individual and on a particular concern with measurement. In this chapter, and the chapters that follow, we turn to the *processes* that support emotional intelligence. We will also be concerned with the expression of EI in real-life behavior. A key theme of this chapter is that emotional intelligence is not simply hardwired into the brain. Part of its acquisition stems also from the process of interaction with parents or guardians, other family members, teachers, and friends. Acquiring the skills required for effective social-emotional functioning is thus dependent on both neural (as the growing brain develops) and psychological processes (as the mind assembles ever more sophisticated internal programs for encoding and responding to emotive experiences).

The Investment Model of Emotional Intelligence

The investment model conceptualizes the development of EI as depending on three qualitatively different (but interacting) processes. The child's level of emotional processing becomes progressively more sophisticated with age, as the control of adaptation shifts from biologically based temperament to self-directed emotion regulation dependent on social learning. The three levels of control of behavior are as follows:

1. *Biology and temperament*   The first layer in the model consists of biologically based temperamental qualities (emotionality, sociability, etc.). This biological substrate is believed to provide the platform and infrastructure for subsequent learning and attendant emotional development.

2. *Rule-based learning of emotional competencies*   The second layer of the model revolves around the learning of crucial emotional skills acquired via behavioral socialization strategies (e.g., modeling of emotional behavior). At this level, in dynamic interaction with temperament, the child learns specific competencies through attachment relationships with significant others (family members, peers, teachers, etc.). Thus, through direct experiences with a variety of structured and unstructured situations in the environment, the child learns "if-then" rules for recognizing emotions in self and others, as well as displaying and expressing emotions.

3. *Strategic emotion regulation development*   The third layer of the model focuses on the formation of self-aware, strategic regulation of emotional behaviors. This process is achieved via coaching or tuition on the part of socialization agents in the child's environment (mainly parents and guardians). Also important is exposure to a host of proximal socialization agents (peers, teachers, etc.). Both temperament, in concert with cognitive and verbal development, and rule-based competencies would then modulate the learning of strategic and insight-based regulatory behaviors.

Figure 5.1 provides a schematic representation of the investment model, which will also serve as a heuristic for organizing the discussion that follows. We begin by covering the role of biological factors in the development of EI. This account is followed by an exposition of the role of socialization practices in helping the child acquire rule-based skills. We then move on to describe the child's learning of self-regulatory competencies.

Parenthetically, "EI" and "emotional competencies" are used interchangeably in this chapter, allowing us to draw freely on the rich body of literature dealing with various emotional competencies. Clearly, some researchers (and we count ourselves among these) prefer to distinguish between these two constructs and not use them interchangeably. Our decision to adopt such an approach in the current chapter, however, frees us to use the literature for more extensive critical analysis.

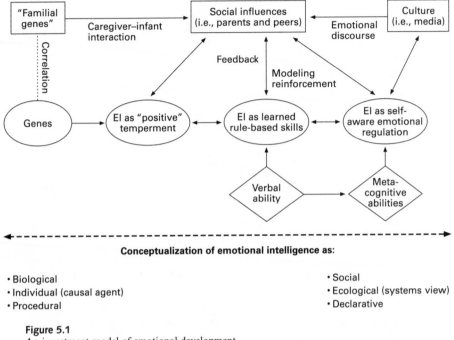

Conceptualization of emotional intelligence as:

- Biological
- Individual (causal agent)
- Procedural

- Social
- Ecological (systems view)
- Declarative

Figure 5.1
An investment model of emotional development

Temperament and the Biology of Emotional Intelligence

Few developmental psychologists would question the notion that a person's biology interacts with personal experience in a complex and enigmatic way to produce emotionally intelligent behaviors (Kagan 1994). Rather than quibble about the relative importance of nature versus nurture, scientists now focus on how nature impacts behavior *via* nurture. While biology predisposes us to emotional behaviors, the form of these behaviors, the situations that elicit them, and the ways that they are expressed remain largely dependent on disparate social and environmental factors. The investment model posits that emotional competencies are determined largely by the way environmental forces impinge on the developing child's biological constitution.

Very young infants have a remarkable ability to perceive emotion signals, discriminate among them, and respond in meaningful ways. These capabilities suggest that emotional competence and adaptability is hardwired and enjoys some independence from experiential factors in cognitive development (Izard 2001). Furthermore some newborns may be

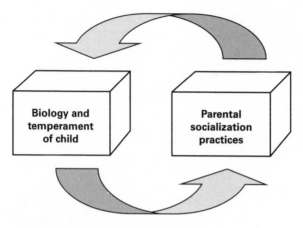

Figure 5.2
The reciprocal relationship between biology and socialization

biologically predisposed to have a low threshold for arousal when confronted with stimulation and novelty (Buss and Plomin 1984). In the first year of life, when faced with uncertainties, these babies may evince particular physical (e.g., elevated heart rate) and physiological changes (e.g., high endorphin levels) that make them very difficult to soothe. Parents, especially "first-timers" (as those who have been in this situation known only too well), often find these overly emotional infant responses to stressful circumstances personally aversive.

As depicted in figure 5.2, human biology and human behavior show reciprocal determinism. That is, there is most likely a bi-directional pattern of effects between parents/guardians and children's emotional behavior (see Denham 1998). Both children's and parents/guardians' temperamental traits influence the emotions they show in dyadic interaction. Accordingly, in the caregiver–child interaction, each dyad member's emotions influence the other's emotional responses during interaction. In turn, these feed into psychosocial functioning or social emotional competence for both parent/guardian and child.

Recent research suggests that certain temperamental qualities may impinge on the growth and development of major facets of emotional intelligence (Halberstadt et al. 2001). Two temperamental qualities, in particular, appear important determinants of emotional self-regulation. The first quality, *emotional intensity* (i.e., latency, threshold, and rise time of emotions), may make the child more (or less) reactive to the effects of stress. The second quality, *attentional processes* (which include, voluntary initiation or inhibition of action), may facilitate the child's efforts to cope with stress.

Temperament affects not only attentional processes and the intensity of emotional experience but also strategies for regulation of emotion. The distress-prone temperament (negative affectivity) may, in fearful settings, promote a style of regulation described variously as clingy, whiny, resistant, or angry (Kochanska and Coy 2002). Research has shown that fearfulness and effortful control were predictors of compliance with mothers' requests in young children ranging in age from 14 to 45 months (Kochanska et al. 2001). Compliance is seen as a prototypical form of self-regulation because the child must change its behavior in accord with parental (and even societal) standards.

Temperament, along with family environment, can impede or facilitate the development of EI through a number of processes (e.g., Izard et al. 2007). For example, children who are predisposed to experience negative emotions may be at risk for emotional dysfunction. The same may hold true for those individuals who live in harsh environments that frequently elicit strong negative emotions. Specific problems include difficulty in regulating emotion arousal and in forming connections between these intense feelings and the appropriate language for articulating them. Also frequent anger experiences might contribute to externalizing aggressive behavior that is likely to elicit strong negative reactions from parents/guardians, siblings, and peers. The negative social feedback in these encounters may amplify the child's already intense anger and further impede the opportunity to acquire emotional competence (Lochman and Lenhart 1993).

Recent evidence also suggests that temperament and social environment contribute to the development of emotional labeling (Izard 2001). The decoding component of emotion labeling and infants' expressive responses to the detection of emotion signals, in particular, has innate determinants (mainly being a function of the emotion perception and expression systems). In infants these systems are highly pre-adapted to facilitate infant–other communication (Magai and McFadden 1995). Of note, studies have shown children's emotional labeling predicts positive behavioral outcomes (especially peer status and academic performance) after controlling for general intelligence (see Denham 1998). Indeed preschool emotion labeling predicts these outcomes four years later, when these children were later assessed in third grade (Izard, Fine, et al. 2001). High scores on emotion perception, in particular, predict positive social behavior, while low scores predict behavioral problems.

Because EI has been conceptualized as partly biologically determined, it has been construed as remaining relatively stable across different developmental phases. Accordingly those low in EI may find it difficult to learn emotional skills at a later stage of development (Taylor et al. 1999). Moreover most view childhood as a critical period for shaping lifelong emotional competencies. The major skills thought to comprise EI may each have crucial periods for their development, extending over years of childhood. Each period represents a window for helping the child acquire adaptive emotional skills as part of the life tasks of that period. If skill acquisition is missed, it makes it that much harder to offer corrective lessons later in life.

Not only may biology affect emotional behaviors; emotion-related behaviors may also affect biology. Thus there is accumulating evidence that emotional interactions between infants and caretakers influence the maturation of the brain involved in emotional awareness and regulation. This interaction can lead to permanent alterations in the morphological development of the orbitofrontal cortex, which, in turn, may shape the capacity of the neocortex to modulate activity in the amygdala and other subcortical structures (Taylor et al. 1999). If the child's interaction with the caretaker is insufficient, or otherwise grossly abnormal, the neural substrate for emotion regulation may be impaired (Schore 2001). In addition developmental delays in language acquisition may impede acquisition of skills for labeling, understanding, and communicating emotion.

Collectively, these findings suggest that the interplay between biological and environmental influences is extraordinarily complex. As a caregiver, teacher, or policy maker reading this book, the implications are perhaps more straightforward than the scientific findings imply. There is clearly value added to providing enriched environmental conditions such that a biological predisposition toward high EI is fostered early in life. Moreover, even if the emotional competence of a child appears low during the early years, there appears scope for influencing biological factors that come into greater prominence as the child matures.

Learning the Rules: Familial Socialization

Family socialization has been theorized to directly impact on the child's social and emotional competency. It also appears to work indirectly on social-emotional competence through the child's understanding of emotions and acquisition of social knowledge. The causal chain follows roughly as follows (see Garner et al. 1994):

Caregiver socialization procedures → Development of child's social knowledge, attitudes, and skills → Crystallization of child's social competence.

Caregiver influences may also act indirectly on the child (e.g., through the observation and modeling of other's emotional responses and competencies; Lewis and Saarni 1985). However, any linear model, devoid of reciprocal effects and feedback loops, may be construed as rather simplistic.

Izard (2001) suggests that EI may reside, in part, upon acquired adaptive skills influenced by temperament but separable from biological substrate. Thus it is highly plausible that EI reflects not only general temperamental qualities but a set of specific aptitudes for learning emotion-regulation skills. The ability to symbolize or label emotions involves inferential or interpretive processes that depend on cognitive development. Language may play a key role in the acquisition of feeling, display, and coping rules. Consistent with these suggestions, Izard (2001) has shown that verbal ability correlates substantially with emotion abilities in young children; that is, conventional intelligence may constrain development of emotional competencies. In the sections that follow we review evidence that these basic, typically rule-bound skills are controlled by socialization processes and the family environment.

Child–Adult Attachment

A major prerequisite for building emotional competencies is the quality of caregiver–child attachment, which serves as the basic foundation for the child's construction of a positive working model of both self and personal relationships. That is, experiences with caregivers, over time, provide the child with the raw materials to build an internal working model of the self and surroundings. Questions such as "am I worthy of being loved?" and "is the world a safe place to be?" form the foundation for a sense of security, self-esteem, and emotional competence (or otherwise). Infants who develop an internal model and form a secure base from which to explore the world, generally feel sheltered from danger and can use this haven to move unhampered into the outside world. Without a secure relationship, emotions can be perceived as unimportant or even threatening (Denham et al. 2003).

Current thinking suggests that the quality of early attachment relations between child and caregivers contributes to the development of prosocial behavior. Thus securely attached children develop internal working models of relationships that incorporate the expectancy that an individual's needs will be responded to and met (e.g., Denham et al. 2003). Securely attached children are held to develop the capacity to respond empathetically to others because they themselves have experienced responsive and empathic caregiving.

Emotional Climate of the Family and Caregiver Expressiveness
The family is the primary context in which children first learn about various facets of emotions, such as how emotions are identified and the various ways to manage affect (Denham 1998). The quality of the emotional climate in the home is due, in no small measure, to two major factors: (1) the way caregivers express both positive and negative emotions, and (2) caregiver reactions to the child's emotional expressiveness. Thus the emotional climate in the home affects children's emotional reactivity and the quality and security of relationships with other family members (Eisenberg, Valiente, et al. 2003).

Familial socialization of emotional competencies is carried out, to a large degree, through the caregivers' attitudes toward the child's emotional expressiveness and how they regulate their child's emotions. Parents/guardians vary with respect to the goals of socialization of emotions in their children (Eisenberg et al. 1998). Thus caregivers who feel it is desirable to express emotions in socially acceptable ways are likely to be supportive of their children's expression of both positive and negative emotions. They are also likely to facilitate the learning and expression of emotions in their child. Other caregivers, by contrast, may believe that negative emotions are detrimental and should therefore be ignored, controlled, or repressed. These parents/guardians are likely to try to teach their children to minimize, ignore, or deny the experience and expression of negative emotion (Saarni 1999). Consequently these children may be less aware of negative emotions in themselves and in others.

Research has shown that parents and guardians, who are high in warmth and positive emotion and low in the expression of disapproval, hostility, and other negative emotions directed toward their children, tend to have socially competent, adjusted children who are also skilled in social understanding (Eisenberg, Valiente, et al. 2003). In addition both parental and family expressiveness (especially positive expressivity) have been associated with children's social competence, emotional understanding, prosocial behavior, and self-esteem. Moreover caregivers who encourage the appropriate expression of emotion in their children are reported to have children who are relatively high in emotion regulation (Gottman et al. 1997).

Why should we expect parents/guardians' emotions directed at the child, or expressed in the family, to be linked to adjustment and social competence? For one, when parents are warm and supportive, children are likely to believe that their parents are concerned with their interests and welfare. Consequently such children are likely to be motivated by feelings of trust and reciprocity (and to comply with, and internalize, supportive parent's standards for appropriate behavior, including demands for self-regulation). Moreover parents who express positive emotions model positive ways of responding to others and to events.

However, the picture is more complex for family expressiveness of negative emotions, where reviews have suggested possible curvilinear relationships according to age and intensity (e.g., Halberstadt and Eaton 2003). The effects may vary with the quantities and intensities of parental negative emotionality directed toward the child (e.g., anger). Thus especially high (or low) quantities of negative affect appear related to deleterious developmental outcomes. Moderate degrees of negative affectivity may be adaptive, especially if expressed appropriately. Caregivers' negative expressivity is likely to produce over-arousal in their children, which weakens regulation and learning in many contexts. For example, Eisenberg et al. (1999) found that parent's reports of punitive reactions to children's negative emotions were negatively related to children's regulation, with regulation and punitive reactions predicting one another over time.

Socialization and Child-Rearing Practices

Data indicate that parental control bears a nonlinear pattern of relations with emotional competence. Thus in preschoolers moderate degrees of control have been associated with optimal levels of emotional competence, whereas both low and high degrees of control have been associated with lower emotional competence (Zahn-Waxler et al. 1979). Parental warmth has also been shown to be positively associated with emotional competence, presumably because secure attachment in infancy is a precursor of later competence in social problem-solving situations. It also appears that parents who are responsive and warm have more socially adjusted children, who are better accepted by their peers (O'Neil and Parke 2000).

When parents are skilled in expressing and coping with aversive emotions, children gain emotional skills that buffer them from the negative effects of stressful events (Gottman 1997). For example, parents' awareness of sadness and tendencies to coach their children about anger were found to have an impact on children's emotional regulation. Specifically, children at age five whose parents possess these meta-emotional dispositions showed less physiological distress, greater ability to focus attention, and less negative playing styles. Moreover, at age eight, these variables were found to predict children's academic achievement.

O'Neil and Parke's (2000) review, based largely on the Social Development Project by the University of California at Riverside, suggests that the strategies parents employ to manage children's negative emotions are associated with children's social and emotional competence. For example, children whose mothers encouraged the expression of negative affect when upset indicated that they would be less likely to use social withdrawal as a coping strategy. By contrast, children whose mothers made more attempts to regulate their emotional expressiveness had less positive affect and more negative affect during a parent–child discussion task. While the mother has a pivotal role, the father's regulation of emotions appears more modestly related to the child's social competence. Children whose fathers reported being more distressed by expressions of negative affect were more likely to report using anger and other negative emotions to cope with distressing events. By contrast, children whose fathers reported using strategies to minimize distressing circumstances were more likely to use reasoning to cope with a distressing situation.

Positive Affect   Positive affect would appear to be important in the initiation of social exchanges and sharing positive affect. Children who are rated happy tend to be liked by teachers, respond more prosocially to peer's emotions, and are seen as more likable by their peers (e.g., Denham 2006). Feeling good in many situations not only greases the cogs of ongoing social interaction but makes it easier for a child to enter the world of their peers in the first place. The enduring patterns of emotional well-being signaled by a happy child are likely to make a positive impression on a preschool teacher. And happier playmates are also easier to like. Although positive emotions are conducive to social competence, there are occasions when this may be inappropriate. For example, Arsenio and Lover (1997) found that happiness shown during preschool conflict is likely not to be well received by a child's peers.

Negative Affect   Sadness, when inappropriately exhibited, is related to teacher ratings of withdrawal and internalizing difficulties. Chronic levels of anger have also been reported as detrimental to the development of social competence. Thus chronically angry children are less likely to meet another's positive overtures in kind and more likely to respond with hostility. In turn, these children's demeanor makes them more difficult, both by omission and commission, to play with.

Socialization of Emotions through Behavioral Techniques

Observation and Modeling Proponents of EI claim that children learn from role models how to process and regulate emotional information and experiences (e.g., Salovey et al. 2000). The emotional competencies that emerge from this learning process presumably influence how children interact with their peers, which, in turn, determines how successful they will be at developing a supportive group of friends. In principle, individuals high in EI have learned from exemplary role models how to process and regulate emotions in order to maintain viable relations with others.

Indeed behavioral research attests to the important role that direct observation and modeling may play in the learning of social and affective responses (Bandura 1965). The basic assumption here is that a child whose caregiver displays constructive EI-related behavior in everyday life (e.g., empathy) is likely to imitate it as part of his or her own behavior. Through observation of parental and other role models, demonstrating specific emotional behaviors (e.g., calmness under pressure), children have been shown to learn and acquire new emotional responses to specific contexts that did not previously exist in their behavioral repertoire (Lewis and Saarni 1985). Saarni (1999) reports that infants as young as 10 to 12 months use their parents' emotional-expressive behavior as a model for their own, for example, when faced with a stranger, or in emotionally ambiguous situations.

Modeling of emotions is essentially teaching by personal example, whether functional (e.g., coping constructively) or dysfunctional (e.g., abusive behaviors) (Epstein 1998). The child is likely to take on the emotional behaviors of parents/guardians, teachers, older siblings, or peers. Parents convey at least as much to their children in this way as they do by direct or indirect rewards and punishment. Caregivers who say "do as I say, not as I do" are fighting a losing battle. Thus parents or guardians who want their children to be emotionally intelligent would do well by providing a model of emotional competency through their own behavior (Epstein 1998).

The different emotional models that children are exposed to partly account for individual differences in emotions. For example, some caregivers model open and free *expression* of negative emotion, whereas others model *suppression* of negative emotions (Hooven et al. 1995). These behaviors are presumably based on parental attitudes and beliefs about the desirability and appropriateness of expressing emotions openly before children. Some parents and guardians also model techniques that are helpful in regulating emotions (e.g., seeking social support), whereas others model dysfunctional modes of emotional expression (e.g., abusive behavior). Indeed infants as young as 10 to 12 months, when faced with a stranger, look to their parent's emotional-expressive behavior as a guide to their emotional reaction, particularly in *emotionally ambiguous* situations (Saarni 1999).

Parents' expressed emotions may model for children what emotions are acceptable in specific social settings, and how to express them (e.g., Halberstadt et al. 2001). For example, parents may express intense, aggressive emotions at a sporting event, moderate the intensity of expression at social functions, and suppress emotional expression in places of worship. Children who typically observe parents suppress emotional displays, in conjunction with verbal displays (e.g., "I need to keep calm"), are likely to internalize such strategies as a first resort when managing their own emotional experiences.

Some children may never have the opportunity to learn how to cope with distressing daily events because of the absence of models demonstrating functional emotional regulation in evaluative situations. Instead they learn to cope with situations in a maladaptive fashion through avoidance behaviors and defensiveness, which eventually interferes with the regulation of emotions. For example, children frequently exposed to temper tantrums and outbursts displayed by members of their immediate family are presumably introduced to poor self-regulatory models (Salovey et al. 2000). Further, given that covert learning of negative affective reactions is possible, a child may learn responses that remain dormant until provided with the opportunity to be enacted in a situation, at some later point in time.

Contingent Reinforcement   According to learning theory, children's emotional competencies are expected to be responsive to environmental reinforcements and contingencies in their early environment. Thus, through their reinforcement behaviors (e.g., praising, scolding), the caregiver may intentionally or inadvertently reinforce certain emotional expressions and extinguish others (Campos and Barrett 1984). Parental encouragement and support for children's open expression help children express emotions acceptably and provide them with ways to deal with emotions in their peer group (Denham 1998). Children who experience repeated familial reinforcement of specific emotional reactions (e.g., pride) in response to given situations (e.g., achieving success) may strengthen and maintain these reactions over time. By contrast, children who suffer painful consequences for the expression of certain emotions may suppress these or similar emotions (e.g., anger when demeaned).

A particular constellation of parenting techniques called "rewarding socialization of emotion" has been said to make a direct contribution to children's social competence (Denham 1998). For example, encouragement and support for children's emotions help them to express emotion acceptably. They also provide children with ways to deal with emotions in their peer group. Furthermore, the combination of parental autonomy, encouragement, and support has been shown to be positively predictive of children's self-regulation (Grolnick and Ryan 1989). By contrast, "punitive socialization" of emotion undermines competent social interaction. Thus, parental use of punitive responses or minimizing of children's emotion is associated with greater incidence of negative emotion (Eisenberg et al. 1999). Furthermore emotionally nonresponsive mothers (and those who express mostly negative emotions) have infants and toddlers who cope poorly with stress, evidenced by increased aggression and reduced social interaction (Zahn-Waxler et al. 1984). These effects likely reflect modeling as well as inappropriate reinforcement of emotion in the child. More severely maltreated children also have difficulty in coping with stress, and with recognizing, expressing, and regulating emotion (Brenner and Salovey 1997; Smith and Walden 1999).

It is readily apparent that socialization and child-rearing practices interact with the child's developmental stage (cognitive, affective, and psychomotor) in shaping emotional competencies. Thus the ability to symbolize or label emotions involves inferential or interpretive processes that clearly depend on cognitive development. Furthermore verbal ability is necessarily a determinant of the child's current measures of emotional understanding, and probably of other facets of EI as well. At the very least the child has to have the requisite receptive vocabulary (a component of intelligence) to understand and respond to these tasks. Because emotion perception and emotion labeling abilities are fundamental to emotion communication and normal social relationships, deficits in these core abilities will contribute to deficiencies in other facets of EI and impede the development of social competence (Izard 2001).

Research suggests that effective learning is influenced by the parents' temperament, although it is often difficult to ascertain the exact mechanism for such effects. Thus empathetic parents are reported to have children who are relatively unlikely to experience personal distress when confronted with a sympathy-eliciting situation. In one study Zahn-Waxler et al. (1979) found that the levels of a mothers' empathy predicted both children's reparation for transgressions and their subsequent level of altruism. Some research provides support for the notion that empathetic parents help their children cope effectively with aversive emotions when distressed (Eisenberg, Fabes, et al. 1991). The specific emotional skills of parents are also important. O'Neil and Parke (2000) found that caregivers who could correctly perceive children's emotion, and were accepting of these emotions (even if they were negative), had children with clearer emotion expression. Furthermore, based on recent neurobiological research, empathic behavior on the part of parents may activate the child's "mirror neurons," causing the child to experience empathic feelings in the specific social context.

Strategic Self-regulatory Behavior

I count him braver who overcomes his desires than him who overcomes his enemies.
—Aristotle

Development of strategic self-regulatory behavior, the third layer in the investment model of EI (see figure 5.1), relates to the development of insightful self-regulation of emotions. In the process of developing self-regulatory skills, children learn to initiate and maintain genuine emotional states, both positive and negative. Children also learn to express these emotions in ways that allows them to meet their emotion-regulation goals (e.g., maintaining positive social interactions). Candidates for emotion regulation are emotions that are aversive or distressing; emotions that are positive but possibly overwhelming; and emotions that need to be amplified for various strategic reasons (e.g., joy).

It appears that how one handles one's emotions may be as important to social functioning—if not more—than one's enduring patterns of expressed emotions (Denham et al. 2003). In the course of their development, children need to learn ways for monitoring, evaluating, and modifying emotional reactions to accomplish their personal goals and enhance emotions that are relevant and helpful and attenuate those that are not (Denham 2006). Children need to learn how to manage emotional intensity when it threatens to overwhelm them, enhancing it when necessary to achieve a goal, and shifting between emotion states. Effective emotion regulation can help children maintain genuine and satisfying relations with others and is instrumental in helping them learn the rules that apply in varying settings. For example, showing too much anger at a peer when slighted can hurt the peer's feelings, but showing too little anger or bravado could make one a target.

In contrast to more basic forms of emotion regulation, strategic emotion regulation depends on the person's *explicit* understanding of self-related goals, social relations, and the particular social and cultural context under consideration. With increased cognitive ability and control of both attention and emotionality, self-regulation shows a distinct developmental progression. Thus it moves from more simple bio-behavioral forms of regulation during infancy and preschool years, to increasingly complex regulative behaviors during early school years, to more planned and strategic forms during adolescence (Kopp 1989; Saarni 2000a). The child's capacity to acquire these skills may be limited by metacognition (i.e., the ability to monitor mental states and to control them adaptively).

During the preschool period, emotion regulation becomes necessary because of the increasing complexity of the demands of the child's social world. Thus primary school children become:

1. increasingly aware of the need for regulation of their emotions;

2. discerning of the connections between their emotion regulation strategies and changes in feelings;

3. more flexible in choosing the optimal ways of coping in specific contexts; and

4. more able to make their own independent attempts at regulation.

By the time they are in the early years of elementary school, children have acquired a flexible repertoire of coping strategies to actively cope with arousal and complex emotions (Eisenberg, Valiente, et al. 2003). These range from attempts to circumvent the stressful situation, choosing different goals, and denying the problem.

The challenges and pressures of the school environment often tax the regulatory skills of children and youth. Preschool and primary school children are not especially skilled at handling conflicts, for example. Initiating, maintaining, and negotiating play; earning acceptance; and succeeding in literacy and numeracy each require young children to keep the lid on their emotions. The increasing complexity of young children's emotionality and the demands of the social world require the child to cultivate emotion-regulation strategies.

With the development of more advanced cognitive and social skills in middle adolescence, abilities such as perspective taking, become more fully developed (Eccles 1999). Adolescents develop a more complex understanding of emotions. For example, elementary school children and adolescents begin to understand that social situations can potentially provoke two different (perhaps even opposite) emotions to emerge simultaneously (e.g., both happiness and sadness at a wedding). They also have an increased awareness of emotional scripts and display rules in conjunction with social roles and are also more adapt at making a distinction between genuine and managed displays of emotion (Saarni 1999). Each of these skills is relevant to the child coping with intensely emotional events.

Socialization of Self-regulatory Behaviors   The investment model (see figure 5.1) predicts that parental coaching or discourse on emotions is the most direct aspect of emotion socialization, contributing to the development of strategic emotion regulation. Coaching consists of, in particular:

1. verbally explaining a complex emotion;

2. directing the child's attention to salient emotional cues;

3. pointing out the relationship between an observed event and its emotional consequences;

4. helping the child understand and manage her or his responses; and

5. segmenting social interactions into manageable emotional components.

Coaching children on emotions and parent–child discourse on various facets of emotions can have a major effect on the child's development of self-directed emotion-regulation strategies. For example, when the child is upset or angry, parents can explicitly teach the child a number of coping strategies. These strategies, which provide a valuable source of exogenous management of emotions, include:

1. *redirecting thoughts and refocusing attention*   for example, "You might get suspended if you beat up your classmate";

2. *positive self-talk*   for example, "I know I can cheer myself up"; and

3. *redefining goals or outcome*   for example, "He can sit in that desk; I want to sit on the opposite side next to Dave anyway."

Parents who adopt an "emotion-coaching" philosophy (see the sidebar for more information) view the child's negative emotions as an intimate opportunity for teaching emotion regulatory and problem-solving ability.

Parents as formal instructors of emotional regulation

Parents' role as formal instructors of emotional regulation becomes increasingly geared to instilling the child with an autonomous understanding of emotion and inculcating a more abstract and sophisticated understanding of the nature of emotion and its regulation. A central aspect in coaching the child is providing reasons for the specific emotional events in the child's life. This includes feedback on the child's emotionally inappropriate behaviors: "Jonas, you may feel a bit jealous that your brother received a toy jeep for his birthday, but he has offered to share it with you; this way you can both enjoy playing with the toy together." Such strategies coach children to consider another's point of view: "Shoving Amelia made her really upset; please go over and say your sorry" and to perceive the social consequences of their behaviors: "Lijuan will get really mad at you if you keep calling her names, and she might not want to play with you anymore."

As such, they tend to problem-solve with the child by discussing goals and strategies with them, setting behavioral limits, and dealing with the challenging situation that led to a particular emotion. Furthermore, when parents discuss emotions with their children, they provide children with a reflective distance from their own feeling states and sufficient space to interpret and evaluate feelings. In addition parent–child discourse provides an opportunity to safely reflect on possible causes and consequences of emotions. What parents and others say to the child, intentionally or unintentionally, may impact on their children's knowledge of emotions. Thus verbal coaching helps the child to formulate a coherent body of knowledge about emotional expression, situations, and cause. When parents use socializing discourse (e.g., "It really hurts and upsets your baby brother when you knock him down"), it not only imparts emotional meaning to everyday events but also fuels the way children figure out how to feel in similar situations that they will encounter in the future (Denham 1998).

Empirical Studies   Research provides support for the pivotal role of parental coaching in the development of emotional competencies and adaptive social behaviors. For example, parents who use coaching procedures when their children become emotional have been found to have children who are better able to physiologically "self-sooth" and calm themselves down when upset. These same individuals also show better peer relations (Rothbart and Derryberry 1981). Children who learn to discuss negative emotions with their parents appear better able to feel sympathy for others, engage in positive behaviors, and are liked more by both the peers and adults with whom they interact (Eisenberg et al. 1997).

Of research conducted, much has focused on the role of the mother. An association has been found between maternal responsiveness to infant's emotional cues and self-regulatory behaviors (Gable and Isabella 1992). Moreover mother-reported positive expressivity in the family was related to higher levels of toddler's self-soothing behavior, whereas mother-reported sadness was inversely related (Garner 1995). In older children maternal acceptance and support were linked to successful coping (e.g., Kliewer et al. 1996).

The wider family also plays a pivotal role in this process. For example, college students and adults from negatively expressive families reported less control than their peers over feelings of anger (Burrowes and Halber-stadt 1987). Parents' verbal discourse with the child, direct instruction, and emotional "apprenticeship" are claimed to be important factors contributing to the development of the child's emotional competencies (Thompson 1998). Accordingly adults who are aware of emotions and freely talk abut them in an intelligent and differentiated manner assist their children in learning how to express, experience, and regulate emotions. The socialization technique of open family discourse about feelings and emotions enhances the child's emotional awareness and allows the child (and significant others) to negotiate shared culturally relevant meanings about experience (Denham 1998). Thus children growing up in families in which talking about feelings is frequent appear better at making judgments about the emotions of unfamiliar adults, at six years, than children growing up in families where talk about feeling states is infrequent (Dunn et al. 1991).

The development of emotion regulation is also supported by parents' efforts directed toward providing their child with coping skills, namely discourse that is more goal-directed than talking about emotions, in the abstract. Gottman (1997) suggests that when parents are skilled in expressing and coping with aversive emotions, children gain emotional skills that buffer them from stressful events. In addition parents' awareness of their own sadness and tendencies to coach their children about anger were found to have an impact on children's emotional regulation. Instruction in problem-solving techniques relates to higher emotional competence in the child, although the effect seems more robust for boys than girls (Jones et al. 2002).

The development of emotion-regulation skills is related to a number of adaptive social behaviors. A longitudinal study showed that knowledge of emotions and emotion regulation at ages 3 to 4 predicted social competence at the kindergarten age (Denham et al. 2003). A number of researchers (e.g., Eisenberg et al. 1998) have presented models in which children's regulatory capacities mediate the relation between parental emotion-related child-rearing practices and children's adaptive social behavior. Specifically, parental expressivity is postulated to work through self-regulatory processes of the child in impacting on adaptive outcomes. Parents who are positive and supportive with their children may help them to manage their distress and cope successfully in stressful situations. In turn, this enhanced regulatory ability might foster the development of social skills and foster positive social interactions. Thus ineffective behavioral regulation has been found to be positively related to externalizing problems, as are constructs such as impulsivity and lack of effortful attention (e.g., Eisenberg et al. 2001; Lengua et al. 1998). Moreover differences in children's regulation predict differences in their social competence, empathy, and conscience (Eisenberg et al. 2000). Findings regarding the relation of internalizing problems to regulation have been less consistent than those for externalizing problem behaviors, although related to low impulsivity.

A number of important but relatively less well researched factors also impact on the development of the child's emotions and emotional intelligence. Several of these are briefly discussed in table 5.1.

Concluding Comments

At present, our understanding of the development of EI is limited and rudimentary. To some extent this assertion is reflected in claims made in the sidebar on the next page. Nevertheless, research demonstrates the existence of systematic individual differences at several levels of emotional functioning, which may broadly be described as aspects of EI. Presumably these components are influenced by biological and socialization/ environmental processes synergistically. Figure 5.3 presents a partial list of causal factors that could plausibly be included in a model of the origins of EI.

Table 5.1
Some potential factors impacting on development of EI in need of future research

Factors	Comments
Personal experiences	Children may glean important information about emotions from their own emotional experiences. Thus, children witness emotions in themselves, think about emotion–event links, and use these relationships in their emotion-related cognitions. Children who are impoverished in their awareness of their own emotional experiences may have parallel deficits in knowing how to respond adaptively to others experiencing similar emotions in their environment.
Peer environment	With increasing maturity, peers become a more salient influence on emotional socialization. Research suggest that when older siblings show a rewarding socialization pattern (i.e., reacting positively to positive emotions and not showing negative reactions to negative emotions), younger siblings demonstrate more emotional knowledge.
Affective environment in school and community	The overall affective environment at the school and community, to which a child is exposed, appears to impact on the child's emotional competence. For example, if teachers or community leaders often express anger or anxiety, children may internalize these affective states and experience them in a variety of situations.
Teachers	Some of the most important emotional learning may take place in informal relationships between child and teacher. Teachers may influence the child's ability to express and regulate emotions in the following two ways: (1) directly—by teaching and coaching—and (2) indirectly—by observational learning or by controlling children's exposure to different situations. Teachers also directly instruct students about how to manage distress.
Media	Watching TV and other forms of mass media provides children with opportunities for observational learning of emotional expression and management. Some TV programs designed for children (e.g., *Sesame Street*) present salient role models who themselves manage emotion arousal in explicit ways. Other programs (e.g., slasher flicks) arouse emotions directly in children that require self-management of arousal.

In this chapter we have structured developmental discussion around a multi-level investment model that may clarify the constructs involved. Consistent with our model, this review suggests that the interaction of biological and social-learning factors is critical for emotional development. Genes influence temperament (together with environmental factors influencing brain development, e.g., nutrition). However, especially in critical periods for development, gene expression is modulated by the social environment. The caregiver–infant interaction is bidirectional. The infant's temperament affects the way parents provide childcare, potentially leading to a vicious circle of conflict and increasingly difficult temperament or to a more benign, mutually rewarding trajectory compatible with the

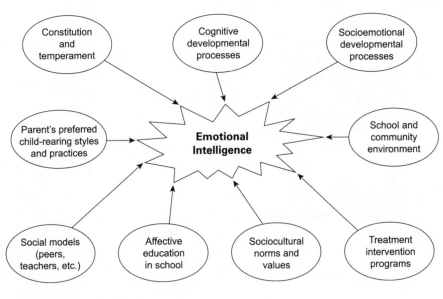

Figure 5.3
Determinants of emotional intelligence

natural inclinations of the child. The unique qualities of parents' interactions (with the individual child) appear to be critical for transmission of environmental effects.

Given these factors, there is a sense that EI resides in the creation of emotionally supportive environments for oneself. We may link high EI to seeking socially supportive environments (e.g., constructive relationships with parents, peers, and teachers) and emotional illiteracy to building environments that are emotionally destructive (i.e., making enemies or choosing poor role models). We can raise EI both by direct training of the child and by providing supportive family and school environments, as described in chapter 8.

A further subtlety is that the child's genes are related to "familial genes"; those of parents, siblings, and other family members, that will influence, often indirectly, the care given to the child. Whatever shared "high EI" genes that parent and child possess may affect the parent and child's temperament directly, as well as increasing the child's EI level through the parent's better quality caregiving. In addition it seems plausible that parents can increase their own emotional intelligence because of their experiences with their children.

A basic tenet of the investment model of EI is that the person possesses a varied repertoire of emotional responses. These responses range from

Stability and change in emotional intelligence across the life span

Generally, EI increases during childhood as a facet of emotional development (Izard et al. 2007). However, there is little hard evidence available on changes in EI during adulthood, although some commentators have made age-related increases in EI a defining feature of the construct. Where age groups have been compared the designs have largely been cross-sectional, making it difficult to draw conclusions about the development of EI over time. For example, Burns et al. (2007) report a series of cross-sectional comparisons for young and middle-aged adults that suggest higher EI in later life, as measured both by self-report and the MSCEIT. Similarly Kafetsios (2004) found age-related increases in the emotion regulation component of EI. The effect sizes for some facets of EI are quite substantial. However, age differences may be a "cohort" effect. That is, because of cultural shifts, younger individuals may be more prone to qualities such as anxiety and neuroticism (Twenge 2000) that influence EI scores. Where age groups have been tracked over time, it has generally been for rather brief durations. For example, Petrides et al. (2007) cite studies showing fairly substantial 1-year test-retest reliabilities for trait EI, similar to other personality traits. Parker et al. (2005) reported comparable levels of EI in college students over a 32-month period. These issues require further data collection. Against the view that emotional wisdom increases with age, we may point to the decline in fluid cognitive intelligence in adulthood (Horn and Hofer 1992), and evidence for affective blunting and loss of openness to feelings in old age (Terracciano et al. 2005).

implicit low-level emotional modulation (temperament), through simple rule-based skills, to more complex and explicit competencies, based on insight and metacognition. Akin to current thinking on emotion development (Izard et al. 2007), this model posits that the varied and rich repertoire of emotional responses is acquired over time and involves the biological, informational, and metacognitive facets of emotions, dependent, in part, on temperament, socialization, and self-regulatory personality processes respectively.

Of critical importance, the model implies that the developmental trajectory of EI depends on the individual's interaction with the environment. The qualities of the distress-prone child, such as hyper-awareness of threat and personal deficiencies, may lead to avoidance of feared social situations. This behavior pattern, in turn, affords fewer opportunities to develop emotion recognition skills, leading to poorer understanding of what happens in emotional situations and hence poorer management of such situations. The resultant skills deficits lead to further avoidance and maladaptive self-beliefs that typically lead to further withdrawal. By contrast, traits that promote engagement with challenging situations, such as sociability, lead to greater opportunities for learning skills for handling exciting (but potentially risky) encounters. Thus temperamental traits may influence emotional development both directly (via individual differences in emotion and attention) and indirectly (through exposure to situations for practicing and learning skills for specific emotional challenges).

Furthermore akin to that proposed for traditional cognitive abilities (Ackerman 1996), the model also indicates why there may be multiple sources of individual differences in emotional competence that are only weakly related to one another. As development proceeds, the range of emotion-regulative mechanisms becomes increasingly varied and differentiated. For example, Derryberry et al. (2003) have described how primitive behavioral strategies for emotion regulation, supported by subcortical brain motivation systems, are, with increasing age, increasingly supplemented by cognitive mechanisms that allow the child to plan and anticipate their actions.

Later in childhood, in concert with biological constitution, modeling, reinforcement, and emotional discourse become increasingly important for the higher level aspects of EI. We reviewed evidence showing how instructional methods influence skill and competence. Again, these processes are bidirectional, in that the child's reactions to emotional instruction will influence parental behavior, with potentials for both delaying and facilitating development. With increasing age, the role of the parents diminishes, and that of other persons, especially peers and teachers, increases. So too does the role of culture.

The model posits that culture has an indirect influence, through parent and educators' beliefs about how children should be raised. For example, we might expect the current zeitgeist to spur parents toward encouraging emotional expression. Such cultural factors should be detectable as cohort effects in longitudinal studies. Cognitive development may constrain emotional development. As discussed above, individual differences in emotional learning in the preschool years appear to be closely linked to vocabulary and verbal ability. Likewise the child appears to require meta-cognitive abilities (Flavell et al. 1995) before self-aware emotion regulation is possible.

The character of EI changes depending on the level of analysis. It is emphasized that these contrasts are relative, not absolute. EI is relatively more biological when conceptualized as temperament, and relatively more social-psychological when conceptualized as self-aware emotion regulation, but both genes and environment are important at all levels. Thus, in keeping with the "differentiation hypothesis," after infancy, multiple mechanisms may operate simultaneously in any given context. The model also provides a basis for distinguishing EI and emotional competence.

The limited empirical research supports only tentative conclusions about the nature of EI development, but the investment model does point toward some priorities for further research. Given valid assessments of aspects of EI in children, careful longitudinal studies are required to investigate their adaptive significance. It is often assumed that superior emotion knowledge (as defined by Izard 2001) confers direct adaptive benefits. However, evidence on causal relationships is limited. A second concern is whether superficially desirable attributes are adaptive. Adult personality traits typically confer both gains and costs, depending on context, as specified by the cognitive-adaptive model (Matthews and Zeidner 2000). Possibly temperament in childhood is similarly ambiguous. For example, negative affectivity may protect the child from potential dangers, and positive affectivity may carry risks associated with impulsive behavior. Alternatively, childhood temperament may be more straightforward in its consequences; adult personality may be more complex because adults learn to compensate for undesirable consequences of dispositional makeup.

Research on the emotional learning mechanisms identified here can be applied to various applied settings. One possible focus is support for parents. Parents whose own EI may be low face the double jeopardy of raising children who may be genetically "difficult," together with their own limited emotional skills (assuming that like most traits, EI is partially inherited). Explicit training in caregiving, modeling, reinforcement techniques, along with instructional and discourse methods might be especially valuable to this group, assuming training is implemented sensitively, without stigmatizing parents as inadequate. In older children, instructional techniques might be implemented in a group setting.

Summary Points: Chapter 5

• The multi-level investment model of EI is showcased in this chapter as a contemporary heuristic framework for understanding and researching the development of emotional competencies. The model posits that the development of emotional knowledge and competencies depends on diverse biological, social learning, and environmental factors and contingencies.

• The first level of the investment model, biologically based temperamental qualities (e.g., reactivity to stress), provides the infrastructure for subsequent emotional learning. Specific temperamental qualities (e.g., strategies for emotion regulation) may facilitate the subsequent development of EI. Emotional competencies are determined, in part, by the way environmental forces impinge on the child's developing biological constitution. The second level of the model consists of the individual's learning of emotional information and rule-based skills and behavioral strategies for emotion control. These skills are acquired largely through behavioral socialization practices, such as role modeling. The third level of the model involves the acquisition of reflective self-regulatory processes, achieved largely through strategic coaching and tuition by primary (e.g., parents) and secondary (e.g., peers) socialization agents.

• Emotional competencies develop through dynamic and reciprocal interactions between the child's biologically programmed temperament, on one hand, and caregiver-child attachment processes and child-rearing techniques, on the other. The development of EI is constrained by the development of general ability as well as specific cognitive competencies, including, perceptual, inferential, interpretive, and linguistic processes.

• Family socialization practices reinforced, for example, by caregiver expressiveness may facilitate the development of the child's emotional and social knowledge, attitudes, and skills and thus shape the child's social competence. Caregiver socialization practices play a pivotal role in the development of EI and cognate abilities, such as empathy.

• The repertoire of emotional competencies is acquired over time, with major facets of EI possibly having critical periods for their development. EI appears to increase steadily during childhood, as a facet of emotional development in general. Enriched environmental conditions may help facilitate the development of EI, particularly if biological predispositions toward EI are fostered early in life. By contrast, there is little empirical evidence on meaningful changes in EI during adulthood, with research clearly required.

6 How Social Is Emotional Intelligence?

Conquest of the outer world does not free the species from the inner world which made its evolution possible. Social life is rooted in emotion and is basic to survival. A comprehensive biology must surely take account of one of man's fundamental properties—his social nature.
—David A. Hamburg

Emotions lie at the center of social experience, providing us with meaning in our lives. Indeed most of what we do in social life, as well as how we do it, is influenced and informed by emotions and the activating social conditions that generate them (Lazarus 1991). Since its inception, the idea that emotions (and meaningful individual differences) have a role in social life is one of the factors that have fueled interest in emotional intelligence (Lopes et al. 2004).

Emotions are deeply embedded in social contexts, reflecting and shaping social processes. Certain emotions (e.g., love, shame) seem to come to life within interpersonal and relational settings. Emotional encounters, however short-lived, typically involve affective involvement with others in a relationship—often supplying some of the most important classes of emotion-inducing events (Parkinson 1996). What people tend to get emotional about can relate to various levels of social interaction, such as the interpersonal (e.g., what others in our surroundings do), group (e.g., what the group does), and cultural level (e.g., norms defining what is of personal concern and emotional significance).

In this chapter we discuss the role that emotional intelligence (EI) plays in social settings. We begin by examining the social nature and functions of emotions and emotional competencies. Next we evaluate research that supports the importance of emotional intelligence in social contexts. We then discuss personality perspectives, focusing on the roles of three major personality factors—neuroticism, extraversion, and agreeableness—in social encounters. We further look at social deviance from a

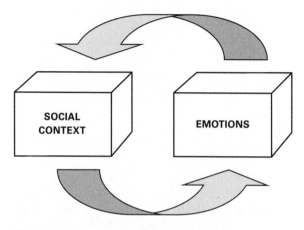

Figure 6.1
Dynamic interaction between emotions and social context

social cognitive perspective, describing the nexus of relations between emotional intelligence, aggression, and impulse control. We conclude by looking at the relatively neglected, darker-side of emotions in social situations.

Emotions in Social Life

As depicted in figure 6.1, emotions are frequently evoked by social events, and emotions in turn influence the course of social reactions. Jealousy, for example, communicates that one feels replaced in a social relationship. It also expresses the desire to be reintegrated into this social relationship. By contrast, sadness, following personal loss, communicates to others the need for immediate social support. Of course, the specific nature of the social relationship between individuals in a social encounter determines, in part, the specific emotions aroused (Parkinson et al. 2005). For example, ridicule by another person can be met by shame, defiance, or disregard—all depending on the nature of the relationship between parties and the current state of the interaction.

Emotions: What Are They Good For?
The ancient Greeks viewed emotions as primitive and irrational passions that needed constantly to be curbed or tamed. Modern theories of emotions, by contrast, posit that emotions are adaptations that have important evolutionary functions critical to survival (Lazarus 1991). For evolutionary theorists, emotions are universal, hardwired affective pro-

---

Functions of Emotions

- Signal meaning of event to self and others
- Enlist social support
- Regulate behavior
- Maintain social control and hierarchy
- Organize activity
- Influence cognitive processing

---

grams that solve recurrent threats to human survival (Lazarus 1991). Indeed Charles Darwin (1872) realized that the communication of emotions has considerable survival value, with emotional expression (e.g., posturing) serving to signal specific messages to others in the group (e.g., beware, snake in the grass), so that behavior and action can be coordinated.

A social-functional view of emotions suggests that emotions signal socially relevant information. This information is of potential use for understanding how to engage successfully in social life and how to interact adaptively with others (Keltner and Kring 1998; Parkinson et al. 2005). The sidebar above gives a summary of these important functions.

Emotions provide us, for one, with invaluable information about the nature and meaning of the social context and what is important to a person engaging in a social encounter. How one feels about a person, object, or episode in the environment acts as an affective barometer, representing the latter's overall personal significance. The very fact that one is upset about something in the course of social interaction, for example, is prima facie evidence that whatever is going on really matters to that person (Scherer 2007).

Emotions also communicate the meanings of events to the self and others. According to Lazarus's cognitive-motivational theory, the expression of emotions serves to communicate core relational themes to the target of the emotional reaction. For example, the expression of fear communicates: "I feel that I am in danger and in need of protection." Facial expressions that are universally recognized as being associated with specific emotions, alert others to the situation, and inform others of threat and situational opportunities and affordances. Presumably high EI individuals would be more accurate in picking up the meaning of the message being communicated and in responding in a more adaptive manner than their low EI counterparts.

In addition emotions serve an important function in facilitating social support. Thus, having been in a traumatic situation, people often want to share the experience, receive justification of emotional feelings, and obtain instrumental social support. At times emotions can go awry, causing psychopathological disturbances. When this occurs, individuals can be helped to recognize and discuss emotions and understand how their social and emotional experiences are related to their intra- and interpersonal difficulties (see chapter 11).

Studies of brain-damaged individuals suggest that the ability to detect and use affective feedback is essential for engaging in, even the most routine, goal-directed activities (Damasio 1994). Emotions also have important organizing functions, helping us shift attention to the challenges, threats, and losses at hand. Thus emotions may interrupt ongoing interactions and behaviors and present a "call for action." In addition certain emotions (e.g., anger) serve as mechanisms of social control, causing others to submit to the social hierarchy.

The information provided by our feelings may often trigger specific strategies; affecting judgment, memory, and style of information processing (Gohm and Clore 2002b). Thus our emotions and current mood can affect information processing by infusing our thoughts, judgments, and behaviors, coloring how we perceive our environment, how we encode, process, and retrieve information, and the way we respond to social situations (Forgas 2001). For example, when we feel good, we see the world as favorable and benign. A positive mood signals to us that we can rely on our existing knowledge in responding to environmental stimuli. By contrast, when we feel sad or depressed, everything seems to be dark and gloomy. Negative affect serves as an alarm signal, alerting us that the environment is potentially dangerous and that we need to pay closer attention to external events. A positive mood has been shown to facilitate creative thinking (Isen 1987), whereas negative mood supports more indepth, deductive or reflective thinking (Sinclair and Mark 1995). We should note that these general trends toward "mood-congruent" thinking are not always realized in specific contexts. Some cognitive processes are more sensitive than others, as described by Forgas (2001).

EI and Adaptive Social Outcomes

The literature has recently provided some promising data in support of emotional intelligence as a reliable predictor of adaptive social outcomes. Some plausible—but not conclusively established—relationships between

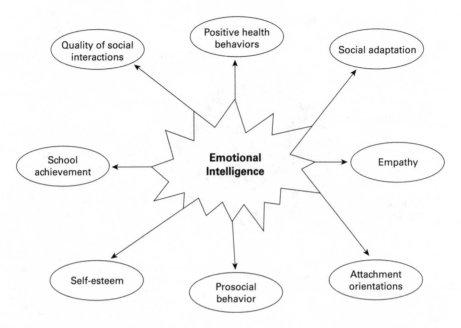

Figure 6.2
Some possible positive relations between emotional intelligence and adaptive outcomes

EI and positive and negative social outcomes, suggested by recent research, are graphically depicted in figures 6.2 and 6.3 respectively. We now briefly discuss the relationship between EI and three different types of adaptive outcomes: social interactions, intimate personal relationships, and health (and well-being).

Social Interactions   Emotions serve social and communicative functions; conveying information about peoples' intentions and both enabling and coordinating social encounters. Clearly, people need to process emotional information and manage emotional dynamics intelligently to navigate the social world, particularly since positive emotion is associated with sociability (Argyle 2001) and negative affect keeps others at bay (Furr and Funder 1998). It follows that emotional competencies are expected to be of pivotal importance for social interactions (Lopes et al. 2004).

Indeed research provides some evidence for the critical role of EI in social relations and adaptation (Brackett et al. 2006). Supportive data have been obtained in studies using both questionnaire and objective measures of emotional intelligence. Generally, questionnaire scales predict various

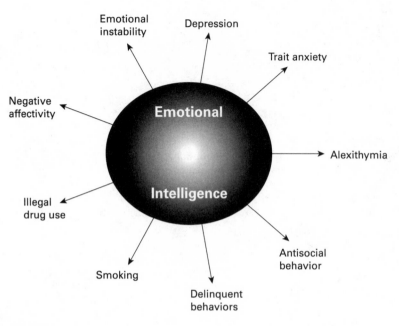

Figure 6.3
Some possible relations between low emotional intelligence and maladaptive outcomes

facets of life satisfaction, including social satisfaction. Schutte et al.
(2001), for instance, reported that EI predicted various self-reported
criteria including empathic perspective taking, social skills, cooperative
responses, and satisfaction with close relationships (see also Austin
2005a). Similarly high EI adolescents who say they are good at managing
other's emotions constructively report having more social support and
satisfaction with support, potentially protecting them from depression
(Ciarrochi, Chan, et al. 2001). Work on temperamental factors in infants
and children (as discussed previously in chapter 5) similarly indicate that
richer emotional competencies are related to prosocial behavior and
better adaptation.

    Brackett et al. (2006) have recently demonstrated that the MSCEIT
predicted real-time social competence—but just for men. A survey of the
literature on the MEIS and MSCEIT (Rivers et al. 2007) suggests that EI
is related to harmonious personal relations and adaptive social outcomes.
Further those high on EI were reported to be more likely to have been
securely attached (Kafetsios 2004) and to keep objects of attachment visible, such as photos of family and letters (Brackett et al. 2004). Among

college-aged individuals, higher scores on the MEIS and MSCEIT have been associated with greater empathy (Ciarrochi et al. 2000), fewer negative interactions with friends (Brackett et al. 2004) and to higher quality of social interactions, as independently assessed by peers (Lopes et al. 2004). Better emotion management, particularly in men, is associated with fewer conflicts and antagonism in college students' relationships with their close friends (Lopes et al. 2003). It appears that managing emotions is consistently most predictive of these social criteria; the other three branches mostly share trivial relations with the social variables assessed (Lopes et al. 2003, 2004).

We will briefly note some limitations of these studies. As in other domains, controlling for personality and intelligence tends to reduce the predictive validity of the EI measures, sometimes making these close to zero (see Day 2004). For example, Austin et al. (2005) found that, with standard personality traits controlled, EI predicted only one out of six outcome criteria (self-reported size of social network). In another study, Bastian et al. (2005) showed that EI predicted at most 6 percent of the variance in life skills. Further, statistically controlling for personality and cognitive abilities substantially reduced the relative contribution of EI, regardless of the measure used. An earlier study (Saklofske et al. 2003) showed that a modest negative correlation between EI and social/emotional loneliness approached zero when personality was taken into account. Correlations between the MEIS and MSCEIT and social well-being also reduce when personality and intelligence are controlled (Brackett and Mayer 2003).

Another limitation is that most of these studies rely on the person's self-reports of their social functioning, which may be biased by self-appraisals. Indeed social well-being may correlate with questionnaire measures of EI precisely because both types of measure reflect how positive the person's self-opinions are. The Lopes et al. (2004) study is better than most in that these authors used another person to assess quality of social interactions in one study, and a structured interview that referred to specific social encounters in a second study.

Intimate Personal Relationships   Intimate interpersonal relationships, such as romantic or marital relations, tend to be both emotion-rich as well as high-conflict social contexts (Fitness 2001). The very intimacy that links two people often lays the groundwork for both emotional highs and lows (Carstensen et al. 1996). Brackett et al. (2005) showed that when couples both score low on EI they report a greater degree of unhappiness with their relationship compared to couples who both score high on EI. Conflicts in relationships often involve a repetitive cycle of emotions (e.g., shame, anger), the initial source of which can be quite trivial (e.g., a snide remark). If allowed to escalate, these conflicts can ruin the relationship.

A recent study by Zeidner and Kaluda (2008) examined the relation of EI to romantic love in 100 newlywed couples considering "actor effects" and "partner effects." Controlling for verbal intelligence, both self-report and ability-based measures showed significant actor effects but failed to account for partner effects. Furthermore EI was not correlated within couples independent of the measure used. Whereas EI is meaningfully correlated with romantic love in both dyadic partners, married persons whose partners are higher on EI are not necessarily more in love with their partners.

Both verbal and nonverbal patterns of dyadic communication and emotion expression may be pivotal for understanding the successful social functioning of couples. These patterns also serve as significant predictors of the quality of intimate personal relations (Gottman et al. 1976). We may assume that good dyadic communication allows partners to openly communicate their own needs, wishes, and desires; to freely experience and express both positive and negative emotions; and to negotiate and reach agreements on central issues in order to resolve conflicts and strengthen emotional bonds.

It stands to reason that the way a couple handles emotionally laden situations has serious implications for the stability of the partnership and perceived satisfaction. Although there is a lack of specific research on EI in this domain, inferences may be drawn based on available evidence from social psychology and emotions research. For example, EI may enter the scene by helping individuals who are high on this dimension maintain positive emotional interactions. In the passages that follow, we further theorize how EI components might contribute to personal relationships.

Perception, Identification, and Expression of Emotions   As discussed in chapter 3, research suggests that people vary in their ability to accurately perceive and communicate emotions. Some individuals are more prone to ignore or misidentify even the most obvious of emotional signals. Others are prone to habitually send ambiguous emotional signals to their partners. EI might help sustain an intimate personal relationship by enabling the open expression of wants and desires, facilitating candid discussion of sensitive issues, and helping a partner decode nonverbal messages.

In general, individuals more sensitive to their partner's feeling states react with greater empathy toward their partners' emotional needs and desires and consequently also experience greater satisfaction with their relationship (e.g., Fitness 2001). Thus couples characterized by open communication tend to express greater satisfaction with their relationships (Christensen and Shenk 1991). Couples who avoid open communication, by contrast, tend to report higher distress levels and a higher rate of relationships that eventually dissolve (Gottman 1994). The latter theme stands at the core of this quote from Veronica Lario, the wife of Silvio Berlusconi, Italy's former prime minister and an alleged womanizer: "To my husband and to the public man, I therefore ask for a public apology, not having received one privately" (*New York Times* quotation of the day, February 1, 2007).

Emotional Understanding   The accuracy and complexity of people's emotional understanding can help decode the intentions, attitudes, motivations, and thoughts of others in their social surroundings (Keltner and Haidt 2001). In the context of intimate personal relationships, understanding of emotions in self and in others can help nurture positive relationships. Poor understanding of emotions in self and others, however, contributes to the misinterpretation of verbal or nonverbal messages, leading to tension and disruption of intimate personal relationships (Fitness 2001).

As suggested in earlier chapters, empathy is likely a key component of emotional intelligence. An empathic person in a close relationship attempts to understand their partner's internal frame of reference (e.g., perspective) in a way that is identical (or very similar) to what the partner is feeling or would be expected to feel (Eisenberg and Fabes 1990). Persons who are empathic have an astute awareness of the other's emotions, picking up on subtle verbal and nonverbal cues.

People, who tend to empathize with their partner's distress are likely to refrain from aggression because of the emotional discomfort induced by the vicarious response to their significant others emotional reaction (Feshbach 1978). Research has found, for example, a positive association between marital adjustment and understanding of the attitudes, role expectations, and self-perceptions of one's spouse (Flury and Ickes 2001). Although empathic accuracy need not lead to empathic behaviors in social situations, empathic accuracy has been shown to be related to one's commitment to intimate relationships, willingness to accommodate partners' problematic behavior, and adjust to the relationship. Particularly, during the formative stages of a relationship, empathic accuracy seems to contribute to positive outcomes.

Fitness (2001) puts all of this into perspective in the following way: "The art of knowing when, why, and how to say you are sorry in marriage, and the ability to practice forbearance under even the most trying circumstances, require many sophisticated emotional skills, including empathy, self-control, and a deep understanding of human needs and feelings" (p. 98). Of note, empathy is linked to showing compassion and forgiveness in the wake of conflict (McCullough et al. 1997). Therefore, in theory, EI enhances the ability of partners to forgive each other and positively contribute to intimacy and satisfaction in a relationship.

Research seems to support this hypothesis. Fitness (2001), for example, found that couples higher on emotional clarity reported less difficulty in forgiving a partner-caused offense than people lower in emotion clarity. These individuals were also found to be happier in their relationship. By contrast, partners characterized by low emotional understanding appear more prone to attack partners and interpret partner distress as hostility. Thus, rather than expressing guilt and remorse, they may act hatefully in return. Over time such reactions are likely to exacerbate conflict and diminish relationship quality. Emotional misunderstandings can also lead to "negative affect reciprocity," where spouses (broadly defined) reciprocate the negative emotions they perceive in their partners.

Emotion Regulation   The ability to successfully maintain, change, or modify emotions, both in self and others, has been claimed to be an important factor contributing to relationship stability and happiness (Fitness 2001). Research suggests that couples higher in marital satisfaction, for example, are capable of reframing negative interactions in a constructive manner, compared to couples reporting less satisfaction (Carstensen et al. 1995). There appears to be an inverted U-curve relationship between expressiveness of emotions and well-being in intimate relations (see figure 6.4). Thus both too much and too little expression of negative emotions may be maladaptive in interpersonal relations.

Because relationship success is a function of how couples handle negative affect, EI would appear to play an important function (see the sidebar). In order for partners to cope successfully with ongoing stresses and emotional fissures, their skill in identifying, understanding, and regulating their own emotions and those of their partners becomes critical (Fitness

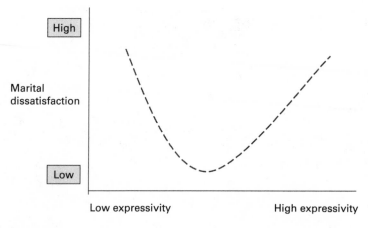

Figure 6.4
Expressivity of negative emotions and marital satisfaction

2001). Overall, the bulk of studies suggest that couples need high EI and a good working knowledge of emotions in the relationship context, to be able to make sense of their own and their partner's emotions. Some of the psychophysiological correlates and consequences of marital dispute are highlighted in the sidebar on the next page. Figure 6.5 takes a slightly broader approach, schematically presenting a number of mediating variables through which EI may work to affect relationship satisfaction. However, it is important to point out that little work has addressed the role of EI directly, although it seems a promising area for future research.

Health and Well-Being   Research points to a modest association between EI and positive health-related behaviors. We note again that relationships between EI and health criteria, certainly in some cases, may nonetheless be an artifact of the confounding of EI with personality, especially where self-report scales are used (e.g., Austin et al. 2005). Leaving aside such concerns, several studies report promising findings. Thus data suggest a modest correlation between EI and dieting and exercising (Saklofske et al. 2007). In addition low EI college students, males in particular, have been reported to be at risk for potentially harmful behaviors, such as illegal drugs, excessive consumption of alcohol, and engaging in deviant behavior (Brackett et al. 2004). Research also points to moderate correlations in a community sample of adults between EI (albeit self-report) and alcohol and drug problems (Riley and Schutte 2003).

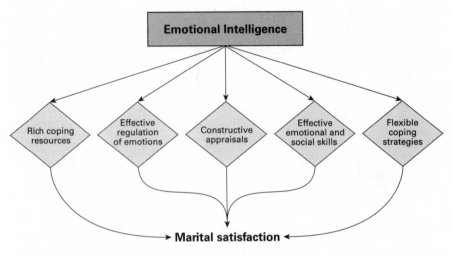

Figure 6.5
Mediating factors in the relationship between emotional intelligence and marital satisfaction

Marital bliss: Emotional intelligence in action?

Research suggests that happy partners are skilled at de-escalating the kinds of destructive interaction sequences characteristic of unhappy partners, tend to respond in a conciliatory fashion during conflict, and report greater marital satisfaction (Gottman 1994). Although happy partners often do express negative emotions in their interactions (e.g., anger, sadness, fear), they also more frequently express love, affection, and good humor in these interactions (Carstensen et al. 1995).

In contrast, unhappy partners are more likely to retaliate and less likely to accommodate their partners during conflict interactions (Fitness 2006). Thus unhappy partners tend to be less likely to inhibit their impulses. They also react destructively when their spouses express anger or behave unreasonably.

And yet a cautionary note is needed, lest one read too much into this research. It is difficult to untangle cause and effect in the above because unhappiness in a relationship may be just as likely to decrease partner's emotional sensitivity to one another as emotional insensitivity may be to decrease happiness in the relationship.

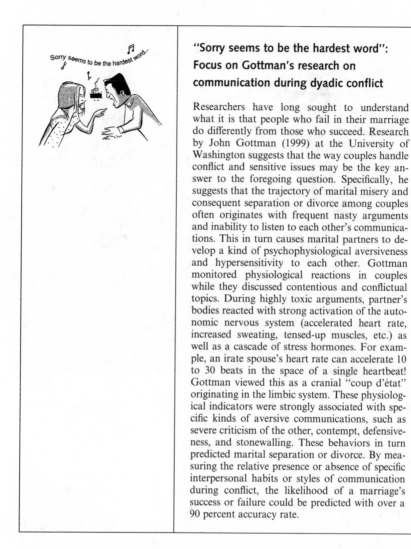

"Sorry seems to be the hardest word":
Focus on Gottman's research on
communication during dyadic conflict

Researchers have long sought to understand what it is that people who fail in their marriage do differently from those who succeed. Research by John Gottman (1999) at the University of Washington suggests that the way couples handle conflict and sensitive issues may be the key answer to the foregoing question. Specifically, he suggests that the trajectory of marital misery and consequent separation or divorce among couples often originates with frequent nasty arguments and inability to listen to each other's communications. This in turn causes marital partners to develop a kind of psychophysiological aversiveness and hypersensitivity to each other. Gottman monitored physiological reactions in couples while they discussed contentious and conflictual topics. During highly toxic arguments, partner's bodies reacted with strong activation of the autonomic nervous system (accelerated heart rate, increased sweating, tensed-up muscles, etc.) as well as a cascade of stress hormones. For example, an irate spouse's heart rate can accelerate 10 to 30 beats in the space of a single heartbeat! Gottman viewed this as a cranial "coup d'état" originating in the limbic system. These physiological indicators were strongly associated with specific kinds of aversive communications, such as severe criticism of the other, contempt, defensiveness, and stonewalling. These behaviors in turn predicted marital separation or divorce. By measuring the relative presence or absence of specific interpersonal habits or styles of communication during conflict, the likelihood of a marriage's success or failure could be predicted with over a 90 percent accuracy rate.

The correlation of EI to behavior may further generalize to more objective assessments such as the MSCEIT. Low EI adolescents (determined using these indexes) are reported to be at increased risk for alcohol and tobacco use (Trinidad and Johnson 2002; Trinidad et al. 2004a, b). Low EI adolescents may be less able to manage emotions resulting from peer pressures to smoke, drink, and use unhealthy substances. By contrast, high EI adolescents may better be able to process social information, including social risk, and employ a wider array of coping strategies to deal with situations that may increase smoking risk. They may also be better able to

Figure 6.6
High EI adolescents appear capable of using a variety of strategies to resist the pressure to use illicit substances

detect unwanted peer pressure, leading to resistance to pressure to use tobacco and alcohol (Trinidad and Johnson 2002; see figure 6.6).

A recent meta-analytic study set out to determine the strength of relationship between EI measures and various health indices (physical, mental, psychosomatic; see table 6.1 for a brief summary of results) (Schutte et al. 2007). On average, EI was significantly and positively related with each type of health indicator, namely physical ($r = 0.22$), mental ($r = 0.23$), and psychosomatic ($r = 0.31$). Furthermore the pattern of relationship between EI and health outcome varied by method of EI assessment, with trait measures showing a significantly higher correlation with mental health compared to ability based measures. The correlation between EI and physical health was significantly lower than the effect sizes for mental and psychosomatic health, perhaps reflecting the relative importance of other causal factors in physical health.

Because emotions provide information about one's relationship to the environment and others, interpreting and responding to that information

Table 6.1
Emotional intelligence and health: Summary of meta-analytic findings

Health facet	N	r
Physical health (e.g., physical symptom level, pain, medical status, physical functioning)	5	0.22*
Mental health (e.g., anxiety, depression)	33	0.23*
Psychosomatic health (e.g., chronoic fatigue, scales assessing mental and physical health interactions)	6	0.31[a]

Source: Schutte et al. (2007).
Note: N = number of effect size indicators; r = the average product-moment correlation between EI and health indicators, aggregated across studies.
a. p is significant at $p < 0.05$.

can direct action and thought in ways that enhance or maintain well-being (Lazarus 1991; Parrott 2002). For this reason EI is hypothesized to predict one's subjective sense of well-being and mental health. A number of researchers have hypothesized that low EI persons, who have difficulties regulating emotions and tend to require more time to elevate their moods following disturbances, are at particular risk for psychopathology (Salovey, Hsee, et al. 1993).

There is some preliminary evidence to support this hypothesis. Thus self-perceived EI is strongly associated with self-reported well-being, more frequent positive affect, life satisfaction, and self-esteem (Gohm and Clore 2002a, b). Also some research suggests that high EI persons experience better mental health and greater life satisfaction (Martinez-Pons 1997, 1998). These individuals similarly report fewer clinical symptoms, including (less, in each instance): anxiety (O'Connor and Little 2003), depression (Saklofske et al. 2003), loneliness (Engelberg and Sjoberg 2004), and borderline personality (Leible and Snell 2004). In addition men with lower EI have been found to engage in self-destructive behavior (Brackett et al. 2004).

In principle, each of these associations could be due to the beneficial effects of incorporating emotional information into how people manage their lives, including making better judgments and having more successful social interactions than others. One line of research shows, however, that EI fails to buffer the effects of daily hassles on psychological health outcomes (Day et al. 2005). Figure 6.7 presents a number of potential mediating factors through which EI may work in impacting health outcomes.

MEDIATING VARIABLES

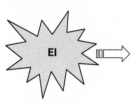

- Limited exposure to stressful events

- Greater resilience

- Richer personal health and
  emotional resources

- More positive emotionality and less
  negative emotionality

- Enhanced optimism

- Wider social support networks

- Adaptive coping mechanisms

- Better self-regulation in maintaining
  health behaviors

Figure 6.7
Some potential mediating factors in the relationship between emotional intelligence and
health outcomes

Because relations between EI and psychological health and well-being are
viewed as a potentially important practical application of the construct
we return to these issues again in chapter 11.

Personality Perspectives on Adaptive Social Behaviors

Thus far we have discussed how EI *may* plausibly confer benefits in social
functioning. It should be apparent from our exposition that direct evidence is skimpier than it should be and that the studies that have been
performed typically use self-report measures of social function, rather
than objective indexes. In this section we turn to another recurrent theme
of this book: the extent that EI adds anything new to existing work on
personality and social outcomes. There are two interrelated issues here.
The first is the role of personality traits as predictors of social behaviors.
The second is the extent to which some people are better socially adapted
than others.

Personality Traits and Social Behavior
In chapter 4 we discussed the five factor model (FFM) that is widely used
as a framework for understanding the social-psychological expressions of
personality. There is extensive research, relating especially to the neuroticism (N), extraversion (E), and agreeableness (A) traits that link these

Table 6.2
How the personality traits of the five factor model predict social adaptation

Criterion for adaptation	Adaptive relationships	Maladaptive relationships	Further comments
Qualities of social relationships	Extraversion— higher social skills Agreeableness— higher satisfaction with relationships	Neuroticism— negative perceptions of others	Personality influences both objective behavior, and *perceptions* of relationships
Intimate relationships	Agreeableness— higher marital satisfaction	Neuroticism, extraversion—higher divorce rate	
Emotion perception			Literature is inconsistent—IQ may be more predictive than personality
Emotion expression	Extraversion— higher positive expressiveness Agreeableness— nonverbal expressiveness	Neuroticism— higher negative expressiveness	Clinically anxious and depressed individuals may show restrictions in expressiveness
Emotion understanding (empathy)	Agreeableness— higher		
Health and well-being	Neuroticism— reduced well-being more vulnerability to illness	Neuroticism—more preventative behaviors Conscientiousness— reduced risk-taking	Clinically anxious and depressed individuals may show damaging health behaviors

aspects of personality to well-being, social skills, social interest and motivation, and perceptions and cognitions of other people (see Matthews et al. 2003 for a review). Table 6.2 shows some of the linkages that have been established by this research (see also chapter 9).

Emotionally unstable individuals (i.e., those high in N) experience a variety of problems, notably greater vulnerability to negative moods that carry over into the social domain and cognitions. Indeed social anxiety and shyness are common in high N persons, who also tend to report less satisfaction both with relationships in general, and with marriage. The probability of divorce is indeed positively correlated with N (e.g., Rogge et al. 2006). Emotional instability also seems to confer vulnerability to social stress: N relates to exaggerated emotional responses to minor social discord (Bolger 1990). There is also an extensive literature linking emotional instability to poorer health (e.g., Goodwin and Freidman 2006).

To some extent the disadvantages of high N relate to a greater willingness to gripe about trivial problems, such as minor physical complaints in the health domain (Stone and Costa 1990). The difficulties of being emotionally unstable may not in fact be as great as reported by high N persons. However, there is increasing evidence that N relates to genuine medical illness, perhaps because higher levels of stress compromise functioning of the immune system (Yousfi et al. 2004). But the news for those with high N is not all bad: it does confer some advantages. This includes greater awareness of potential health problems, leading to early diagnosis (Mayne 1999), and greater willingness to preempt potential threats by sustained effort (Smillie et al. 2006). Awareness of threat may be a spur to effective action.

Extraversion–introversion is defined in part by level of sociability. Thus it comes as no surprise that extraverts, who are more talkative and socially expressive than introverts, tend to possess superior verbal social skills (e.g., Berry and Sherman-Hansen 2000). However, extraversion also relates to influence and dominance in social relationships, and being overbearing toward others has its disadvantages. Extraversion relates to narcissism, for example (Bradlee and Emmons 1992), which is associated with inflated self-importance and exhibitionism. The self-confidence that such individuals' project may help in creating a good first impression, but closer acquaintance tends to reveal the flaws associated with the trait. These flaws may also contribute to the higher incidence of divorce in extraverts (Furnham and Heaven 1999). Extraverts are also more prone to potentially self-damaging, impulsive behaviors such as sexual promiscuity (Eysenck 1976). Thus extraversion has distinctly mixed adaptive outcomes. Social self-confidence may indeed help persons make friends and influence them, but arrogance and impulsivity may be damaging, especially to longer term relationships.

The third trait we have highlighted here is agreeableness. The trait shares a defining feature with EI: high empathy. Highly agreeable persons tend to be altruistic, cooperative, and trusting, whereas those low in A are cold and unsympathetic. In common with E, A relates to social involvement and greater satisfaction with social relationships. However, A differs from E, in that it relates to nurturance and affiliation with others, rather than dominance and influence: nurturance and dominance are independent facets of personality in social settings (Trapnell and Wiggins 1990).

Thus the benefits and costs of being agreeable differ from those of extra-version. High A facilitates interpersonal cooperation and mutual loyalty, and indeed that relates to marital satisfaction. Berry and Sherman-Hansen (2000) obtained data by coding videos of people in conversation. Agreeableness was related to nonverbal social skills, such as expressing interest in the other person that enhanced the quality of the social interaction.

Even so, in some contexts, agreeable people may be too nice for their own good. High A is linked to difficulties in handling interpersonal conflicts and competitive situations, and tendencies to be deferential and submissive. Even empathy may have its disadvantages. In group situations, empathizing with someone may lead the person to favor them unfairly, at the expense of fairness within the group as a whole (Batson et al. 1999). We could imagine that an empathic juror in a criminal case might be swayed by either the victim's sufferings or the accused person's broken home; trial lawyers are likely not averse to playing on such emotionally infused judgments.

The evidence that standard personality traits predict a wide range of social-behavioral criteria raises two important issues for our analysis of emotional intelligence. First, we reiterate a methodological point we make throughout this book—many popular measures of EI appear confounded with personality. Associations between EI and social criteria may be incidental to the influence of personality traits, which may be a more fundamental factor, as previously discussed. For example, Bar-On's (2000) EQ-i picks up extraversion, agreeableness, and low neuroticism. By extension, it would be astonishing if it failed to predict relevant social criteria, such as self-reported social skills and satisfaction with social interaction. Studies using the MEIS or MSCEIT (e.g., Lopes et al. 2004; Trinidad et al. 2004a, b) may be on a firmer footing because the confounding is relatively minor. Establishing the incremental validity of EI measures over above personality and intelligence will be important for future research.

The second issue is whether dispositional variables actually predict some overall adaptation (i.e., people who are globally superior in handling social encounters) or *styles* of social interaction that carry both benefits and costs. To address this issue, we present a brief theoretical account that emphasizes the processing bases for social adaptation, followed by discussion of how individuals of differing EI may vary in the major social processes involved.

Personality Traits and Adaptation to Social Challenges

Matthews and Zeidner (e.g., 2003) have outlined a "cognitive-adaptive" theory of personality that specifies how dispositional traits relate to individual differences in adaptation. It proposes that the individual's level of adaptation is most directly dependent on a multiplicity of acquired skills. Social skills are seen here as being heterogeneous in nature: they may be verbal or nonverbal, explicit or implicit, directed toward an instrumental goal or directed toward providing emotional support. Some skills are primarily cognitive (e.g., good social perception, understanding, and memory; see Weis and Suess 2005). Others relate to emotion (e.g., effective regulation and communication of emotion; Scherer 2007). Skills also appear to be somewhat specific to context. For example, the skills needed to dominate a business meeting are not the same as those required for sustaining an intimate relationship. Skills must be *learned* within some social and cultural setting. Space precludes further discussion of the conceptualization and assessment of social skills (see Norton and Hope 2001), but we take here the position that social skills are made up of a number of separable components.

Matthews and Zeidner (e.g., 2000) also propose that skills are executed within a dynamic process of interaction between the person and the environment, a process that may lead to the person's typical performance falling short of their actual competence or potential. They argue that during development, genes and early learning determine a number of basic processing characteristics that provide a platform for subsequent skill acquisition. Indeed it is easier to learn skills for talking to strangers if one has good verbal working memory, fluent speech production, and psychophysiological stress tolerance. The child that has difficulties in keeping track of the conversation and reacts to strangers with high emotional arousal is liable to have difficulties in acquiring these social skills (see chapter 5).

In addition children acquire not just the skills themselves but beliefs about their level of skills and styles of emotional response to the contexts in which the skills are performed. Bandura's (1997) work on self-efficacy highlights how beliefs about personal competence can support or undermine actual functioning. Similarly a large literature on evaluation anxieties, including test and social anxiety, demonstrates that negative beliefs about personal competence can disrupt execution of the skills concerned (Zeidner and Matthews 2005). Thus social adaptation reflects not just skill learning but personal factors (e.g., self-efficacy) that determine whether the person performs the skill at its true level of competence.

Dynamic factors are critical in adulthood too. The learning, execution, and modification of skills operate over extended time periods. Adaptation reflects the dynamic interaction of actual competencies, self-regulation, and feedback from social encounters (Wells and Matthews 1994). Both benign and harmful patterns of interaction may develop. For example, a talented entrepreneur (possessing actual skills for business interactions) gains confidence in using those skills (self-regulation), which in turn supports successful outcomes in business (profitable partnerships and deals). The entrepreneur becomes increasingly engaged in business activities, leading to refinement of social skills and increasing self-efficacy and self-understanding. Conversely, the socially anxious person may have some relatively minor deficits in social skills. Coupled with an excessively negative self-appraisal and dysfunctional self-regulation (e.g., excessive worry about social failure), the person's social encounters do not go well (and may even be perceived as being less successful than they actually are). The person then tends to avoid challenging social events, leading to loss of opportunities to enhance social skills and to disconfirm negative beliefs; a process that may result in social phobia (Alden and Taylor 2004).

The argument so far suggests that we can identify globally functional and dysfunctional styles of interaction with the social world. Perhaps there are some emotional geniuses brimming with skills and confidence who adapt easily to every conceivable social challenge. However, there are reasons for caution in accepting this position. A general point is that the dynamic process just described is often context specific. Skills, by their nature, are linked to a well-defined set of stimuli (Anderson 1996). Self-efficacy and other aspects of self-knowledge are also typically described as being situation-specific (Cervone 2000), although personality studies suggest some generalization across contexts (Judge et al. 2002).

Similarly Matthews and Zeidner (2003) argue that the major personality traits correspond to styles of dynamic interaction that are linked to specific contexts. In other words, traits relate to (partly unconscious) choices of environmental specialization. Figure 6.8 illustrates an adaptive perspective on extraversion-introversion. The assumption is that extraverts are specifically adapted to the demands of "high-pressure" social environments, such as interacting with strangers. Information-processing routines such as good divided attention and fluent speech production support the learning of skills needed for social challenge (e.g., speed of verbal response). Performance skills are supported by congruent components of

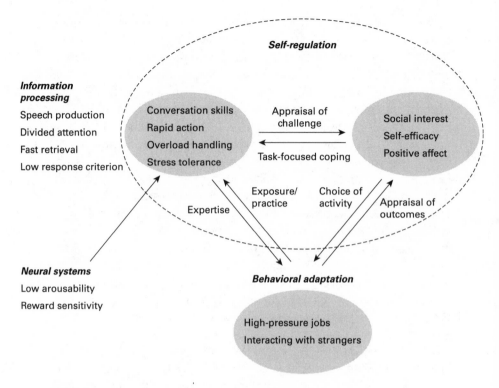

Figure 6.8
Styles of adaptive self-regulation supporting extraversion

self-knowledge, including social self-efficacy, interest and motivation, and positive emotional responses to social interaction. Social skills and self-confidence work together through generating constructive appraisals of social challenges, and adaptive, task-focused coping. Successful outcomes confirm positive self-beliefs, and motivate the extravert toward further exposures to social challenge, affording the opportunity for further enhancement of skill (practice makes perfect). Thus the extraverted individual may indeed be seen as more "emotionally intelligent," but in relation to a restricted set of social contexts.

By contrast, the introverted person lacks the social skills and self-efficacy to function effectively in challenging social settings. However, the evidence shows that there are other contexts in which introversion is adaptively neutral, or even beneficial. Introverts show no particular difficulties in dealing with close friends or life partners; indeed being patient rather than impulsive may be advantageous. Introverts also have an advantage in settings requiring sustained solitary effort and reflection. To the extent that EI involves self-reliance, good impulse control, and the ability to resist boredom and distraction, we might even say that introverts are more emotionally intelligent. The point here, of course, is that the label is not very informative: both extraverts and introverts have their particular social-emotional strengths and weaknesses, matching the social environments to which they are best suited. Bill Clinton, for example, was renowned as an effective and engaging political speaker, but displayed weaknesses in impulse control around women.

A similar perspective may be presented for agreeableness. The basic foundations of the trait are less well understood than those of extraversion, but as indicated above, agreeableness relates to specific skills for maintaining emotional engagement with others, coupled with self-knowledge that sustains supportive perceptions of others (Jensen-Campbell and Graziano 2001). A virtuous circle is likely to ensue: the high A person's positive statements about others and expressions of empathy will elicit more supportive behaviors from others, reinforcing the value of the social encounter.

Again though, the success of the interpersonal stance depends on the context. If other people are not in fact benign and aim to exploit the person concerned, high A will tend to increase vulnerability. As we saw before, low A individuals appear to be at an advantage in competitive situations. Yet again, the same individual may appear to be emotionally intelligent or unintelligent depending on the nature of the social challenge. Specializing for one kind of social environment carries costs of loss of adaptiveness to others.

Social Failures and Transgressions: EI or Personality?

Next we look briefly at social mistakes and misdemeanors. Are they a sign of some general lack of EI, or of more limited weaknesses linked to specific personality traits? We look briefly at exaggerated negative emotions, an issue that we return to in more depth in chapter 7. We will look too at the dispositional factors that relate to the various social failings linked to impulsivity and aggression.

Excessive Negative Emotionality   As noted previously, emotional instability (high N) is linked to a general tendency to experience negative emotions more frequently and more intensely. Negative emotions are not in themselves maladaptive, but in certain social contexts they may cause problems. Emotional individuals may respond to minor criticisms by flaring up or breaking off the conversation, responses that may impede future interaction with the other person concerned. Empirical studies have confirmed that high N persons are especially sensitive to interpersonal disagreements (Bolger 1990). Such sensitivities may be seen as a part of the general stress vulnerability linked to N. We will discuss dispositional stress vulnerability in more detail in chapter 7, but for now, we note that heightened awareness of social threats is not necessarily globally maladaptive. The high N person might have a jump start in detecting lack of sincerity or respect from others: again, the adaptive value of threat sensitivity depends on the actual level of threat in the social environment. In extreme cases, though, such tendencies are more clearly maladaptive, and may lead to social phobia, as discussed in chapter 11.

Aggression and Antisocial Behavior   Another type of social malfunction refers to more direct acts of aggression (or other behaviors) that are harmful to others. Several different sources of such behavior should be distinguished. Impulsive behaviors may have no aggressive component, as when an individual simply does something careless without due reflection. Recklessness appears to relate to failures to judge risk appropriately and to low conscientiousness (Gullone and Moore 2000). Aggression itself may either be reactive or proactive (Crick and Dodge 1996), although the two forms often occur together (Miller and Lynam 2006). *Reactive* aggression is an anger response to some perceived provocation that includes verbal or physical retaliation. Soccer fans may recall Zinedine Zidane's violent head-butt of an Italian player, who, allegedly, insulted his sister, during the 2006 World Cup. Lashing out at others in this way is linked most strongly to neuroticism (the anger is disproportionate) and also to low agreeableness (Caprara et al. 1996; Miller and Lynam 2006).

Proactive aggression refers to acts committed more cold-bloodedly in order to obtain some instrumental goal. A mafia boss and his henchman may commit acts of violence to support their illicit business, or a playground bully may profit from relieving other children of their lunch money. Aggression of this type is linked especially to low agreeableness but not to neuroticism (Caprara et al. 1996; Miller and Lynam 2006). In its more extreme forms it reflects personality disorders or abnormal traits including antisocial personality and psychopathy (see chapter 11).

We note briefly that antisocial dispositions are supported by cognitions and dynamic person–situation interaction similar to the prosocial traits described in the previous section (see Matthews, Zeidner, et al. 2002). Aggressive children show distortions in their perceptions of others, seeing them as being more hostile than they actually are, coupled with fast retrieval of aggressive solutions to "solving" social problems (Lochman and Dodge 1994). Dynamically, dealing with interpersonal difficulties by aggression operates as a self-fulfilling prophecy that reinforces dysfunctional cognitions: aggressive behaviors evoke actual hostility and deterioration of relationships. Reckless impulsivity may relate to biases in information processing, such as poor inhibition of dominant responses and misperception of risk (see Matthews, Zeidner, et al. 2002). There may also be social-cognitive elements, for example, relating to the person's willingness to violate social norms for orderly behavior.

Doing dumb things, lashing out in anger, and preying on others are all behaviors that are undesirable, no two ways about it. But are they really emotionally unintelligent? If so, can they be attributed to a single, unitary EI or to multiple, independent competencies? Reckless impulsivity (linked to EI as a deficit in self-control) appears to be primarily cognitive rather than emotional in nature, although oversensitivity to rewards signals likely plays a part. Impulsivity is not entirely maladaptive, however. Indeed it may bring benefits in terms of opportunistic gains, impressing others by bold actions, and freedom from the time costs of more conscientious behaviors such as prolonged study (Matthews, Zeidner, et al. 2002). The cognitive disinhibition that is implicated in impulsivity may also contribute to imaginative, unusual thoughts that support creativity. Supporting this proposition, creative artists tend to be impulsive, disorganized, and rebellious (Eysenck 1995).

Proactive aggression entails too personal gains to the extent that the aggressor is successful in using violence for their own ends. Björkqvist et al. (2000) showed that social intelligence relates to both (indirect) aggression and to peaceful conflict resolution. Their study suggests that socially intelligent persons may use a variety of strategies, including aggression, for dealing with conflict situations. By contrast, more empathic individuals use less direct and indirect aggression but make more use of conflict resolution, compared with those low in empathy. Below we discuss Machiavellianism, as a form of antisocial EI, where the person uses their social skills to manipulate others for personal profit. For example, in professional sports, it is not unknown for players to needle an emotionally vulnerable opponent in the hope of provoking an emotional response that will cause the perpetrator to be dismissed from the field or court.

Thus we can only define EI as nonviolent to the extent that we place empathy (and other facets of agreeableness) at its core or if we conceive EI as necessarily infused with moral values. There is, of course, a conflict here between the interests of the individual (which may be served by "intelligent" aggression) and the interests of the community (which often are not). Reactive aggression appears more clearly maladaptive, in creating hostile patterns of interaction with others, which are likely to be damaging to the person concerned. We noted previously that neuroticism, although it may be adaptive in terms of elevated awareness of real dangers, tends to disrupt personal relationships.

EI, Personality, and Social Adaptation   Earlier in this chapter we set out a case showing that EI is broadly adaptive for handling social encounters. It is not hard to see how the person may benefit from empathic understanding of others, skills in conversation and negotiation, and constructive expression of personal emotions. However, our analysis of personality factors points toward some challenges for identifying EI as the key to productive social relationships. Standard personality traits are robustly predictive of a variety of social criteria, and social dispositions are central to some traits, notably extraversion and agreeableness. Studies using questionnaire measures of EI may simply be picking up these personality effects. In such instances it is unclear what EI predicts once personality effects are controlled.

We have seen too that studies showing that personality traits or EI predict some measure of social competence may be misleading, since the individual's competence in one area may be balanced by lack of competence in others. The theoretical account of personality that we have outlined suggests that the specialized social skills needed for success in one social domain, such as business, may prove unhelpful, or even counterproductive in others. Likewise undesirable, antisocial behaviors are not necessarily emotionally unintelligent (to the extent they support the individual's personal ambitions). The more extreme forms of impulsivity and aggression are generally maladaptive, but we have seen that there are qualitatively different patterns of antisocial behavior that need to be distinguished from one other. Next, we will develop the argument that emotional dispositions tend to carry both benefits and costs by exploring "the dark side" of EI.

The Darker Shades of Emotional Intelligence

By and large, researchers and practitioners alike have focused on the positive features and merits of EI, touting its adaptive value for both the individual and group in social situations. While the social benefits of emotional competencies are readily apparent, as amply evidenced in this chapter, researchers have generally ignored the potential costs and practical complications in applying EI in real life social situations. In the section that follows, we reflect on the darker side of EI and especially the circumstances under which core attributes of EI may be maladaptive.

Foreclosure on Emotional Disclosure

Emotion disclosure and expression has been associated with positive physical and psychological outcomes (Pennebaker et al. 1988). Thus relative to those who repress their emotions, persons who express their painful or traumatic emotions—to providers of professional or social support, or in writing—were reported to gain psychologically from emotional disclosure and suffer from fewer somatic symptoms. However, some recent studies have questioned this assumption (see Bonanno 2004). These studies suggest that greater disclosure of negative emotions may increase rumination, negative affect, and depression, prolonging negative affects (Nolen-Hoeksema 2001). Moreover, when people are working through past experiences, this perspective is likely to direct people to focus selectively on concrete features of their experience and lead them to relive experiences, serving to increase negative arousal (McIssac and Eich 2004). In turn this strategy makes cognitive analysis of one's emotions difficult. In brief, emotion self-awareness and disclosure can turn out to be a double-edged sword.

The Costs of Psychological Mindedness

A number of clinical researchers have recently raised the possibility that persons who are psychologically minded and have richer emotional competencies as personal resources may be wiser and more emotionally competent. At the same time these individuals may feel less happy and less satisfied emotionally. Accordingly psychologically minded individuals who constantly appraise-reappraise their situation often feel disappointed with the seeming superficiality of others in their surroundings and often experience unrequited social insight. These psychologically minded people may be less able to allow people and things to pass them by in a relatively smooth and uncomplicated manner, thus experiencing negative affect, loneliness, and depression (Vachon and Bagby 2007).

There is in fact some evidence to suggest that emotion perception and understanding are related to higher levels of depression, hopelessness, and suicidal ideation, as well as lower self-esteem (Vachon and Bagby 2007). Apparently, excessive attention to one's emotion can be directly related to stress. Presumably too much attention to emotion leads to rumination, increasing the feeling of being besieged by life events.

Compassion Fatigue

The ability to both empathize and view the world from the perspective of others is typically viewed as a positive characteristic of individuals high in emotional intelligence. Indeed empathic ability is a critical construct in the therapeutic process. It is commonly held that clients often get better during psychotherapy because therapists empathize with their condition, feel their pain and suffering, and are emotionally "there for them" (Sabin-Farrell and Turpin 2003).

Ironically it is precisely this empathic ability and concern that makes mental health workers especially vulnerable to experiencing the traumatic feelings of the sufferer, plausibly through the mechanism of emotional contagion. Empathic behaviors may extract a serious cost and be harmful to one's well-being and health, often leading to a sense of distress, helpfulness, and isolation. This secondary trauma, referring to the stress resulting from helping a traumatized person (Figley 1995), has been variously termed "compassion fatigue," "vicarious traumatization," or "secondary traumatic stress." Although robust empirical evidence for compassion fatigue is scant, individual case studies do provide clinical support for this phenomenon. As aptly phrased by Figley (1995): "There is a cost to caring. Professionals who listen to clients' stories of fear, pain, and suffering may feel similar fear, pain, and suffering because they care" (p. 1).

Eavesdropping and Negative Emotional Leakage

The ability to decode subtle emotional cues in gauging the internal state of others, although generally viewed as a key facet of EI and of benefit in social interactions, can also be a mixed blessing. Whereas the recognition of positive emotional states may lead to positive outcomes, the recognition of negative emotional states may have deleterious effects. Thus people generally find it uncomfortable to express negativity in a verbal and direct manner, with negative feelings and feedback more likely communicated through indirect means (e.g., "leaky" nonverbal channels or by voice intonation). It may be assumed that high EI individuals can more easily eavesdrop on the negative emotions of others. In turn, this may prove harmful because it allows one to understand precisely the type of information (e.g., envy) that others are reluctant to express (Elfenbein and Ambady 2002).

Blissful Emotional Ignorance

Contrary to the commonly held positive value of elevated emotion perception, several studies have found that low emotion perception may sometimes be good for one's psychological health and well-being, at least in the short term. Ciarrochi et al. (2002), for example, reported that individuals high in emotion perception reported more depression, hopelessness, and suicidal ideation (relative to counterparts low in emotion perception). The authors suggest that people who are poor at perceiving their emotions might actually be *less* sensitive to the effects of stress, possibly because they repress what they feel or may not actually realize they are being affected adversely.

Another study by Simpson et al. (1995) demonstrated that dating couples can be motivated to inaccurately perceive each other's thoughts and feelings; this "working misunderstanding" may actually protect the couple from stress. Similarly research has shown that the tendency to not think about thoughts and feelings (i.e., low psychological mindedness) is associated with lower anxiety, depression, and paranoia (e.g., McCallum and Piper 2000).

Disutility of EI in Organizational Settings

As shown in the sidebar, EI may not be adaptive across all possible forms of social and organizational interaction; the particular value of an emotional skill may vary with social setting. Before applying EI to various social and organizational contexts, an essential step is to precisely identify the specific contexts, needs, and purposes for which emotional skills are being applied. For example, in occupational settings, disparate occupations may require different types of interpersonal interaction. In some jobs (e.g., social work) one interacts emotionally with others during most of their time on the job. Inside such professions there is a real need to have frequent interchanges with clients at an emotional level and high EI skills are expected to be functional here. However, in other jobs (e.g., systems analyst) one interacts with people a smaller percentage of the time. The need to be able to recognize and manipulate others' feelings is relatively unimportant, and being too socially conscious and expressive (e.g., spending too much time socializing with others in the office corridors)

Where more emotional sensitivity may be less

• A leasing agent in a large San Diego residential complex who, out of compassion, agrees to waver the $50 fee for late payment of rent for financially hard-pressed residents. In doing so, the agent may be violating company policy and may risk being censured by management.

• An oncologist who is so emotionally involved with her patients that she spends much of time with patients in psychological ventilation and providing emotional support rather than in medical treatment. The oncologist may be harming rather than helping, the patient.

• An assembly line supervisor who is overly empathic to his subordinates' needs and wants may not feel comfortable in exercising authority and fails to lean on subordinates hard enough to get the job done in time. The supervisor may fall behind in his production schedule and not meet company production quotas, thus risking his own job.

---

may, in certain instances, interfere with job productivity. Prefacing what we have to say in chapter 9, the advantages of EI at work may depend on the emotional demands of the job (Wong and Law 2002).

Negative Side of Positive Self-Esteem

EI has frequently been related to social cognitive beliefs of positive self-concept and self-esteem, but such beliefs are not necessarily adaptive. Thus researchers have identified a "dark side" of self-esteem, including excessive self-enhancement, narcissism, and the denial of personal or social problems (Baumeister et al. 1996). These features, particularly, narcissism and trait self-enhancement, relate not only to self-esteem but also to relationship difficulties (e.g., Campbell et al. 2000).

Furthermore self-esteem has been found to be a driver of interpersonal aggression (Baumeister et al. 1996), with children higher in self-esteem also being higher on aggressiveness. Ironically classroom bullies are shown to have higher, rather than lower, self-esteem. Aggression is also frequently observed to be related to classroom popularity. It has even been suggested that aggression is little else than social intelligence devoid of empathy (Björkvist et al. 2000).

Bullies may manipulate others through various techniques, including emotion-laden strategies, for their own ends (Sutton and Keogh 2000). Contrary to conventional wisdom, bullies tend to hold positive self-perceptions (David and Kirstner 2000). Moreover adolescents with sociopathic tendencies are often able to regulate the emotions of others to their own benefit; should they be considered emotionally intelligent?

Machiavellianism

It is better to be feared than loved—if you can't be both.
—Niccolo Machiavelli

Clearly, the acquisition of emotional skills, such as regulation of emotion in others, does not ensure socially or emotionally intelligent behavior. As noted by Kristja'nsson (2006): "the sobering fact remains that Goleman's conception of EI fails to make any substantive moral demands on the content of intelligent emotions" (p. 53). Indeed one can use EI skills not only to help others but to manipulate others for personal ends—as is the case in Machiavellian individuals. Perhaps closer to home, business managers and leaders, who control major organizational information and resources, are often in the position to manipulate members of the organization toward their self-serving goals. These individuals may alter their followers' internal motivation and harness it manipulatively to achieve their own self-serving and often undesirable aims (Bass 1996). Or as blithely stated by Waterhouse (2006): "nothing in any EI construct precludes someone with high EI from being an immoral person" (p. 253).

Concluding Comments

Research on EI offers promise for better understanding of why relationships may flourish or prove disappointing. The core functions of EI are critical for the outcomes of interactions with others. These functions include effective processing of emotions, managing problematic emotions, and the expression, sharing, and communication of emotions. To a considerable extent EI appears to overlap with earlier notions of social intelligence (see chapter 1). A successful social psychology of EI would have much to contribute to practical issues such as remediation of social anxiety and stress, marriage counseling, greater work effectiveness, and treating various forms of deviance including violence and substance abuse. We have seen too that empirical studies confirm that both self-report and objective tests of EI predict a range of outcome variables that may reflect social competence. However, we should caution that effect sizes are often modest in magnitude, and outcome variables are often questionnaire measures rather than objective indexes. So the impact of EI on real-life social functioning remains uncertain.

As in other domains, much remains to be done before good understanding can be reached. There is extensive evidence that the personality traits included in the five factor model predict the same social criteria that are hypothesized to relate to EI. It is unclear how much existing EI measures can add to personality in predicting these criteria. Researchers need to identify specific niches within this large research area in which EI is clearly more important than personality (and conventional IQ). Beyond problems of overlap with other constructs, whether some people are generally better socially adapted than others remains problematic. Analysis of personality data suggests that strengths in one area of social functioning are often balanced by weaknesses in others. Indeed there is a "dark side" to EI, including overly high self-esteem, awareness and expression of negative emotion, empathic identification with others, and selfish emotional manipulation.

In sum, EI may be too broad and ill-defined a concept to capture the adaptive trade-offs involved. Someone that is highly empathic and sensitive will likely show a different pattern of strengths and weaknesses than someone who is an assured manipulator of other people. We may need a more definitive account of the different facets of EI in order to better comprehend the personal dispositional factors that contribute to social successes and failures. Finally, both personality and social-psychological research also highlight the importance of situational factors in generating dynamic interactions among people that are critical for adaptive processes. Current models of EI require considerable work and reformulation before they can capture these dynamic processes.

Summary Points: Chapter 6

• Contemporary research suggests a pivotal role for emotions in social life, and so has fueled interest in theory, research, and applications of EI. Social encounters frequently evoke strong emotions, and these emotions often influence the course of the social interactions and inform much of what we do.

• Emotions serve as affective barometers, providing us with critical information about the nature and meaning of the social environment that may be useful for understanding how to interact successfully with others. Emotions serve a number of important adaptive functions in social life; for example, signaling socially relevant information and facilitating social support.

• It has been claimed that EI is adaptive for handling social encounters, with high EI persons benefiting from empathic understanding of others and adaptive skills in constructive communication of context-appropriate emotions. Further EI has been implicated in a wide array of adaptive social outcomes. These include: satisfaction with life and social relationships, higher self-esteem and well-being, harmonious close personal relationships, empathic perspective taking, receipt and provision of social support, greater self-control in social situations, and diverse health outcomes.

• Some researchers have ignored the costs and practical complications in applying EI in real-life social situations, generally failing to address the "darker side." In and of itself EI is not infused with moral values, but it may be misused for personal gain and personal self-serving ends. Further emotional disclosure and excessive expressivity of emotions following trauma may lead the person to relive traumatic experiences, and thus exacerbate negative arousal and affectivity. High EI individuals may also show exaggerated sensitivity to the demands of stressful environment, as well as excessive empathy in personal and clinical interactions, resulting in "compassion fatigue."

• Certain methodological problems may be found in the literature examining associations between EI and adaptive social outcomes. First, the associations reported show modest correlations. Second, many popular measures of EI may simply be confounded with personality or ability. Thus it is presently unclear to what degree EI predicts adaptive social behavior with relevant individual difference variables statistically controlled. Third, there is little direct evidence of the unique value of EI in social settings, with much of the findings based on self-report measures of social functioning rather than objective indicators. Finally, social skills are context-specific, so it is difficult to identify a globally functional or dysfunctional style of interaction with the social world.

7   Grace under Pressure? Emotional Intelligence, Stress, and Coping

How a man rallies to life's challenges and weathers its storms tells us everything of who he is and all that he is likely to become.
—St. Augustine

In contrast to daily routine stressors, disasters like that which occurred during 9/11, the floods of New Orleans, and the 2004 Indian Ocean Earthquake are outside the typical range of human experiences, and are usually met by everyone in the community with intense fear, terror, or helplessness. Thousands of people were seriously injured or met their death during each event, whereas others emerged unscathed, though in a state of shock and disbelief after being exposed to horrific events. Traumas such as these tax our need to think the world is predictable and basically just (Van der Kolk and McFarlane 1996). The ubiquity of the emotional responses manifested by individuals faced with psychological trauma has recently been recognized in the clinical syndrome known as posttraumatic stress disorder (PTSD). This diagnostic category gathered together a seemingly disparate group of clinical phenomena, including hypervigilance, flashbacks to traumatic event, and nightmares to name a select few (Freedy and Donkervoet 1995).

Even so, the prevalence of those with symptom criteria for PTSD after such events is often modest. Despite substantial distress after 9/11, for example, most people reported adapting to the situation without substantial mental health symptoms (Galea et al. 2002). Thus, whereas a significant percentage of primary victims of *traumatic* events develop posttraumatic symptoms, the majority do not. In view of the substantial individual differences observed in negotiating stressful events and coping with disaster questions arise: Can emotional intelligence play a meaningful role in how people cope with and react to stress, both in the short and long term? Can emotional intelligence (EI) help buffer against stress reactions, supporting more adaptive coping and more positive outcomes? Such questions relate to exposure to grave events, such as those experienced during 9/11, as well as routine stressors and hassles, and normative life events. For example, Graves et al. (2005) found that, among people who chose to write about the events of 9/11, high scorers on the Salovey et al. (1995) trait meta-mood scale (TMMS) tended to use more emotional language. The authors suggest that this form of emotional expression may have helped the writers to cope with the stress of the event (Pennebaker 1997). More generally, does emotional intelligence play a pivotal role in coping and adaptive outcomes? We examine this important issue in the chapter that follows.

It is readily apparent that successful coping depends on the integrated operation of rational as well as emotional competencies (Salovey et al. 2000). Accordingly the different constructs referred to as "emotional intelligence" throughout this book, may contribute to the successful regulation of emotion and coping. Researchers have posited that effective coping with the demands, pressures, and conflicts evident at work, in educational contexts, and in social life, is central to the EI construct (Bar-On and Parker 2000). Indeed the scientific merit of emotional intelligence plausibly rests in demonstrating that it is a coherent quality of the person that underpins adaptive coping.

In the chapter that follows we examine current thinking and research investigating the role that EI might play in the coping process. A brief description of key conceptualizations of coping is followed by a discussion of the proposed pattern of relations found between coping and emotional intelligence, with an emphasis on a number of mediating variables in the emotional intelligence–coping relationship. We then briefly summarize the state of recent empirical research and conclude with a critical analysis of the EI–coping interface.

What Is This Thing Called Coping?

Whether 'tis nobler in the mind to suffer the slings and arrows of outrageous fortune or to take arms against a sea of troubles and by opposing end them?
—William Shakespeare

Stressful events, running the gamut from daily hassles to communitywide disasters, are environmental demands, pressures, or constraints that challenge one's coping capabilities. Broadly speaking, coping involves a person's efforts to manage the demands of a person–environment transaction that is appraised as stressful (e.g., Folkman 1991). These constantly changing efforts can be cognitive or behavioral, direct and indirect. Accordingly, when the demands of a potentially stressful situation (e.g., presenting an important proposal before the company's CEO) are perceived as stressful, efforts are directed at regulating emotional stress and/or dealing with the problem at hand in order to manage the troubled person-environment transaction (e.g., see Lazarus 1990).

Although a wide array of taxonomies of coping strategies are currently available, researchers appear to have converged on the following three categories:

1. *Problem-focused coping*   The individual solves the problem by removing or circumventing the stressor (e.g., carefully planning for a major presentation before the company's board).

2. *Emotion-focused coping*   The person regulates, reduces, channels, or eliminates aversive emotions associated with the stressful encounter (e.g., seeking emotional support from friends).

3. *Avoidance coping*   The individual employs strategies that are designed to circumvent or avoid the stressful situation via the use of person-oriented (e.g., seeking of others) or task-oriented strategies (e.g., watching TV).

These three pivotal forms of coping are graphically depicted in figure 7.1.

Figure 7.1
Three forms of coping: problem-solving, emotion-focused, and avoidance

Because problem-focused coping is expected to alter the actual terms of the individual's stressful relationship with the environment, more favorable cognitive appraisals and a more positive response to the stressful situation (in most situations over which the person has control) should come as a result. By contrast, emotion-focused and avoidance coping may be viewed as an effort to avoid the stressor. Problem-focused coping tends to predominate when people believe that something constructive can be done about the situation. Emotion-focused coping, by contrast, tends to predominate when people believe that the stress is something that must be endured (Lazarus and Folkman 1984). Emotion-focused and avoidant coping, however, might be adaptive under conditions of minimal environmental control (Zeidner and Saklofske 1996). Exactly why this might be the case is taken up in the passages that follow, where we define the concept of adaptive coping.

Adaptive Coping

Adaptive or functional coping behavior is seen as a "buffer" that absorbs the impact of stressful events. It in turn protects the individual from the immediate, damaging effects of stress (e.g., physiological disturbance). It also maximizes the chances of "rising to the challenge" and making the most of any opportunities for personal gain that the situation affords. Conversely, maladaptive coping involves failure to resolve the situation successfully, and may even exacerbate the problems that the individual is experiencing. The transactional model of stress and coping (Lazarus 1991; Lazarus and Folkman 1984) offers several basic working assumptions impacting on conceptualizations of adaptive coping:

1. Coping strategies should not be prejudged as adaptive or maladaptive. Rather, the concern must be *for whom* and *under what circumstances* a particular coping mode has adaptive consequences.

2. Coping effectiveness must be demonstrated empirically against some criterion for a successful outcome of the encounter (see Zeidner and Saklofske 1996).

3. Coping is a process embedded in context. Thus responses vary across contexts, change over time in response to external conditions, and alter as a function of the skill with which it is applied. For example, coping strategies found to be effective in the context of disputes at work might not be adaptive in the context of family disputes.

4. Coping efforts should not be confounded with coping outcomes (Lennon et al. 1990).

Emotional Intelligence and Coping

When angry, count four. When very angry, swear.
—Mark Twain

It's what happens before you count to five which makes life interesting.
—David Hare

What are the specific mechanisms through which emotional intelligence might help in coping with stress? To begin with, researchers have claimed that EI may help one circumvent or avoid stressful encounters. Plausibly, emotionally intelligent individuals have less stress because they conduct their personal affairs in environments that produce fewer frustrating events. These individuals may be adept at identifying, and then avoiding, potentially dangerous social contexts (Epstein 1998). There is presently, however, little empirical evidence supporting this claim. Indeed, contrary to this hypothesis, adaptive success may require engaging with, and successfully managing, aversive situations. For example, studies of social anxiety suggest that avoidance of stressful circumstances undermines self-confidence and hinders the acquisition of social skills (Wells 2000).

Rather than avoiding stressful encounters, the person high in EI may learn more quickly in social and emotional situations relative to others. Similar to learning differences between people on aptitude tests, emotionally intelligent individuals might make coping "mistakes" less often until an adaptive style is learned. By contrast, individuals low in EI might try the same maladaptive coping strategy (like rumination) over and over again.

Another viable explanation for relations between EI and coping with stress is that emotionally intelligent individuals may have more constructive thought patterns. On the one hand, low EI individuals may tend to ruminate unproductively about their problems. On the other hand, high EI individuals may more faithfully observe the procession of their thoughts, and their impact on emotion. As a result these individuals may find it easier to identify faulty appraisal and to correct maladaptive construal (Epstein 1998). Individuals who make sense out of their feelings have also been shown to have greater rebound from induced negative mood and reduced rumination (Salovey, Stroud, et al. 2002).

Yet another explanation for relations between EI and coping with stress is related to the regulation and repair of negative emotions. Those skilled at regulating emotions appear better able to repair negative emotional states (e.g., engaging in pleasant activities as a distraction from negative affect). Further, high EI individuals are thought not to be overly sensitive to disapproval and to worry less about things that are beyond their control. Another key emotional skill may be effective disclosure of past personal traumas. For example, Pennebaker (1997) has shown that the simple act of disclosing emotional experience (through writing) improves a person's physical (e.g., improved immune function) and mental health (e.g., absence of depressive symptoms). The disclosure process appears to restructure emotionally disturbing experiences, giving these experiences a coherent and meaningful place in the person's life.

Emotionally intelligent individuals may also have richer emotional and social coping resources compared to their less emotionally intelligent counterparts (Epstein 1998). EI has thus been hypothesized to work through social support, equipping the individual with the necessary skills and social connections required to build an extensive and supportive social network (Salovey et al. 1999). In times of need, emotionally intelligent individuals are better able to rely on these networks to provide an emotional buffer against negative events (Salovey et al. 2000).

Finally, it has been claimed that individuals with high EI may engage in active coping during stressful situations (e.g., Epstein 1998). EI has been associated with the competencies to clearly perceive, differentiate, and repair one's own emotions. By this line of reasoning, people high in EI perceive their feelings clearly in a stressful situation and believe they are capable of managing their emotions. In short, "a time-honored principle of effective coping is to know when to appraise a situation as uncontrollable and hence abandon efforts directed at altering the situation and turn to emotion-focused processes in order to tolerate or accept the situation" (Folkman 1984, p. 849).

Figure 7.2 presents a number of possible key mediating factors in the emotional intelligence–coping relationship. It is evident from this figure and the accompanying passages that the scope of individual differences in coping linked to emotional intelligence is very broad indeed. Some of the mediating mechanisms (e.g., adaptive regulation) refer directly to coping with emotion. Other mechanisms, such as managing exposure to stressors, are more likely to influence emotion indirectly, depending on the outcome of the encounter. However, it is unclear which of these various mechanisms should be related to EI, personality, and/or ability factors. Given this uncertainty, the place of EI in the nomological network connecting different stress-related constructs remains uncertain. Further, evidence for the importance of personal resources in mediating the EI-coping interface is sparse and in need of empirical instantiation.

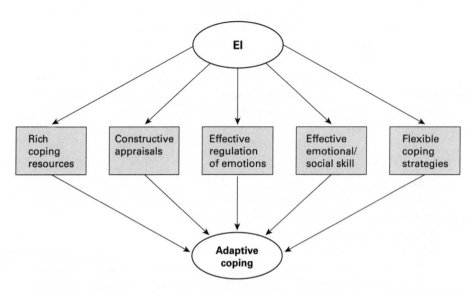

Figure 7.2
Hypothesized factors mediating the emotional intelligence-coping relationship

Do Emotionally Intelligent Individuals Cope Better with Stress?

Research devoted to uncovering relations between EI and effective coping strategies has generally touched on two related issues. The first, rather simple, issue has involved determining how EI measures correlate with established coping scales, for example, the choice of coping strategy. The second, more subtle, issue has involved ascertaining whether coping mediates associations between EI and well-being.

Two research strategies have been used in testing whether EI relates to choice of coping strategy. The first is to relate EI to the person's general style of coping. There are various questionnaires that seek to assess the broad classes of strategy that people use, such as the problem-focused, task-focused, and emotion-focused strategies previously described. In addition to studying these general preferences, the coping strategies used to manage some specific event may be investigated. For example, we might ask Thai people how they coped with the trauma of the 2004 Indian Ocean Earthquake. This approach may bring us closer to the person's actual coping, in context, than does assessing general coping style (see Zeidner et al. 2006).

Several studies have correlated measures of EI with scales for coping style. These cross-sectional studies suggest associations between EI and various aspects of coping (Zeidner et al. 2006). Two such studies found that questionnaires for EI related to more use of rational coping, and less use of emotion-focused coping (Petrides et al. 2007; Saklofske et al. 2007). Goldenberg et al. (2006) reported that the Schutte et al. (1998) EI scale correlated with three coping factors, which they labeled as (1) problem-focus, (2) cognitive reappraisal and restraint, and (3) seeking social support and expressing emotion. Studies conducted by the present authors (Zeidner et al., in preparation) also link EI to a preference for problem-focus over emotion-focused strategies. Fewer studies have attempted to link objective tests of EI to coping, although Goldenberg et al. (2006) found that correlations between the MSCEIT and their coping scales barely exceeded chance levels. Similarly Burns et al. (2007) found that once personality and ability were controlled, the MSCEIT was unrelated to coping style. Their study confirmed that the TMMS relates to higher levels of active (e.g., problem-focused) coping.

A second research strategy is to assess coping with a specific challenge. Salovey et al. (2002) had their participants perform difficult cognitive tasks, under high time pressure, and assessed their coping. Most of the correlations between the TMMS and situational coping were nonsignificant. However, the study did show that the mood repair scale related to appraising the tasks as less threatening, and to reduced usage of "passive coping" (e.g., denial). Interestingly the series of studies reported by Salovey et al. (2002) suggested an association between the TMSS scales and reduced secretion of cortisol, a hormone that may index stress response. Also a recent study by Ramos et al. (2007) examined the effects of EI on emotional distress in a sample of 144 adult women exposed to a stressful video showing scenes of sexual assault. These researchers found that the clarity and repair subscales of the trait meta-mood scale were related to less negative emotional responses and intrusive thoughts. Thus higher emotional clarity and repair may lead to less personal distress, which enables individuals to adapt to stressful encounters.

A recent study (Fellner et al. 2007) tested for various questionnaire scales as predictors of coping during performance of tasks requiring facial emotion processing. High EI should be adaptive in this context. Trait Emotional Intelligence Questionnaire (TEIQue) scales correlated in the range −0.20 to −0.30 with situational avoidance and emotion-focused coping, but with the Big Five controlled, no significant correlations were found. Similar results were obtained with the TMMS.

Only one study thus far seems to have employed an objective measure (i.e., the MSCEIT) rather than questionnaires to ascertain whether EI predicted coping with task stressors (Matthews, Emo, Funke, et al. 2006).

In this study three elements of stress response—task engagement, distress, and worry—were measured using the Dundee Stress State Questionnaire (Matthews, Campbell, et al. 2002). EI was associated modestly with lower distress and worry, and with reduced use of emotion-focused and avoidance coping, strategies likely to be maladaptive in the performance context. With the Big Five controlled, EI related to less worry and avoidance coping, providing some support for the MSCEIT as a predictor of stress processes.

The EI and Coping Interface: Unresolved Issues

Empirical data considering how EI relates to coping leave many issues unresolved. One issue is the extent to which findings are simply a consequence of the well-known confounding of EI scales with personality. Biases toward positively framed coping strategies, and away from negatively framed strategies, are exactly what might be expected on the basis of the overlap between EI and (1) high extraversion and (2) low neuroticism (see chapter 4). Although some studies have neglected to control for personality, others have showed associations between EI and coping that remain significant with personality traits controlled (e.g., Gohm and Clore 2002). A second issue is that both EI and coping scales may actually reflect stress outcomes. Petrides et al. (2007) EI scale includes items for general mood, and the example item they give for their emotion-focused coping scale (i.e., "feel worthless and unimportant") seems more like a symptom of maladaptive coping rather than a strategy that someone would choose to manage emotion. If both EI and coping scales are picking up moods and stress symptoms, it is not surprising that the two measures correlate, but the data tell us little about the coping process.

A third issue is that EI appears to be a considerably more robust predictor of general style of coping than of measures of actual coping in a specific situation. In line with the previous comment, EI scales may simply pick up generic attitudes about self-efficacy and coping, which are not necessarily indicative of a person's choice of strategy for dealing with specific stressors. It is possible, though, that the weakness of EI as a predictor reflects the task challenges used to induce situational stress. Perhaps EI would relate more strongly to coping with social stressors.

A fourth issue is that EI, rather ironically, relates to using rational task-focused coping in preference to emotion-focused strategies (e.g., Saklofske et al. 2007). The problem-focus of high EI persons appear to be at variance with these individuals being more in touch with their emotions, and better able to manage emotion. One study using the TMMS

(Gohm and Clore 2002a) obtained results more consistent with definitions of EI in showing that the TMMS scales related to strategies such as seeking emotional social support. Even here the clarity scale of the TMSS, however, related to active, planned coping.

Across these various types of study, research appears to converge in pointing to a positive association between EI and problem-focused strategies and a negative association between EI and emotion-focused (and avoidance) strategies. It is tempting to conclude that EI simply relates to greater use of more positively toned strategies and less use of strategies that focus on negative aspects of challenge. However, research has yet to establish that general EI plays some unique role in the coping process. Research using more narrowly focused mood-regulation questionnaires such as the TMMS appear promising, especially as (1) these measures may be less confounded with personality than extant EI questionnaires (Gohm and Clore 2002a), and (2) Salovey et al.'s (2002) study showed evidence for meaningful psychophysiological correlates. Objective tests for EI appear to be more modest predictors of both coping and well-being/ stress outcomes; even so, the MSCEIT has some modest incremental validity with respect to personality and ability (e.g., Matthews, Emo, Funke, et al. 2006).

Mechanisms Linking EI to Coping and Stress Outcomes

Unfortunately, the mechanisms linking EI constructs to coping and stress outcomes remain obscure. For example, our recent studies with the MSCEIT have failed to show that EI moderates stress response as expected (Matthews, Emo, Funke, et al. 2006). A promising mediating mechanism is coping through seeking emotional social support, which has been implicated both in the effects of self-reported (Goldenberg et al. 2006) and performance-based EI (Zeidner et al., in preparation). However, it is important to differentiate *availability* of social support from *coping* by seeking support. As discussed in chapter 6, various studies show that EI relates to perceptions of the size and quality of social networks (e.g., Lopes et al. 2003). Thus availability of social support may be a product of superior social skills rather than a process linked to coping. The emotionally intelligent person may simply make friends more easily, regardless of stress. Some evidence in favor of mediation by coping comes from studies by Ciarrochi, Wilson, et al. (2003), who showed that troubled adolescents are less likely to seek help if they are low in emotional competencies, even when social support is potentially available.

Studies that have investigated EI, coping, and mood-regulation within specific contexts (e.g., Matthews, Emo, Funke, et al. 2006) should be better-suited than studies using global coping measures for identifying mediating mechanisms, but this promise has yet to be fully realized. The personality and situational factors that moderate the impact of EI on coping remain relatively obscure. It has also yet to be established that the coping styles characteristic of high scorers on tests for EI actually confer any direct benefits in terms of well-being, behavioral adaptation, or health.

Emotional Intelligence, Personality, and Stress Vulnerability

A pivotal issue, so far not well understood, is whether EI relates to *vulner-ability* toward stress. That is, do stressful events bring out differences in coping and adaptation between the emotionally intelligent and unintelligent? Cross-sectional studies correlating measures of EI with questionnaires for stress and coping tell us nothing about vulnerability. The issue awaits further research, but we cannot leave the topic without discussing the well-established role of personality factors, and especially neuroticism (N), in stress vulnerability.

By contrast with research on EI, there is solid evidence from longitudinal studies that N predicts vulnerability to future stress outcomes (see Matthews et al. 2003). Intriguingly, as shown in figure 7.3, there are at least two paths to vulnerability revealed by longitudinal studies of emotional responses to life events (e.g., Ormel and Wohlfarth 1991). More neurotic individuals react to events with elevated, possibly excessive negative affect. In addition N predicts future adverse events; it seems that

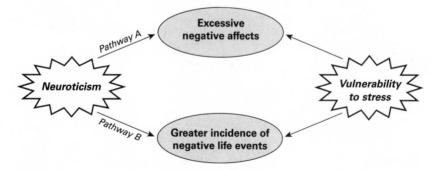

Figure 7.3
Mediating mechanisms of neuroticism and vulnerability

behaviors typical of the trait such as interpersonal arguments increase the likelihood of high N persons experiencing life events. To some degree these individuals bring stress on themselves. More fine-grained investigations demonstrate several mediating processes that contribute to stress vulnerability. These processes are discussed in the passages that follow.

Bias in Information-Processing   Neuroticism relates to negative biases in information-processing that tend to increase salience of threat. Typically studies have investigated trait anxiety, which is highly correlated with N (or clinical anxiety, as further discussed in chapter 11). Thus anxious individuals tend to divert their attention toward sources of threat, to infer that ambiguous stimuli and situations are threatening, and to be preoccupied by themes of danger and personal vulnerability (Mathews 2004). Biases in the component processes supporting attention can be demonstrated using objective data from performance tasks such as the emotional Stroop test (Matthews and Wells 2000). Studies report bias even when threat stimuli are presented subliminally (Mathews 2004), indicating that bias is in part unconscious. The increased worry of high N participants when completing cognitive tasks is depicted in figure 7.4.

Bias in Cognitive Content   Highly neurotic individuals typically report a variety of negative beliefs about themselves and their place in the world. They tend to overestimate the severity of threats and to underrate their own capacity to cope (Matthews, Derryberry, and Siegle 2000). Bias in the content of cognition is often explained by schema theory. Beck (e.g.,

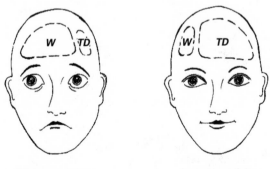

High neuroticism   Low neuroticism

Figure 7.4
Information processing in high and low neuroticism individuals (W = worry, TD = task-directed processing)

Clark et al. 1999) proposed that the person's core self-beliefs are organized as a schema in long-term memory. A depressed person's schema typically represents irrational beliefs that the person is worthless and their future is hopeless, whereas anxiety relates to beliefs in personal vulnerability to threats. The schema may also encode specific fears such as phobias or traumatic events. For example, following 9/11, a vulnerable individual might develop a schema encoding beliefs that a further terrorist attack in New York was highly likely, generating unrealistic apprehensions. Negative self-schemas in turn relate to biases in appraisal and coping. Neuroticism is linked to elevated threat appraisal and—resembling the EI research reviewed above—to a greater use of self-critical emotion-focused strategies, and less use of problem-focused coping (Endler and Parker 1990). Table 7.1 presents a number of possible

Table 7.1
Neuroticism (anxiety) and facets of attention

A. *Content*   High N individuals are hypothesized to exhibit selective attentional bias favoring processing of information that represents threat. Due to hypervigilance, high N persons are particularly sensitive to personally dangerous or ego-threatening stimuli and constantly scan their environment in search of ambiguous stimuli that may serve as potential sources of threat to their well-being. Thus they attempt to maximize the probability of threat detection by allocating a disproportionate amount of resources to threat stimuli. Due to negative threat schemata, high N persons tend to be biased in processing more self-detrimental than self-enhancing information, and their cognitive stores are more replete with threat-related information.

B. *Capacity*   High N, relative to low N persons, are characterized by low working memory capacity. Their negative cognitive schemata predispose them to divert attentional resources to threatening stimuli in their immediate environment so as to maximize the probability of detecting threatening environmental stimuli. They find it difficult to concentrate on the target stimulus in presence of irrelevant stimuli, both external and internal (worry, irrelevant thought). Because worry and irrelevant thoughts absorb part of the degrees of freedom of the cognitive processing system, fewer resources remain free to process task-related stimuli, particularly on complex tasks requiring large amounts of working memory capacity.

C. *Distractibility*   High N is associated with increased susceptibility to distracting stimuli in the immediate surroundings. The constant scanning to detect threatening stimuli requires diverting processing resources away from the current task to extraneous sources of stimuli. Due to increased distractibility, high N persons experience difficulty in focusing on task-related stimuli and may suffer from cognitive decrements in performance. This is due, in part, to their tendency to allocate attentional resources to irrelevant thoughts and threat-related stimuli.

D. *Selectivity*   High N persons attend vigilantly to anticipated aversive stimuli in surroundings, scanning ambiguous stimuli in a broad fashion while no danger is identified. But, once detecting threat stimuli, they turn to a more narrow focus. The elevated anxiety of high N individuals in an ego-threatening situation results in narrowing of attentional span and lower cue-utilization and narrowing of attention to self.

Source: Adapted from Eysenck (1992) and Zeidner (1998).

mechanisms through which the anxiety facet of N may affect attention and cognitive processing.

Bias in Mood-Regulation and Metacognition   Mood-regulation refers to how persons understand and control their own emotional state. Anxiety is often accompanied by excessive, prolonged worry, and similarly rumination about problems is common in depression (Matthews and Funke 2006). Mood-regulation is a feature of *metacognition*, which reflects an internal perception-action cycle. People monitor their own states of mind, and if these states are appraised as unduly negative or inappropriate for current circumstances, they will implement strategies for modifying cognitive or emotional states. Some strategies are behaviorally mediated, such as engaging in pleasurable activities (Thayer 1996). Others are internal, in that the person tries to suppress unwanted moods and thoughts, or seeks to reappraise the mental state in a more positive light (Gross 1998).

The ability to regulate moods successfully is often seen as a defining feature of emotional intelligence. However, the maladaptive styles of mood-regulation described by, for example Salovey et al. (1995), are known to relate to high N and related traits. Negative affectivity is linked to excessive self-focus of attention; the person tends to be absorbed in their own inner world as they brood on their problems (Wells and Matthews, 1994). Self-focus tends to amplify negative moods, increase the accessibility of dysfunctional beliefs, and interfere with attention to the outside world, so adaptive task-focused coping becomes more difficult (Wells and Matthews 1994). Not only are high N persons preoccupied with their own mental states, but they also implement maladaptive regulative strategies (e.g., rumination) that, counterproductively, tend to perpetuate worries and negative beliefs (Wells 2000). Anxiety relates especially to "meta-worry," that is, being worried about one's own worries. Such metacognitions tend to inflate the importance of the person's negative thoughts, again perpetuating worry.

The various biases just described work together to increase vulnerability to stress in high N individuals (see Suls 2001). Information-processing biases exaggerate the salience and severity of external threats and activate negative beliefs encoded in the self-schema. The distorted appraisal of the threat and personal capability that results often leads to maladaptive coping, and failure to take direct, problem-focused actions that might be effective. The high N person's style of mood-regulation and metacognition perpetuates worry and rumination, and entrenches negative self-beliefs.

The maladaptive patterns of social interaction related to N that we described in chapter 6 can be understood in this light. Social threats are often difficult to evaluate; it may be hard to tell if people are laughing at us or laughing with us (Matthews 2004). Further uncertainty derives from the frequent need to maintain good relations with the threatening person (e.g., a critical family member), and the tendency for aggressors to disguise the nature of threat (e.g., spreading office gossip behind the victims back). Dealing with social threats effectively may require a degree of self-reflection and suspicion of others. However, the high N person's cognitive biases are likely to lead to misreading social situations and overreacting to minor disagreements. Indeed there is a literature on social anxiety demonstrating that this trait can lead to self-perpetuating, dysfunctional cycles of social interaction, dominated by exaggerated threat appraisals that lead to social withdrawal (e.g., Ledley et al. 2006).

Given the substantial correlations observed between many scales for EI and low N, these EI measures will (and do) predict stress vulnerabilities of the type just described. The low EI person, just like the high N individual, will be prone to maladaptive regulation of personal emotions and of interactions with others. Once again, we are faced with the question of what research on EI—especially as operationalized by questionnaire assessments—can add to the existing, much richer literature on N as a stress vulnerability factor. We make a few tentative suggestions in the passages that follow.

Competency in Emotion Management

As we have seen, N relates to strategies for monitoring and regulating mood of the kind often attributed to low EI. However, EI may relate to competencies in mood management over and above the role of N. The broader trait may not fully capture how the person understands and controls their inner emotional world. The attention, clarity, and repair factors of the TMMS may index some specific competencies of this kind that, plausibly, contribute to stress tolerance. For example, Fernandez-Berrocal et al. (2006) showed that clarity and repair scales relate to better mental health and adjustment, even with low self-esteem controlled.

Emotion-Focused Coping

We have suggested that existing studies linking EI to *less* use of emotion-focused coping may be flawed by their use of negatively toned scales (e.g., self-criticism) or even scales that pick up emotional symptoms rather than coping. Pennebaker's (1997) work introduced the idea that writing about emotions thoughtfully may help resolve emotive challenges and stress. Empirical studies have largely failed to address how EI may relate to the constructive use of emotions in coping, for example, in understanding and coming to terms with the negative emotions elicited by stressful events (see Epstein 1998).

Communication Competencies

Scherer's (2007) analysis of emotional competencies highlights communication competencies, including effective emotion perception and emotion expression. EI may relate to specific deficits in these processes, over and above any influence of N. Affective biases in perception and attention may interfere with accurate perceptions of the emotions of others. In general, N is not linked to any overall deficit in perceptions of others (Lippa and Dietz 2000). Still, although EI may be more predictive of emotion perception, in a recent study we failed to find any association between several leading EI questionnaires and accurate perception of emotional microexpressions (Fellner et al. 2007). It may also be important to look at contextual factors. Lieberman and Rosenthal (2001) found that extraversion related to better decoding of social cues only in a multi-tasking situation that tended to overload attention. Perhaps EI is only advantageous in situations of social overload or stress. The expressive side of communication competence may also be linked to EI. Anxiety and depression relate to reduced or maladaptive facial expression of emotion (e.g., Renneberg et al. 2005), and future research might explore whether low EI relates, for example, to constricted emotional expression or to expression of emotions inappropriate to the situation.

A final comment on stress vulnerability is in order. We should not assume that N and low EI are necessarily maladaptive in the larger scheme of things. In the previous chapter we introduced the cognitive-adaptive theory of personality that proposes that traits typically confer both benefits and costs, depending on the situation. Cognitive-adaptive theory offers an account of N on this basis (Matthews 2004). The cognitive biases supporting heightened awareness of threat may be advantageous for early detection and preemption of threat, for example, by avoidance or through sustained effort. Advantages of N in anticipating possible threat are evidenced, for example, by studies showing that N and anxiety relate to greater sustained effort in demanding work environments (Smillie et al. 2006), to readiness to take early action to deal with health problems (Mayne 1999), and to slower speed in vehicle driving (Matthews 2002). Conversely, the costs of high N come into play when the threat cannot be avoided, and must be confronted directly, and cognitive distortions and overload of attention interfere with effective action (e.g.,

Zeidner and Matthews 2005). Similarly emotional intelligence may signal both strengths and weaknesses, as explored in the previous chapter. In the next section we develop the argument that the advantages of high EI may be situation-specific.

Challenging the Conventional Wisdom on Emotional Intelligence, Stress, and Coping

Many accounts of EI (e.g., Bar-On 2000) assume that people can be rank-ordered in terms of their personal coping efficacy, reflecting a coherent set of underlying competencies for handling affectively loaded encounters. The simple causal chain is that emotional competence leads to more effective coping that in turn leads to more positive outcomes, that is:

Emotional intelligence → Effective coping → Adaptive outcomes

However, the transactional perspective we have developed (Matthews and Zeidner 2000) presents challenges for this position.

First, *competencies may be largely independent of each other.* If EI represents a coherent psychological construct, then different competencies should be correlated. With respect to stress, the various, distinct mechanisms for adaptive coping should correlate. Individuals who are effective at mood-regulation should thus possess a richer and more effective repertoire of coping strategies and should be adept at resolving conflicts. However, competencies identified with EI might not be positively correlated. For example, a ruthless CEO might be highly effective in managing others' behaviors to attain corporate goals but lack empathy. Conceivably, handling emotive situations might be influenced by a variety of unrelated competencies. If so, EI (like "stress") might be a useful umbrella label for a broad area of inquiry, but the term should not be assumed to identify a single, global construct.

Consider, for example, the competencies contributing to "managing emotions," one of the core abilities contributing to EI, described in chapter 3. Multiple factors might contribute to difficulties in emotional management (see also Gross and John 2002). Thus a problem with anger at work might variously reflect temperamental irritability, misappraisals of others as hostile (information-processing), brooding on themes of injustice and retaliation (self-regulation), or lack of skills for dealing with specific sources of frustration such as an uncooperative coworker (knowledge). It is far from clear that these different sources of dysfunctional anger management can be grouped together as lack of EI.

Second, *coping strategies may not be universally adaptive or maladaptive*. It is assumed that the coping strategies linked to EI, such as use of problem-focus in place of emotion-focus, are generally effective. However, as previously discussed, we cannot usually partition coping strategies into those that are adaptive and those that are not. The outcomes of coping are complex and multifaceted. In other words, operationalizations of EI may not signal overall adaptive advantages but rather qualitatively different patterns of costs and benefits related to the preferred mode of coping.

Third, *adaptations may be situation-specific*. People with high EI should express it in a variety of situations. For example, individuals with good impulse control appear able to resist qualitatively different impulses. However, this need not always be the case; consider, for example, the alcoholic patient who might be good at resisting most impulses but not drinking alcoholic beverages. Research on EI has neglected situational moderators by almost exclusively operationalizing coping and stress through global measures. As discussed in the previous chapter, personality research suggests that each trait is adaptive in some contexts but not others (Matthews et al. 2003; see also figure 7.5).

In our research (Matthews, Emo, Funke, et al. 2006), we are beginning to find some contexts in which EI is not adaptive (e.g., managing high workloads), but there may be allied situations (team performance) in

Figure 7.5
Coping strategies may be adaptive or maladaptive depending on the specific situation: The case of the clumsy waiter and the happy family

which one or more EI constructs does moderate stress response. At this point we simply do not know which contexts are most relevant, and there is an urgent need for studies focusing on the role of EI in facing specific types of challenge. Thus it appears that interpreting EI as representing some global coping ability is misconceived. It is difficult to categorize coping strategies as generally adaptive or maladaptive (except, perhaps, in the case of dysfunctional strategies associated with clinical disorders). Likewise individuals cannot be classified as more or less adapted in some generic sense: individual differences in adaptation to external demands and pressures appear to be context-bound, and contingent on the criteria used to define "adaptation." Adaptive coping in a given situation depends on a variety of independent competencies, and their interaction with unique features of the situation itself.

Summary and Conclusions

The literature suggests that emotional intelligence may serve as a buffer against stress and support adaptive coping. Currently empirical studies suggest particular coping strategies are only weakly related to outcomes. Because existing research literature does not support the notion of a continuum of adaptive competence, there are no accepted criteria for rating the outcomes of events in terms of overall adaptive success or failure. More generally, it is central to the transactional approach that emotions must be understood within the specific context in which they occur. Although the concept is superficially appealing, the bulk of the evidence suggests that we cannot identify EI with emotional adaptability. Thus we are skeptical that EI will be shown to be an aptitude central to adaptive coping. Yet we are not dismissive, in that specific constructs labeled as EI may prove to add to existing understanding of the stress process. Progress of this kind requires: (1) clear conceptual and psychometric discrimination of the multiple constructs related to emotional competency, (2) a strong focus on mediating mechanisms, (3) a strong focus on situational moderators of EI constructs, and (4) an emphasis on building causal models using data from experimental and longitudinal studies.

Summary Points: Chapter 7

• Adaptive coping with psychological stress depends on rational and emotional competencies operating interactively. The EI literature assumes that effective coping with stressful encounters is central to the EI construct.

Thus it has been claimed that EI may buffer against stress reactions and play a meaningful role in how people cope with a wide array of stressful encounters, ranging from daily hassles and major life events to traumatic community disasters.

• EI has been claimed to serve as a personal resource in facilitating adaptive coping. The scope of individual differences in coping linked to EI is, however, very broad. Thus high EI individuals may avoid or circumvent stressful or potentially dangerous social conditions in the first place; possess richer emotional and social coping resources to negotiate stressful encounters; learn and apply context-relevant coping strategies more quickly; show more constructive thought patterns and ruminate less; be more skilled at regularly repairing emotions; enjoy richer social networks to provide an emotional buffer against negative events; and show greater coping self-efficacy. Presently evidence supporting these variables mediating the EI-coping interface is meager; additional research is needed.

• The literature suggests that EI is only weakly related to coping strategies. It does, however, point to a positive relationship between EI and action-oriented coping strategies and a negative relationship between EI and use of palliative and avoidant strategies. EI also appears to be a more robust predictor of general coping styles than measures of actual coping in a specific context. Indeed EI may not signal overall adaptive advantage but rather qualitatively different patterns of costs and benefits related to specific modes of coping. Each of these results appears measure-dependent, with self-report measures showing more robust relationships than ability-based measures.

• Current thinking suggests that it may be misplaced to construe EI as representing some global coping capacity. As coping experts have noted, it is difficult to classify coping strategies as generally adaptive or maladaptive. Individual differences in coping appear context dependent and adaptive coping depends on an ensemble of independent competencies and their interaction with the unique features of the situation. Thus adaptation to stress may be situation-specific, and individuals with high EI may not express their abilities across situations.

• Research is needed to examine the unique role of EI in factors not currently captured by facets of the five factor model of personality, such as attention to emotions, emotional clarity, adaptive disclosure of emotions, and emotion repair. Additional empirical research is also needed to convincingly demonstrate EI plays a unique role in the coping process.

IV EMOTIONAL INTELLIGENCE IN ACTION

8 Schooling Emotional Intelligence

I have never let my schooling interfere with my education.
—Mark Twain

This chapter explores the potential role of emotional intelligence in educational settings. We begin this chapter with a brief overview of some of the problems currently facing educators, and they serve as a backdrop for introducing social and emotional learning in the schools. Next we examine the evidence for a relationship between emotional intelligence (EI) and school performance. We then evaluate current practices, generally going under the name of social and emotional learning (SEL) and suggest future guidelines for the development and assessment of these programs.

Education in the Twenty-first Century: A New Vision?

Perhaps because of increased globalization, educational reform currently appears to be a key political agenda in most countries. Recently in Germany, for example, a series of testing programs have sprung up around the country, based on that nation's relatively poor standing on the global assessment known as the Programme for International Student Assessment (PISA). Similarly, in the United States, Congress passed the "No Child Left Behind (NCLB) Act" in 2002 in order to increase the number of students who achieve minimal state achievement standards. In the spirit of the cultural zeitgeist in favor of emotions (see chapter 1), many of these countries are also looking to improve the emotional climate of their schools, with school safety one of the leading indicators of a school's success under NCLB legislation.

Beyond policy and legislature there appear a number of reasons for considering more than just the academic standing of children in school. For example, recent analyses concerning the status of American youth and families concluded that the United States is a nation at risk in regard to many social indicators (Nation et al. 2003). Thus schools are witnessing discernible levels of violence, bullying, dropout, and youth suicide. These negative behaviors have taken a toll on student's emotional well-being and social adjustment, documented by rising rates of childhood depression, emotion-related illnesses, and expressions of fear and hopelessness (McCombs 2004). Violence and antisocial behavior in the schools is not a theoretical abstraction, but rather something that affects many students daily, who live in fear for their safety.

Indeed the last decade of the twentieth century was characterized by some commentators as the "decade of violence in schools" (Aronson 2000). The recent events at Virginia Tech—where Seung-Hui Cho, a student of that institution, shot and killed 32 people before committing suicide—suggest that violence may have spilled over to higher education as well. For children and young adults across the globe who suffer from bullying and daily personal harassment and attack, life in the classroom is often problematic. The recent concern over shootings in the United States led many schools in that country to adopt a zero-tolerance policy for aggressive behaviors such as classroom bullying (Espelage and Swearer 2003). The US Department of Health and Human Services followed with the launch of a multiyear national bullying public awareness and prevention campaign in 2003. Although American schools are hit hard by school violence, this problem is by no means restricted to the United States. Violence has become a problem of major international concern as a host of countries across the globe (e.g., Australia, Germany, Greece, England, Ireland, Italy, Japan, Norway, and Scotland) have reported similar problems of bullying and violence in schools (see Espelage and Swearer 2003 for a review on research on school bullying).

A reasonable number of today's students may have adequate cognitive ability but are said to be lacking in emotional intelligence (see figure 8.1). Given the prevalence of violence and crime alluded to in the preceding paragraphs, there is clearly a need to reform the climate of contemporary schools. Proponents of EI and emotional literacy programs in the schools argue that this may be best achieved by instituting dramatic changes in the social atmosphere of the classroom. Traditional education may also neglect the "positive psychology" of classroom learning. Jenson et al. (2004) point out that the climate in the classroom is often negativistic, with hard-pressed teachers more likely to express disapproval than praise for students. These commentators indicate a need to retool instructional techniques to promote the mastery and "flow" experiences that are the

Figure 8.1
The importance of fostering emotional intelligence in the school should not be underestimated, even if we eventually realize our goal of making all children academically smart

hallmark of positive engagement (e.g., a cooperative learning environment). In short, there appears a need to produce social environments that will make schools more humane and compassionate.

As the postindustrial society evolves, the rapid and complex cultural changes of the past and those of the predictable future may make emotional and social competencies crucial requirements for adaptive and successful functioning of children and youth, along with their continued adaptation as adults. Although rarely considered a necessary component of education in the past, social and emotional skills may be as critical for the basic knowledge repertoire of all children as reading, writing, and arithmetic (Greenberg et al. 2004). Although academic achievement and social and emotional learning are often assumed to compete in a zero-sum game, and that schools must choose between the two, many experts now contend that there is no reason to believe that one is achieved at the expense of the other (e.g., see Hawkins et al. 2004).

Emotional Intelligence and Educational Attainment

A casual inspection of publications on EI in the popular media shows that these competencies are frequently touted as being meaningfully predictive of important educational criteria. Does your child have difficulties coping with stress and assignments? Or do they have problems relating to peers at their school? The argument is that low emotional intelligence is at play. Training EI in schools may indeed offer a solution to educational problems, but interventions must be soundly based in psychological theory and careful definition and analysis of emotional competencies. In fact, much as was the case for Head Start Programs when first introduced, EI programs are becoming inculcated in the schools. Do these programs have sufficient theoretical grounding? Are hypotheses related to intervention tenable? Have evaluation studies been rigorously designed? Answers to these questions speak to the viability of EI programs as providing meaningful change to the individual and the wider educational community.

Theoretical Basis

It is thought that, compared to their less emotionally intelligent counterparts, students with high-levels of EI might also be more motivated and be high achievers in the classroom (Zins et al. 2007). Learning may be promoted by emotional skills said to include higher motivation, self-control, and effective self-regulation, along with social skills such as forming constructive learning partnerships and avoidance of damaging antisocial behaviors. EI has been claimed to be directly predictive of student success, as well as indirectly mediating success by protecting students from barriers to learning such as mental distress, substance abuse, delinquency, teen pregnancy, and violence (Hawkins et al. 2004).

Proponents of this SEL approach suggest that EI-linked prosocial behaviors are related to positive academic outcomes (Zins et al. 2007). One of the reasons for the popularity of EI among educators (and a basic working assumption underlying the implementation of programs for teaching emotional skills in the classroom) is that EI plays a critical role in improving children's academic motivation, learning, and achievement. Indeed recent research has suggested that the process of learning is itself of a social nature. Because numerous elements in classroom learning are relational and social, emotional skills are said to be essential for the successful development of cognitive thinking and educational outcomes (Elias et al. 2001).

Empirical Research

If, in the immortal words of the 1960s song by Mickey and Sylvia, "Love will make you fail in school," the question arises: Will controlling your emotions (through EI) make you succeed in school? A number of commentators (e.g., Romasz et al. 2004) have further claimed that the acquisition of social and emotional skills are a prerequisite for students before they can benefit from the traditional academic material presented in the classroom (see Humphrey, Curran, et al. 2007). A glance at the literature suggests that high EI, as evidenced by rich social and emotional skills, can be instrumental in the acquisition of knowledge and in the development of cognitive abilities (Caprara et al. 2000; Wentzel 1994). Emotional competence also appears to help students pay attention in the classroom (Trentacosta et al. 2006). A review by Denham (2006) shows consistent relationships between emotional and social competencies and school achievement in elementary school children. Children's prosocial behaviors (e.g., empathy) have been found to be associated with elevated school performance in reading and spelling (e.g., Feshbach and Feshbach 1987), and are also predictive of performance on standardized achievement tests (Malecki and Elliot 2002; Welsh et al. 2001). Halberstadt and Hall (1980) reviewed studies showing a positive relationship between nonverbal sensitivity (i.e., emotional awareness and perception) and laboratory-based cognitive outcomes in children—although these were found to relate only weakly to traditional measures of cognitive skills. Some experimental work suggests that exposure to empathy training has a positive effect on children's achievement in schools, and also increases self-esteem and lowered aggression (Feshbach and Cohen 1988).

A study conducted by Parker et al. (2004) among 667 high school students reported a moderate correlation of $r = 0.33$ between EI scores and academic success, with the correlation slightly higher among females than among males. Students in the top academic group had higher levels of a variety of interpersonal, adaptability, and stress management abilities than the other two groups. Studies on EI and scholastic performance have also been conducted with college student populations. Overall, the data collected has yielded contradictory results. Some researchers have reported modest positive associations between emotional and social competencies and college success. Parker et al. (2004, 2006) reported that first-year students who persisted in their studies were significantly higher than those who withdrew on a broad range of self-reported emotional and social competencies. Parker et al. (2004) also found that EQ-i scores were modestly associated with GPA in college students, but this result may plausibly reflect the confounding of the EQ-i with low anxiety and other personality factors that are known to relate to college grades. Amelang and Steinmayr (2006) reported that when controlling for ability and personality, in both high school and adult samples, neither ability nor trait EI contributed in an incremental fashion to academic performance. Other studies show negligible associations between EI and college exam scores (Newsome et al. 2000; O'Connor and Little 2003), particularly when cognitive ability and personality are controlled (Barchard 2003).

Indirect Evidence

Low EI has been shown to be a key ingredient in a variety of deviant behaviors, particularly those linked to emotional deficits (Roberts and Strayer 1996). EI has been reported to be negatively associated with deviant school behaviors (e.g., being excluded or expelled from school) in a sample of 650 grade 11 students in Britain (Petrides et al. 2004). Similarly EI was reported to be negatively related to deviant behaviors (tobacco and alcohol use) in a sample of American adolescents (Trinidad and Johnson 2002).

Figure 8.2 presents some of the posited mediating factors between EI and academic attainment. At present, we concur with Amelang and Steinmayr (2006): "The results concerning the incremental validity of both ability and trait EI regarding achievement criteria remains ambiguous and necessitate further research" (p. 460).

Academic, Social, and Emotional Learning in the Classroom

Education is an admirable thing, but it is well to remember from time to time that nothing that is worth knowing can be taught.
—Oscar Wilde

How can some of the current problems in education be ameliorated? An increase in expenditures on public education is one frequently suggested fix. Curiously enough, there appears to be a serious disconnect between public spending on education and school performance, so increased spending will not necessarily by itself do the trick. Thus, while total federal, state, and local expenditure on education has increased substantially in the United States, over the past few decades, for example, the academic achievement scores for students has failed to reflect this increase. Indeed, if children reject education, the solution may lie in a radical change in the content, structure, or process, rather than increased expenditure on current forms of teaching and learning.

A number of experts involved in SEL programs (e.g., Zins et al. 2007) have contended that the best way to remedy issues plaguing the school

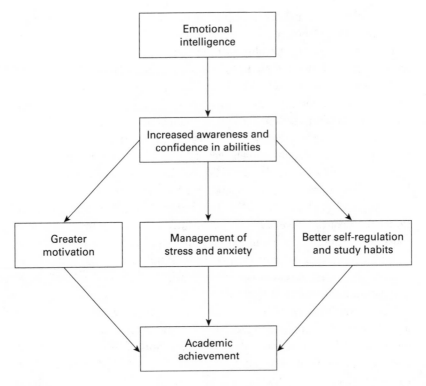

Figure 8.2
Variables mediating the relationship between emotional intelligence and academic success

system is by thoroughly revamping the school program, including both curricular content and classroom procedures. According to these educators, schools have traditionally focused their energies and resources in promoting the development of students' cognitive skills and academic achievement—with less than impressive results. Because students are not systematically educated in affective competencies, basic values, social skills, and moral reasoning across the school years, students are not given the crucial foundations and skills for becoming caring, empathic, responsible, and compassionate citizens. As has been demonstrated by extensive research, one of the many correlates of classroom bullying and antisocial behavior is the lack of empathic and self-regulatory skills (Olweus 2001). In fact, social and emotional education has been coined the "missing piece" in school life—that part of a school's mission that, while always close to the thoughts of many teachers, somehow eluded them (Elias et al. 1997). The trend of bringing emotional literacy into schools makes emotions and social life themselves key topics for learning and discussion, rather than treating these most compelling facets of a child's life as irrelevant intrusions. It is of note that in the past, the teaching of EI was generally seen as being the responsibility of the parent, but now this responsibility seems to have shifted largely to the school system.

The emotional literacy movement, which the EI bandwagon has latched on to, coincides with a "new look" in education, requiring that the traditional focus on intelligence be supplemented by a strong concern with social and emotional skills. On one hand, to be educated means to be cognitively intelligent, knowledgeable, and well versed in the sciences, humanities, and the arts. On the other hand, to be educated means to be kind, caring, considerate, responsible, trustworthy, conscientious, honest, and prosocial (Elias et al. 2001). This approach requires that the traditional focus on intelligence be supplemented with a major emphasis on social and emotional training and development. Thus one possible solution toward solving some of the problems of the educational system is to balance the focus on school achievement with a focus on students' social and emotional learning outcomes.

Yet, at the same time, the reality of schools' funding often may dictate a preference for emphasizing cognitive achievements rather than non-cognitive skills. Furthermore the implementation of SEL programs may also incur additional costs, such as training resources, designated classrooms, and class time that a strapped school system may find difficult to bear. One important consideration in favor of the implementation of SEL programs is the singular benefit and return on investment associated with delivering programs. Thus Zins et al. (2007) report that the Seattle Social Development Program had a very high cost per student serviced: $4,590. However, at the same time it had benefits of $14,426 for each student, or $3.14 per dollar spent. Examples of demonstrated benefits include improved educational outcomes (e.g., test scores, graduation rates), reduced crime, lowered substance abuse, and decreased teen suicide attempts.

Current Social and Emotional Intervention Programs in the Schools

It is a capital mistake to theorize before you have all the evidence. It biases the judgment.
—Arthur Conan Doyle

This section briefly examines social and emotional learning programs (SEL)—an umbrella term that provides a common framework for programs with a wide array of specified outcomes. Prior to NCLB legislation in the United States, a plethora of social and emotional learning (SEL) programs designed to cultivate social-emotional competencies in the schools sprung up. While still widely represented, the number of these has diminished slightly in recent times, however, as schools struggle to meet adequate yearly progress (AYP) on traditional achievement indicators. The programs designed to foster EI in the classrooms fall under the general rubric of social and emotional learning programs (SEL), referring to the process through which children enhance their ability to integrate thinking, feelings, and behaving to achieve life tasks (Zins et al. 2004). A broad spectrum of EI intervention programs designed to teach emotional competencies in the school is now available, including, social skills training, cognitive-behavioral modification, self-management, and multimodal programs (Topping et al. 2000).

Curricular-based SEL programs seek to educate children about the value of EI as well as to foster the development of specific skills in these areas (e.g., recognition of emotions in self and others, empathy, conflict resolution; see reviews by Cohen 1999a–c; Zins, Weisserg, et al. 2004). In addition these programs are purported to enhance educational achievements in the classroom, an issue we discuss shortly. These programs can also be integrated into whatever instructional unit is currently being taught in the classroom. Given that children can learn by observing and modeling real, as well as symbolic, representational models, curriculum-based emotional learning comes naturally with many of the liberal arts. For example, children can learn much about various feelings when reading literary works that depict characters with the tendency to experience specific emotions (e.g., sadness). Children can observe how characters express and display their emotions, what makes the characters feel as they do, how the characters cope in response to their feelings, and how effective are the various methods of coping employed. This form of affective learning proceeds throughout the educational system, and as the literary or artistic scenarios become more complex, so does emotional learning seeking to promote the development of social and emotional competencies.

Working Assumptions of SEL Programs

The development and implementation of EI-focused educational programs in the classroom rests on a number of working assumptions. One basic assumption underlying current attempts to educate students in EI in educational settings is that emotional competencies are modifiable attributes, so these can be meaningfully trained and improved through educational programs (Elias et al. 2001). Whereas the components of EI appear being capable of being learned both inside and outside the home, the classroom, as a more formal arena than the family setting, may be a particularly useful source of generalized EI skills that may be applied to other structured environments (e.g., the workplace).

Furthermore EI has been assumed to be positively related to academic achievement and productive experience in the world (Elias et al. 1997). This is one of the presumed reasons for the keen interest in the construct in educational circles. It is further assumed that affect and cognition work synergistically, that schools will be most successful in their educational mission if they make a systematic attempt at integrating efforts to promote manifold facets of a child's personality through cognitive, social, and emotional learning.

Another basic assumption underlying current programs is that caring relationships form the foundations of genuine and enduring learning in schools. Schools are assumed to be social settings, with learning viewed primarily as a social and highly interpersonal process. Given that the teaching-learning process is of a social nature, students ought to learn best in collaboration with their teachers and in the company of peers and supported by parents and school staff. Because social and emotional factors play such an important role, schools must attend to this aspect for the benefit of students.

Popular SEL Programs

The idea that students' emotional and social problems can be addressed through school-based programs became popular among educational reformers during the 1990s. The Nueva School in Hillsborough, California, was one of the first to start an emotional literacy program, and New Haven implemented such a program in public schools districtwide. Once established, the concept of EI has proved itself a catalyst to the thinking and planning of educators and policy makers. The Collaborative for Academic, Social, and Emotional Learning (CASEL) at the University of Illinois reports that more than 150 different emotional literacy programs are being used today by thousands of American schools. Programs seeking to inculcate emotional and social competencies go under a variety of names, such as "life skills training," "self-science," "education for care," "social awareness," "social problem solving," "social competency," and "creative conflict resolution."

It is beyond the scope of this chapter to extensively survey all EI intervention programs or emotion-based curricular materials available on the
market today (for a survey of several prevalent programs, see Cohen,
1999a–c; Zins et al. 2007). Table 8.1 briefly describes salient features
(i.e., objectives, program foci and activities, EI content, assessment
results) underlying the most popular and frequently referenced of these
programs.

As is readily apparent from inspection of table 8.1, current EI intervention programs target a wide array of objectives. These include improving
social, communication, and life skills (problem-solving strategies, assertiveness training); modifying emotional regulation and coping techniques;
effective peer-relation training; fostering conflict resolution and responsible decision making skills; promoting health; preventing alcohol, tobacco,
and drug use; reducing violence; developing self-esteem; and enriching
linguistic experiences (see Zins et al. 2007). Furthermore programs vary
widely with respect to their systematic coverage of the major components
of EI. Whereas some programs target relatively few elements directly
related to EI (e.g., Seattle Social Development Project), others (e.g., Promoting Alternative Thinking Strategies, or PATHS) cover quite a number of important components of EI. For example, in PATHS, awareness
and regulation of emotions, perspective taking, conflict resolution skills,
coping with stress, and several other related concepts are all subject to
intervention. The objectives most frequently targeted by prevalent EI
programs, as represented in table 8.1, include (1) problem-solving, (2)
awareness and understanding of emotions in self and others, (3) impulse
control, (4) emotion regulation, (5) coping with environmental stress and
negative emotions, and (6) perspective taking and empathy.

The majority of programs have not made raising student EI levels an
explicit target of the intervention. SEL programs can, after the event, be
related to the over-arching construct of EI, by identifying specific components in the program description and in curricular materials. However,
these components are not always specified as program objectives in the
planning stage, nor are they consistently assessed during the evaluation
phase. Even when programs have been designed according to a specific
model of EI (e.g., the four-branch ability model; see table 8.2), the
effectiveness of such programs have not been evaluated to date. Typically
programs also fail to capitalize on the increasing research-based understanding of development of emotional competencies, as reviewed in chapter 5. Thus, even for programs that have some demonstrable efficacy, it

Table 8.1
Selected social-emotional learning intervention programs, including source, population, goals, EI content, and evaluation results

Program	Source	Population	Goals	EI content	Evaluation results
Improving Social Awareness– Social Problem-Solving Project	Elias et al. 1986; Clabby and Elias 1999	Grades K–12, with emphasis on elementary and middle school	Improve problem-solving skills; enhance involvement; increase behavior and interpersonal effectiveness	Students are taught skills in areas loosely overlapping with EI: awareness of feelings; self-control, anger, and stress management; emotion-focused coping, adaptability; and perspective taking. Students are taught to recognize emotions in pictures and facial expressions related to emotions. Emotional lessons merge naturally into reading and writing, health, science, and social studies.	An initial evaluation of this program (Elias and Clabby, 1992) showed that it reduced the impact of typical middle school stressors. Follow-up evaluation six years later documented long-term gains in children's prosocial behavior, sense of efficacy, and a reduction in pathology and socially dis-ordered behaviors (aggression, vandalism). Program participants showed higher levels of positive prosocial behavior and lower levels of antisocial and self-destructive behavior. Elias et al. (1991) reported that students who had received a two-year social decision-making program in elementary schools showed higher levels of positive prosocial behavior and lower levels of antisocial self-destructive, and socially disordered behaviors when followed up in high school four to six years later than did the control students who had not received this program.

Promoting Alternative Thinking Strategies (PATHS)	Greenberg et al. 1995	Grades K–12, with emphasis on younger children	Improve children's ability to: understand, express, and regulate emotions; understand perspective of others; solve social problems	(1) Understanding, discussing, expressing and regulating negative emotions (e.g., anger); (2) controlling impulses; (3) empathic understanding of other's feeling	Program was effective for both low and high risk special students in grades 2 to 3 in improving emotional fluency and the range of vocabulary in discussing emotional experiences, in understanding of emotions, and efficacy beliefs regarding management of emotions and developmental aspects of some elements of emotions.
Resolving Conflicts Creatively Program (K–12)	Aber et al. 1998	Grades K–12	Reduce youth violence by promoting constructive anger control and conflict resolution skills; improve inter-group relations; foster a caring and peaceful community of learners	(1) Identifying one's own negative feelings in conflict situations; (2) regulating anger in one's self; (3) taking the perspective of others and empathizing with other's feelings	The program was evaluated based on two waves of developmental data. Those receiving a high number of lessons had a significantly slower growth in self-reported hostile attributions and teacher-reported aggressive behavior, compared to children receiving a low number of lessons (Aber et al. 1999). Patti and Lantieri (1999) report that more than 87 percent of the teachers said that RCCP was having a positive impact on their students. Also, about 92 percent of the student felt well about themselves and 64 percent of the teachers reported less physical roles.

Table 8.1
(continued)

Program	Source	Population	Goals	EI content	Evaluation results
Yale–New Haven Social Competence Promotion Program	Shriver et al. 1999	Grades 5–8	Develop a sense of self worth; foster socially skilled and positive relations with peers and adults; engage in positive, self protective practices; feel motivated to contribute responsibly and ethically to peer group, family, school, and community	Feelings awareness, emotion-focused coping, and adaptability; self-management (e.g., self-monitoring, self-control, stress management, persistence, emotion-focused coping, adaptability); feeling awareness and perspective taking	The K–12 curriculum was implemented gradually over a four-year period, thus enabling the school district to learn from the implementation. Rather informal surveys were conducted of teachers, parents, administrator, and student satisfaction (Shriver et al. 1999).
Oakland's Child Development Project	Child Development Project Report (CDPR 1999)	Grades K–6 particularly high-risk children	Build a caring and fair school community by nurturing basic values and helping students become caring fair and responsible citizens.	Empathy and impulse control	CDP was evaluated in three separate studies. The first study followed up children from K to grade 4, with longer term assessments in grades 6 to 8. The second assessed two programs and two comparison schools while the third assessment involved six US districts. Results in all three studies point to the central importance of a caring school community for the development of personal and social qualities (e.g., social competence, concern for others) and academic orientations (motivation, liking for school) and qualities that help students avoid the risk of problematic behaviors.

Source: Adapted from Zeidner et al. (2002).

Table 8.2
Emotional literacy in the Middle School Program (ELMS): Activities designed to cultivate emotional intelligence

I *Perception of emotion* These activities are designed to enhance students' perception of instances of nonverbal (mainly facial) expressions of emotions in their immediate surroundings. Teachers introduce the topic by showing students an array of pictures depicting faces revealing various emotions. Students are asked to identify the specific emotions depicted, provide examples of other aspects of the face that may reveal different emotions, try to account for the circumstances leading to the emotion, and so on. Students then work on a class project requiring the identification and assembly of facial expressions of emotions in the media (newspapers, advertisements, comic strips, etc.). The end product of this assigned project is the creation of a mobile or collage depicting various human expressions of emotions, which is then discussed in class.
II *Use of emotions* These activities are designed to enhance students' insight into how emotions impact upon thinking. In order to set the stage for thinking about the effects of advertised products and services on the way we think and the consumer attitudes we develop, classroom students explore the ways through which TV commercials influence emotions. Students are asked to think about the emotional triggers that commercials use and how they may affect their thoughts. In an assigned classroom project, students create a poster depicting a variety of commercials, analyzing: the audience targeted by the commercial, the various components used to influence emotions, the specific emotions the commercial was designed to elicit, and the thoughts these emotions may facilitate. The finished projects are presented and discussed in class.
III *Understanding of emotions* These activities are designed to enhance children's understanding of the causes of emotions. After introducing the idea that different emotions have different causes, and that a particular circumstance or event can lead to different emotions, students are assigned to a project requiring them to assemble pictures of objects, events, or people that may trigger different types of emotions. The completed products (collages, posters, etc.) are discussed and elaborated upon.
IV *Management of emotion* These activities are designed to help students analyze ways to handle emotions and to assess the effectiveness of regulating emotion. After a brief introduction, students are asked to recall specific emotions they experienced and to try to analyze the "triggering" event. Students are also asked to recall how they dealt with the emotion and to think of how they could have managed their emotions more effectively. As part of a class project, students are assigned the preparation of a poster depicting different ways of handling emotions.

may be a stretch to claim that they influence EI rather than some more specific and context-dependent set of skills (Goetz et al. 2005). An interesting exception is a pilot intervention for Head Start children, reported by Izard et al. (2004), that is based on Izard's theory of emotional competence (see chapter 5). Training four-year-olds in emotion labeling, recognition, and vocabulary led to improved teacher ratings of emotional competence several months later. The authors point to some limitations of the studies, including insufficient program monitoring, but overall these results are suggestive.

Evaluation of Current SEL Programs

Some programs have attracted few systematic evaluations (e.g., Yale–New Haven Social Competence Promotion Program), whereas others have enjoyed systematic evaluations (e.g., PATH). Some evaluation studies may be construed as "one-shot", while others have conducted follow-ups after five years or more (Elias and Clabby 1992). Lopes and Salovey (2004) aptly point out that only a limited number of SEL programs have been rigorously evaluated, using adequate comparison groups, and longitudinal designs. An evaluation of current SEL programs by Zins et al. (2004) found general agreement in the effectiveness of recent school-based prevention programs in reducing maladaptive behaviors related to school success. Thus a selected number of programs (e.g., Promoting Alternative Thinking Strategies, Seattle Social Development Project, Resolving Conflicts Creatively) have undergone rigorous evaluations, and the results appear to be promising (Weissberg and Greenberg 1998). Wilson et al. (2001) conducted a meta-analysis of 165 published studies of the outcomes of school-based prevention programs, ranging from individually focused counseling to behavior modification programs. Programs were shown to be helpful in reducing delinquency and nonattendance, all important for school success.

A summary provided by Zins et al. (2004) shows that SEL programs with differing focal points helped improve school performance, attitudes, and behaviors. Zins et al. (2007) also show that students who participate in high-quality SEL programs have improved attitudes toward school, a higher sense of self-efficacy, a better sense of community, and greater trust and respect for teachers. These students were also found to have positive school behaviors such as more prosocial behavior, more classroom participation and involvement in positive activities (e.g., sports), fewer absences and suspensions, as well as fewer classroom disruptions and incidences of interpersonal violence. In addition their performance in school may be enhanced in terms of improved learning-to-learn skills, and improved skills in math, language, arts, and social studies (see table 8.3).

Recently Roger Weissberg and Joseph Durlak have undertaken a meta-analysis of more than 700 studies of the outcomes of youth development, SEL, character education, and prevention interventions. The researchers divide the field into three kinds of study: (1) school-based interventions that promote social and emotional learning (SEL), (2) after-school programs, and (3) programs for families. Full results of this labor-intensive analysis have not yet been published, although some pre-

Table 8.3
Focus on competencies targeted by social and emotional learning (SEL) programs

Competency	Sample qualities
1. Self-awareness	Knowing what one is feeling, accurately assess self strengths, etc.
2. Self-management	Regulating emotions for stress management, impulse control, etc.
3. Social awareness	Empathizing with others, taking the perspectives of others, etc.
4. Relationship skills	Cooperating with others, negotiating skills, etc.
5. Decision making	Making good decisions based on ethics, evaluating results, etc.

Note: EI skills and competencies, as cultivated and trained in programs, are firmly believed to be able to help students become more socially, emotionally, and academically competent, and grow to become more responsible and productive members of society. Zins et al. (2007) argue that SEL interventions may be enhanced through explicit focus on these five key emotional competencies. They find that evaluations of SEL programs consistently show these programs to achieve, for example, their goals of "improving" peer relations, thus helping students make good decisions and promoting healthy student development.

liminary findings are reported at the Web site of the Collaborative for Academic, Social and Emotional Learning (CASEL: http://www.casel.org/sel/meta.php). Generally, indications from the initial analyses are promising. An initial meta-analysis by Durlak and Weissberg (2005), encompassing more than 300 studies of school based interventions, reported wide-ranging benefits. Accordingly, when compared to their nonprogram counterparts, students who participated in SEL programs were reported (1) to be ranked at least 10 percentile points higher on achievement tests, (2) to have higher GPAs, (3) to have significantly better attendance records, (4) to like school more, (5) to show more constructive (and less disruptive) classroom behavior, and (6) to be less likely to be disciplined or suspended. However, not all reviewers have reached optimistic conclusions about SEL programs in schools. For example, Kristja'nsson (2006) questions whether SEL programs are setting overambitious goals that cannot be attained in practice. He also asks whether EI programs may simply promote self-serving manipulation of others, as opposed to supporting moral development.

A further meta-analysis (Durlak et al. 2007) focused on the effectiveness of targeting four different social-emotional contexts for intervention: the school, the family, the wider community, the family and school relationships (e.g., parental involvement in afterschool activities). The meta-analysis showed significant improvements (against various outcome criteria) in all of these contexts except community involvement. The effect sizes ranged from 0.34 to 0.78; the largest effect sizes (>0.70) were found for school-based interventions that targeted either classrooms or the whole school. The review also illustrates some of the common limitations of research in this field. Only 24 percent of the studies initially sampled provided any quantitative data, and 85 percent of these outcome data were based on questionnaires, which as discussed elsewhere in this book, are vulnerable to artifacts. The authors also report that only 74 percent of the measures reached acceptable standards for reliability, and evidence for construct, predictive or discriminant validity was provided in 48 percent of cases. Few studies attempted to follow up the persistence of gains in social-emotional functioning over time. In the one in which follow-up evaluations were common (enhancement of parenting practices), gains were well maintained at follow-up. Durlak et al. (2007) arrive at the reasonable conclusion that enhancing social-emotional competence by targeting social systems such as the school and the family may be as effective as working with individual children.

Problems, Pitfalls, and Fissures

In this section we discuss a number of basic conceptual and methodological problems that appear to challenge current EI intervention programs and earmark some desired features and principles for future EI programs. The following issues plague a number of current programs:

Minimal EI Relevant Content   Notably, what is puzzling about some current "EI" programs is the lack of relevant content of these programs. Whereas various facets of EI (e.g., emotional perception, emotional regulation) are implicit in models developed to promote social and emotional competencies, these facets have rarely been the foci of preventive interventions. Thus a violence reduction or conflict resolution program may include a module focusing on anger management as a means to help participants control violent behavior and reduce aggressive and offending behavior, without making this the focus of the program. A cursory examination of table 8.1 shows that aside perhaps from the PATH program, none of the other programs specifically addresses all major facets of EI.

In most of the programs listed only one or two facets are addressed. A major problem in assessing the effectiveness of EI interventions is that few programs were specifically designed to serve as primary prevention or similar programs for promoting, developing, or fostering EI skills. Thus most of the programs cited by Goleman (1995a) as supporting the effectiveness of EI interventions, for example, were not designed for this purpose. Instead the programs were designed for other purposes (e.g., promoting conflict resolution skills, enhancing problem-solving skills, reducing drug use, and preventing school violence or teenage pregnancy.).

Protean Nature of Some SEL Programs   Zins, Weissberg, et al. (2004) define SEL as the process "through which we learn to recognize and manage emotions, care about others, make good decisions, behave ethically and responsibly, develop positive relationships, and avoid negative behaviors" (p. 4). According to Zins et al. (2004) five person-related competencies are included in most SEL programs: (1) *self-awareness* (e.g., identifying and recognizing emotions), (2) *social awareness* (e.g., respect for others), (3) *responsible decision making* (e.g., evaluation and reflection), (4) *self-management* (e.g., impulse control), and (5) *relationship management* (e.g., negotiation). Inspection of these curricular contents shows that they are extremely broad. Thus practically everything "under the sun is" encompassed under the SEL umbrella, with programs lumping together character development, moral reasoning and behavior, decision making, antisocial and prosocial behavior, as well as highly divergent issues comprising school discipline, drug abuse, pregnancy, ethical and moral behavior, prosocial relationships, alienation, dropping out, and school failure. A related problem is trying to tease out the effects of EI components in multiple-component, multiple-year studies that target multiple outcomes.

Atheoretical and Unclear Focus of Some SEL Programs   Many current programs are highly fragmented, with separate programs to promote psychological health, enhance school bonding, teach problem-solving skills, reduce bullying and teenage violence, prevent dropping out, and so forth. In fact, nationally, schools are implementing a median of 14 practices to prevent problem behaviors and to promote safe environments (Zins, Weissberg, et al. 2004). One unsettled issue is what content schools should focus on? Some skills, such as managing feelings, can not be learned through explicit instruction alone. Children can be helped to procure these skills within stimulating learning environments that create opportunities for children to practice and provide constructive feedbacks, with teachers also as the role models (Lopes and Salovey 2004). However, it is unclear how much of this should be formal instruction or experiential learning. Moreover it is uncertain what approach works best for students coming from disparate social or cultural backgrounds. Already it is difficult to compare the effectiveness of EI intervention programs because these programs often have targeted different facets of EI in different or developmental age groups. Thus EI programs for younger children tend to focus on building a "feelings vocabulary" and recognizing facial expressions of emotions. EI programs for middle-school students, by contrast, often address impulse control and emotion regulation. Finally, programs targeting high school students generally focus on the role of emotions in helping students resist peer pressure to engage in risky behaviors (e.g., sexual behavior, drug or alcohol use, aggression, and violence). Additional research is needed for showing which content of SEL programs is most developmentally appropriate and congenial to various subcultures.

Small Effect Sizes and/or Lack of Rigorous Methodology Proving Efficacy A major concern of some studies is that the size of program effects is often small, so the clinical significance of the changes in the dependent measure is often uncertain. For example, in assessing the effects of the Resolving Conflicts Creatively Program (RCCP) program, small and inconsistent effects were found (Aber et al. 1998). The authors claim that this result is not surprising since children's developmental trajectories toward aggression and violence are multiply determined (and RCCP targets only some causal factors). Moreover many descriptions are replete with anecdotal material supporting the effectiveness of these programs, rather than hard data. A case in point is Goleman (1995a) who presents the testimony of one of the teachers from the New Haven program for innercity children about one of the female participants. It goes like this: "If she hadn't learned to stand up for her right during our Social Development classes she almost certainly would have been an unwed mother by now" (e.g., Goleman 1995a). Also program evaluations frequently rely on self-reports of student, teachers, or parents, rather than observational or behavioral data (e.g., Lantieri and Patti 1996), with the outcomes poorly defined.

Transferability of Emotional and Social Skills Another concern is that students may not transfer the skills taught in an EI course to real life. One can teach students knowledge of specific skills (e.g., like knowing the ingredients for baking a cake; akin to declarative knowledge) without students being able to use them effectively in social situations (e.g., bake an actual cake; akin to procedural knowledge). Clearly, the practical use of social-emotional skills extends beyond abstract knowledge to motivation and situation-dependent knowledge needed to use the skill "in the heat of the moment." Indeed this proposition resonates with much of our previous criticism of current assessments of EI; the procedural aspects of this construct are rarely taken into account (see Roberts, Schulze, et al. 2005).

A still further problem in the evaluation of emotional intelligence programs is that we really do not know *how* they work (Salovey, Bedell, et al. 1999). Even staunch advocates agree that we will only be able to speak to the optimistic claims about EI programs (e.g., reducing drug use and violence) after they have been subjected to rigorous, controlled evaluation. Because recent standards adopted by educators to assess the efficacy of interventions are exceedingly rigorous, certainly in the United States, this is no trivial undertaking (see the Department of Education government Web site at http://www.ed.gov/admins/lead/account/consolidated/index.html).

Guidelines for the Development and Evaluation of Social and Emotional Learning Programs

Thus far we have seen that SEL programs have had some successes (Zins, Weissberg, et al. 2004) but further progress is likely to depend on development of interventions that have a stronger psychological rationale, and are more rigorously evaluated. The following guidelines have been suggested for constructing SEL programs (Zeidner et al. 2002). The guidelines are consistent with "best practice" recommendations of educational psychologists and experts in pedagogy.

Base EI Intervention Programs on a Solid Conceptual Framework
EI intervention programs should be based on a solid theoretical framework, permitting a clear definition of EI and a coherent rationale for program objectives and methods for achieving them (Elias et al. 1997; Zins et al. 1997). An array of models, ranging from those based on behavioral modification and learning theories to those specific to EI, may potentially serve as frameworks both for identifying and understanding the processes and factors involved in developing effective intervention strategies. Settling on a valid definition of EI and the identification of critical EI behaviors represents a first step in the process. Clearly, different

conceptualizations of EI would lead to different intervention programs and techniques, varying operational measures, and perhaps even different postulated outcomes.

At this stage our recommendation is that the program should be explicitly based on one out of the several alternative conceptualizations previously described. An ability-based conceptualization (see chapter 3) would support training of specific competencies such as emotion perception and regulation of affect. Such a program should be evaluated against changes in objective test scores and indexes of behavior. A "mixed" conception, including elements of personality, might train the person in qualities such as impulse control and adaptive coping with stressful encounters. A more personality-focused program may be evaluated against "softer" (but validated) outcome criteria such as indexes of stress and well-being, and teacher or parent ratings of adjustment. By contrast, programs based on over inclusive accounts of EI are unlikely to succeed. In addition it is important to specify those components of EI that are to be targeted. For example, interventions designed to combat violence may need to focus on interpersonal aspects of EI, whereas intrapersonal competencies may be central to programs designed to foster improved academic study skills.

Carefully Specify Program Goals and Behavioral Outcomes

The next challenge is to decide on the specific program goals for the target population under consideration (Zins et al. 2000). Program goals should be targeted at strengthening those components of EI that form the basis of the conceptual framework underpinning the program. Once the universe of discourse on EI is clearly mapped out, it should be fairly straightforward to develop operational program objectives (and procedures designed to achieve these objectives). Program developers should thus state the desired outcomes of the EI training program in terms of the specific skills to be learned (e.g., "the sixth-grade student will be able to label 6 positive and 6 negative emotions after the fourth session of the EI training program"). Targeting specific skills entails the developer having some preexisting scheme that differentiates specific components of EI, and valid measures for each skill.

Identify the Educational, Social-Cultural, and Developmental Context for Program Implementation

The specific educational, social, and cultural contexts in which EI programs will be implemented needs to be identified from the outset (Zins et al. 2000). Otherwise, efforts may be directed at the wrong targets or social-cultural context, and may prove inappropriate. Relevant constituencies that need to be identified upon inception include student age and cultural group, school milieu and culture, teacher and administrative staff characteristics, and the broader community. EI programs should strive to foster appreciation of diversity. They should be sensitive, relevant, and responsive with regard to the ethnic, gender, and socioeconomic composition of students. These programs should also take into account the various needs and demands placed on the faculty and staff delivering the instruction and services (Elias et al. 1997).

Furthermore instructional methods and program content should be developmentally appropriate for the ages (and the grades) at which the program is being delivered (e.g., see Shriver et al. 1999). Thus EI programs should be based on developmentally appropriate, sequential, preschool to high school classroom instruction (Cohen 1999a; Zeidner et al. 2002). For example, a program designed to improve student's skills in identifying, expressing, or understanding different emotional states, should be structured according to a developmental hierarchy—beginning with basic emotions (e.g., happy, sad, or angry) and proceeding to more complex emotional states (e.g., jealous, guilty, or proud).

Fully Integrate EI Programs into the School Educational and Instructional Curriculum

As the social and emotional learning field has developed it has moved away from short-term, sporadic efforts focused on specific problems and toward comprehensive multiyear interventions designed to affect a wide range of behavioral outcomes (Nation et al. 2003). Ideally EI programs should not be taught as "add-ons" to the regular curriculum; they should be fully integrated into the overall academic program (Elias et al. 1997; Salovey et al. 1999). Accordingly an emerging strategy in this framework is not to create a special class for teaching emotional skills but to complement regular academic subjects by blending lessons on emotions with other topics (e.g., arts, health, or science). Thus students can learn how to harness emotions in gym; how to handle stress, anxiety, or frustration in math class; or how to empathize with another's plight when reading powerful literature (Salovey et al. 1999). Indeed one would not expect lasting changes to happen unless the program's principles become part of the entire school's culture (Patti and Lantier 1999). Furthermore effective EI programs should be an essential ongoing part of children's education over the course of their schooling. Thus plans should be made to provide the intervention over multiple years (Zins et al. 1997). It is the ongoing process that provides repeated opportunities for students to discover more about themselves and build these competencies as they develop (e.g., Cohen 1999a).

Make Provisions for Practice and for Generalizing the Domain of Emotional Skills across Different Classes of Behavioral Performance

Social skills may not automatically be applied to every social task and situation encountered, and it is important to ensure transfer of appropriate skills across time and contexts. To produce meaningful effects on specific target behaviors, it appears necessary to include opportunities for students to practice emotional skills in meaningful emotion-laden contexts. Consequently special efforts should be made to promote generalization of EI skills acquired in the classroom to nonclassroom contexts. One way of doing so would be to provide students with ample opportunities to practice emotional competencies both in and out of the classroom. For example, some youth development programs are based on after-school activities, whereas others seek to involve family members in social-emotional training (Durlak et al. 2007). Thus the curriculum should include strategies to facilitate generalizations across settings, individuals, and academic subjects. In this respect the cultivation of emotional competencies is similar to the cultivation of cognitive skills: it is absolutely essential to practice what is learned as well as to obtain environmental feedback on one's performance.

Professional Development of Program Personnel

It is essential to adequately prepare teachers and other staff involved in EI programs so that they can fulfill their professional role in implementing EI interventions. Because nothing in the standard curriculum prepares teachers for this type of affective experience, many teachers are often reluctant to tackle a topic that seems so foreign to their training. Therefore plans must be made to provide the staff that will deliver the program with sufficient knowledge, skills, and expertise. Professional development programs would appear requisite before and during program implementation, including periodic on-site consultations for staff.

Use Robust Experimental Designs for Assessing Program Effectiveness and Valid and Reliable Assessments

EI intervention programs should be backed by rigorous evidence of effectiveness and employ the principles and criteria used by evidence-based intervention programs. Wherever feasible, future research should employ experimental designs in which experimental units (classrooms or students) are randomly assigned to experimental or control groups, thus assuring the initial equivalence of experimental and control groups. It is noted that the large majority of SEL intervention programs implemented and assessed to date have employed quasi-experimental designs. For example, they frequently do not obtain pre-test scores before the implementation of the intervention. Furthermore the study should obtain data on long-term outcomes of the intervention, in keeping with principles of evidence-based interventions, so that researchers can judge whether or not the EI intervention effects are sustained over time.

To assess program outcomes, it is critical to use reliable and validated measures of EI and its components, rather than employing generic measures of emotional and social skills. Standardized measures of EI are needed to allow comparison of data across projects. Note that most current EI measures have been developed for adult populations, with few current measures specifically designed for school-aged populations (notable exceptions include downward extensions of the EQ-i and MSCEIT, though validity evidence for both is meager). Notwithstanding, there is an urgent need to use appropriate criterion measures to assess the impact of EI for school-aged children and youth. It is important also not to neglect the existing metrics for competence and adjustment provided by standard personality and ability tests. Such measures are often much more strongly validated and better understood than the EI scales (chapter 3). Given the overlap between EI and existing constructs, it is important to differentiate changes that can be uniquely attributed to the development of EI from changes in personality and ability. It may also be valuable to investigate interactions between EI and conventional traits. For example, Petrides et al. (2004) have found that high trait EI aids classroom achievement in children that are low in IQ, perhaps because the trait helps them manage the academic and emotional challenges posed by their lack of cognitive aptitude.

Concluding Comments

Overall, despite the problems in the conceptualization, measurement, and validation of the EI construct, the concept of EI has proved itself a catalyst and "soupstone" to the thinking and planning of educators and policy makers with respect to training social and emotional skills in the schools. Proponents of EI have supported and added impetus to the trend of bringing emotional literacy into schools and making emotions and social life key topics for learning and discussion. EI research has recognized the potential for using the school setting as a context for learning and teaching emotional skills and competencies. The school and community might be used as a means of training emotional competencies for real life, and fostering the development of specific skills in these areas (e.g., empathy). In general, EI research has been consistent with a rising tide that children's emotional learning is not outside the mandate of the school and should be fostered within education.

Further research is clearly required to better understand how to teach students to be emotionally intelligent and productive members of society (Roberts et al. 2007). We need to know more about how educators make decisions to adapt evidence-based programs, what constitutes positive adaptations that enhance program outcomes, which elements are essential to success, and what ecological conditions are needed for training to be beneficial. The work on SEL has made significant progress in these directions. However, as in the case of organizational studies (see chapter 9) there is a need for greater methodological rigor and a stronger focus on the psychological mechanisms that mediate the impact of successful interventions.

In sum, the jury is still out on the successful schooling of EI. Even so, it would seem premature to dismiss the potential value and importance of school-based EI interventions. We await systematic program planning and evaluation studies, based on the suggested guidelines above, to better inform us whether EI can be effectively schooled. Conceivably too there is room for developing programs with a closer match to contemporary knowledge of emotional skills and competencies.

Summary Points: Chapter 8

• Educators have been inspired to tackle the contemporary problems of schooling by promoting social-emotional learning. Training competencies such as constructive problem-solving, impulse control, and finding enjoyment in learning may remedy deficiencies in social functioning and support academic learning. However, for these benefits to be realized, rigorous development and evaluation of interventions is necessary.

• Academic learning may be enhanced by emotional skills that maintain motivation and self-control, together with social skills supporting teamwork and avoidance of damaging antisocial behaviors. Research thus far suggests that social-emotional competencies are modestly correlated with academic attainment in samples of schoolchildren, but evidence from studies of college students is conflicting.

• Various intervention programs designed to enhance emotional competencies in the school have been developed. They include social skills training, cognitive-behavioral modification, self-management, and multi-modal programs. Broadly, such programs often appear to be effective in improving school performance, attitudes, and behaviors, as evidenced by meta-analyses. However, enthusiasm for intervention should be tempered by recognition of methodological deficiencies. The role of EI in successful practical programs is typically unclear, and evaluations of success often lack rigor.

• Initial efforts at intervention point the way toward improving current emotional learning programs. Guidelines for success include basing programs on a solid theoretical framework, identifying educational and socio-cultural contexts, specifying goals and outcomes explicitly, integrating programs into the curriculum, training program personnel adequately, and using rigorous experimental designs for program evaluation.

• EI has been an important catalyst for interest in social-emotional learning in schools. The extent to which psychological understanding of EI may translate into better educational practice remains open to question, but education remains an important arena for the application of EI knowledge.

9 Work and Emotional Intelligence

Companies use a lot of energy trying to increase employee satisfaction. That's very nice of them, but let's face it—work sucks. If people liked work they'd do it for free.
—Scott Adams, creator of the Dilbert cartoon franchise

Emotional intelligence (EI) is frequently claimed to be an essential ingredient in what it takes to become a productive and contented organizational citizen. Indeed many companies are now committed to the idea of Corporate Social Responsibility (see table 9.1). For example, the leading global car manufacturer—Toyota—has a messaging campaign that implies hiring is not so much cognitive abilities, technical expertise, or skills. Good corporate citizenship is instead what is being sought in new recruits. Companies are now scouting for people who are compassionate, reliable on the job, productive teamworkers, and care both about their coworkers and their job (i.e., emotionally intelligent individuals). It is readily apparent that EI has become an integral part of the discussion surrounding effective organizational recruiting and placement, functioning, leadership, and training—issues which we deal with in this chapter.

As the information age continues to evolve, the wider economic system is constantly being transformed. Modern organizations are experiencing a variety of rapid changes and transitions, including proliferation of new technological developments; increased privatization; worldwide information exchange; restructuring and downsizing; outsourcing; and an increasingly diversified workforce (e.g., Burke and Cooper 2006). As a consequence of these global trends, organizations are experimenting with a variety of innovative processes at work, including more flexible organizational structures, greater emphasis on creativity, and new leadership styles.

In this evolving business world, people need both cognitive and technical skills, along with a broad arsenal of emotional and social skills, to

Table 9.1
Selected facts and figures from businesses that are committed to a philosophy of corporate social responsibility: The new yardstick for successful organizations?

Definition Corporate social responsibility (CSR) is "the continuing commitment by business to behave ethically and contribute to economic development while improving the quality of life of the workforce and their families as well as the local community and society at large" (World Business Council for Sustainable Development).
Toyota "Being a good corporate citizen starts with hiring lots of good citizens. What's a good corporate citizen? It's not about awards or mission statements or press releases. It's about people. People who care about what they do and how they do it. And at Toyota, we know these people pretty well, because we hire them every chance we get." (Recruitment Ad, *Scientific American*, August 2006).
The Body Shop, Ben and Jerry's, Whole Foods All have socially responsible founding philosophies.
Sun Microsystems Has a CSR initiative and publishes a corporate social responsibility annual report. Initiatives including sharing "groundbreaking assistive technologies" for free to people with disabilities.
Microsoft Number one in the eighth-annual Harris Interactive/*Wall Street Journal* ranking of the world's best and worst corporate reputations, largely on the back of the philanthropic activities of Bill and Melinda Gates.
Hewlett Packard The number two "best corporate citizen" published by *Business Ethics* in 2006; cited for its Digital Village Program, which establishes computer centers in villages in Africa, Asia, and Latin America.

succeed at work. Socioemotional competencies demanded in the modern workforce include, for example, passion for working effectively toward achieving group goals, communication and negotiation, and effective leadership skills. In fact, because most adults in today's world spend more of their waking hours at work than any other place—with the number of hours spent at work steadily on the rise—the workplace is one of the best settings for examining the role of EI in real-life settings, as well as for reaching adults and fostering their social and emotional competencies (Cherniss 2000a, b). Table 9.2 presents a number of claims (some exaggerated, some plausible, and some clearly unjustified) about the importance of EI in the workplace.

The roots of EI in organizational settings may be traced to classic management theory and practice (Gowing 2001). Indeed many of the strategies used in early assessment centers evaluated noncognitive abilities akin to EI (e.g., social awareness). These abilities were found to be pre-

Table 9.2
Claims with minimal supporting evidence about the importance of emotional intelligence in the workplace

Claim(s)	Source(s)
EI predicts successful behaviors at work, at a level exceeding that of intelligence.	Copper and Sawaf 1997; Goleman 1998; Weisinger 1999
Emotional competencies are a better predictor of success at the workplace than cognitive abilities or technical skills, recommending that emotional competencies be included as a method for improving senior-level hiring practices.	Cherniss and Goleman 2001
Use of EI for recruitment decisions leads to 90-percentile success rates ... what distinguishes top performers in every field, in every industry sector, is not high IQ or technical expertise, it is EI. (p. 91).	Watkin 2000

Note: Some of these claims have subsequently been retracted by the authors.

dictive of successful performance in managerial positions in many corporations. Over three decades of psychological assessment research has further vindicated the importance of taking social and emotional competencies into consideration when attempting to predict occupational effectiveness (e.g. Boyatzis 1982; Howard and Bray 1988). Increasingly these issues are being framed in terms of EI (e.g., Cherniss 2000a; Jordan et al. 2007). Could EI be the key that unlocks the gate to productivity and job satisfaction for all? Not all are convinced. There is an increasingly vocal group of critics of EI emerging within organizational psychology (see Murphy 2006a). Murphy (2006b) concludes that the emerging science of EI provides grounds for optimism, but much basic and translational research is needed to realize the potential of EI in the workplace.

In this chapter we set out to present current thinking and research on EI in various facets of organizational life. We begin with a brief description of the importance of emotions and related competencies in the workplace. This is followed by examining the evidence for the claimed role of EI in determining valued organizational outcomes (i.e., occupational performance and success, job satisfaction, organizational citizenship, and leadership behaviors). The chapter concludes with a discussion of efforts made in training emotional skills and competencies in the workplace.

The Role of Emotions in Organizations

Emotions are frequently viewed as useful sources of information that can help us interpret and navigate our social environment (chapter 6). At the workplace affective processes saturate daily life and routines; from periods of interest, pride, and joy, to moments of boredom, sadness, anger, and disgust (Ashforth and Humphrey 1995; Pekrun and Frese 1992). However, the importance of emotions in the workplace has generally been given short shrift in organizational thinking. Whereas research on emotions in mainstream psychology experienced a renaissance in the 1990s, the role of emotions at work did not enjoy a similar revival until the turn of the millennium.

One possible explanation for this state of affairs is that cognitive, motivational, and performance factors have been viewed as being more urgent for occupational life than emotions. Traditionally the workplace has been viewed as a highly logical, rational, and orderly environment, with cognitive intelligence *the* most important predictor of performance in many jobs. Because emotions were viewed as antithetical to rationality they were glossed over, disparaged, or relegated to a relatively minor status (Ashkanasy et al. 2002). A pejorative view of emotion in occupational contexts may partly account for the frequent attempts to control the experience and expression of emotions at work. Indeed, except for clearly circumscribed conditions (e.g., a high status task member giving feedback to subordinates), expressions of negative emotions are often discouraged in the work setting (Ashforth and Humphrey 1995). By contrast, if expressed in moderation and in appropriate circumstances, positive emotions appear to be approved in most work settings (e.g., at amusement parks—but not recommended for extensive use at funeral parlors).

However, the zeitgeist has offered an alternative view on the interface of reason and emotions. Current research in the cognitive and affective sciences suggests that rationality is well served by emotions and that emotions are, in fact, necessary for sound judgment and decision making (Damasio 1994). Affect may further have an important role as processing increases in complexity, with specific moods affecting cognition in different ways. Thus more and more psychologists have realized that emotions are a central element of organizational life. It is of note that the spiralling research on EI over the past decade or so has, perhaps inadvertently, catalyzed the resurgent interest in emotions in organizations and its emergence as a flourishing area of research (Ashkanasy and Tse 2000).

Work and emotions are most plausibly construed as being reciprocally determined. On the one hand, an individual's profession is among the primary determinants of emotional life and a sphere of existence that really matters, certainly in Western society (i.e., workplace → emotions). Work, with its importance for a person's well-being, self-esteem, income, and so-

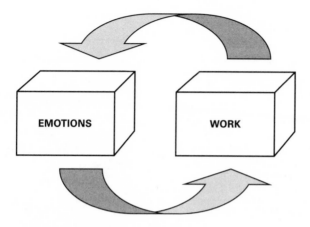

Figure 9.1
Reciprocal relationships between emotions and work

cial status, is a major source of both positive and negative emotions. Success or failure at work may influence the individual's affective development and health through the mediation of emotions. On the other hand, emotions are among the primary determinants of behavior and achievement at work, impacting upon individual productivity, well-being, and social climate (i.e., emotions → work). Thus emotions may influence work-related cognitive and motivational processes, which in turn affect task and social behavior, and performance outcomes (see figure 9.1).

However, the diverse emotions expressed in the workplace are slippery and difficult to classify (Rafaeli and Sutton 1989). Depending on the perspective adopted, the same emotion can be viewed as positive or negative. For example, the smile of a customer service representative may be construed as friendly by customers, but artificial, negative, and patronizing by the same (or another) customer service representative. One tentative typology of emotions at the workplace (Pekrun and Frese 1992) is that which attempts to specify the universe of work-relevent emotions (see table 9.3). Two major dimensions—valence (positive vs. negative) and focus (task vs. social)—partition the domain of emotions in the workplace into four discrete categories.

Emotional Competencies at Work

Typically EI is seen as a *fluid* (potential) ability from which emotional experiences and learning situations build *crystallized* ability describing learned competencies (see Matthews, Zeidner, et al. 2002). In practical

Table 9.3
Taxonomy of work-relevant emotions

	Valence	
	---	---
Focus	Positive	Negative
Task-related	• Enjoyment	• Anger
	• Hope	• Sadness
	• Relief	• Shame/guilt
	• Pride	• Boredom
	• Gratitude	• Jealousy
Social-related	• Empathy	• Contempt
	• Admiration	• Social anxiety
	• Sympathy	• Embarrassment

Source: Adapted from Pekrun and Frese (1992).

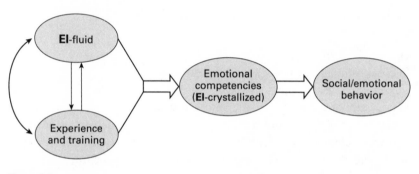

Figure 9.2
Emotional intelligence, emotional competencies, and social-emotional behavior

settings, such as the workplace, actual competencies or skills, including assertiveness, service orientation, and initiative, may be more important than potential ability. Thus it is important to evaluate the actual emotional competencies demonstrated by employees that translate EI into "on the job" capabilities. For example, in order to be able to actually empathize with another's plight, one needs to have learned the specific empathic skills that translate into caring and compassionate pastoral counselling, effective psychotherapy, or bedside nursing (Cherniss and Goleman 2001). Figure 9.2 presents a schematic for the conceptual relationship of fluid EI and crystallized competencies to work outcomes.

As depicted in figure 9.2, EI works through specific competencies to impact on work behaviors and success. Within this general framework a large array of competencies have been claimed to be critical for success in occupational settings (e.g., see Boyatzis et al. 2000; Cooper and Sawaf

Table 9.4
Two-dimensional conceptualization of emotional intelligence

	Self	Others
Identification of emotions	Self-awareness Identification and differentiation of emotions	Sympathy Empathy
Regulation of emotions	Self-regulation Coping with stressful encounters	Regulation of others' emotions Conflict resolution

1997; Weisinger 1998). For example, Goleman (1998) lists 25 different competencies necessary for effective performance in various occupational contexts (see also chapter 4). Thus confidentiality is touted as important for loan officers and priests, while trust and empathy appear vital for psychotherapists, social workers, and marriage counselors. It is of note that of the 180 competence models identified by Goleman (1998), over two-thirds of the abilities deemed essential for effective performance were identified as emotional competencies.

A useful taxonomy, presented in table 9.4, is based on the cross-partitioning of two major facets of EI, namely *emotional competencies* (emotion identification vs. emotion regulation) and *target* (self vs. others). This cross-partitioning of these two facets forms a four-category specification of the universe of discourse for EI in organizational settings (Goleman 2001).

Practical Utility of EI at Work

Much of the interest surrounding EI in organizational settings is based on the working assumption that EI can play a major role in making the workplace a more productive, profitable, and enjoyable place. The combination and integration on the part of the individual of explicit cognitive knowledge and tacit emotional knowledge may help us see what pure logic overlooks and thereby help us steer the best, safest course to success. Thus EI has been claimed to be related to a wide array of organizational results, ranging from process to outcome measures. In this section we examine the claims and supporting evidence for the claimed practical value of EI with respect to occupational outcomes typically valued in research and practice. As Antonakis (2004) soberly comments, "we have had enough propositions and armchair speculation regarding the utility of EI. Now we want to see data" (p. 179).

Job Performance

It is well established that general ability predicts anywhere from about 10 to 30 percent of the criterion variance in job performance, leaving about 90 to 70 percent of the variance in success unaccounted for (e.g., see Jensen 1998). The unexplained percentage of success appears to be, in large part, the consequence of complex (perhaps even chaotic) interactions among hundreds of variables playing out over time. Nevertheless, this well replicated finding has led researchers and practitioners alike to predict various parameters of occupational success via noncognitive variables, of which the concept of EI appears a prime candidate.

The concept of EI has even greater appeal since it is also claimed to be useful when evaluating ongoing functioning and the well-being of employees at critical stages of their careers (i.e., selection, placement, training, and promotion). In addition, as aluded to previously, EI appears valid for gauging the impact and intervention effectiveness of organizational change and restructuring (see also Bar-On 1997). As one group of writers has argued: "If the driving force of intelligence in twentieth century business has been IQ, then … in the dawning twenty-first century it will be EQ" (Cooper and Sawaf 1997, p. xxvii).

As noted above, a number of rather fantastic claims have appeared in the popular literature and the media about the significant role of EI in the workplace. Thus EI has been claimed to validly predict a variety of successful behaviors at work, at a level exceeding that of intelligence. In the *Times* article that helped popularize EI, Gibbs (1995) wrote, "In the corporate world … IQ gets you hired but EQ gets you promoted" (p. 59). In no small measure this argument rests on claims that EI assists people in "teamwork, in cooperation, and in helping others learn how to work together more effectively" (Goleman 1998, p. 163). Inside conventional wisdom, because each of these factors is thought to impinge on an organization's success, EI is given great status.

Various facets and components of EI have been claimed to contribute to success and productivity in the workplace. Thus EI is claimed to predict occupational success because it influences one's ability to succeed in coping with environmental demands and pressures (Bar-On 1997). Workers endowed with high EI are also claimed to be particularly adept at designing projects that involve infusing products with feelings and aesthetics (Mayer and Salovey 1997). More emotionally intelligent individuals are said to succeed at communicating in interesting and assertive ways, thus making others feel better in the occupational environment (Goleman 1998). Furthermore it has been claimed that EI is useful for

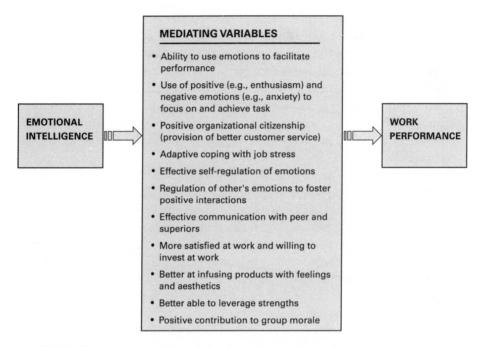

Figure 9.3
Mediating factors in the relationship between emotional intelligence and performance

group development, since a large part of effective and smooth team work is knowing each other's strengths and weaknesses and leveraging strengths whenever possible (Bar-On 1997). Figure 9.3 presents a number of potential factors mediating the relationship between EI and job performance.

It is important to underscore that the assessment of EI for occupational purposes is only cost-effective to the extent that it provides additional information to that provided by measurement of established ability and personality constructs. Thus EI measures must demonstrate not just criterion and predictive validity, but also incremental validity, with respect to existing tests. Establishing predictive validity is made more difficult by the lack of convergence between different types of EI test (see chapters 3 and 4). There is a serious problem with divergent validity in the EI domain; it has not been established that questionnaire measures of EI add much that is new to orthodox personality assessments.

A priori there is reason to be skeptical of EI proving itself more useful than intelligence tests in the area of personnel selection. Overall, conventional intelligence tests do quite a reasonable job of predicting occupational criteria (e.g., see Hunter and Schmidt 1998). A review of the literature by Hunter and Hunter (1984) suggests that cognitive abilities have a mean validity for training success of about 0.55 for all known job families. In addition ability tests appear valid across all jobs in predicting job proficiency. The validity coefficients vary by both outcome (higher for job training and lower for job performance) and job complexity (higher for greater job complexity). Almost without exception, personality-like measures are more modestly predictive of job performance than ability measures.

Several reviews point out that empirical studies of EI and job performance have obtained inconsistent results (e.g., Jordan et al. 2007; McEnrue and Groves 2006). Sometimes EI is indeed correlated with performance, typically measured with supervisor ratings, but several studies have failed to find any association. Even when the correlation between EI and performance is significant, it is typically small in magnitude, and the majority of studies fail to control for the overlap of EI, personality, and general intelligence. Studies are also weakened by methodological problems such as over-reliance on subjective ratings, small samples, poor documentation of samples and jobs, and lack of a clear rationale for predicting effects of EI. Perhaps in consequence, the field is over-reliant on unpublished studies that have not been subjected to the rigors of peer review (see Van Rooy and Viswesvaran 2004).

As an example of some of the better work being done in the area, we will describe a study using Chinese samples reported by Law et al. (2004), using the authors' own questionnaire. Their study is notable because they used a "multimethod" approach that obtained ratings of respondents' EI both from those people themselves and from others that knew them, including parents and coworkers. Interestingly the ratings of self and others were not very highly correlated. In one sample, teenagers' ratings correlated 0.21 with those of their parents; in a second sample, workers' ratings correlated 0.41 with those of supervisors. The latter sample was made up of 165 workers in a cigarette factory. These individuals, together with coworkers and supervisors, also rated their task performance, interpersonal facilitation, and job dedication.

We cannot do full justice to the various results of this study, but several findings stand out in the set of correlations given in table 9.5. First, look at the upper left quadrant of the table. The person's own ratings of EI are quite highly correlated with their ratings of task performance and related work behaviors. Now look at the lower right quadrant. A similar pattern is found for the supervisors' ratings: EI correlates with performance at

Table 9.5
Selected correlations between self-ratings and supervisor ratings of emotional intelligence and performance

	Self-rating				Supervisor rating			
	EI	Task	IF	JD	EI	Task	IF	JD
Self-rating								
EI	—							
Task	0.54	—						
IF	0.65	0.47	—					
JD	0.67	0.58	0.78	—				
Supervisor rating								
EI	0.38	0.32	0.19	0.32	—			
Task	0.18	0.31	0.17	0.30	0.51	—		
IF	0.20	0.19	0.26	0.27	0.57	0.44	—	
JD	0.23	0.27	0.26	0.39	0.58	0.63	0.69	—

Note: Task = task performance, IF = interpersonal facilitation, JD = job dedication.

0.51. But now look at the lower left quadrant, which shows how self- and supervisor-ratings correlate. The level of agreement is modest. For example, the person's own rating of their task performance correlates 0.31 with the supervisor's rating. Although not shown in the table, ratings obtained from peers (other workers at the same level) showed a similar level of agreement. Indeed, peer and supervisor ratings of EI and performance were themselves moderately correlated. On the face of it, the lack of agreement suggests a problem with the validity of the ratings, calling into question the findings of the study. Much of the variation in response seems simply to reflect the "method" for obtaining the data, namely by the type of person doing the ratings.

Law et al. (2004) used a form of structural equation modeling to try to separate such method variance from "true" variation in EI and performance. The results confirmed that most of the variation (70 percent) relates to method factors, but some variance (25 percent) can be attributed to underlying traits of EI, task performance, and other work behavior traits. More important, the *self-rating* of EI (i.e., a standard questionnaire assessment) correlates modestly but significantly ($r = 0.18$) with *supervisor* rating of task performance. Law et al. (2004) showed that this small contribution to predicting the supervisor rating remains significant with personality traits controlled. Thus, although the study concludes that "EI might be a good predictor of job performance" (p. 494), it in fact suggests rather weak criterion validity for EI. The multivariate analysis also highlights the extent to which both self- and other-ratings of EI and work performance may simply reflect method factors.

A recent meta-analysis showed weak criterion validity for most EI measures (estimated true correlation ρ of about 0.20) (Van Rooy and Viswesvaran 2004). Criterion validity was similarly modest for both objective (MEIS) and questionnaire assessments of EI. Notably the correlation between EI and performance was higher for performance assessments based on ratings (ρ = 0.26) than for assessments based on objective records (ρ = 0.14). When controlling for IQ, EI accounted for only about 2 percent of the variance in occupational criteria, whereas IQ added 31 percent to measures of EI. However, EI added to the predictive power of the Big Five personality traits, and even the modest criterion validities that the study demonstrates may be practically useful in certain circumstances. The authors suggest that using EI measures for personnel selection may generate significant savings and improvements for organizations.

Although the importance of EI for job performance has clearly been overstated in some quarters, there may be certain types of "people-oriented" jobs for which EI is most relevant. In other words, job type may be a "moderator factor" that determines whether or not EI correlates with performance. Wong and Law (2002) found that the predictive power of EI was dependent on the employee's rating of the emotional demands of the job, but Côté and Miners (2006) failed to confirm this hypothesis. A slightly different notion is that EI may be especially important for jobs requiring emotional labor (i.e., actively managing emotional expression in support of work goals). Salespersons, for example, need to project enthusiasm irrespective of how they feel. Daus (2006) summarizes studies suggesting that EI may promote more effective emotional labor in service-based occupations.

Côté and Miners (2006) tested whether effects of EI may be moderated by cognitive intelligence, as Petrides et al. (2004) have shown in the educational context (see chapter 8). The idea is that high intelligence will typically support good work performance irrespective of emotional competencies. However, if the person lacks cognitive ability, they may be able to compensate through superior EI. Côté and Miners (2006) obtained supervisor ratings of performance for 175 university employees (in non-academic jobs). They also administered the MSCEIT, personality, and intelligence tests. Analysis of the data showed that MSCEIT score correlated moderately but significantly (at 0.32) with ratings of performance, but with other variables controlled, the contribution of EI to predicting performance was trivial. However, the interaction between EI and cognitive intelligence was significant (explaining 2 percent of the variance). As hypothesized, EI made no difference when cognitive intelligence was high, but EI was positively related to performance among the less intelligent.

Côté and Miners (2006) also discuss the potential problems of using supervisors' ratings of performance, as many studies do. Ratings may be biased by the extent to which the supervisor likes the employee. In essence, high EI employees may be more likeable—not necessarily more competent—than low EI employees. In fact in the Côté and Miners (2006) study, by far the strongest predictor of rated performance ($r = 0.60$) was a measure of the quality of relationship between supervisor and employee. In addition the authors discuss the possibility that high EI employees are simply good at self-presentation (impression management); perhaps EI helps workers fool their bosses into thinking they are doing a better job than is in fact the case. Côté and Miners (2006) argue against such factors as a cause of the effects of EI their study shows, but they also accept that more research is needed on such issues.

For the present, by contrast with the impressive predictive validity of general intelligence, there is little evidence that suggests an essential role of tests of EI in real-world selection and assessment applications (see also Murphy, 2006b). Further work is needed to determine the precise circumstances in which assessment of EI may in fact be of value, by systematically investigating the roles of work demands, contextual emotional challenges, and the performance index of interest. There is also little evidence that EI is related to promotion and that EI can help individuals achieve promotion once they get a foot in the door. Indeed a recent study (Amelang and Steinmayr 2006) based on a German community sample ($N = 207$) used a structural equation modeling approach to show that general intelligence and conscientiousness related to professional status, but EI had no causal effect.

Job Satisfaction

Theory, and some empirical research (e.g., Kafetsios and Zampetakis 2008; Sy et al. 2006), suggests that emotionally intelligent individuals report greater satisfaction at work Why should this be so? First, high EI individuals purportedly utilize their ability to appraise and manage emotions in others, thus enabling them to foster interactions that help boost their morale and that of the group. This, in turn, helps contribute positively to well-being and job satisfaction for all. Second, when compared to their low EI counterparts, high EI individuals may be better at regulating their emotions to reduce job stress. Third, supervisors who are emotionally intelligent are more adept at helping workers manage their emotions, buffering them from negative events that diminish job satisfaction. Finally, emotionally intelligent managers tend to foster a positive work environment that enhances job satisfaction (Sy et al. 2006). These managers are adept at nurturing more positive interactions between employees, which fosters cooperation, coordination, and organizational citizenship behaviors contributing both to enhanced performance and job satisfaction.

Presently, empirical research supporting the direct role of EI in enhancing job satisfaction at the workplace is meager. Bar-On (1997) reports a meaningful relationship between total EI scores (based on the self-report EQ-i measure) and job satisfaction in a sample of 314 participants (mainly salespersons, teachers, college students, and nurses). Specifically, about 20 percent of the variance in work satisfaction was predicted by 3 subscale scores taken together, namely self-regard, social responsibility, and reality testing. Such findings might be expected on the basis that the Bar-On scale is saturated with neuroticism variance (see chapter 4), a personality trait that is known to relate to job satisfaction (Matthews et al. 2003).

However, the nature of the EI-job satisfaction link is not invariant across different occupations. Another study using the EQ-i (Slaski 2001) studied 224 middle and senior managers from a large UK supermarket chain. In addition to EI, data were gathered on measures of distress, morale, quality of working life, and general mental health. Management performance was gauged by assessments of immediate line managers who were asked to rate the frequency of specific behaviors (e.g., setting objectives). Total EQ-i scores were meaningfully related to quality of work satisfaction ($r = 0.41$), morale ($r = 0.55$), distress ($r = -0.57$), and general mental health ($r = 0.50$) but only very modestly related to managerial performance ($r = 0.22$). Even these weak relationships need to be qualified since the correlations failed to statistically control for general ability or personality factors.

Another study (Sy et al. 2006) examined the relationship between employee's and manager's EI, on one hand, and employee's satisfaction and performance, on the other. Data were collected from 187 food service employees from nine different locations for the same restaurant franchise. Employee's EI was positively associated with job satisfaction and performance. Also, manager's EI had a more positive correlation with job satisfaction for employees with low EI, but not for performance. More research is needed to substantiate the causal mechanisms underlying the reported relationship between EI and job satisfaction.

Positive Organizational Attitudes and Behaviors

A spate of publications has linked EI to positive organizational citizenship (i.e., attitudes and actions in the workplace that benefit working relationships and contribute to a positive working climate). Thus Abraham (2005) contends that EI would both augment organizational citizenship behaviors and enhance organizational commitment. Similarly Jordan et al. (2002) argue that organizational commitment is moderated by EI, with high EI individuals more likely to generate high affective commitment—even during times of stress and instability. Unfortunately, these theoretical models have not yet been substantiated by empirical data; their validity remains to be vindicated.

Even so, some empirical studies provide evidence in support of the link between EI and affective outcomes that might be subsumed under the heading of "positive organizational citizenship." These include altruistic behavior, career commitment, and affective commitment to the organization (Carmeli 2003); interpersonal sensitivity and prosocial tendencies (Lopes et al. 2005); altruism and compliance (Carmeli and Josman 2006); satisfaction with other group members and with the communication within their group (Lopes et al. 2005); job dedication (Law et al. 2004); customer orientation (Rozell et al. 2004); conflict resolution styles (Jordan and Troth 2002); affective tone in negotiations (Foo et al. 2004); and willingness to change (Vakola et al. 2004). These findings need to be replicated across different occupations and in large representative samples. Some studies also suggest that the relationship between EI and citizenship may be more nuanced than a general advantage for those high in EI. For example, Côté and Miners (2006) showed that EI related more strongly to behaviors related to the organization than to individuals within it. A high EI person might be prepared to defend the organization but not necessarily to help coworkers in need.

EI and Transformational Leadership

Although different definitions of leadership abound in the literature, the term, broadly defined, refers to the mobilization of resources toward the attainment of organizational goals (Yukl 1997). Accordingly leadership involves choosing organizational objectives; planning and organizing work activities in order to accomplish group objectives; motivating others to achieve the objectives; maintaining cooperative interpersonal relationships and teamwork; and enlisting support from people outside the group or organization to promote organizational goals.

Over the past two decades or so, social and emotional competencies have become integral to any discussion of effective leadership (Goleman 1998). Leadership is frequently viewed as an emotion-laden process, both from the perspective of leader and follower. In their book "Primal Leadership," Goleman et al. (2002) argue that in essence, the major component of leadership is *emotional*. In fact great leaders move us emotionally and ignite our passions and inspire the best in us. Thus, at its roots, the fundamental task of leaders is to prime good feelings in followers. Emotional competencies, it has been argued, can be important at every stage of the process linking effective leadership and work group outcomes (Ashkanazy and Tse 2000).

The link between leadership and EI has not always been apparent. Personal resources, intelligence, and cognate abilities have traditionally been regarded as the primary factor in effective leadership. According to this view, to be a successful leader, one should be smarter than others. However, while there is some empirical support for the notion that good leaders are smart, the actual relationship between general mental ability and leadership effectiveness is quite weak. Thus cognitive intelligence, particularly under highly stressful conditions, has not been shown to be a good predictor of leadership, as leaders need to be flexible, inspirational, and oriented toward the future. In fact a recent meta-analysis found that "the relationship between intelligence and leadership is considerably lower than previously thought," with a corrected correlation coefficient of only 0.27 (Judge, Colbert, and Ilies 2004, p. 542). This finding suggests that IQ accounts for only about 8 percent of the variability in leadership effectiveness, with the remainder partly accounted for by social, emotional skills, and motivational variables. While some authors (e.g., George 2000) have written compellingly about the logical relationship between EI and leadership (see figure 9.4), the hard evidence is difficult to come by.

Whereas leaders were once seen to plan, monitor, and control the overall running of an organization, in today's more service oriented industries, leadership roles entail motivating and inspiring others to foster positive attitudes toward work and creating a sense of commitment among employees (Hogan et al. 1994). These contemporary demands have changed the way we view and assess leadership. They have also placed new demands on leadership training programs to develop these skills in evolving leaders and on organizations involved in leadership selection to identify them in potential candidates (Palmer et al. 2001, 2002).

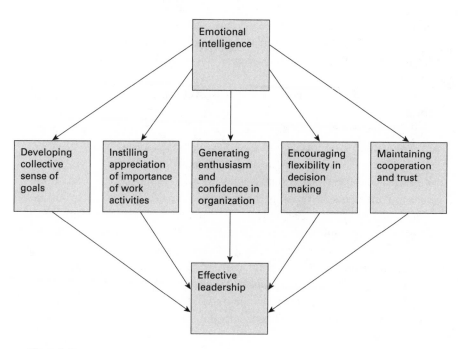

Figure 9.4
Mediating factors in the relationship between emotional intelligence and leadership

EI research on organizational management and leadership has focused on a set of leadership qualities subsumed under the umbrella term of *transformational* style of leadership (Bass 2002). Transformational leadership is characterized by the following attributes: (1) charisma and articulation of a vision of the future—the leader transmits a sense of mission that is effectively articulated, instills pride, faith, and respect, and has a gift of seeing what is really important; (2) intellectually stimulating—arouses followers to think in new ways and emphasizes problem solving and the use of reasoning before taking action; (3) individualized consideration—the leader pays attention to individual differences among peers and subordinates, delegates projects to stimulate learning experiences, provides coaching and teaching, and treats each follower as a respected individual (Yamarino and Bass 1990).

Transformational leaders excel because they develop clear and compelling visions. They also inspire their followers to work toward those visions through their use of language, storytelling, and other communication devices. The ability to communicate in ways that evoke the desired emotional response requires emotional intelligence (Ashkanasy and Tse 2000). Bass (2002) relates EI to transformational leadership via a host of mediating variables, including coping, hardiness, moral reasoning, and optimism.

EI is viewed as a prerequisite for successful transformational leadership for a number of reasons (Barling et al. 2000). Indeed it has been claimed that EI is a foundational element of charisma, vision, and careful attention to the personal needs and qualities of the individual follower (Prati et al. 2003). Transformational leaders, it is claimed, will use charismatic authority and transformational influence and induce collective motivation in team members in order to improve team performance. Transformational leaders are further said to be in touch with their own and their follower's feelings and "lead from the heart." Whether it is charting a grand vision for the future, mediating among diverse stakeholders, or providing corrective feedback to a struggling subordinate, leaders must draw on the abilities associated with emotional intelligence. Ashkanasy and Tse (2000) attribute this power to the charismatic leader exercising control over his or her own emotions, as well as controlling other member's emotions.

Critical Perspective   Several authors have disputed whether EI is integral to leadership (e.g., Locke 2005). For example, Antonakis (2003, 2004) questions to what degree high levels of emotional appraisal are needed in organizational leadership. Clearly, normal individuals are known to be perfectly capable of demonstrating the appraisal skills necessary for leadership, without resorting to inordinate levels of charisma. But it is unclear why leaders should refrain from displaying anger or sadness, as charisma is frequently based on an emotional appeal that might include anger, disgust, and so forth. Former British Prime Minister Margaret Thatcher was known both for her charisma and her lack of empathy for the victims of social and political change.

It appears then that proponents of EI offer a circular argument by listing inspirational leadership as an emotional competency essential to effective leadership (Locke 2005). By asserting that leadership is an emotional process, proponents are also appearing to disparage and denigrate the critical role played by rational thinking in the leadership process. Furthermore, although the morale of employees is important, for sure, it is not an end in itself divorced from effectiveness. Good leadership is more than promoting a positive emotional climate and worker morale; it revolves around consistent rational thinking by a mind that is able to grasp and integrate all the facts needed to make the business succeed. In short, as aptly phrased by Locke (2005): "Leadership is not primarily about making people feel good; it's about knowing what you are doing and knowing what to do" (p. 429). Indeed emotional leadership in the absence of actual achievement may be positively dangerous. Executives in the failed Enron Corporation continued to make convincingly bullish statements about the company's prospects even as its finances disintegrated, leaving many with worthless stock. One may wonder whether willingness to follow a transformational leader is a sign of emotional intelligence or stupidity.

Empirical Research   A number of studies have vindicated the relationship between EI and key facets of transformational leadership. For example, Bass (2002) presented empirical evidence indicating that social and emotional intelligences are better predictors of transformational leadership than cognitive intelligence. Additional studies point to relationships between various facets of EI and leadership (Barling et al. 2000; Skinner and Spurgeon 2005). However the data are not entirely consistent, with some studies even reporting contrary findings (Palmer et al. 2001).

A recent study by Rosete and Ciarrochi (2005) provides a good example of the strengths and weaknesses of research in this area. The authors administered the MSCEIT to a rather small sample ($N = 41$) of executives working for a large Australian public service organization. They measured leadership effectiveness through (1) five-point ratings made by the person's direct manager, and (2) a 360 degree rating that combined the person's own ratings with the judgments of other personnel. The study showed that the MSCEIT correlated moderately with the manager's rating of the person's *style* of leadership (how they achieved their level of performance) but was unrelated to ratings of actual performance (what they achieved). Analysis of the 360 degree ratings showed that the MSCEIT correlated with two out of five features of leadership (cultivating productive relationships and exemplifying drive and integrity). Despite these rather ambiguous findings, the authors happily conclude that "higher EI was associated with higher leadership effectiveness" (p. 380). One might equally infer that EI relates to style rather then effectiveness of leadership. The researchers also attempted to control for personality and intelligence, showing that perceiving emotion—but no other branch—predicted leadership with these factors controlled. Although the study provides evidence linking MSCEIT scores to qualitative features of leadership, it also shows how slippage from equivocal data toward an oversimplified conclusion may result.

There are further some inconsistencies in the details of leadership studies. Rosete and Ciarrochi (2005) found that "strategic EI" (understanding and managing emotion) related to ratings of leadership but "experiential EI" (perception and assimilation) did not. However, another rather similar study of 38 supervisors in a large manufacturing organization (Kerr et al. 2006) found that it was experiential, rather than strategic, EI that predicted ratings of supervisory leadership performance. Both studies support a role for EI in leadership but without consistency in the relevant facets of EI, it is difficult to say much more about why EI may be important.

When all of the available research is considered collectively, the evidence seems to support the hypothesis that EI is linked to various indexes of transformational leadership style, although it is unclear which facets are critical. Future research would benefit from a number of improvements, such as using practicing leaders (rather than students), gathering data on leadership in more objective ways, using ability-based (rather than self-report) measures of EI, and controlling statistically for personality and IQ. Some studies (Rosete and Ciarrochi 2005) have done so, but much more remains to be done to discover the underlying psychological processes and contextual factors that influence the relationship. For instance, what are mediating and moderating factors in this relationship? What kinds of leadership tasks and functions are most affected by the leader's emotional intelligence? Are there certain kinds of followers who are more affected by the emotional intelligence of the leader than others? We leave it to research in the future to address these more sophisticated questions about the connection between emotional intelligence and leadership. For now we provide a summary in figure 9.5 of the relationships between EI and various organizational variables and outcomes.

Training EI Competencies at the Workplace

Based on the working assumption that EI is malleable during adulthood and can be trained, there is a growing impetus toward the provision of personal and workplace interventions that purport to increase EI (Zeidner 2005). It is, of course, assumed that personal and societal benefits will follow from investment in programs to increase EI. That is, specific emotional competencies (e.g., emotion perception) will have important consequences for how individuals perform in organizational settings, how they cope with stress and conflict, and react affectively to the environment. Whether the motivation is to promote greater organizational

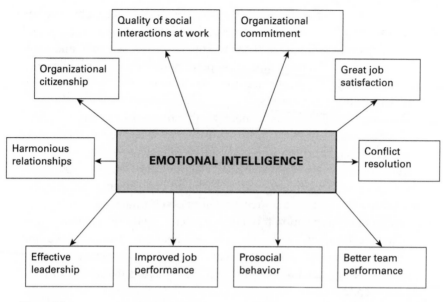

Figure 9.5
Emotional intelligence and organizational variables and outcomes

productivity and competitiveness, or physical health and well-being, the workplace may be one of the best settings for examining the role of EI and for reaching adults and fostering their EI (Cherniss 2000).

Currently there are a variety of training programs designed to promote emotional skills and competencies in the occupational environment. For example, police departments have adopted training designed to help officers better manage their own reactions and those of others in conflict. Similarly physicians have been given training on how to be more empathetic toward their patients and to their families (Cherniss et al. 1998). In effect the American industry spends about $50 million each year on training competencies, and much of these programs focuses on social and emotional abilities (see Cherniss 2000a, b).

The workplace appears to be a most appropriate setting for systematic efforts to improve EI competencies, for a number of reasons. First, emotional competences are claimed to be critical for maintaining effective performance on the job. As noted in this chapter, emotions at work have been shown by some studies to influence work decision making and performance, job satisfaction, and helping behavior. It has been claimed that about two-thirds of the competencies linked to superior performance are emotional or social qualities, such as self-confidence, empathy, and the ability to get along with others (Boyatzis 1982). Second, many workers enter the workforce without the necessary emotional competencies and social skills that will enable them to cope with the demands and challenges on the job. Third, compared to other potential sites for implementing interventions, the workplace often has available means for providing necessary training experiences.

Overall, it is difficult to determine whether or not EI training programs at the workplace are effective to any meaningful degree, with reviewers differing in their conclusions. Based on their survey of the intervention literature in the domain of management, Cherniss and Goleman (2001) conclude that interventions targeted at EI-based competencies are effective and tend to enhance such desired outcomes as self-awareness and rapport. In addition self-motivation training (e.g., lecture and discussion) can help in fostering creativity and harnessing stronger achievement drive and business performance. Thus they conclude: "Taken together, all these interventions demonstrate that it is possible for adults to develop EI competencies (p. 214)."

In a recent review of research focusing on EI in organizational settings (Jordan et al. 2007), EI is evaluated as being an important potential personal resource for organizational contexts. Thus EI is claimed to be particularly related to organizational performance and outcomes in tasks where there is a clear emotional skill required for successful performance (e.g., sales, customer relations). A meta-analysis conducted by Burke and Day (1986) seems to support this conclusion. These authors found that managerial training programs had an average effect size of over one standard deviation for human relations training and about two thirds of a standard deviation for self-awareness.

However, with several notable exceptions (e.g., the theory-based EI program systematically assessed by Ashkanasy et al. 2006), few organizations actually test the EI training programs they implement (Caruso and Wolfe 2004; see Landy 2005, 2006). Cherniss et al. (1998) report the results of a recent survey of companies conducted by the American Society for Training and Development. Of the 27 companies claiming to have tried to promote emotional competence through training and development, more than two-thirds did not attempt to evaluate the effect of these efforts. Those who had, relied primarily on employee opinion surveys. Evidently, when it comes to EI, hard-nosed companies become soft and they simply do not insist on hard evidence.

In order to maximize the effectiveness of EI training programs, Cherniss and Goleman (2001) offer a number of useful guidelines, including

Table 9.6
Proposed guidelines for development of emotional competence training programs in the workplace

| **Preparation for Change** |
| Before change can take place, efforts should be made at assuring the motivation, commitment, and self-efficacy of members of the organization. Accordingly, people are likely to be motivated to improve emotional competencies if they are convinced that such a change will lead to desirable consequences. Efforts to improve emotional competencies should begin with an assessment of the competencies most critical for organizational and individual effectiveness. If employees are ready, motivation and commitment can be strengthened by helping them to set specific meaningful and realistic goals. Training programs will be more effective if they include activities designed to help learners develop positive expectations for the training and greater self-efficacy. |
| **Doing the Work** |
| The next step involves training and development of members of the organization. Emotional and social change needs to occur in a safe and supportive setting, and the relationship between trainers and learners becomes crucial in defining how safe and supportive the learning environment is for the learners. It is assumed that live models that demonstrate the skills and competencies to be mastered are more effective than simply focusing on declarative knowledge. Training should involve experiential learning rather than lecture and discussion, with ample opportunity for the learners to practice the new skills in as many domains as possible. About a dozen sessions are needed; receiving feedback on practice is particularly valuable. Training materials should encourage the learners to anticipate what barriers and problems they might encounter when they begin to apply what they have learned in their day-to-day lives. Then they learn how these might affect them emotionally and what they might do to deal with these problems. |
| **Evaluation of Training Efforts** |
| Training efforts should be evaluated to determine not just whether people feel good about them but also whether they produce meaningful changes in on-the-job behavior. This is especially important for EI promotion efforts because there is often greater skepticism about whether such work is useful. Even managers who recognize that EI is important for individual and organizational success may question whether a training initiative can bring about significant improvements in these competencies. Evaluation research should be used to help program managers see why and how a training effort works and ways in which it can be improved in the future. |

Source: Adapted from Cherniss et al. (1998).

creating an encouraging and supportive environment for intervention, using models of desired skills, inoculating against setback, and providing follow-up support (see table 9.6). They claim that these guidelines appear to have had some success. The modern training protocol that is derived from such guidelines is briefly described in table 9.7.

Proponents of EI programs at the workplace have claimed that the development and training of emotional competencies requires deep changes and the re-tooling of ingrained habits of thought, feeling, and behavior (e.g., see Cherniss et al. 1998; Goleman 1998). The limbic system, one of

Table 9.7
Protocol for training EI skills in the workplace

Phase 1 Competencies required by the organization are identified and a careful diagnosis is made of the specific skills in which the client is lacking, in order to help bridge the gap between demanded skills and present skills. The program trainers make an effort to help the clients appreciate the benefits of mastering those competencies as well as socializing them to the process of acquiring them through cognitive, behavioral, and physiological changes.
Phase 2 Clients are trained to improve their ability to identify their own emotions and to distinguish them from the emotions of others. Clients are also taught to improve their ability to use multiple and increasingly subtle cues to identify emotions in their co-workers. Learning skills of emotion perception, understanding, and regulation requires that EI training be experiential, based on repeated practice and role playing with feedback.
Phase 3 Clients are encouraged to form social support groups with similarly minded people for the purpose of practicing their newly acquired EI skills and providing mutual reinforcement.
Phase 4 The last phase of the training protocol involves systematic assessment of the outcomes (cognitive, social, emotional, and behavioral) of the intervention. Valid and reliable measures of the program outcomes need to be taken.

the oldest parts of the brain in evolutionary terms, does not "understand" words or concepts. Thus any successful effort to improve emotional intelligence must be active and experiential, not just verbal and cognitive. Accordingly there are strong response habits that must be altered in emotional learning and existing neural pathways must be weakened and eventually extinguished before new ones can be established. What this means, in practice, is that the learning process requires repeated practice over a much longer time. Thus learners must enter the process with a high degree of motivation, and there must be considerable guidance and support to help them maintain motivation until a new way of thinking becomes second nature (Cherniss et al. 1998). Otherwise, following a short-term training and development program, participants will simply get a short-term buzz of energy that lasts no more than a few days or weeks, after which they fall back into whatever their habitual mode was before.

One example of an experiential training program is the Emotional Competence Training program, developed at American Express Financial Advisors in 1992 and since used by managers in that company and several others in the United States (Cherniss and Adler 2000; Goleman

1998). There are several versions of the program, but the one that has been found to be effective involves about 40 hours of training, divided into two group sessions of two or three days each, which are separated by a month or two. Carefully selected, doctoral-level psychologists who understand the special challenges involved in implementing such a program in work organizations deliver the program. Although there are some didactic segments of the program, much of it involves highly experiential activity, such as role playing, simulations, and the like. The program covers a number of topics, including the role of emotion in the workplace, different ways of expressing how we are feeling, the impact of "self-talk" on feelings and behavior, active listening, and norms for the expression of emotion at work.

Concluding Remarks

This chapter discussed the theory and evidence supporting the claimed role of emotions and EI in the workplace. Overall, EI is currently evaluated as being an important and potentially valuable personal resource for organizational settings, purportedly related to tasks where there is a clear emotional skill required for successful performance (e.g., customer relations). Accordingly EI is shown to modestly predict an array of organizational outcomes, ranging from job performance to job satisfaction, organizational citizenship, and leadership.

As noted, the traditional predominance of rationality as the major paradigm for researching occupational settings has been indirectly responsible for the neglect of the role of emotions at work. However, the recent popularization of EI as a salient psychological construct has lead to an upsurge of interest and has spawned a sizable literature on both emotions and emotional competencies at the workplace. Yet there is much that remains to be learned about emotion in this setting. For example, relatively little is known about the situational and cognitive antecedents of positive and negative emotions when on the job. Furthermore information on the phenomenology of work-related emotions, the consequences of emotions, or the prevention, optimization, and modification of emotional behavior while performing one's occupational duties is sparse and in need of further investigation. It is of note that both researchers and practitioners have shown less interest in the potential positive functions of emotions than in the potential dysfunction caused by negative emotions in an organizational environment (see chapter 10 for our take on this issue).

More research is needed to discover the contextual factors that influence the relationship between EI and organizational leadership and other criteria. For instance, what are the kinds of leadership tasks and functions that are most affected by the leader's emotional intelligence? Are there certain kinds of followers who are more affected by the emotional intelligence of the leader than others? What are the types of work environment in which high EI is most advantageous? Another gap in the research is neglect in empirical studies of mediating processes. For example, what factors control the association between job performance and supervisor ratings found in some studies? Is the high EI worker (1) genuinely more proficient at the immediate tasks performed, (2) better at self-promotion, (3) better at forming good working relationships with others, or (4) simply more likeable? These more sophisticated questions about the connection between EI and workplace behavior should call for more research.

Overall, however, the current excitement surrounding the potential benefits from the use of EI in the workplace may be premature or even misplaced. The relationships reported in the literature are far from consistent, and additional research is needed to replicate and extend existing knowledge as well as uncover mediating processes through which EI works to explain various types of job outcomes. EI appears to be related very modestly to performance and a number of affective outcomes, although the evidence for performance effects is very limited and often contradictory. Much of the reported predictive validity of EI measures—particularly self-report—may be a product of their overlap with standard personality factors, although a few studies have shown incremental validity for EI.

From a practical point of view, there is little empirically based evidence, generated from representative samples of respondents in different occupational categories, and published in peer-reviewed journals, to indicate that EI measures do reliably and incrementally predict criteria of job success and well-being, above and beyond that predicted by standard ability or personality measures. Notwithstanding claims by proponents of EI at the worksite with respect to the role of EI in career assessment, EI should probably not be included as part of every standard job selection or classification battery. Instead, EI should be used only where warranted by the job description. Accordingly, when particular emotional skills are part of the job description (e.g., empathy or conflict resolution), it would seem important to assess EI. By contrast, in those jobs where adequate emotional skills are really minimal, there is little sense in assessing EI. At present there is an urgent need for sound taxonomic research

Table 9.8
Job features that enhance the relevance of emotional intelligence

Obtaining benefits from EI in occupational settings requires attention to a long-standing issue in organizational psychology: the "criterion problem" of valid assessment of work performance and other job-related behaviors (Guion 1998). Accordingly, it is not only overt job proficiency that is important for the organization but also other classes of behavior that contribute meaningfully to the organization's goals and mission, such as willingness to support others, to apply extra effort and volunteer for assignments, and to maintain personal discipline, integrity, and honesty. These behaviors are captured by terms including organizational citizenship and contextual performance (Motowidlo 2000). It seems plausible that we can analyze overt job descriptions for the relevance of EI. Below are features of jobs that may particularly enhance the relevance of EI (Schmit 2006):
1. The job involves emotionally charged situations and emotional labor; for example, oncologists face long-term interactions with emotionally demanding family of patients.
2. Performance depends on expression of positive emotion, as in customer service, sales, recruitment, and marketing.
3. The job requires creative problem solving (assuming this to be facilitated by emotion), as would be the case in advertising.
4. The organization is required to confront change; EI helps employees to manage the stress of changes in business strategy and working practices.

that focuses on determining the EI constructs that are crucial for the performance of particular jobs and identifying the relevant EI measures that best assess these affective constructs. Table 9.8 delineates a number of job features that may enhance the relevance of EI.

A number of training programs designed to promote EI at the workplace have been implemented and reported in the literature. Unfortunately, these programs are, by and large, seriously flawed from a program planning and evaluation perspective. Thus these training programs are typically not grounded in a solid conceptual framework, they fail to be based on appropriate experimental designs (e.g., randomized trials), and have been lacking in systematic evaluations that include repeated assessment and tracking over time to gauge delayed or prolonged effects. An additional problem is that the reviews of EI programs at work often include, under the rubric of EI interventions and training programs, worksite programs that have existed in the past (e.g., sensitivity training). The success of these commonplace and longstanding programs is inappropriately taken as evidence for the effectiveness of EI programs. At present the value of EI-based training programs remains uncertain. A final thought is that it remains unclear whether training in EI should benefit the worker or the organization. Is the intent to train self-aware, emotionally literate employees who can take decisions that best serve their own interests—or to enhance productivity and inculcate loyalty to the organization? Happy workers may be productive workers, but personal and organizational interests do not necessarily coincide. Sometimes the emotionally intelligent choice may be to put personal needs first.

Summary Points: Chapter 9

• It is widely believed that emotional competencies are important in the workplace. Skills in communication, teamwork, handling pressure, and leadership seem to have been neglected by organizational psychologists. Organizations may be able to increase productivity and improve employee well-being through assessment and training of EI. However, much work on EI in organizations lacks rigor, and there is a risk that it may prove to be no more than another business fad.

• Work and emotions are reciprocally related. Successes and failures at work generate emotions that may feed back to influence job performance, health, and other work behaviors. Understanding the interplay between work and emotion requires the identification of emotional competencies that determine whether the employee can manage work demands adaptively.

• A major focus for research has been to test whether measures of EI predict job proficiency. Studies have compared various scales for EI with conventional intelligence tests and personality questionnaires. Although some studies show modest associations between EI and job performance, meta-analysis suggests that EI is of limited practical utility as a predictor. IQ is generally a stronger predictor of performance. Research is now focusing on moderator factors that may influence the strength of the association between EI and proficiency, such as the extent to which the job is people-oriented or dependent on emotional labor.

• Research has also been directed toward occupational criteria in addition to job proficiency. There is some evidence for EI relating to affective outcomes including job satisfaction, and organizational commitment and citizenship, although high EI does not necessarily produce across-the-board improvements in relation to affective criteria. High EI has also been linked to effective leadership, especially transformational leadership dependent on charisma and inspiration.

• American industry spends millions of dollars each year on training programs intended to enhance social and emotional abilities. Systematic attempts to improve EI in the workplace may confer a number of organizational and personal benefits. However, as with the educational training programs reviewed in chapter 8, it is often difficult to evaluate the effectiveness of workplace interventions, due to a lack of rigor in study design and evaluation methods. Suggested guidelines for improving training effectiveness include creating a supportive environment for intervention, providing models of desired skills, inoculating against setback, and providing follow-up support.

• Hopes are high that a focus on EI will contribute to remediation of many of the problems faced by the modern workforce. There is some empirical evidence showing that tests of EI relate to a variety of organizational criteria, although validity coefficients are often modest. However, systematic research matching facets of EI to specific job competencies is needed in order to substantiate the relevance of EI to the workplace.

10 Emotional Intelligence and the Toxic Work Environment

Life is just one damn thing after another.
—Elbert Hubbard

It's not sure that life is one damn thing after another. It's one damn thing over and over.
—Edna St. Vincent Millay

Frequently described as the Black Plague of the postindustrial era, psychological stress has become a major problem, threatening individuals, organizations, and whole societies. For example, US industry loses approximately 550 million working days per year due to absenteeism; it is estimated that 54 percent of these absences are in some way stress-related (Elkin and Rosch 1990). The total cost of stress to American organizations, including losses due to absenteeism, reduced productivity, compensation claims, health insurance, direct medical expenses and other factors adds up to more than $300 billion a year (American Institute of Stress 2002). A large proportion of premature deaths in western countries are also attributed to stress-related illness. Among physical and mental disorders linked to stress are coronary heart disease, infectious disease, sleep disorders, chronic respiratory ailments, and depression (House 1981; Shirom 2003).

Indeed organizational stress appears a global problem. Research has demonstrated highly comparable levels of stress in workers in various occupational settings across the globe. A National Institute for Organizational Safety and Health (NIOSH 1999) report suggests that between 26 and 40 percent of workers often find their jobs stressful. A review by Mack et al. (1998) discusses a variety of sources of work conditions (e.g., heavy workload), levels of stress, and personal characteristics that cause workers to be susceptible to stress. In recent years, social trends ranging from the introduction of new technology, economic globalization, and increasing conflicts between the demands of work and home have been seen as exacerbating occupational stress (e.g., Burke and Cooper 2006).

Emotions are on-line indicators of the meanings we attach to environmental events in real time (see chapter 7). Our emotions and feelings on the job capture our personal understanding of ongoing workplace events involving the challenges, threats, and losses that a job provides. When we believe we are successfully coping with a challenge we tend to feel good about ourselves; failure to cope effectively makes us feel bad. Thus emotions evoked on the job are capable of providing us with rich information we can tap into, informing us of the various dynamic transactions and relational meanings that we share inside our organizational environment. In the best-case scenario this emotional awareness may alter our thinking and behavior in such a way as to allow us to negotiate organizational challenges in a more adaptive (and productive) manner. Furthermore, to the extent that a better understanding of emotions will help workers reach organizational goals, and thus give organizations a competitive edge, emotional issues may be critical for organizational success (Ashkanasy et al. 2002).

In this chapter we set out to present current thinking and research on the pivotal role of EI in coping with the stress, violence, and the ego-threatening complexities of organizational life. We begin with a brief description of sources of occupational stress, move on to discuss the potential outcomes of stress at work, and then touch briefly upon violence and aggression at the worksite. The chapter concludes with a discussion of the contribution of EI research to training coping skills in the workplace.

Organizational Stress

Emotional intelligence (EI) has figured prominently in the literature as a pivotal factor said to impact upon stress, coping, and adaptive outcomes (see chapter 7). Proponents of emotional intelligence (e.g., Goleman 1998) have recently claimed that a better understanding and regulation of one's emotions may dramatically enhance personal coping capabilities at the workplace and impact favorably on adaptive outcomes. Accordingly EI should be systematically related to individual differences in coping, which in turn should confer generally more or less successful outcomes on the individual.

What Is Occupational Stress?

Following the transactional model of stress (e.g., Lazarus and Folkman 1984), a number of occupational psychologists (Beehr and Newman 1978; Kohler et al. 2006) have conceptualized stress in organizations as a dynamic interaction between the person and the environment. Accordingly job stress arises in an occupational situation that has demands, constraints, and opportunities that are perceived to threaten (or to exceed) a person's attentional resources and coping capabilities. This interaction between occupational conditions and the worker's attentional resources result in a meaningful change (disruption or enhancement) of the worker's physiological or psychological condition, such that the person is forced to deviate from normal functioning.

From the transactional perspective, to understand the experience of work stress, one must consider both the subjective and objective environment that the individual is encountering. In addition one needs to consider stable individual differences that influence both the nature and strength of, occupational stresses that are perceived, coping resources and responses that are available and utilized, and emotional and physical well-being. Figure 10.1 depicts key factors in job stress according to the transactional model.

Sources of Occupational Stress

Over three decades of systematic study in the area of occupational stress have generated a substantial body of evidence on interacting factors that contribute to stress in the workplace (Cooper et al. 2001; Spielberger and Reheiser 2005). Work stress can be caused by factors such as too much or too little work, time pressures and deadlines, having too many decisions, fatigue from the physical strains of work (assembly line), excessive travel, supervisor/coworker bullying, emotional labor, having to cope with frequent changes in the workplace, and errors in making financial decisions (Cooper et al. 2001).

Interestingly job requirements to regulate negative emotions and express positive emotions are by themselves a frequent source of stress and physical symptoms (Schaubroeck and Jones 2000). In sum, almost every job description will include factors that for some individuals, at some point in time, will be a source of pressure. Table 10.1 presents some of the major categories of work stress, based on a taxonomy suggested by Cartwright and Cooper (1996). The table brings out the multifaceted nature of sources of stress. Some sources are innate in the work activities

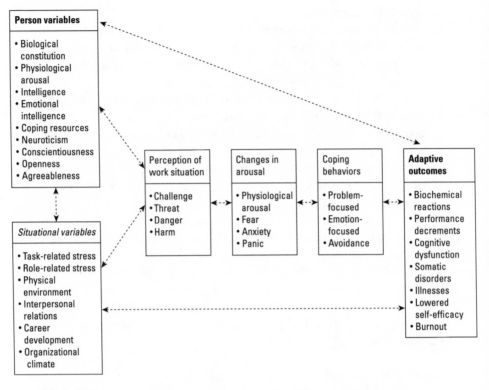

Figure 10.1
A transactional model of occupational stress and coping

performed, such as excessive workload and pressing deadlines. Some sources feed off the person's goals and values, such as failure to win promotion, or disruption of home life due to work demands. Still other sources are interpersonal, such as poor relations with coworkers and customers. The emotionally intelligent employee needs not just to be a good coper but also a multitasker in juggling diverse sources of demand, and setting priorities so as to focus on coping on those demands that are most pressing.

Outcomes of Occupational Stress
As noted by Repetti (1993), "Work can be hazardous to your health" (p. 368). The literature suggests that occupational stress can adversely affect a variety of outcomes, including job satisfaction and performance, family problems, and a person's physical and mental health (e.g., the in-

Table 10.1
Sources of occupational stress

1. Factors intrinsic to the job, task, or workplace This category includes physical conditions and task-related sources of stress (Schuler 1980). Specific sources of stress include poor physical working conditions; for example, inadequate lighting, crowded space, and lack of privacy. Task-related sources of stress include, for example: work overload/underload, lack of autonomy, and shift work. French and Caplan (1973) differentiate between quantitative overload, where a worker has too much to do, and qualitative overload, where a task is too difficult for the worker. Research suggests that work overload is indeed a major source of stress with important health implications (Cooper and Marshall 1978). Both qualitative and quantitative overload produces a variety of different symptoms of psychological strain, such as: job dissatisfaction, tension, and low self-esteem. More chronic and serious consequences include coronary heart disease, escapist drinking, and absenteeism.
2. Role in the organization Key dimensions of perceived role-related stress include ambiguity, conflict, and powerlessness. Role ambiguity arises when a person has inadequate information about the work role or lack of clarity about work objectives; about work colleague's expectations of the work role; and scope and responsibilities of the job. If employees do not know what their duties are, for example, they may hesitate to make decisions. Role ambiguity has been linked to job stress and high levels of anxiety, along with poor productivity, lower job satisfaction, and higher job-related stress (Kottkamp and Travlos 1986). Role conflict evolves when behaviors expected by others in the organization are inconsistent (Hamner and Tosi 1974). Role conflict exists when an individual in a particular work role is torn by conflicting job demands or is engaged in things she really does not want to do (Cooper and Payne 1978). Kahn et al. (1964) reported that role conflict was related to job stress, high job-related tension, and lower self-esteem. Powerlessness, another major source of job stress, refers to the perception that an individual cannot control outcomes. Lack of control over outcomes has been linked to high anxiety, job dissatisfaction, low self-esteem, and poor job performance (Kottkap and Travlos 1986).
3. Problematic relationships with others at work Another source of stress on the job involves the poor relationships between group members, including subordinates, colleagues, and clients (Cooper and Marshall 1978). This is manifested by low trust, low supportiveness, and low interest in listening to and trying to deal with problems that confront organizational members. Some data suggest that negative interactions with coworkers and employees and clients and supervisors are the most frequently reported source of work-related stress. This is related to a person's need for acceptance and interpersonal recognition. When these interpersonal relations are not satisfactory to an individual, stress results (Schuler 1980).
4. Career development This category includes the threat of job loss, underpromotion, demotion, and derailing, having reached a career plateau, early retirement, or unclear career future. A source of fear involves the threat of job security and status incongruity (e.g., frustration at having reached one's career's ceiling; Cooper and Marshall 1978). Transitions and organizational changes are frequently viewed also as being extremely disruptive.

Table 10.1
(continued)

5. Organizational structure, climate, and culture This category subsumes stressors related to being in a particular organization and its organizational milieu and culture. This may include, for example, lack of a person–role fit. The mismatch and gap between job demands and requisite knowledge, skills, and abilities will result in high strain for workers especially in service-based jobs. Threat to an individual's freedom, autonomy, and identity is a source of stress for many. Also personal and sexual harassment have assumed increasing prominence as a source of stress at the workplace. Human service jobs may also pose demands that are different from those of other professions because workers must use themselves as the technology for meeting the needs of clients, who in turn do not always express gratitude or appreciation. Stress associated with organizational climate, including measures of perceived job design, leadership, and relationships with coworkers, have been found to be related to worker satisfaction and alienation in these domains. A variety of sources of job stress in this category (e.g., workload, role conflict) have been reported to predict job dissatisfaction, psychological symptoms, and various risk factors for coronary heart disease (French and Caplan 1973). Career stress is associated with multiple negative outcomes (Ivancevich and Matteson 1987).
6. Home/work interface Managing the interface between work and home can be a major source of stress, particularly for dual career couples or those experiencing financial crises. By providing more flexible work arrangements and adopting family-friendly employment policies, this source of stress may be ameliorated.

Source: Adapted from Cartwright and Cooper (1996).

cidence of coronary heart disease) (Schuler 1980; Shirom 2003). The indirect costs of stress are reflected in a variety of indexes of social pathology, including levels of substance abuse, high divorce rates, mortality rates, and accident statistics. Stress may also result in higher incidences of aggressive behaviors, accidents, and thefts in the occupational environment. Furthermore work stressors may feed into the family and social environment, becoming a potential source of disturbance that subsequently pervades the whole quality of an individual's life. Over the past two decades a substantial amount of research on job stress has been conducted. Much of this research focus has examined the potential consequences of stress on criterion variables such as job satisfaction, job burnout, and morbidity. The literature has consistently shown that perceived stress on the job is related to employee health and well-being (e.g., Michielsen et al. 2007; see also Holt 1993; Jones and Bright 2007; McEwen and Lasley 2007; Schnall et al. 1994).

Following French and Caplan (1973), it is useful to differentiate between quantitative overload ("too much to do") and qualitative stress ("task is too difficult"). Research by Cooper and Marshall (1978) suggests that quantitative overload is indeed a major source of stress with important health implications. At the same time both qualitative and quantitative overload produce an array of different symptoms of psychological strain: job dissatisfaction, tension, low self-esteem, threat, high cholesterol levels, and tobacco abuse. More chronic and serious consequences include coronary heart disease, escapist drinking, and absenteeism.

Coping with Occupational Stress

Proponents often see effective coping with stress as central to EI (Spielberger and Reheiser 2005), although, as we saw in chapter 7, the role of EI in coping has not always been confirmed. Broadly, current thinking among EI researchers (e.g., Salovey, Bedell, et al. 1999) suggests that the way people identify, understand, regulate, and repair emotions (in self and others) helps determine coping behaviors and resulting adaptive outcomes.

Research suggests that most people do not cope very well with organizational change and transitions, and consequently suffer long-term adverse mental and physical health (Cherry et al. 2006; Head et al. 2006). In fact coping with, and managing, work stress is often more complex than dealing with stressful events outside work. The challenge results from inherent constraints within the work environment, which restrict the range of acceptable coping responses and limit individual control. These demands emphasize the potential importance of emotional competencies in coping with the stresses of current work environments.

Newman and Beehr (1979) identified four strategies used to cope with work stress: (1) changing one's work environment, (2) changing one's behavior, to accommodate to existing work conditions, (3) changing one's physical conditions (e.g., diet, exercise), and (4) changing psychological conditions (e.g., planning ahead). Cartwright and Cooper (1996) suggest that work-related stress and routine daily work hassles elicit more task-oriented or problem-focused than emotion-focused strategies. This outcome resonates with others findings. For example, Lazarus (1991) observed that individuals used higher levels of problem-focused than emotion-focused coping when negotiating with stressful events on the job. However, there are concerns that typical coping scales capture the dynamic behaviors employed in dealing with workplace stressors. Dewe (2003) suggests that coping may be better conceptualized as functionally distinct patterns of behaviors such as the use of coping strategies that facilitate one another, or using one strategy as a "fallback" following the failure of the initial coping attempt.

In relation to the conventional categories of coping, problem-focused coping may be preferred to emotion-focused coping because opportunities to discharge emotions in the workplace are generally restricted. Cross-sectional studies have typically found that use of problem-focused coping relates to greater well-being in the workplace, whereas emotion focus and avoidance tend to relate to stress symptoms (Welbourne et al. 2007). Also the literature suggests that adaptive coping with occupational stress should lead to positive outcomes, such as heightened job satisfaction, fewer psychosomatic symptoms, and decreased anxiety (Spielberger and Reheiser 2005). Hence, if EI is eventually found to be meaningfully related to coping, high EI individuals should benefit from positive job outcomes. However, the relationship between coping and well-being at work may not be entirely straightforward, and it is difficult to establish that coping has a direct causal influence. Pearlin and Schooler (1978) surveyed the effectiveness of coping in four realms: work, marriage, parenting, and household economics. Whereas coping responses were successful in the sense of reducing strain in the final three putative domains, they had relatively little effect on strain resulting from work, indicating that the effectiveness of coping may vary across different contexts. A recent longitudinal study (Amiot et al. 2006) confirmed that problem-focused coping may influence well-being, but data also suggested that stress influences later choice of coping strategy. Potentially EI might influence both choice of coping stategy in response to stressors, and the effectiveness with which a strategy is implemented. Plausibly, emotion-focused coping might work better for emotionally intelligent individuals.

Research suggests that whereas individual coping efforts may not be particularly effective in organizational settings, group coping, operationalized as social support, might be especially effective (Schabracq 2003). Thus, in the workplace, where many influential stress factors are beyond an individual's control, individual coping strategies may be less potent than "higher level" strategies (involving the support of groups of workers or entire organizations). That is, job stressors may be among the problems that are not amenable to individual solutions, but depend on highly organized cooperative efforts that transcend those of the individual—no matter how well developed ones' personal resources.

La Rocco and Jones (1978) suggest that while the coping strategy of social support bears a direct main effect on job-related strains (e.g., job dissatisfaction), it has a buffering effect on health-related variables, including psychological and somatic outcomes. Furthermore emotion-focused coping was found to be positively related to strain. These findings suggest that palliative forms of coping are not adaptive with respect to job stress, or alternatively, that emotion-focused coping is simply a reaction to high levels of job stress (rather than a cause). These authors conclude that little is to be gained by exhorting human service professionals to change their ways of coping, because individual coping has little impact on job strain. Stress management and counseling programs are often seen as ways of enhancing coping at work. However, although there may be benefits to supporting employees in efforts to take control over circumstances at work, research has typically shown modest or even no benefits from interventions targeted at the individual (Cartwright and Cooper 2005).

Emotional Intelligence and Stress Vulnerability

We saw in chapter 7 that measures of EI are at least somewhat predictive of stress and coping. We might expect that strategies favored by the more emotionally intelligent such as using task-focused coping and seeking social support would help one manage stress effectively. However, the issue has not attracted much research, and most reported studies have not been especially sophisticated. Some studies (e.g., Slaski 2001) have demonstrated correlations between stress indexes and EI scales in the context of investigating other criteria such as performance and satisfaction. A study relating MSCEIT scores to work performance in a finance company also showed that EI related to better ratings of interpersonal facilitation and stress tolerance (Lopes et al. 2006). One of the more thorough studies of this kind, collected data from 330 people in human service professions (e.g., doctors, nurses, and teachers), including the SSRI, in a Polish translation. Oginska-Bulic (2005) found that EI correlated at -0.23 with perceived stress at work. The SSRI also showed similar correlations with some more specific facets of occupational stress including work overload, lack of control, and lack of support, although the EI scale proved to be a poor predictor of health status. In similar vein, a study using a Spanish version of the TMMS (Duran et al. 2004) found that EI related to lower levels of burnout, and also to greater work engagement.

Various factors may mediate effects of EI on occupational stress. Two that have been researched are the person's ability to handle organizational change, and the ability to manage emotional labor. Vakola et al. (2004) surveyed 137 professionals and found that an EI questionnaire predicted more positive attitudes toward organizational change. A scale for using emotions for problem-solving was the most predictive. Petrides and Furnham (2006) found that trait EI was, in part, linked to lower job stress via perceived job control. It is plausible that a greater sense of control would mitigate harmful effects of change. Curiously Petrides and Furnham also reported a strong direct path from EI to lower stress in men but not in women.

Organizational change also featured in a study of the impact of nurses of a major hospital restructuring in Alberta, Canada (Cummings et al. 2005). The authors investigated the role of leadership in mitigating effects of restructuring on various indexes of stress such as emotional exhaustion (similar to burnout) and psychosomatic symptoms. Leadership styles were differentiated based on Goleman's (e.g., 1998) analysis. Those nurses who worked for "resonant" leaders experienced fewer negative emotional symptoms and reported better workgroup collaboration, by contrast with nurses who had emotionally unsupportive leaders. Resonant leaders are those who are tuned to their own and others' feelings. They aim to build harmony and positive working climates. This style of leadership may be successful in mitigating potentially harmful organizational changes.

In the previous chapter we noted that EI may relate to "emotional labor" (managing emotions to support the mission of the organization: Daus 2006). Mikolajczak et al. (2007) point out that emotional labor may be a source of stress because it creates conflict between authentic feelings and those required by the employer. They suggest that "deep acting"—transforming one's inner feelings—may be more effective for coping with stress than "surface acting"—modifying the external display of emotion. Surface acting may promote emotional dissonance and requires more effort to maintain, leading to stress symptoms that may include burnout. Mikolajczak et al. (2007) investigated trait EI as a predictor of emotional labor and burnout in a sample of nurses. The study showed that trait EI related to less emotional labor (both surface and deep acting), and to less burnout and somatic stress symptoms. Some evidence was found for the associations between trait EI and stress symptoms being partially, but not fully mediated, by emotional labor, as hypothesized.

Most of the studies reviewed failed to control for confounding of self-report EI with personality. However, Vakola et al. (2004) and Mikolajczak et al. (2007) showed that EI had incremental validity for predicting at least some stress criteria, over and above the personality traits of the FFM. Mikolajczak et al. (2007) used a nonstandard adjectival measure that may not have been ideal for this purpose. More generally, it is well established that as with stress in general (see chapter 7), the neuroticism trait predicts various organizational criteria including low job satisfaction

Figure 10.2
Little attention has been paid to the interaction between EI and work demands in generating stress; does the "suit" have high or low EI?

and other indexes of negative affect (Judge et al. 2004; Matthews et al. 2003). More research is needed on what scales for EI can add to existing personality measures in predicting organizational stress. For example, Mikolajczak et al. (2007) showed incremental validity for EI in relation to burnout and emotional labor, but not with somatic stress symptoms as the criterion. Another weakness of the sparse research in this area is that little attention has been paid to the interaction between EI and work demands in generating stress, which is a key feature of the transactional perspective presented here (see figure 10.2).

Next we discuss major sources of stress and tension in the workplace: violence, bullying, and aggression.

Going Postal: Violence and Bullying in the Workplace

Workplace violence is a widespread and particularly stressful and disturbing aspect of organizational life (see Schat and Kelloway 2005a for a review). The media has sensationalized acts of bullying and workplace aggression to the extent that "going postal" has become part of the vernacular of organizational discourse (Douglas and Martinko 2001). This topic has been dealt with under various different headings, including "mobbing," "bullying," "harassment," "aggression," "incivility," "inter-personal abuse," and "victimization." All these terms describe unpleasant and potentially harmful interpersonal behaviors at work (Baron and Newman 1996). Workplace violence ranges from minor acts of incivility (low-intensity deviant behaviors) to extreme antisocial behavior, which harms both organizations and its members. It also includes sexual harassment, which is a growing concern within organizations.

Over 20 percent of the human resource managers participating in a recent survey reported that their organizations had experienced workplace violence since 1990. An additional 33 percent reported that there had been threats of violence in their workplace. Furthermore, according to another survey, 2 million Americans were the victims of physical attacks in the workplace, 6 million were threatened, and 16 million were harassed within the previous year (Bulatao and VandenBos 1996). Nonphysical aggression is also common; as many as 69 percent of respondents in a still further survey reported experiencing verbal aggression at work (Pizzino 2002).

This section focuses on workplace bullying (i.e., mobbing), one of the most frequent forms of workplace aggression and a major source of occupational stress. Bullying is characterized by repeated and persistent negative acts toward one or more individuals, with the situation typically involving a perceived power imbalance between aggressor and victim (Salin 2003). Bullying may encompass a variety of different behaviors, including verbal aggression (e.g., slandering or gossiping), aversive organizational politics (e.g., withholding needed information or support), social seclusion and isolation, and physical aggression (e.g., pushing, shoving).

Workplace violence may be construed as both a workplace stressor, on one hand, and a stress outcome, on the other. As a *stressor*, workplace violence is very costly from both a society and individual perspective. The organizational costs of workplace aggression are legion: reduced individual productivity, high frequency of absenteeism and worker turnover, and intent to leave the organization (Keashly and Jagatic 2000; Salin 2003). In addition victims of workplace violence report decreased job satisfaction, psychological distress, and stress-related somatic illnesses. Given the serious social and personal problems that occur when workplace aggression takes place, studies aimed at rectifying and understanding this phenomena are clearly warranted.

As a stress *outcome* workplace violence is associated with expressions of hostility and frustration, with sources including restructuring, downsizing, and other organizational changes (Hoel and Cooper 2000). Baron and Neuman (1996) suggest that uncertainty and change in the workplace (e.g., budget cuts) are related to physical aggression. Furthermore aggression has been found to be associated with dissatisfaction and stress at work, including high workload, time pressure, and deficient communication channels (Baron and Neuman 1996). Thus stress at work may lower aggression thresholds (Hoel and Cooper 2000) and employees may try to elevate their own status under conditions of change by lessening other employee's prestige or eliminate opposition.

The question of why people injure, offend, or unjustly treat each other at work has emerged as an important research area in management. Recent explanations emphasize the interaction between individual differences and situational (organizational) factors in accounting for workplace aggressions (Salin 2003). With respect to organizational factors the structure of most modern organizations, as group-based hierarchies, may play an important antecedent role in workplace bullying. Thus violence at work (as well as other forms of bullying) commonly involves a power gap or imbalance between perpetrator (e.g., supervisor) and victim (e.g., subordinate). In fact one common explanation of workplace aggression is the perpetrator's need to assert control and dominance over the victim. In many countries supervisors, who are higher up in the work hierarchy, appear to make up a clear majority of all bullies or instigators of incivility (Salin 2003). Also in many countries women, who traditionally have less power and status than men, seem to report more victimization than men at work (Zapf et al. 1996). Indeed organizational power differences are often connected with societal power differences and bullying often overlaps with related phenomena such as sexism or racism in the workplace. In addition bullying appears to be particularly prevalent in institutions (e.g., prisons) where dominance and power imbalances are strongly emphasized. Thus members of the subordinate group in the hierarchy appear to receive the lion's share of "negative liabilities," including interpersonal aggression.

In some organizational cultures bullying and other forms of harassment seem to be more or less permitted. In fact bullying appears to flourish when the organizational leadership is weak or "laissez faire," failing to develop anti-bully policies at the worksite, to monitor bullying, and to punish perpetrators. Failure to react to bullying behaviors on part of the management might be interpreted by workers to mean that the organization tacitly accepts aggressive behaviors if it achieves organizational goals or leads to greater productivity (Salin 2003). That being the case, the perpetrator may perceive the costs as very low.

Individual differences, including personality traits, perceptions, attitudes, and beliefs, may also play an important causal role in the bullying process. Thus some research suggests that workplace bullying is related to the aggressor's hostile dispositional style and heightened tendency to attribute hostile intent to the actions of others, even when these actions were ambiguous (Dodge and Coie 1987). Furthermore some research suggests that employees who attribute negative work outcomes (e.g., failure to meet deadlines) to causes that are external to themselves (e.g., deliberate sabotage by subordinate), and who also perceive these outcomes as being stable, intentional, and controllable, are more likely to experience anger and to express that anger outwardly toward others at work compared to employees who do not exhibit these attributional tendencies (Martinko and Zellars 1998).

Why are some individuals in the same organizational status in the hierarchy targeted more than others for bullying? Prior research suggests that three broad categories of victim-centered variables can reliably predict such experiences in organizations. First, certain personal characteristics may put individuals at risk for bullying and aggression. Thus persons who are high in such characteristics as trait anger, inability to control emotions, and low life satisfaction may put themselves more frequently at risk for interpersonal conflict at work (Douglas and Martinko 2001). Some research suggests that it is aggressive persons who are more likely to provoke others and be victimized than those who are less aggressive (Aquino and Bommer 2003). Thus, whereas some workers become targets of aggression because they behave passively, others are chosen because they exhibit threatening, aggressive, or irritating behaviors. Past studies show that people who possess these characteristics may knowingly or unknowingly create the social conditions that lead them to become frequent targets of others' harmful actions.

A second category of victim variables consists of strategic behaviors that people might use to defend themselves from interpersonal mistreatment, such as tactical revenge (Tripp and Bies 1997). Finally, there is evidence that indicators of social status, such as hierarchical position (Aquino 2000) and race (Sidanius and Pratto 1999), can predict victimization. The majority of victims of aggression failed to see themselves as personally responsible in the emergence of the bullying episode, pointing an accusing finger at the aggressor, in the hope that this will eventually lead to the latter's dismissal from the organization (Zapf 1999). Studies also show that socially attractive people are less likely to be victimized (Furr and Funder 1999).

There is a striking lack of research on EI and workplace violence, and we have introduced the topic in part to draw attention to the need for study of the issue. However, research in other domains suggests some promising lines for future research, which we will outline. Focusing first on the EI of the aggressor, it is in some ways reasonable to predict that the less emotionally intelligent will be more likely to perpetrate acts of bullying. We saw in chapter 6 that low EI relates to a variety of difficulties in interpersonal relationships (e.g., Lopes, Brackett, et al. 2004). Specifically, the likelihood of aggression may be elevated by lack of empathy for the victim, poor self-control over angry impulses, and misperceptions of hostility in others. The "reactive" form of aggression, namely lashing out in anger (Miller and Lynam 2006), may directly reflect poor emotional control. On the other hand, in looking at the "dark side" of EI, we also saw that self-esteem, which tends to overlap with EI, is elevated in bullies (Baumeister et al. 1996). Indeed we could see "socially intelligent" aggression from which the perpetrator gains as a form of Machiavellian EI. For example, an employee hoping for a promotion might seek to undermine a rival by spreading false rumors. In studies using questionnaire assessments of EI we might expect negative associations between EI and aggression to predominate. Self-report scales for EI correlate with several major traits linked to lower anger and/or aggression including emotional stability (less anger), agreeableness (greater empathy, lower aggression), and conscientiousness (fewer antisocial actions at work: Ones, Viswesvaran, and Schmidt 1993). However, the employee's scope for employing aggression intelligently suggests a more nuanced picture may be desirable.

Turning from perpetrator to victim, we cannot simply blame victims for being so low in EI that they invite acts of aggression. Thus, as just described, some personality characteristics linked to victimhood, such as aggressiveness itself (Aquino and Bommer 2003), might prove to be linked to EI scales. Beyond personality factors, some of the skills described in ability models of EI (see chapter 3) plausibly contribute to countering aggression effectively. Accurate emotion perception may contribute to detecting early signs of hostility in a coworker, and high emotion understanding could give insights into the reasons for hostility. Perhaps the most important branch is emotion management, as suggested by other research on interpersonal relationships (Lopes, Brackett, et al. 2004). The highly emotionally intelligent person may have the social skills to defuse aggression and establish cooperative relationships with potential enemies.

Should organizations focus on enhancing EI as an intervention for workplace aggression? We saw in chapter 8 that one of the targets for social-emotional learning in education is violent behavior (Zins et al. 2007) so perhaps comparable programs training recognition of hostility, empathy, and anger management (of both self and others) would be of value. (There may be a dilemma regarding the extent to which an aggressive individual merits training, as opposed to being fired or otherwise sanctioned.) Despite growing organizational interest in interventions for violence, few programs have yet been implemented or evaluated (Schat and Kelloway 2005b), so work on EI might potentially make a useful contribution.

From the lens of EI, organizational culture promoting emotional intelligence and organizational citizenship at the worksite is expected to reduce bullying and aggressive behavior on the part of a superior. In addition this may allow subordinates to deal with aggression in a more assertive and adaptive manner, creating bonds of mutual obligation and reciprocity (Aquino and Bommer 2003). Thus, in organizations encouraging and cultivating emotional and social skills and discouraging aggressive behaviors when unwarranted, a lower incidence of bullying behavior and workplace mobbing is expected. When empathy, prosocial behaviors, and positive citizenship behaviors are promoted and central, there is little tolerance for workplace bullying and mobbing. Further research, however, is needed to substantiate these assumptions.

Management of Occupational Stress

Different taxonomies have been offered to classify organizationally based stress management and training intervention programs. One scheme classifies interventions designed to reduce stress at the worksite by the *target* of intervention, namely (1) the individual, (2) the organization, or (3) the individual–organization interface. Interventions that focus on the individual (Cartwright and Cooper 2005) include stress education activities (e.g., identifying sources of stress), counseling, relaxation programs, and employee skill training (e.g., assertiveness training). Organization-focused interventions (Hurrell 2005) may be directed toward changing workload and/or work procedures or improving macro-level factors in the organization (improved selection, restructuring, organizational development). Interventions focusing on the organization–individual interface center on improving personal–organizational interface (e.g., improving emotional or practical skills of employee or management to match job descriptions and requirements).

Cartwright and Cooper (1996) have distinguished three levels of intervention for stress at the worksite (see also Cooper et al. 1996; Hurrell 2005). The first level, *primary prevention*, involves stress reduction, including modifying environmental stressors by direct action to eliminate negative impact on the individual. *Secondary prevention* involves mainly stress management, designed to teach employees who are high risk for stress to cope with demands at work in a more adaptive manner. The third level, *tertiary prevention*, involves programs targeting employees who have suffered from high degrees of disabling stress. The programs are generally "employee assistance programs," which focus on dealing with outcomes or consequences of the stressful situation. In any case, the latter two levels deal with stress management rather than modifying environmental stresses. Hurrell (2005) suggests that primary interventions that change objective working conditions appear to provide the most effective approach, but he cautions also that interventions are often poorly designed and evaluated. Ivancevich and Matteson (1987) provide a slightly different classification scheme. These researchers identify three possible areas for intervention in the workplace: (1) reducing intensity and number of stressors, (2) helping the individual modify perception or appraisal of potentially stressful situations, and (3) improving the range of competencies in coping with stress.

Despite a growing number of studies on occupational stress, there have been rather few evaluations of interventions that target employees' efforts to cope with the stress of the workplace. Stress management programs are rarely evaluated adequately, and, as they typically comprise multiple modules, it is difficult to asses the effectiveness of any specific component, such as enhancement of coping (Cartwright and Cooper 2005). Some promising results emerge from specific studies. For example, Bekker et al. (2001) trained workers in assertiveness, coping, relaxation, and realistic thinking. Compared to a control group, trainees experienced less somatic complaints and less stress, along with more use of active coping and social support seeking. As with other research on coping, it is difficult to judge whether changes in coping exerted a causal influence on well-being. Hurrell (2005) reviews participatory action research (PAR), in which groups of employees work with outside experts to identify problems and develop appropriate interventions. Some, but not all, interventions of this kind have produced benefits; Hurrell concludes that interventions focusing on job redesign are more effective than those that focus on stress in a more global sense. Thus, we are in need not only of evidence-based effective interventions but also an understanding of the key psychological processes that can be targeted to improve coping and well-being. A process-based model for intervention is necessary to understand the role of EI in coping with occupational stress.

Practical Suggestions from the EI Literature

The EI literature is replete with practical suggestions for coping with occupational stress. We will cover these only briefly as few have much evidentiary basis in research on EI. Caruso et al. (2006, pp. 202–203) offer this appraisal of workplace programs: "Our concern regarding the explosion of training programs has to do with their lack of rigor and theoretical underpinnings. We have seen many programs labeled as EI programs whose content bears no resemblance at all to either emotions or to intelligence. Unfortunately, the term has become a convenient marketing tool more than a body of professional practice." Caruso et al. (2006) are referring to training for EI in general, but the comment equally applies to programs focusing on stress. Some of these practical suggestions are incorporated in the training programs discussed in the previous chapter, although they are rarely evaluated formally. Cooper and Sawaf (1997), in their popular book on *Executive EQ*, recommend a three-step strategy for managing emotional energy. These steps are (1) acknowledge and feel—rather than deny or minimize—the emotion experienced, (2) listen to the information or feedback the emotion is giving you (e.g., if one experiences anger or sadness, one should ask: what principles, values, assets, resources, or goals are at stake), and (3) guide or channel the emotional energy into an appropriate constructive response. The underlying assumption of these authors is that emotions are an energy that is neither good nor bad. What is important is how you respond to it. Presumably, by applying this three-step strategy, one can learn how to better cope with aversive emotions and stress at the worksite and achieve better adaptive outcomes.

Goleman (1998) writes that emotionally intelligent people, best able to handle stress, often have a stress management technique they call on when needed, whether it's a long bath, a workout, or a yoga session. According to Goleman, regular daily practice of a relaxation method seems to reset the trigger point for the amygdala (recall, this is that mechanism in the brain thought to control emotions), making it less easily provoked. The neural resetting gives us the ability to recover more quickly

Table 10.2
Some practical tips in the literature for managing stress

Emotional diary
Cooper and Sawaf (1997) suggest that stress can be managed through an emotional diary or morning notes. According to these authors, a worker should spend two or three minutes every morning clearing away the frustrating, trivial stuff that echoes in their head and plants seed of confusion in their heart. Workers are advised to write whatever they feel and keep the log handy throughout the day. The theoretical and empirical basis for these suggestions is uncertain.
Humor
Weisinger (1998) suggests that humor is the best medicine for coping with stress, serving as a distraction to turn us away from whatever distressful emotions we may be having. He suggests it might be helpful to create a humor-filled environment, with silly photographs, jokes, and humorous situations. Furthermore the individual can try to look at coworkers and the boss through a 'hidden-camera' perspective, observing them in an absurd, whimsical, or silly perspective rather than in a serious way.
Mental imagery
Weisinger (1998) advances the use of mental imagery as a way to cope with stress. Thus we can visualize ourselves in almost any situation, and visualize the outcome of a particular situation. Here mental imagery can galvanize us into activity by visualizing ourselves doing the activity. By identifying, refining, and practicing in our mind the steps necessary for successfully staying on course, it is easier for one to be motivated to carry out the steps in real life. Thus one can imagine oneself relaxing, calling up in minds tasks which one feels are unmotivated, imagine oneself struggling with the task, gaining composure, succeeding, and feeling good.

from "amygdala hijacks" while making us less prone to them in the first place. The evidence for this hypothesis is problematic at best. Additional practical suggestions and tips are presented in table 10.2. Unfortunately, little empirical support is generally offered to back up the suggestions put forth.

Concluding Comments

This chapter discussed the theory and evidence supporting the claimed role of EI in coping with stress at the worksite. Overall, EI is currently evaluated as being an important and valuable potential personal resource for coping with the threats, challenges, and affordances of *organizational* settings, purportedly related to tasks where there is a clear emotional skill required for successful performance (e.g., sales, customer relations, helping professions, and school teaching). Enhancing EI is potentially an important strand of workplace interventions for organizational stress.

Regretably, however, relatively few studies have addressed employee's efforts to cope with the stress of the workplace, and the literature is relatively silent about the ways that employees cope with transitions in the workplace. The implications of current research on coping in occupational settings for the role of EI are complex. On one hand, theory would suggest that individuals high in EI would show a preference for problem-focused over other forms of coping when something can be done to alter the source of stress. However, when little can be done to alter the source of stress, constructive emotion-focused coping should be the most adaptive, although maladaptive strategies such as excessive self-criticism and brooding or ruminating on problems may make matters worse. Unfortunately, there is little published research that conclusively identifies the most effective strategies, and further research is needed to test these hypotheses.

Even so, given the research that suggests that individual coping efforts are not very effective in making a difference at the workplace, it is highly questionable to what extent the coping strategies typically used by emotionally intelligent individuals would be helpful to them. Overall, the role of EI in impacting on the effectiveness of macro-level interventions would be expected to be minimal. Furthermore there are no peer-reviewed studies in the literature, to our knowledge, that systematically looked at the relationship between EI, coping, and adaptive outcomes in specific occupational settings. One focus for future research may be on group-based interventions such as PAR; given the associations between EI and social functioning discussed in chapter 7, high EI may be advantageous to collective efforts at redesigning the workplace to alleviate stress. It is unknown whether emotionally intelligent group problem solving can be trained, though. Thus we are in urgent need of studies that enable persons to report events or stressful encounters that are important to them in specific occupational sites, how they cope with them, and the role of EI in coping with occupational stress.

Summary Points: Chapter 10

• Work stress is becoming increasingly prevalent across the globe, contributing to loss of productivity, absenteeism, workplace violence, and ill-health. As discussed in chapter 7, EI may influence the extent to which the person copes adaptively with external pressures and regulates their own emotions. Hence high EI may be especially important for negotiating the "toxic" workplace.

• Understanding of organizational stress is based on the transactional model introduced in chapter 7; broadly, stress arises when the person is overwhelmed by the demands of the workplace. Sources of stress include factors intrinsic to the job (e.g., time pressure), threats to personal goals (e.g., lack of career progression), and the social environment of the workplace (e.g., hostile coworkers). Effective coping with multiple potential stressors is essential for mitigating the various adverse outcomes of the stress process.

• Despite expectations that EI should make an important contribution to managing stress, the issue has not attracted much research. A few cross-sectional studies show negative correlations between EI and occupational stress indexes. However, it is unclear that EI improves over standard personality traits such as neuroticism in predicting occupational stress. Existing research has also neglected the person–situation interaction that is central to the transactional model.

• Workplace aggression and bullying, ranging from minor incivilities to sexual harassment and extreme violence, is an especially disturbing source of workplace stress. Violence may be construed as both a source and an outcome of stress, within the dynamic perspective of the transactional model. Individual difference factors may be relevant to both aggressive behavior, and to becoming a target for harassment and bullying. Emotionally intelligent workers may be more effective at solving problems without resorting to violence, and at defusing confrontations with potential aggressors. Research is needed on whether EI promotes a more civil organizational climate that mitigates against violence.

• Organizational stress may be managed both through objective changes to the physical and social environment of the workplace, and through supporting individual efforts at coping with the pressures of the job. Popular books on EI are replete with practical suggestions for emotionally intelligent coping in the workplace. A focus on EI may be important for the workplace interventions described in chapter 9. However, little systematic research has been conducted, although the approach may be promising.

• Although a plausible case may be made that EI is a necessary antidote to the various forms of organizational stress, this topic is sorely in need of research. However, EI may be of little relevance to the macroenvironmental factors that render a workplace toxic; often it is more effective to change the organization than to change the individual.

11 Emotional Intelligence in the Clinic

I am now the most miserable man living. If what I felt were distributed to the whole human family there would not be one happy face on the earth.
—Abraham Lincoln

Some of the most extreme examples of emotional dysfunction are shown by people suffering from clinical disorders. Patients suffering from depression are beset with irrational foreboding and dread of the future. Individuals with impulse-control disorders may act out emotionally in bizarre ways including starting fires and kleptomania. Autistic children may be so deficient in social-emotional functioning that they cannot even connect with their own parents. We might loosely say that such people are deficient in emotional intelligence. Mental illness often seems to involve experiencing inappropriate or excessive emotional reactions in specific contexts, such as excessive anxiety where unwarranted, or poor management of emotions, such as lashing out in anger or ruminating continuously about the emotions evoked in a stressful encounter.

The example of Abraham Lincoln illustrates the need for caution in making an easy equation between emotional disorder and lack of emotional intelligence (EI). A recent biographer (Shenk 2005) argues that Lincoln was prone to clinical depression, as evidenced by two severe breakdowns in which talk of suicide alarmed his friends. Although more stable in later life, a melancholic temperament was central to his personality. Shenk claims that he learned not just to cope with chronic unhappiness but to channel the insights gained from struggling with depression into political leadership. Depression gave Lincoln patience, determination, empathy, and clarity of vision. We suspect Lincoln would not have scored highly on the EQ-i, Schutte Self-Report Inventory (SSRI), or other questionnaires that reward a cheerful self-confidence. Nonetheless, he offers a model for a different kind of EI. Thomas (1952) quotes the *New*

York Herald: "Plain common sense, a kindly disposition, a straightforward purpose, and a shrewd perception of the ins and outs of poor, weak human nature have enabled him to master difficulties which would have swamped any other man" (p. 497). Thomas observes that Lincoln sought to appeal to reason, but remembered that the mind is best reached through the heart. Lincoln was not a paragon of EI in all respects; his tendency to deal with his wife's mood swings by withdrawing emotionally would not please marriage counselors. Nonetheless, Shenk's (2005) biography shows how emotional disorder can accompany, and even feed remarkable social-emotional gifts. Shenk also emphasizes that Lincoln's depression was never "cured."

A biography shows what is possible, but tells us little about what is typical of emotional disorder. Many sufferers fail to integrate their condition into their lives adaptively as Lincoln did; indeed one of his cousins, Mary Jane Lincoln, died in the Illinois State Hospital for the Insane, after a confinement of 21 years. In this chapter we will look at whether we can attribute low EI to individuals with disorders linked to social-emotional impairments. A central problem that EI faces in gaining a foothold in clinical practice is the diversity of mental disorders (Vachon and Bagby 2007). The clinician's staple—the *Diagnostic and Statistical Manual* (DSM-IV-TR-IV: see First et al. 2004)—recognizes dozens of separate mental disorders. Emotional problems are common to a wide range of diverse conditions (sometimes emotional dysfunction may be a by-product of other pathologies). Both generalized anxiety and depression might both be linked to low EI through excessive, unrealistic negative emotion, but to the clinician these are separate disorders, diagnosed on the basis of different symptom clusters, and requiring different approaches to treatment. The notion of EI may be simply too broad to be useful in clinical psychology.

Nevertheless, several authors (e.g., Parker 2000, 2005; Vachon and Bagby 2007) have argued that EI merits more attention in clinical psychology. A striking example is provided by *alexithymia* (Taylor 2000), meaning difficulty in understanding and verbalizing emotions. Deficiencies in other facets of normal EI (see chapter 1), such as consistently misinterpreting the emotions of others or failure to express and cope effectively with one's emotions (see chapter 7), might also contribute to mental illness. Curiously alexithymia is not considered to be a clinical disorder in the DSM-IV-TR-IV.

This chapter will explore recent work on EI and its potential contribution to clinical psychology. Before doing so in considerable detail, we will review how EI might fit into the diagnostic systems clinicians use to understand mental disorder, and the potential practical value of work on EI to clinical understanding.

Diagnosis and Categorization of Mental Illness

Current understanding of mental disorder is based on a well-established—though sometimes controversial—framework. Development of a disorder depends on two factors: a *diathesis* and a *stressor*. The diathesis refers to underlying traits, such as personality factors, that make the person vulnerable to disorder. However, even if the diathesis for a disorder is present, it will remain latent until an external stressor precipitates an episode of mental illness. Lincoln recognized this distinction in his own writings (see Shenk 2005, pp. 85–87). He distinguished a "general cause"—being of nervous temperament—from "special causes," including the harsh Illinois winter, the absence of friends, and the imminence of marriage. These days we would refer to these special causes as environmental stressors or life events.

Figure 11.1 graphically depicts the relationship between diathesis, possible sources of stress in the familial environment, and disorders in social communication.

The personality trait of neuroticism (N, see chapter 4) is seen as a diathesis for various emotional disorders, including anxiety and depressive disorders (e.g., Harkness et al. 2002). However, high N is not itself a disorder; many individuals with an emotionally unstable personality function perfectly well within society, despite their proneness to negative

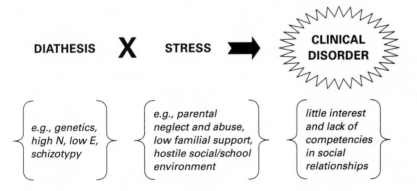

Figure 11.1
Diathesis-stress model of disorders in social connection

moods. These persons are believed to be especially vulnerable to developing a clinical disorder following certain kinds of trigger stressors. For
example, the loss of a family member may initiate clinical depression.
The low N individual, lacking the diathesis for these disorders, will experience stress and unhappiness for a time but will manage to cope with the
stressor without developing clinical symptoms.

The DSM system distinguishes the underlying, stable diathesis and the
full-blown mental illness. Axis I disorders, such as anxiety and mood disorders, are defined as sets of distinctive symptoms, representing a distinct
episode of illness. Axis II disorders refer to more stable traits, such as
abnormalities of personality and mental retardation, which do not necessarily cause severe disruption to living. Axis II disorders may be seen
as predispositions to axis I disorders, although the distinction between
the two types of disorder is not always clear-cut (Widiger and Shea
1991). DSM-IV treats axis II conditions as discrete categories—the
person either has the disorder or does not. However, abnormal personality traits, like traits that are "normal," are dimensional constructs rather
than all-or-nothing conditions (Widiger et al. 2002). Indeed vulnerability to severe emotional dysregulation and clinical disorder may simply
correspond to excessive levels of neuroticism (e.g., Larstone et al. 2002).
Studies of EI in the clinical context have been concerned with both axis
I disorders, especially emotional disorders, and with abnormal traits
that may act as diatheses (Matthews et al. 2002; Vachon and Bagby
2007).

How might EI fit into this diagnostic system? Answering this question
again confronts us with the problem of the uncertain causal status of EI,
discussed as early as chapter 1 (i.e., whether EI is a core latent trait that
influences behavior, or whether it is an outcome, a superficial quality of
behavior driven by other factors). Some of the behaviors characteristic
of mental illness can readily be described as "emotionally unintelligent,"
but labeling outcomes in this way is not informative about the sources of
mental disorder. The more interesting issue is whether low EI acts as a
diathesis or predisposition toward developing clinical disorders. Could
we perhaps define abnormally low EI as an axis II disorder that renders
the person vulnerable to more severe disorders? Different facets of EI
might predispose the person toward different mental illnesses. If so, measurement of emotional intelligence—and especially estimating the person's EI prior to the onset of illness—might prove a powerful diagnostic
tool for the clinician.

Practical Applications

The emerging science of EI may potentially inform understanding of both the underlying processes that generate mental disorder and therapeutic strategies. The mental condition of an individual person, such as Lincoln, is harder to understand than textbook descriptions of abnormal psychology might suggest. Generalized anxiety patients all meet a common set of diagnostic criteria, but each individual differs in the precise nature of their fears and concerns, and the environments that trigger anxiety and coping strategies (Wells 1997). Nevertheless, a central part of abnormal psychology involves understanding the underlying processes that generate the overt symptoms of the disorder. These processes can be understood both neurologically (e.g., abnormalities in neurotransmitter functions) and psychologically: we will focus mainly on psychological models here.

Anxiety research (e.g., Matthews and Funke 2006; Wells and Matthews 2006) identifies a set of distinct processes that appear to contribute to pathology. Broadly speaking, clinically anxious individuals are excessively aware of, and attentive to, threat stimuli. They also have distorted beliefs about their place in the world that exaggerate their personal vulnerability. They also regulate their anxious emotion and worries maladaptively, for example, by using thought control strategies that serve to maintain awareness of anxiety. Could theories of EI help us better understand these processes that serve to initiate and perpetuate mental illness? We focus here on the *proximal* influences on mental disorder; the immediate psychological causes that may be uncovered by clinical examination. Distal causes such as genetics and the family environment are also important, but beyond our present scope.

Understanding the role of low EI in mental illness may help the clinician in diagnosis and choice of therapy for the patient. A good neuropsychological model of impaired EI—something that is currently some way from being realized—might support drug treatments. At a psychological level clinicians may be able to develop behavioral or cognitive interventions that are tailored to the particular weaknesses of the low EI person. For example, a cognitive therapy that depends on the patient's insights into their own condition might not be a good bet for such a person, given their difficulties in self-understanding (Parker 2000). It may also be possible to treat directly the core components of EI such as poor emotion perception or impaired mood regulation.

Table 11.1
Three loose clusters of disorders of "low emotional intelligence"

Category	DSM axis 1	DSM axis 2
Emotional disorders	Mood disorders	"Neurotic" personality disorders: dependent borderline Obsessive compulsive
	Anxiety disorders	
Impulsivity and aggression	Impulse control disorders not elsewhere classified (e.g., kleptomania, pyromania)	Antisocial personality disorder
	Disruptive behavior disorders (e.g., conduct disorder)	
Social disconnection	Schizophrenia	Schizoid and schizotypal personality disorder
		Developmental disorders: autism, Asperger's syndrome

A good deal of this chapter addresses the role that low EI may play in selected disorders. In reviewing mental disorder, we will address three broad types of pathology. Table 11.1 summarizes three aspects of emotional vulnerability that map onto various axis I and axis II disorders in DSM-IV-TR-IV. For each of these three broad (and admittedly heterogeneous) areas of pathology, we will look at how symptoms may relate to low EI and what some of the key underlying emotional and cognitive processes might be.

First, we will look at disorders for which excessive negative emotion is central, including the various anxiety and mood disorders. One issue here is whether EI adds anything new to the notion of "neurotic" personality as a "vulnerability factor" (see also chapter 4). We have included some of the DSM-IV-TR-IV abnormal personality traits on the basis of their linkages with emotionality and neuroticism (Widiger et al. 2002), but each disorder refers to a constellation of symptoms that are not restricted to emotionality. For example, borderline personality refers to instability in relationships and impulsivity as well as to emotional reactivity.

The second type of pathology refers to poor impulse control, especially in states of emotion. In children, these conditions are described as "externalizing," including impulsive aggression, hyperactivity, and other conduct problems. In adults, we will refer to personality disorders such as antisocial disorder frequently found in deviant groups such as criminals. Part of the popular appeal of EI (1995a) has been that criminality may be reduced through raising the EI of vulnerable individuals, and there are quite successful school programs directed toward impulsive conduct problems (see chapter 8).

The third cluster of conditions refers to major difficulties in social interaction, typified by difficulties in understanding and communicating with others. In children, prototypical conditions here are high-functioning autism and Asperger's syndrome. In adults, we will focus on the schizoid personality, in which the person typically lacks both the motivation and the social skills to form meaningful relationships. Table 11.1 also refers to schizophrenia as a condition of this kind, but we will not discuss it much here due to space limitations and the complexities of this research. We note briefly that social withdrawal is common in the more passive forms of schizophrenic psychosis, and there is scope for research on loss of EI in this condition.

In the final section of the current chapter we will review the implications of our review for therapy. We will look at what research on EI may offer to treatments for alexithymia, dysfunctional patterns of mood regulation (e.g., rumination), and problems in expressing and communicating emotion.

The Emotional Disorders

A man who has not passed through the inferno of his passions has never overcome them.
—Carl Gustav Jung

Table 11.2 summarizes some of the better-known anxiety and mood disorders, which represent two separate groups of conditions in DSM, although anxiety and depression are often comorbid with one another. Mood disorders also include various types of bipolar disorder, in which positive moods ("mania") can be as problematic for the person as negative moods. Evidently emotional dysfunction is central to these disorders, but can we really say that low emotional intelligence is a source of pathology? In this section we look at whether excessive negative emotion should be seen as emotionally unintelligent, and some of the underlying processes that might link emotional disorders to low EI, and at research on *alexithymia*.

Table 11.2
Principal symptoms of some anxiety and mood disorders in DSM-IV

Generalized anxiety disorder
• For more than half the days in at least 6 months, patient experiences excessive anxiety and worry about several events or activities
• Patient has trouble controlling these feelings
• Other anxiety and worry symptoms include feeling restless, tired, and irritable; may have trouble concentrating and sleeping
• Symptoms cause distress or impair work, social or personal functioning

Obsessive-compulsive disorder
• Patient must have obsessions or compulsions (or both) that cause severe distress, and interfere with social or personal functioning
• Obsessions: Recurring, persisting thoughts, impulses or images inappropriately intrude into awareness and cause marked distress or anxiety. Patient tries to ignore or suppress these ideas or to neutralize them by thoughts or behavior.
• Compulsions: Patient feels the need to repeat physical behaviors (checking the stove to be sure it is off, hand washing) or mental behaviors (counting things, silently repeating words). These behaviors aim to reduce or eliminate distress, but they are not realistically related to the events they are supposed to counteract.

Panic disorder (with or without agoraphobia)
• Patient experiences recurrent panic attacks, defined as the sudden development of a severe fear or discomfort that peaks within 10 minutes. During this discrete episode, four or more of the following symptoms occur:
Chest pain or other chest discomfort
Chills or hot flashes
Choking sensation
Derealization (feeling unreal) or depersonalization (feeling detached from self)
Dizzy, lightheaded, faint, or unsteady
Fear of dying
Fears of loss of control or becoming insane
Heart pounds, races, or skips beats
Nausea or other abdominal discomfort
Numbness or tingling
Sweating
Shortness of breath or smothering sensation
Trembling
• For a month or more after at least one of these attacks, the patient has had one or more of the following concerns:
Worry that there will be more attacks
Worry as to the significance of the attack or its consequences (for health, sanity, etc.)
Material change in behavior, such as doing something to avoid or combat the attacks

Posttraumatic stress disorder
• Patient has experienced or witnessed an unusually traumatic event that involved actual or threatened death or serious physical injury to the patient or to others, and patient felt intense fear, horror, or helplessness
• Patient repeatedly relives the event through, for example, intrusive recollections, distressing dreams, "flashbacks," accompanied by distress and physiological reactivity to cues that symbolize or resemble the event
• Patient repeatedly avoids thinking about the event, and situations that recall the event
• Patient has numbing of general responsiveness; for example, feels detached from other people

Table 11.2
(continued)

Social phobia
• Patient strongly, repeatedly fears at least one social or performance situation that involves facing strangers or being watched by others. Patient specifically fears showing anxiety symptoms or behaving in some other way that will be embarrassing or humiliating.
• Phobic stimulus almost always causes anxiety, which may be a cued or situationally predisposed panic attack
• Patient either avoids the situation or endures it with severe distress or anxiety
• Either there is marked distress about having the phobia or it markedly interferes with the patient's usual routines or social, job, or personal functioning

Major depression
• At least one major depressive episode (i.e., in the same two weeks), the patient has had five or more of the following symptoms, occurring for most of nearly every day. Either depressed mood or decreased interest or pleasure must be one of the five:
Mood   Patient reports depressed mood or appears depressed to others
Interests   Interest or pleasure is markedly decreased in nearly all activities
Eating and weight   Marked change in appetite or actual weight
Sleep   Patient sleeps excessively or not enough
Motor activity   Patient's activity is agitated or retarded
Fatigue   There is fatigue or loss of energy
Self-worth   Patient feels worthless or inappropriately guilty
Concentration   Patient is indecisive or has trouble thinking or concentrating
Death   Patient has repeated thoughts about death/suicide or made a suicide attempt
• Symptoms cause clinically important distress or impair work, social, or personal functioning

---

An Excess of Emotion

Central to the anxiety disorders are unrealistic, irrational fears, while depression centers on prolonged, deeply negative moods and associated themes of hopelessness, helplessness, and lack of self-worth. Loosely, we might assume that it is not emotionally intelligent to experience high levels of anxiety or depression when objective circumstances are not especially threatening or harmful. However, such an assumption does not take us very far; the reasoning is circular if we say that low EI causes emotional disorder, and then infer lack of EI from the disorder itself.

In fact there is rather little evidence on levels of EI shown by clinical patients, although as discussed in chapter 4, questionnaire measures of anxiety, depression, and other expressions of negative emotion tend to correlate negatively with self-reported EI (e.g., Fernandez-Berrocal et al. 2006; Malterer et al. 2008; Petrides et al. 2007; Summerfeldt et al. 2006). Smaller ($r < 0.30$) associations exist between the MEIS/MSCEIT and these measures (Rivers et al. 2007). EI may also relate to traits for abnormality and pathology in nonclinical samples (Bar-On 1997). In college students, low scores on the TMMS correlate with various abnormal personality traits linked to negative emotion, including borderline, avoidant, and dependent personality (Leible and Snell 2004).

Goldenberg et al. (2006) recruited a community sample of stress-vulnerable individuals and compared SSRI (Schutte et al. 1998) and MSCEIT scores for three groups: those reporting having received treatment for depression, those treated for other conditions, and those who had not sought treatment. As expected, the depression group had a lower mean SSRI score than the controls. By contrast, MSCEIT scores for both the treatment groups were actually *higher* than those for the no-treatment group. Goldenberg et al. (2006) speculate that high MSCEIT scorers may be more motivated to seek treatment than low scorers, and that treatment may elevate scores on the MSCEIT. Ciarrochi, Wilson, et al. (2003) have also reported that emotional competence relates to willingness to seek help with emotional problems when necessary. Nevertheless, the association between the MSCEIT and emotional pathology remains ambiguous.

As discussed previously in chapters 4 and 7, relationships between low EI and excess negative emotion may simply reflect the overlap of both qualities with the neuroticism trait. Other FFM traits that overlap with self-report EI may also be a factor. Figure 11.2 shows the patterning of

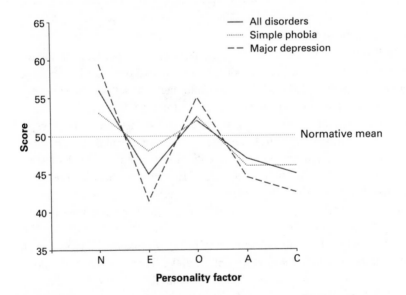

Figure 11.2
Personality characteristics of people reporting diagnoses of emotional disorders during their lifetimes compared to the norm

the Big Five in a group of people reporting at least one diagnosis of emotional disorder during their lifetimes), compared with controls (Trull and Sher 1994). Similar patterns are seen for specific disorders (simple phobia, depression). The study is significant because it used a structured interview to assess diagnostic status. In addition to high N the emotional disorder group also exhibit low extraversion, agreeableness, and conscientious, three traits that tend to be linked to self-report EI (see chapter 4). Trull and Sher's finding that openness was higher in the emotional disorder group chimes with Ciarrochi, Wilson, et al.'s (2002) suggestion that high EI may render the person more sensitive to negative experiences.

Even if it were established that low EI is uniquely related to emotional disorder, we would still have the problem of determining whether low EI is a *cause* or an *outcome* of the disorder. If EI is viewed as more malleable than standard traits, it is quite plausible that an episode of mental illness would lead to loss of emotional competence. The traits of the FFM, in fact, appear to be reciprocally related to emotional disorder. High N, and other traits including social introversion, increase the risk of developing the disorder, as evidenced in longitudinal studies (e.g., Harkness et al. 2002; Surtees and Wainwright 1996). However, the emotional maladjustment that follows may itself influence personality, until the disorder is successfully treated (Barnett and Gotlib 1988). Given the overlap between "trait" EI and personality, we anticipate that studies of EI will provide comparable results. It is unknown whether low EI adds to vulnerability over and above the FFM or how EI might change during an episode of severe anxiety or depression.

We note briefly that almost nothing is known about how bipolar disorders might relate to EI. The issue is of interest because behaviors that may be seen during manic or hypomanic phases illustrate how *positive* emotions may contribute to unintelligent behavior. The patient may conceive wildly impractical schemes, or engage in pleasurable but risky behaviors such as promiscuous sex or high-stakes gambling. Conflicting data on personality in bipolar patients have been reported. One study (Akiskal et al. 2006) assessed personality when patients were not in fact experiencing an acute episode of mood disturbance. It confirmed that individuals vulnerable to bipolar disorder are high in N, but also found evidence for elevation of some extraverted traits, including energetic and assertive qualities. Given that E typically relates to higher EI, the implication is that it is unclear whether trait EI (low N/high E) would be elevated in bipolar disorder.

Process Factors

We may get a clearer picture of how pathologically low EI might operate as a risk factor if we can identify some of the key underlying processes that make the person vulnerable to developing emotional disorders. Perhaps processes specifically linked to EI play a key role that has been missed in existing accounts of vulnerability. Does the inability to read other people's emotions generate pathology? Or does the inability to manage emotions constructively generate pathological disturbances? An extensive research literature on antecedents of emotional disorders implicates numerous specific cognitive and biological factors in vulnerability (e.g., Alloy and Riskind 2006), in addition to the more broadly defined personality traits already discussed. It is unclear whether research on EI can add to understanding of the various vulnerability factors.

In fact we have introduced some of the key processes already when discussing subclinical stress and anxiety (see chapter 7). Patients suffering from both anxiety and mood disorders show similar—but more pronounced—biases in cognition to individuals high in neuroticism, negative affectivity, and trait anxiety. Biases include focusing attention on threats, holding excessively negative self-beliefs, regulating mood through worry and rumination, and metacognitions that it is important to monitor and control one's mental state. Abnormalities in metacognition may be one of several factors that transform "normal" anxiety into clinical disorder. For example, panic disorder patients believe it is important to monitor bodily sensations in case they signal an imminent health crisis, such as a cardiac arrest (Wells 1997, 2000). In fact excessive awareness of physical and emotional symptoms may itself lead to pathology, including panic attacks. Dysfunctional metacognitions may also contribute to harmful rumination in depressed patients (Papageorgiou and Wells 2004).

What can research on EI add to current understanding of emotional pathology? It might identify key processes in mental adjustment that have been neglected in existing research. For example, Scherer's (2007) analysis points toward the importance of communication competence, taking in both emotion perception and emotion expression. Depression and anxiety may also relate to deficits in communicating and expressing emotions (e.g., Renneberg et al. 2005).

There is growing interest in whether clinical patients are deficient in the perception of emotions. Some studies do indeed suggest a general impairment. For example, Surguladze et al. (2004) found that depressed patients showed a deficit in recognizing both mildly unhappy and mildly happy faces. Ambady and Gray (2002) review evidence that depression also relates to poorer performance on more naturalistic, socially infused perception tasks such as the Profile of Nonverbal Sensitivity (PONS; Rosenthal et al. 1979). Other studies suggest that deficits are specific to certain disorders and emotions, but there is little consistency across these studies. For example, Montagne et al. (2006) showed that social anxiety related to lowered sensitivity to angry faces. By contrast, Joorman and Gotlib (2006) found that social phobics appeared to be more sensitive than both controls and depressed individuals to anger; while Philippot and Douilliez (2005) failed to find any evidence that social anxiety relates to misinterpreting facial emotion. It may be that there is no basic processing deficit in at least some of these disorders, and the effects reported are dependent on contextual factors. Philippot and Douilliez (2005) suggest that social phobics may be sensitive to stimuli of personal relevance, rather than negative social stimuli in general. Edwards and Weary (1993) suggest that depressives are especially motivated to monitor the social world around them, due to their social insecurities. Sometimes this motivation may increase sensitivity to a range of social cues; at other times excessive sensitivity may be counterproductive in making sense of the social world (Ambady and Gray 2002).

Finally, it is unclear exactly what the theory of EI predicts. On the one hand, the simplest assumption is that, if we link emotional disorders to low EI, these conditions should relate to some general impairment in emotional perception. On the other hand, if some *oversensitivity* to emotion is implicated in clinical disorders, then we would predict enhancements in perception of the kind found by Joorman and Gotlib (2006). The theory does not appear to be specified in sufficient detail to make sense of the complex empirical findings.

Alexithymia

Alexithymia is a construct derived from clinical observations that may be especially relevant to deficiencies in EI (Taylor and Bagby 2000). The term "alexithymia," coined by Sifneos (1972), literally means lack (*a*) of words (*lexis*) for emotion (*thymos*). In various disorders, including "psychosomatic" disease, panic and eating disorders, some patients show difficulties in verbalizing their feelings. Alexithymics may be especially prone to misattribute somatic sensations to disease, contributing to disorders such as hypochondriasis, essential hypertension, and functional gastrointestinal disorders (Taylor 2000). The most popular means of assessing alexithymia are given in table 11.3.

Table 11.3
Assessing alexithymia: The Toronto Alexithymia Scale

Test description	Sample constructs and items
Alexithymia may be measured as a continuous trait using the widely used Toronto Alexithymia Scale-20 (TAS-20: Bagby et al. 1994). This 20-item Likert type scale asks respondents to rate the items using a 7 point scale from "completely disagree" to "completely agree". The TAS scale yields information on three constructs given in the next column.	1. Difficulty identifying feelings and distinguishing between feelings and the bodily sensations of emotional arousal (e.g., "I am often confused about the emotion I am feeling") 2. Difficulty describing feelings to other people (e.g., "I find it hard to describe how I feel to people") 3. Externally orientated thinking, reflecting a preference for concrete details of everyday life over imagination, fantasy, and inner experience (e.g., "I prefer to watch "light" entertainment shows rather than psychological dramas")

At a process level, alexithymia appears to relate to fundamental differences in encoding and processing emotions. Several studies confirm that alexithymia relates to various deficits in processing emotional information, including recognition of verbal and nonverbal emotion stimuli, identifying emotions of others, and recalling emotion words from memory (e.g., Lane et al. 1996; Luminet et al. 2006). These effects appear to be specific to emotional stimuli (Luminet et al. 2006). Alexithymia may also be associated with deficits in the automatic processing of high arousal emotional stimuli, leading perhaps to difficulties in understanding symptoms of bodily discomfort (Vermeulen et al. 2006). Alexithymia has also been linked to deficits in interpersonal functioning related to difficulties in perceiving, communicating, and expressing emotion during interactions with others (e.g., Spitzer et al. 2005).

Alexithymia appears especially relevant to EI because it relates specifically to difficulties in processing emotion, rather than general negative affectivity. Table 11.4 summarizes the extent to which the two dimensions are comparable. Various studies have addressed the relationship between EI and alexithymia using empirical data (Vachon and Bagby 2007). These studies typically show substantial positive correlations between questionnaire measures of EI and lower alexithymia. The associations may in part reflect shared personality variance, given that alexithymia correlates with neuroticism and introversion, traits that substantially correlated with self-report EI. A study that employed a large nonclinical sample confirmed that alexithymia and EI are distinct, though positively correlated constructs (Parker et al. 2001).

Table 11.4
Comparison of EI and alexithymia along key dimensions

Dimensions	Emotional intelligence	Alexithymia
Origins	Emotions and ability research	Clinical observations (medical, psychiatric)
Type of variable	Individual difference (ability/competence)	Individual difference? Personality disorder?
Broader category	Social intelligence	Affect regulation disorder
Dimensionality	Multidimensional	Multidimensional
Intelligence link	Interpersonal and intrapersonal	Intrapersonal and interpersonal
Emotional continuum	Entire continuum	Low end of continuum
Information processing	Cognitive processing of affective data (e.g., recognition, storage)	Deficit in affect processing and elevating processing to conceptual stage
Factor structure	Three to four factors	Three factors
Biological underpinnings	Biological determinants unclear—possible genetic factor	Neurobiological determinants attested (deficits in bi-directional transfer of information among hemispheres, anterior cingulate cortex activity)
Etiology	Primary socialization and social learning	Biology and attachment processes
Related features	Empathy, social skills, assertiveness, etc.	Limited empathic capacity, social conformity, tendency toward actions, etc.
Intelligence correlates	Moderately related to verbal intelligence	Negligibly related to intelligence
Personality correlates	Unclear—function of scoring technique	Positively correlated with N and negatively correlated with E and O
Links to clinical disorders	Unclear	Widespread incidence in variety of clinical disorders
Intervention prospects	Good	Poor (particularly conventional psychotherapy)
Intervention focus	Social-emotional skill training	Focus on labeling and discerning inner experiences and emotions

Objective tests for EI (e.g., MSCEIT) appear to be modestly correlated with lower alexithymia (Parker 2005). Correlations between scales of the MSCEIT and TAS are typically around −0.30 or so (Lumley et al. 2005; Warwick and Nettelbeck 2004). Lumley et al. took various measures related to emotional functioning and regulation and developed a confirmatory factor model. The authors distinguished an "implicit self" factor, defined by the MSCEIT subtests, from an "explicit self" factor defined by questionnaire measures including the TAS, the TMMS of Salovey et al. (1995), and a scale for emotional coping. Once again, a sharp divide appears between self-report and objective tests. Lumley et al. (2005) also distinguished an "other self" factor defined by a clinical interview rating scale and an assessment for alexithymic traits by another person. The authors conclude that emotional ability is not a unitary construct.

Alexithymia has important treatment implications in clinical psychology (Parker 2005). Whether it represents a stable diathesis factor for mental illness is open to debate, although prospective studies are now starting to appear in the literature (e.g., Rufer et al. 2006). So far as EI is concerned, developments in theory and research on alexithymia may help identify promising new research areas and processes such as verbalizing feelings that may be linked more strongly to EI than to general negative affectivity. We are left with the issue of whether EI will actually add anything new to the concept of alexithymia in clinical practice. Lumley et al.'s (2005) study shows that objective tests for EI measure qualities quite distinct from self- and other-reported alexithymia, but the clinical relevance of the MSCEIT has yet to be demonstrated in patient groups.

Concluding Remarks

On the face of it, it is reasonable to describe some of the core attributes of emotional disorders as emotionally unintelligent (see Salovey et al., 1999), such as misperceptions of threat, unrealistically low self-concept, excessive awareness of negative mood, and use of dysfunctional regulative studies that prolong worry. In terms of Scherer's (2007) analysis, faulty appraisals, regulation, and communication all seem to feature in all or most of the disorders reviewed. The relevance of the four-branch model (Mayer et al. 2000) appears harder to establish. Some conditions, notably obsessive-compulsive disorder (OCD), appear to relate to difficulties in assimilating emotion into thought. In OCD, intrusive thoughts that elicit anxiety themselves become a source of threat for which the person feels responsible; thoughts of harming one's child might be seen as equivalent to the act itself (Salkovskis 1999). Impairments in mood-regulation, along

Table 11.5
Why has emotional intelligence had so little impact on the clinical psychology of emotional disorders?

Data on EI typically come from nonclinical samples rather than patients, and therefore are of little direct use to clinicians working with patient populations.
Accounts of EI neglect the component processes that may be key to disordered monitoring, understanding, and regulation of emotions. The current clinical psychology of emotional disorders makes use of a rich array of process-based constructs, substantiated by extensive empirical evidence (see Alloy and Riskind 2006).
Accounts of EI neglect the dynamic processes that may be critical to emotional pathology (Wells and Matthews 1994, 2006). Conceptualizing EI as a set of stable traits does not contribute to understanding how disorders arise from maladaptive patterns of person–environment interaction. For example, mood-regulation strategies are highly sensitive to situational factors (e.g., Gross 1888; Gross and John 2003); conceptualizing mood-regulation in terms of traits (as in the TMMS) fails to inform on how dysfunctional cycles of regulation may develop and impair the person's ability to handle environmental challenges.
Studies of subclinical symptoms fail to control for neuroticism and other personality traits known to be implicated in disorder.
Clinicians already have concepts and tests of alexithymia that may capture the most important features of low EI for emotional disorders. Although EI may be psychometrically distinct, it is unclear what it adds to alexithymia.

with maladaptive coping (see chapter 7), suggest that managing emotions may be deficient in patients. The role of understanding emotion is unknown, and the empirical studies cited above do not suggest a consistent general deficit in emotion perception. Empirical studies imply that self-report measures of EI are likely to be sensitive to disorder, although there is little evidence to suggest that lower MSCEIT scores will be seen in patients.

Overall, despite some promise, EI has had little impact on the clinical psychology of emotional disorders (Matthews et al. 2002; Vachon and Bagby 2007). Table 11.5 presents a number of reasons why we believe this might be the case.

Disorders of Impulse Control

The ruling passion, be it what it will;
The ruling passion conquers reason still.
—Alexander Pope

Goleman (1995a) implicated self-control as a master aptitude for EI, but it has received relatively little attention in research. However, clinical psychology recognizes impairments in self-control as central to disorders typified by impulsive behaviors. Axis I disorders that meet this criterion tend to be florid and somewhat unusual, and relatively little studied, certainly in relation to EI. Kleptomania and pyromania both involve behaviors committed in response to increasing tension, followed by pleasure, gratification, or relief after the theft or fire-raising, implying maladaptation in mood-regulation. Trichotillomania—recurrent hair-pulling—is similar.

Rather better known are the axis II personality disorders that may contribute to impulsivity in everyday life contexts (including criminality). The most problematic of these disorders for society is antisocial personality disorder. Diagnostic criteria in DSM-IV-TR include impulsivity, irritability, and aggressiveness, and consistent irresponsibility. It overlaps with the concept of psychopathy, which covers (1) impulsive and antisocial behaviors and (2) deceit of others and allied emotional deficiencies (Hare 1999). Borderline personality was covered in the previous section because of its link to affective instability, but impulsivity and inappropriate anger are also listed as diagnostic criteria in DSM-IV-TR. Histrionic personality also relates to excessive emotionality (in conjunction with attention seeking) but also to disinhibited behaviors such as shallow sexual encounters.

Disorders related to impulsivity are also important in child psychiatry. Conduct disorder corresponds, at least loosely, to adult antisocial personality. Defining features include aggression, destruction of property, deceitfulness or theft, and serious violations of rules such as persistent truanting. Indeed a broad range of conduct or "externalizing" problems, including delinquency, substance use, and risky sexual behaviors, may reflect a single underlying syndrome (Cooper et al. 2003). By contrast, children with attention-deficit/hyperactivity disorder (ADHD) are not generally willfully antisocial, but exhibit serious inattention, and/or restlessness, and/or behavioral impulsivity.

Factor analytic studies of continuous abnormal traits (reviewed by Matthews et al. 2003) suggest that we should distinguish antisocial conduct (linked to low agreeableness and "psychoticism") from disinhibition and sensation seeking (linked to extraversion). In fact impulsivity as a trait has proved rather difficult to localize precisely within conventional personality models (Zuckerman 2005). The most harmful form may be what Zuckerman terms "impulsive aggression," a concept referring to striking out at others, verbally or physically, when angry.

In addition to various forms of socially inappropriate behavior, there are several indications of lack of EI in these (somewhat diverse) conditions. First, social-emotional deficiencies are common in antisocial and conduct disorders. Psychopaths are deficient in empathy for others, so they feel little guilt or remorse over the harm they do (Hare 1999). They also appear to experience a more general poverty of emotion, with limited depth of feeling, and are perceived by others as being unemotional. Similarly, while some children with conduct problems are overemotional, a subgroup possessing callous-unemotional traits may be identified (Loney et al. 2003). These young psychopaths show little concern for others, impaired moral understanding and empathy, and tend to be more predatory in their violent activities than other children with conduct problems. Dylan Klebold and Eric Harris, the teenaged Columbine killers, may provide an extreme example (although, of course, it would be glib to attribute their actions to lack of EI). A *Time* magazine article titled "Bad to the Bone" (December 27, 1999) quotes psychiatrist Donald Black thus: "What's frightening is how cold and calculated all this was, with no regard for the consequence. They view it through their perverse world view, not seeing it as others would, which is a characteristic of antisocials." At a psychobiological level there is evidence that antisocial personality disorder relates to low arousability, as measured by indexes of the autonomic nervous system (Zuckerman 2005). Such individuals may be deficient in their emotional responses, and they may also need to commit extreme, exciting acts in order to counter the boredom that results (Raine 2002).

Although lack of empathy is seen as a hallmark of low EI, some psychopaths may also show social skills that would seem to indicate high EI (see Hare 1999). Con-men and -women are often adept at gaining the trust of others in order to defraud them. Such persons appear charming and pleasant, implying that, in some respects, social competence can be differentiated from empathy. The counterpart in normal personality is the Machiavellian personality, which relates to manipulative traits as discussed in chapter 6.

In other persons, conduct disorder is linked to over- rather than underemotionality. Aggression is often divided into cold-blooded proactive aggression and reactive aggression whereby angry outbursts follow some real or perceived provocation (Coie and Dodge 1998). Reactively aggressive children show particular difficulties in interpersonal interaction (Vitaro et al. 1998). These individuals tend to be low in agreeableness but also high in emotional instability (Caprara et al. 1996). Thus there is some overlap with emotional disorders and borderline personality, and such children do indeed tend to be prone to internalizing as well as externalizing problems.

Thus far we have delineated some features of impulse control and conduct disorders that may be linked descriptively to emotional intelligence. Unfortunately, there is rather little relevant empirical evidence. A few studies (reviewed by Rivers et al. 2007) link lowered MSCEIT scores to indicators of deviance such as drug use, but these studies did not address the clinical status of their participants. Riley and Schutte (2003) found that self-report EI related to both drug and alcohol abuse; other work suggests such associations may be dependent on standard personality traits (Austin et al. 2005; Brackett and Mayer 2003).

It is widely believed that psychopathy relates to deficits in social cognition and information processing. Most prominent are tendencies toward hostile attributions (Vitale et al. 2005). The psychopath believes the world is unpredictable and dangerous, and violence is justified by the survival imperative. Moral reasoning and judgment are also impaired; victims of violence are seen as getting what they deserved. Similar attitudes are found in aggressive children, including those with conduct or externalizing disorders. Such children tend to appraise others as hostile, to evaluate aggressive or confronting behaviors as successful coping options, and to access rapidly specific aggressive responses (Coie and Dodge 1998). Such distortions of appraisal might be labeled as emotionally unintelligent, in line with Scherer's (2007) analysis. Indeed, recent research by Malterer et al. (2008) shows that whereas the repair and attention scores of psychopathic individuals were lower than those of controls, the clarity scores of psychopaths were higher than those of controls. The authors conclude that "individuals with primary psychopathy are both less likely to attend to emotion cues and less able to revise their mood states once emotions are experienced" (p. 742).

Aggression—and other expressions of impulsivity—may relate to a neurocognitive system for effortful control, which inhibits the child from engaging in risky behaviors. Frick and Morris (2004) suggest that reactive aggression, associated with emotional outbursts, reflects a combination of high emotionality and low effortful control. Proactive aggression, by contrast, is not primarily emotion-driven. Aggression may also relate to distortions of the self-schema analogous to those seen in the emotional disorder, but centered on relations with others rather than personal self-worth and vulnerability (Matthews et al. 2000). Wallace and Newman

(2004) suggest that psychopaths are deficient in self-regulatory control, leading to a lack of adequate evaluation of response tendencies, such as violence. In addition implicit memory processes tend to generate powerful but inappropriate aggressive responses—reminiscent of the rugby football dictum that one should get one's retaliation in first. Probably multiple mechanisms contribute to aggressive behaviors (see Frick and Morris 2004), with different mechanisms more prominent in different impulsive-aggressive disorders.

As with emotional disorders some authors have identified emotion processing as critical to antisocial personality; perhaps the psychopath neither sees nor feels the victim's pain. Blair et al. (2004) propose that lack of empathy is linked to a brain system that processes sad and fearful emotional displays. A processing deficit in this system renders psychopaths insensitive to the suffering of others, and interferes with their moral socialization. To test this hypothesis, Blair et al. (2004) recruited a sample of psychopathic prisoners from high-security London jails. They showed that, compared to a control condition, these individuals tended to be generally poor at recognizing facial emotion, but the deficit was greatest for fear faces. Supportive data were also obtained in a study of children with psychopathic tendencies (Stevens et al. 2001). The clinical relevance of such findings was supported in a correlational study of children that showed the ability to recognize sad and fearful expressions (but not other emotions) was inversely related to both level of affective-interpersonal disturbance and impulsive/conduct problems, as rated by their teachers (Blair and Coles 2000).

However, other studies have arrived at different conclusions (e.g., Kosson et al. 2002). Glass and Newman (2006) studied a fairly large sample of 111 psychopathic criminal offenders but failed to find any deficits in facial emotion recognition. Across the various studies there appears to be a stronger trend toward an emotion recognition deficit than seen in emotional disorders. However, as Glass and Newman (2006) state, the conditions that reveal affective deficits in psychopathic individuals require further investigation.

Psychopathy might relate to alexithymia because both conditions relate to an impoverished emotional life (Haviland et al. 2004), but the little empirical research available fails to substantiate any clear relationship (Louth et al. 1998). Kosson et al. (2002) review various other studies of psychopathy and emotion processing; some of which show deficits and some of which do not. The precise nature of emotional deficits in psychopathy remains unclear. As with emotional disorder we can loosely describe low EI as a feature of the disorders of impulse control. However, thus far it is unclear how the theory of EI can help add to current clinical understanding of these disorders.

Disorders of Social Connection

Some disorders are typified by social disconnection, in which the person seems to lack both the ability and the motivation to form close relationships with others. We will make no attempt to do justice to the large research literatures relating to autism, Asperger's syndrome, schizoid personality, and related conditions. Our purpose is mainly to draw attention to the apparent failure of social-emotional competence in these disorders. It is surprising that they have not received much attention from researchers on EI, given the importance of interpersonal functioning in accounts of the construct.

Autism and Asperger's Syndrome

Perhaps the most dramatic such condition is autistic disorder (i.e., autism; see Lainhart 1999). DSM-IV-TR lists diagnostic criteria in relation to three types of functional impairment that must emerge before the age of three: These are impairments in (1) social interaction, (2) communication and language, and (3) in range of interests in behavior. The related condition of Asperger's disorder is similarly defined, without delays in language development. Asperger's patients are typically within the normal range for general intelligence, although the majority of autistic persons score as being subnormal on standard intelligence tests. It is difficult to distinguish "high-functioning" autistic and Asperger's patients (Ghaziuddin and Mountain-Kimchi 2004).

High-functioning autism appears, on the face of it, to dissociate cognitive and social-emotional intelligence. The individuals concerned appear to have normal cognitive reasoning abilities but have great difficulties in relating to others. They are said to lack a "theory of mind" (Baron-Cohen 1995) that would allow them to understand other people. Even those individuals that are articulate and insightful compare themselves to "anthropologists on Mars" (Sacks 1995). They are forced to work out from observation and reason how to behave around other people. Frith (2004) describes Asperger's syndrome as involving an extreme egocentrism, in which the person cannot take the perspective of others. Indeed the person with Asperger's may even have trouble understanding that other people may have different perspectives to themselves. The person must actively attempt to compensate for the lack of the implicit, unconscious competencies that contribute to normal social interaction.

Social impairment is evident in emotions also. Corresponding to difficulties in perspective-taking is a lack of empathy, which tends to frustrate other family members. Complex emotions may be especially hard to comprehend (Blair 2003). In an autobiographic account, Lawson (1998) thus writes:

> I find emotions interchangeable and confusing. Growing up I was not able to distinguish between anger, fear, anxiety, frustration, or disappointment.... I could tell the difference between a comfortable and an uncomfortable one, but I didn't know what to do with it.... [With age] I have learned to recognize the subtle differences between anger, frustration, and disappointment, and understand why I feel these things. (cited in Howlin 2004, p. 105)

Such accounts imply that autism and Asperger's should relate to alexithymia, and indeed the conditions overlap (Fitzgerald and Bellgrove 2006). Studies have also shown deficits in emotion perception, although it is unclear whether deficits are specific to face processing or reflect a more general deficit (Dawson et al. 2004). Impairments may also be a consequence of abnormal strategies for scanning faces; high-functioning autistics tend to look at the mouth rather than the eyes, and to avert the gaze entirely during emotion-laden interactions (Klin et al. 2002).

Like other axis II conditions, high-functioning autistic symptoms may be seen as the expression of a continuous trait or traits. Baron-Cohen and his colleagues (e.g., Wakabayashi et al. 2006) have developed the Autism Spectrum Questionnaire, which provides the researcher with a so-called AQ (see http://www.wired.com/wired/archive/9.12/aqtest.html, where you can actually take the test). It assesses in adults and adolescents five traits linked to autism: social skill, attention switching, attention to detail, communication, and imagination. The scale effectively discriminates autistic patients from normal controls. It shows some overlap with the five factor model (FFM; see Austin 2005b; Wakabayashi et al. 2006), but correlations are no more than moderate. The papers cited found correlations typically in the 0.3 to 0.4 range between AQ and neuroticism, low agreeableness, and introversion. Austin (2005b) notes that some of the subscale reliabilities are rather modest (around 0.6), and her factor analysis recovered only three out of five scales, indicating a need for instrument refinement. Nevertheless, the questionnaire represents an interesting attempt to identify continuous traits for autism that may pick up some aspects of EI.

However, we should be cautious in viewing Asperger's syndrome or high-functioning autism as a paradigm for low EI. These conditions relate to complex patterns of abnormality; some of which, such as motor functions, have nothing to do with emotional intelligence. Asperger's relates to specific neurological deficits (Frith 2004), and it is unclear whether the same brain systems are implicated in low EI within the normal range. Furthermore, at the psychological level, the deficits appear to be primarily cognitive in nature. These include, for example, an underdeveloped theory of mind, or an executive dysfunction that impairs organization, planning, and flexible problem-solving. Seeing Asperger's as the low point of a continuum of levels of EI might then entail taking a strongly cognitive view of deficits in emotional competence, a view incompatible with many of the theories of EI that we have reviewed.

Schizotypal and Schizoid Personality

Additional personality disorders may contribute to lack of interest and competence in social interaction, including abnormal traits that may provide a diathesis for schizophrenia. The symptoms of *schizotypal* personality in DSM-IV-TR bear at least a passing resemblance to Asperger's syndrome: "a pervasive pattern of social and interpersonal deficits marked by acute discomfort with, and reduced capacity, for, close relationships as well as by cognitive or perceptual distortions and eccentricities of behavior" (First et al. 2004, p. 359). Likewise *schizoid* personality refers to "detachment of social relationships and a restricted range of expression of emotions in interpersonal settings" (First et al. 2004, p. 357). Although both conditions are diagnostically distinct from autism/Asperger's making the correct diagnosis is often challenging for the clinician (Wolff 2000). One important difference is that schizotypy relates to unusual and original thinking, and even to artistic creativity in some cases, but autistic individuals tend to be literal, detail-oriented, and narrowly focused in thinking. Nettle (2006) showed that poets and visual artists tend to show schizotypal but not autistic traits, whereas mathematicians show the opposite pattern. Similarities between autism and personality disorder relate especially to the "negative symptoms" associated with schizophrenia and its attendant personality disorders (i.e., flattening of affect, loss of verbal and emotional expressiveness, and lack of social motivation). Like autistics, schizotypal individuals appear to have difficulties in conceptualizing and reasoning about mental states (Langdon and Coltheart 1999).

Schizotypy can be measured as a continuous trait with distinct facets (e.g., Mason and Claridge 2006) relating to positive and negative symptoms and to cognitive disorganization. Facets representing negative symptoms such as lack of affect, anhedonia, and social disengagement appear to be most relevant to EI. Waldeck and Miller (2000) found that schizotypal individuals were poorer at identifying positive, but not negative, emotions on the Izard Emotion Recognition Test. They point out that more robust deficits in emotion recognition are found in schizophrenic patients. This study also tested social skills. It appears that schizotypal individuals were aware what is appropriate behavior but failed to implement social norms into their own behavior. Studies using the TMMS have confirmed that schizotypy relates to poorer mood regulation, as well as elevated negative affect (Berenbaum et al. 2006; Kerns 2006). Kerns (2006) established a fairly strong association between the negative facet of schizotypy and emotional confusion, defined in part by low TMMS clarity about emotion. Negative schizotypy also relates to alexithymia (Gooding and Tallent 2003). As with autism, there is at least a loose correspondence between schizotypy and low EI, but it is unclear how reference to EI would benefit clinical understanding.

Implications for Therapy

As noted throughout this chapter, the impact of research on EI on clinical practice has been rather slight. Psychotherapists already have fairly effective techniques for treating the disorders we have reviewed whose origins predate recent interest in EI by several decades. Matthews et al. (2002) point out that many of the concerns of EI are prefigured by cognitive-behavior therapies (CBTs). Based on the insight that emotional dysfunction often reflects faulty cognition (Beck 1967; Ellis 1962) CBTs aim to restructure thinking to foster both realism and optimism. Contrary to popular opinion, CBT is not just a matter of talking through problems with a patient. It aims to change implicit as well as explicit cognition by addressing unconscious cognitive influences on behavior in addition to the contents of awareness. The therapist builds an individual case conceptualization, based on the relevant cognitive theories of disorder (e.g., Beck 1967), that specifies how abnormalities in cognition play out into behavioral dysfunction within the circumstances of the person's life (see Wells 1997). The specific interventions used may then be tailored to the case conceptualization.

Intervention in CBT is often directed toward "emotionally unintelligent" cognition. For example, Beck (1967) pointed out how depressives make false inferences about their lack of worth from daily events (e.g., overgeneralizing from a single personal failure). The patient may be directed toward participation in behavioral experiments that focus attention on personal competencies and accomplishments, and constructing a more positive self-schema, with consequent benefits for mood and behavioral functioning. In addition to targeting the content of self-schemas, therapy may also be directed toward dysfunctional processes, such as "automatic thoughts," seemingly spontaneous negative cognitions, and images that occupy consciousness. Thus—to the extent that emotional pathology can be attributed to cognitive factors—CBT already draws upon a wide range of theories and practical techniques.

What might EI add to current practice? Greenberg and Pascual-Leone (2006) identify four goals for working therapeutically with emotion that are common to a variety of schools of therapy. First, it is important that the client is aware and accepting of emotions (typically, negative emotions). Arousing and managing negative emotions in the course of therapy sessions may be important for eventual success: "the distressing affective experience must be activated and viscerally experienced by the client" (Greenberg and Pascual-Leone 2006, p. 615). They caution also that the experience alone is not sufficient for progress in therapy. Second, appropriate emotion-regulation must be addressed: some clients overregulate and some underregulate. Third, it is important to reflect on emotion. Awareness of disturbing emotions should be followed to develop new personal narratives that allow more constructive emotional management. Fourth, the most fundamental goal of emotion-directed therapies is to transform emotions positively. For example, maladaptive anger can be transformed into adaptive sadness, leading to eventual acceptance of the emotion.

Although there are several therapeutic means to these ends, including psychodynamic and cognitive approaches, Greenberg (2006) advocated an explicitly emotion-focused approach to therapy. The therapist should act as an "emotions coach" who helps people become aware of, accept and make sense of their emotional experience. It is thus especially important that the therapist is able to empathize with, sooth and support the client. Indeed this issue points toward the importance of the clinician's (as opposed to the client's) EI. Figure 11.3 illustrates the need for the therapist to cope effectively with the emotional demands of therapy.

Figure 11.3
An extreme case of compassion fatigue

With this general background in mind, we will focus especially on two issues where the study of EI may, in fact, make a unique contribution. The first is treatment for alexithymics: their difficulties in understanding and communicating their own emotions make them especially challenging for psychotherapists (Parker 2000). The second issue is whether research on EI highlights emotional competencies that may have been neglected in existing approaches to therapy. We will briefly look at what EI may offer to therapies concerned with mood-regulation and with emotion expression.

Treatment for Alexithymia

Clinical interest in alexithymia in part reflects clinicians' difficulties in working with patients with this condition. Therapies that rely on the patient developing insight into their condition are often ineffective, and alexithymia itself is hard to treat directly (Taylor 2000). (Of course, some therapies, such as traditional behavior therapies and drug treatments, require no insight at all.) Indeed alexithymics may drop out of

treatment as the therapy stagnates and both the client and therapist become increasingly frustrated (Pierloot and Vinck 1977). Cusack et al.
(2006) report data showing that alexithymia correlated at −0.39 with perceptions of treatment helpfulness, in a sample of men who had accessed
professional therapy services for various reasons. The study showed that
alexithymia also related negatively to a self-measure of the bond formed
between client and therapist.

Several clinicians have been motivated to develop therapies that are
especially geared to the needs of alexithymics: our account here draws on
reviews by Parker (2000) and Vachon and Bagby (2007). Krystal (1979,
1988) noted that in alexithymic patients with psychosomatic diseases, psychotherapy sometimes seemed to exacerbate physical symptoms to the
point of serious illness. He developed a multi-step strategy for treatment
that aimed to help the patient accurately label and verbalize emotions. He
claimed that over time, alexithymics were able to improve their understanding and communication of emotions, leading to improved social
functioning. It may also be important for the therapist to be emotionally
expressive, in order to model how specific emotions may be attached
to specific interpersonal situations. Group therapy may be valuable for
some clients with alexithymia because feedback from other group members may help the alexithymic understand how his or her behavior influences others emotionally (Swiller 1988). However, as Swiller sagely points
out, if groups contain more than a small number of alexithymics, interactions are unlikely to add insight. A few studies supporting the benefits of
such treatment options exist (Parker 2000; Spitzer et al. 2005).

Treatment for Disorders of Mood Regulation

The importance of targeting dysfunctional mood-regulation strategies
such as rumination is well-established. As noted earlier, Salovey et al.
(1999) explicitly link rumination to low EI. Purdon (2004) reviews the
various treatment options. She points out that "thought-stopping" techniques intended to condition the patient to cease ruminating through use
of an aversive stimulus are ineffective. Voluntary attempts to suppress
thoughts may actually lead to a later "rebounding" of the thoughts
concerned. It is important instead to address the underlying cognitive pathology that generates rumination and worry through modifying dysfunctional beliefs and attentional processes.

Wells (2000) has identified maladaptive metacognition as important in
the etiology and maintenance of emotional disorders. Anxiety patients
are prone to meta-worry (worry about worry), whereas depressives under-

estimate their control over ruminative thought and tend to believe that rumination is in fact a productive coping strategy (Papageorgiou and Wells 2004). Wells and his colleagues have developed and evaluated several specific techniques for metacognitive therapy. These include:

1. explicit analysis of the patient's beliefs about metacognition;

2. facilitating flexible control over thoughts through training the person to focus attention externally rather than internally;

3. modifying dysfunctional beliefs about metacognition; and

4. decatastrophizing emotion; that is, addressing beliefs that negative emotion signals disaster or pathology.

Generally, Wells and Matthews (1994) advocate a state of detached mindfulness as the goal for therapy, namely being able to monitor one's thoughts in a detached, objective manner without having those thoughts trigger negative affect or worry. Teasdale et al. (2000) have also developed meditative techniques intended to train development of "nonjudgmental" awareness of thoughts, feelings and bodily sensations without becoming upset by them.

In similar vein, Ciarrochi and Blackledge (2006) advocate what they call mindfulness-based emotional intelligence training. It focuses on skills such as being able to deal with unpleasant emotion when inevitable or necessary for action (effective emotional orientation), using emotion as information, being able to "emotionally defuse" threatening feelings and self-concepts, and sustaining effective action orientation. A theme here is that effective action in the world depends on being mindful of unpleasant emotions and managing them constructively. The therapy aims to build acceptance of unpleasant experiences and learning to become detached from emotions that may interfere with the pursuit of valued activities. Loosely, the idea appears to be that it is more emotionally intelligent to learn to live with negative emotions than to try to reassemble people's language-based models of the self and its weaknesses (as cognitive therapy does). The effectiveness of this approach remains to be evaluated systematically.

Emotion Expression and Treatment

Established treatment methods already target emotion expression, but much of the emphasis is on the ways in which expressing emotions may be problematic. For example, social phobics often believe that their visible display of anxiety will lead other people to denigrate them: an erroneous belief that can be treated, for example, in behavior experiments in social interaction (Wells 1997). One of the more novel contributions of EI may be its focus on the benefits of being emotionally expressive, and the role of therapy in encouraging expressiveness.

In an important synthesis of the literature, Kennedy-Moore and Watson (1999) review the therapeutic relevance of emotional expression, and we will paraphrase their arguments here. They point out that people often believe that venting negative emotions is effective in coping with them. The contemporary zeitgeist, of course, favors letting emotions out, as opposed to bottling them up. However, the advantages of venting are not so clear-cut. It may be a symptom of excessive distress rather than a solution to it, and venting may even intensify distress. High levels of grief following bereavement predict a poorer long-term outcome (Bonanno 2004); a certain amount of emotional avoidance may even be adaptive in this context. Venting, as an angry tirade, for example, can elicit negative reactions from other people. People may find expressions of distress overwhelming, frightening, or even boring. Pennebaker (1992) reports that following the 1989 San Francisco earthquake, residents were seen wearing t-shirts stating "Thank you for not sharing your earthquake experience."

Kennedy-Moore and Watson (1999) go on to propose that the person must not just vent distress, but understand it and communicate it to other supportive people (including therapists). They list four potential benefits of emotional expression, *provided that it functions adaptively*. First, it can free the person from the psychologically and physiologically harmful effects of emotion suppression, consistent with Pennebaker's (1992) studies of emotional disclosure. Second, emotion expression is necessary for the person to gain self-understanding through exploring their feelings. The clinical patient may need support from a therapist to avoid being overwhelmed by strong emotion. Third, expression may motivate constructive coping efforts. Fourth, adaptive expression of emotions supports interpersonal relationships, by enhancing intimacy and connection with others, leading to greater availability of social support.

Thus, in line with Greenberg and Pascaul-Leone's (2006) view that experiencing negative emotions is necessary (but not sufficient) for successful therapy, treatment may be enhanced through techniques that focus on the expression of the emotions felt. Kennedy-Moore and Watson (1999) provide numerous examples. In brief, some of the principal areas of application are as follows:

Emotional Constriction in Depression   Depressed individuals often have trouble expressing emotions other than a passive general misery. This expressive style can interfere with communication and relationships with others; the depressed person may be perceived as unresponsive, disengaged, or even hostile. It is important to cultivate awareness of positive emotions, empathy, and more effective interpersonal communication.

Traumatic Emotion   Kennedy-Moore and Watson (1999) point out that the survivors of trauma often vacillate between being overwhelmed by strong emotion and periods of emotional numbness. Helping clients express their feelings adaptively, as they create new perceptions of themselves and the traumatic event, contributes to a "middle ground" of emotional expression in which survivors can process and resolve their emotions.

Marital Therapy   Couples may become locked into destructive interpersonal cycles, including but not limited to mutual hostility. Therapy may be directed toward modifying the rigidity of expressive roles that the protagonists adopt. Couples can learn to recognize and step back from maladaptive emotional expressions and to reinterpret their spouse's emotions with greater insight and compassion.

Emotion Expression in Health Psychology   Data are somewhat inconsistent, but it is possible that chronic emotional suppression is implicated in the etiology or progression of cancer (Nyklièek et al. 2002). It may thus be important to help cancer patients express painful emotions, but there is rather little evidence that interventions of this kind are effective (Kennedy-Moore and Watson 1999). There is stronger evidence that hostility is a risk factor for cardiovascular disease, and cognitive-behavioral anger management programs may be helpful (e.g., Deffenbacher et al. 1994).

Concluding Comments

Overall, there should be a natural match between clinical psychology and emotional intelligence. Emotional dysfunction is pervasive across a wide range of disorders, including but not limited to the classic emotional disorders. Furthermore, some of the key processes identified in theory and research on EI are also implicated in emotional disorder. We have discussed the clinical importance of distorted appraisals of emotive events, poor impulse control, maladaptive mood-regulation, and deficits in the communication and social expression of emotions. Interest in EI also seems to mesh with increasing interest in direct targeting of emotions in therapy (Greenberg 2006). Potentially therapists might screen clients for facets of low EI as an aid to diagnosis, target the key processes supporting EI in therapy, and accommodate to the client's emotional strengths and weaknesses in building the therapeutic partnership.

However, EI rarely figures explicitly in clinical practice, for several reasons. A basic difficulty is that EI is something of a fifth wheel. Clinicians can already draw upon a range of theoretically based emotional constructs in case conceptualization including neuroticism, alexithymia, and various dimensions of abnormal personality. It is unclear what EI can add. Also the construct of EI may simply be too broad to be useful; it is not helpful to lump together mood disorder, antisocial personality, and autism.

A more fine-grained approach that evaluates abnormality in cognitive and emotional processes in detail is needed, and the broad categories of emotional functioning described in theories such as that of Mayer et al. (2000) tend to obscure the fine but critical detail needed in clinical psychology. The example of Lincoln with which we opened the chapter shows how predispositions to mental illness may have emotional benefits as well as costs. The neglect of process-based analyses in favor of broad functional descriptions that we have already noted contributes to the problem. Finally, the broad-brush approach of much EI research does not lend itself to specific therapeutic interventions. It is unfortunate that operationalizations of EI, especially in the self-report domain, may conflate symptoms and outcomes with underlying causal processes. Although treating emotional problems is critical, much more work on the pathology of EI is needed before the field will have much of immediate practical value to contribute.

Summary Points: Chapter 11

• Some of the most extreme examples of emotional dysfunction are shown by people suffering from clinical disorders. Low EI may constitute a vulnerability factor or "diathesis" for a range of pathological conditions. Perhaps treatments for lack of EI could help individuals with conditions including emotional disorder, poor impulse control, and autism.

However, there are some difficulties finding clinical utility from work on EI. The example of Abraham Lincoln shows that a predisposition to melancholy is not necessarily accompanied by low EI. A more fundamental difficulty is that emotional pathology takes many different forms, as recognized in the multiplicity of disorders recognized by clinicians. The concept of EI may simply be too broad to be useful in clinical practice.

• The emotional disorders are typified by excessive negative affect (depression and anxiety) and negative cognitions and thinking styles. Questionnaire measures of anxiety and depression correlate quite highly with self-report scales for EI. However, these associations may be mediated by personality factors, such as neuroticism and introversion, that tend to be elevated in emotional disorder patients. Studies of EI might identify process factors, such as impairments in emotion perception, that increase vulnerability to disorder. Thus far experimental findings are equivocal. A related research area focuses on the construct of alexithymia (difficulties in verbalizing and processing emotion). Studies of alexithymia suggest that impairments in encoding emotion may contribute to emotional disorder.

• Clinical psychology recognizes impairments in self-control as central to disorders such as that of the antisocial personality, in which destructive, impulsive behaviors are common. Social-emotional deficiencies are frequent in such disorders but may take different forms. Psychopaths are "underemotional" in that they lack depth of feeling, emotional arousability, and empathy. By contrast, reactive aggressiveness is associated with rapidly escalating anger under provocation. Various neurological and cognitive concominants of impulsivity and aggressiveness have been identified that broadly suggest deficiencies in EI. Thus far, though, work on EI has added little to clinical understanding of these conditions.

• High-functioning autism provides a dramatic dissociation of intellectual and emotional capabilities, which are apparent especially in deficits in understanding and connecting with other people. Individuals with this condition lack empathy and display various deficits in emotion processing. Other disorders of social disconnection are schizotypal and schizoid personality disorders, which may relate to vulnerability to psychosis. Flattening of affect, loss of verbal and emotional expressiveness, and lack of social motivation seen in these conditions suggests a deficit in EI. However, as with other disorders, it is unclear how labeling individuals as low in EI adds to current clinical understanding.

• There is a growing interest within clinical psychology in "emotion-directed" therapies that aim to transform emotions positively. Understanding of abnormally low EI has the potential to contribute to developing such therapies. Such methods might be especially valuable for alexithymic patients, or for anxious and depressed patients in whom mood regulation is maladaptive. Another promising therapeutic avenue is to focus on emotion expression, addressing difficulties such as constriction of expression, traumatic emotions, and interpersonal hostility. Thus far the needed translational research on EI is lacking.

• By contrast with other applied domains, work on EI has found little direct application within clinical psychology despite its potential relevance. The broad-brush approach of much EI research has not led to specific therapeutic interventions. However, a finer grained approach focusing on pathology in specific emotional processes offers the hope that understanding of EI may eventually contribute to improvements in emotion-directed therapy.

V   EMOTIONAL INTELLIGENCE...REVISITED

12 Emotional Intelligence: Known, Unknown, and Future Directions

A man who reviews the old so as to find out the new is qualified to teach others
—Confucius

As underscored throughout chapters of this book, the emotional intelligence (EI) construct remains intriguing but also mysterious, slippery, and elusive. This state of affairs constrains somewhat scientific measurement and theory-based applications. Despite extensive scrutiny and systematic research there appears relatively little consensus over how EI should be conceptualized, assessed, and practically implemented. Clearly, there is a need to more carefully delineate that which is scientifically grounded and permissible in real-life settings from endeavors that are pseudoscientific at best.

This concluding chapter aims at providing a final snapshot of this newly minted construct. Specifically, we set out to distinguish the knowns from the unknowns in relation to three paramount concerns of EI research: conceptualization, assessment, and applications. We begin each section by discussing the *knowns*, namely assertions that may be made with some degree of confidence, elucidating what are essentially sources of consensus concerning the status of emotional intelligence. We then move on to discuss the *unknowns*, namely those controversial issues for which there is less agreement among scientists and practitioners. We hope that this concluding chapter, aimed at providing "straight talk" about the current status of EI research, will provide both an executive summary and the essential take-home message(s) that the reader can readily digest.

Conceptualization of Emotional Intelligence

We cannot study EI if we do not know what it is. The different accounts of EI reviewed in this book typically contain common elements.

Perceiving, understanding, regulating, and communicating emotions are all commonly seen as central to EI (Roberts et al. 2007; Scherer 2007). However, once we start to look at the details of the different EI models, fissures appear. In chapter 1, we compared the search for EI to the search for the—possibly mythical—island of Atlantis. As with attempts to localize Atlantis it is far from clear that different EI researchers are actually describing the same entity. Despite the research there appears to be little beyond a somewhat superficial description of the major functions of emotional intelligence. Thus, it is presently unclear whether EI:

1. refers to explicit or implicit knowledge of emotion;

2. is cognitive or noncognitive;

3. refers to a basic aptitude or to some adaptation to a specific social and cultural milieu; and/or

4. is a single entity, or a multiplicity of different constructs to which the same label has been affixed?

Arguably, a primary task in any scientific endeavor is the systematic mapping out of the major components and facets in the universe of discourse under consideration (Kerlinger 1973). However, it is difficult to obtain a satisfactory definitional framework for the EI construct. Nevertheless, most researchers would likely agree that popular definitions are too overinclusive to be useful. Defining EI as a "laundry list" of virtually every positive quality of character, *except* for cognitive intelligence, accomplishes little (see especially chapter 4). The question then is what does a conceptual analysis of the EI construct yield? This is the main topic addressed in the three sections that follow.

Conceptualization: Knowns

EI Is a Multifaceted Construct That May Be Best Studied from Multiple Perspectives As demonstrated throughout the book (see chapters 2 through 4, in particular), different conceptions and definitions of EI have been proposed, leading to different operational measures of the construct. The various psychometrically adequate scales for EI appear to be measuring disparate constructs. This assertion is supported most clearly by the weakness of correlations between objective tests and questionnaires based on self-report (e.g., Warwick and Nettelbeck 2004), but other instances may be found. For example, Austin (2005a) studied chronometric (i.e., time-based) measures that, by analogy with cognitive research, should correlate with scores on EI tests. Although a distinct emotional-information processing factor was identified, it failed to correlate significantly with *overall* EI scores from two leading assessments.

There is probably a consensus that trait EI may be studied separately from ability-based EI. However, it remains unclear if there is a single overarching "trait" EI dimension or if the various questionnaires may be picking up multiple, largely independent traits. Some questionnaires do exhibit a strong general factor (e.g., Bar-On 2004; Petrides and Furnham 2003), whereas others do not. Tett et al. (2005) extracted independent factors from their questionnaire that they labeled as self-orientation, other-orientation, and emotional sharing. As they point out, the first two factors correspond to Gardner's (1983) intra- and interpersonal intelligences, conceived as separate personal intelligences. By contrast, the Mayer et al. (2000b) model does not sharply separate emotion regulation in self and others. Thus, although it is agreed that EI may encompass multiple domains, it remains unclear how many separate domains should be discriminated, and whether general factors may identified within each domain.

EI Overlaps with Other Constructs   A major issue is how EI should be aligned with other dimensions of ability and personality. The degree of overlap of EI with other constructs appears to be measure dependent, with each EI construct relating differently to other factors. For example, objective measures of EI, in keeping with an "ability model," correlate between 0.30 and 0.40 with general intelligence, and rather less with personality traits (chapter 3). Comparably, Brackett et al. (2007) reported that ability-based (but not self-rated) EI correlated with social competence in men when personality was statistically controlled, even in real-time social conditions. Further psychometric studies may succeed in locating an EI ability factor inside the multi-stratum model for ability advanced by Carroll (1993; chapter 3). Even so, it is unclear whether the MSCEIT converges with the objective abilities that may be defined using information-processing tasks (Roberts et al. 2006). Multiple, perhaps unrelated, abilities may contribute to objective emotional competence.

By contrast, questionnaire measures for EI overlap with standard personality traits to a degree that often appears excessive. As discussed in chapter 4, the most egregious example is Bar-On's (2004) EQ-i, which correlates around 0.80 with low trait anxiety and general psychopathology. Other questionnaires appear to possess more unique variance, but still show substantial intercorrelation with personality, raising the thus-far unanswered question of how personality and EI traits should be interrelated within a common structural model. The onus is on researchers working within a mixed- or trait EI model to develop factor structures that specify the relationship between EI and standard personality traits as latent constructs.

Frustrating, at least for the present authors, is the limited progress that has been made in this direction. Petrides and Furnham (2001) claim that trait EI is a lower-order construct within the five factor model (FFM; see chapter 4), but their data frequently show that different facets of trait EI load on different factors. Some facets attach to the standard Big Five, whereas others define a separate factor. As with ability models, it seems attractive to place EI within some larger multi-level model, but again, we may find that we have multiple constructs that do not define any general overarching trait of EI. Indeed, our analysis of standard personality traits made in various chapters (see especially 4 and 6) support just such a conclusion.

EI Relates Meaningfully to Various External Criteria   As shown in chapter 6, there is a growing body of evidence showing that various scales for EI correlate robustly with a variety of outcomes that plausibly signal social-emotional success. Both the MSCEIT and various questionnaires purportedly assessing EI correlate with measures of well-being and social engagement and competence. Validity coefficients tend to be higher for questionnaires, but in this case they are amplified by confounding with personality traits linked to social adjustment, such as extraversion. Given the overlap with personality and ability already noted, a critical issue is whether tests for EI show incremental predictive validity with key factors, including general intelligence (or g) and the Big Five, statistically controlled. Evidence for incremental validity is, however, mixed. Several studies fail to show that scales for EI predict important criteria (e.g., academic success) with other traits controlled, while still other studies demonstrate the obverse (see chapter 8). It is fair to conclude that EI may improve over general intelligence and the five factor model in predicting some criteria, but the incremental validity is modest.

EI Relates to Exceptionality   A common tactic for gathering validity evidence for ability and personality measures is to show that they discriminate groups that are exceptional in terms of, for example, their intellectual capabilities, social maladjustment, or pathology. Support for the validity of EI may be found from similar sources. Case studies of emotionally gifted individuals provide some informal but persuasive evidence (Oatley 2004). Quantitative differences in EI scores have been shown for groups such as therapists, psychiatric patients, and prisoners (e.g., Bar-On 2004; Schutte et al. 1988). Echoing a common theme these studies neglect, however, the possible confounding influences of personality and ability. The association between EI and (lack of) alexithymia has been important in establishing the clinical relevance of the construct (chapter 11). However, for each exceptional group, findings may vary with the measure of EI employed. For example, Zeidner, Shani-Zinovich, et al. (2005) showed that intellectually gifted children obtained elevated scores on the MSCEIT but were lower in self-reported EI, demonstrating a failure of convergence.

EI Follows a Well-defined Developmental Trajectory   There is an extensive literature on social-emotional development in children that predates work on EI (chapter 5). Recently Izard et al. (e.g., 2001, 2007) has shown how competencies in emotion perception and emotion knowledge may influence the developmental process. There appears to be a fairly well-defined sequence of markers of emotional development, beginning with the simple expressive and regulatory behaviors of the infant, and culminating in active, insightful self-regulation sensitive to the social and cultural environment (Saarni 2000a, b). In chapter 5 we proposed that emotional competencies may be attached to the following three separate aspects of the developmental sequence:

1. Basic temperaments shaped by innate biological attributes.

2. Social learning of rule-based adaptive behaviors (e.g., emotion display rules).

3. Development of self-reflective insight.

As the child's repertory of skills for handling emotional encounters becomes more differentiated with age, emotional competencies too may become more diverse, consistent with our view that EI is often used to refer to disparate and distinct constructs.

Conceptualization: Unknowns
We may contrast these emerging areas of consensus with several issues on which researchers are divided, sometimes sharply. A hard core of enthusiasts for EI continue to promote the validity of the construct as measured through objective tests (Mayer et al. 2004), self-report (Petrides

et al. 2007), and in applied settings (Jordan et al. 2007). Advocates for EI can rightly point toward the accumulation of validity evidence reviewed in previous chapters of this book as grounds for optimism. Others are more skeptical. Brody (2004), for example, challenges the psychometric status and predictive validity of ability tests of EI. By contrast, Landy (2005) claims that much of the applied work fails to meet elementary scientific standards, such as availability of data to other researchers. Even if it is accepted that empirical studies are rigorous, the suspicion may be that the phenomena observed (e.g., rating one's response to vignettes of doubtful personal relevance) lack ecological validity and are of minimal relevance to real-life emotional functioning. A final possibility is that the story of EI is neither one of unalloyed success nor of unmitigated failure (Roberts et al. 2007). It may be that the research has added usefully to understanding of individual differences in emotional functioning, even though it falls short of the lofty ambitions of the pioneers of the field.

Is There Evidence for Multiple Emotional "Intelligences" and Do They Share Any Common Element(s)?   It is perhaps ironic that although one of the roots of the EI construct is the notion of multiple intelligences (e.g., Gardner 1983), researchers in the field typically propose a general factor of EI, supported by multiple facets. The assumption seems to be that legitimizing the construct requires it to resemble a g factor for the emotions. The awkward truth—that two of the main conceptualizations (ability- and questionnaire-based EI) are largely unrelated—fuels a turf war over which construct is the "true EI." For example, Petrides, Furnham, et al. (2007) criticize Mayer et al.'s (2000b) ability model as being inconsistent with models of differential psychology, awkward to score, and lacking concurrent and predictive validity. The view that EI should be studied as an ability and "trait EI" may be investigated separately as a part of personality studies offers a partial resolution to the issue. However, the multiplicity of constructs labeled as "EI" appears to go well beyond this duality. As we have pointed out in previous critiques (e.g., Matthews, Zeidner, et al. 2002; Roberts, Schulze, et al. 2005), there are a variety of distinct ways of conceptualizing EI as a construct open to objective measurement.

Matthews, Zeidner, et al. (2006a; Roberts et al. 2007) suggest that there may be no general EI factor. There may instead be several distinct types of construct, each loosely labeled as EI but quite distinct psychologically. These authors list four types of construct that may be differentiated psychometrically in terms of the basic processes that support them, and in terms of their adaptive significance. Different forms of "EI" include basic temperamental factors such as positive emotionality, emotional self-confidence acquired by social learning, emotional information-processing as revealed by chronometric studies, and emotional knowledge and skills linked to specific contexts. The list is not exhaustive. For example, knowledge might be further broken down into explicit emotional knowledge (as featured in the MSCEIT) and implicit emotional knowledge and procedural skills. A possible basis for EI in implicit knowledge has been especially neglected despite recent interest in implicit features of personality and unconscious priming processes. The general point is that using the label of EI for several distinct constructs is liable to cause conceptual confusion. Table 12.1 presents multiple types of constructs that may contribute to emotional competence.

There are additional reasons from emotion theory to question whether an overarching EI construct is expected to generalize across different domains and measurement methods. One feature of many emotions theories is that there are multiple basic emotions supported by distinct neurological and cognitive systems (e.g., Oatley and Johnson-Laird 1995; Scherer 2001). For example, fear and anger are supported by different neurobiological subsystems (Panksepp 1998). Thus it is not self-evident that individual differences in the functioning of, say, the fear system, which is localized in structures including the amygdala, will relate to individual differences in systems of anger or disgust. It could reasonably be argued that EI relates not to individual emotions but to a super-ordinate emotion-regulation system located anatomically in the frontal lobes (see Rolls 1999). However, in our view, EI researchers have done too little to separate emotion regulation from meta-emotional regulation, which may be supported by different brain systems. Also surprising is the paucity of research evaluating whether individual differences in regulation generalize across the basic emotions. Clearly, these are important research questions that would advance the field if addressed with rigorously designed studies.

What Are the Most Appropriate Criteria for Evaluating the Importance of EI? We would like to know which areas of real-life functioning are affected by EI (as well those for which EI is not important). A fundamental difficulty confronting researchers is deciding what independent criteria for social-emotional competence should be predicted by EI measures. Most research exacerbates this problem in using self-report scales to assess

Table 12.1
Multiple types of construct that may contribute to emotional competence

Construct	Possible measure in chapters	Equivalent in IQ research	Key processes	Adaptive significance	Developmental influences
Emotionality temperament	Scales for Big Five personality EQ-i ECI	None that are direct, though links to openness	Neural and cognitive processes controlling arousal, attention, and reinforcement sensitivity	Mixed: most temperamental factors confer a mixture of costs and benefits	Genetics and early learning
Emotional self-confidence	SSRI subcomponents TEIque subscales	Self-assessed intelligence	Self-concept and self-regulation	Predominantly but not exclusively positive: presumed similar to self-esteem	Learning and socialization: mastery experiences, modeling, etc.
Emotional information processing	Emotional Inspection Time, Emotional Stroop	Choice reaction time, inspection time, working memory	Specific processing modules	Uncertain: Is speed of processing necessarily adaptive?	Genetics and early learning
Emotional knowledge and skills	MSCEIT, LEAS, SJTs	Crystallized intelligence (and related aptitudes)	Multiple acquired procedural and declarative skills	Adaptive within context for learning; may be irrelevant or counter-productive in certain other contexts	Learning, socialization and training of specific skills and knowledge

both predictors and outcomes, with criterion contamination thus coming into play. For example, questionnaires for EI include items that refer to positive mood, optimism, and confidence; the very same criteria that many researchers wish to predict. Indeed too little research has used objective behavioral criteria, though in the few isolated instances where this information has been collected, evidence tends to be mixed. On the one hand, some studies do suggest that scales for EI may predict objective physiological (Salovey et al. 2002) or performance-based (Austin 2005a) criteria. On the other hand, the MSCEIT fails to predict attentional and working memory performance under stress (Matthews, Emo, et al. 2006). EI questionnaires also fail to predict learning to use emotional information in a multiple-cue discrimination task and other tasks requiring attention to facial emotion (Fellner et al. 2006, 2007).

What Should the Status of Ethical and Moral Behavior Be in EI Models?   Another issue is the extent to which ethical and moral behavior should be part and parcel of the EI construct. As pointed out in chapter 6, the selfish, Machiavellian individual may possess EI in the sense of perceiving other's emotional weaknesses and then proceeding to manipulate them. At the extreme, individuals with antisocial personality disorder may possess social skills that allow them to exploit others (Harpur et al. 2002) despite deficiencies in other areas of emotional functioning. In short, "no EI construct precludes someone (sic) with high EI from being an immoral person" (Waterhouse 2006, p. 253).

There is also a tension between EI in the sense of fitting in with the social expectations of others and EI in the sense of making insightful autonomous decisions about the value of social norms. EI as an index of conformity to consensus views (chapter 3) suggests the former; EI as critical to transformational leadership (see chapter 9) implies the latter. It is unclear how EI relates to conflicts between personal and societal values. If one lives in an unjust and tyrannical society, is it more emotionally intelligent to make the compromises necessary to avoid arrest, or to risk one's life in striving to change the situation and perhaps the society?

What Are the Dynamic Processes Underlying EI?   It is perhaps ironic that much research revisits one of the less attractive aspects of intelligence research. There is a tendency to present ability as a static set of constructs, while ignoring the processes that support intelligent interaction with the external environment (see Corno et al. 2002). Describing EI as a laundry list of desirable qualities, unrelated to any independent psychological theory, is the most obvious example of this sort of problem. Research on EI offers many pointers to key processes, but few definitive answers. Emotional intelligence has thus variously been attributed to fundamental brain processes (Rolls 2007), to basic information-processing routines (Austin 2005a), and to high-level cognitive processes such as appraisal and coping (Zeidner et al. 2006). However, the research does not identify clear pathways to superior adaptation: for example, that EI leads to more accurate perceptions of others, which in turn leads to greater benefits from social interaction.

More subtly, research on EI frequently ignores the person to situation interaction that has become fundamental to personality research (Magnusson 1976). The basic point is that the expression of EI may vary—perhaps radically—depending on the surrounding environment. Individual differences in EI may be more apparent in some contexts than in others, and EI may be adaptive in some settings but harmful in others (chapter 7).

Borrowing from Caspi and Bem's (1990) account of person to situation interaction, we can identify three forms of interaction, related to the above, that remain almost entirely unexplored:

1. How do high EI persons filter and interpret the social world around them (reactive interaction)?

2. What kinds of behaviors does the high EI person provoke in others (evocative interaction)? Perhaps (consciously or unconsciously) the high EI person elicits more cooperation and support from other people, whereas the low EI person rubs them the wrong way.

3. How does EI relate to choosing and shaping social environments (proactive interaction)? For example, low EI may be associated not just with a liking for harmful drugs (Trinidad et al. 2004a, b) but also for picking friends that are a bad influence.

Is EI Related to Adaptation?   Calling EI a type of ability signals that it refers to individual differences in adaptation. Within this perspective the high EI person is, in some sense, better adapted to social-emotional functioning than the low EI person. At the extreme, tests may assign people to an emotionally elite upper class or to an emotionally illiterate underclass. The view that those scoring highly on EI tests possess a genuine superiority needs empirical support, especially as self-reports of competence are sometimes viewed as suspect (see chapter 4). The vision of the pioneers of tests for EI appears to have been that high EI is unequivocally adaptive (see chapter 3). To enjoy high EI is to enjoy a variety of benefits, including life satisfaction, emotional connections with others, and occupational success. As shown throughout this book, researchers differ sharply in their assessments of whether these predictions have been confirmed. Furthermore there appears to be a "dark side" of EI (or some of its specific operationalizations), including overconfidence, narcissism, Machiavellian social manipulation, and inflated self-esteem (see chapter 6).

What is needed is a cost-benefit analysis of the qualities conferred by EI (in its different versions). As discussed in chapter 6, personality traits such as extraversion, agreeableness, and even neuroticism typically benefit the individual in some environments and contexts, while imposing costs in others. Similarly, it is likely that high trait EI has both advantages and disadvantages, depending on circumstances. By contrast, abilities should be generally adaptive, but it is questionable whether the empirical evidence really shows major adaptive benefits for high scorers on the MSCEIT and other ability tests. Matthews, Zeidner, et al. (2002) raised the possibility that high scores signal adaptation not through true objective competence but via social conformity, namely being more emotionally in tune with typical members of one's own culture.

Recommendations

Table 12.2 includes a list of recommendations that we would like to make based on our review of conceptual issues undertaken throughout this book. These recommendations serve as possible research topics for interested students or otherwise show important issues that we would like to see resolved in time for a second edition of this book. The list is by no means definitive and the astute reader may well be able to add to it.

Assessment of Emotional Intelligence

The case that reliable and valid assessment of EI is central to building a science of EI is straightforward to make and is generally accepted by researchers (see chapter 2). Approaches to measurement of the EI construct have generally been understood as a distinction between ability (chapter 3) and "mixed" (chapter 4) models of the construct. The ability model suggests that EI may be assessed by objective tests, whereas mixed models have inspired self-report approaches.

Table 12.2
Recommendations for theory development that may move the field of emotional intelligence forward

Recommendation	Current status	Challenges in implementing
Conceptualize EI as a distinct domain, separate from standard personality and ability spheres	Current models describe some key functions such as perception, understanding and regulation of emotion.	Standard measures of personality and ability relate to emotional functioning; it is unclear what is truly distinctive about EI. Research needs clear criteria for stating which qualities "belong to" EI and which do not.
Explore true multi-domain concepts of EI (i.e., separate multiple constructs that may not be closely related)	Research has inspired some distinctive conceptions of temperament, learning, information processing, etc.	Most researchers in the area believe in an over-arching EI construct akin to g for general intelligence. This construct may not exist. Delineating a set of more modest aptitudes, competencies, and traits may be less inspirational.
Distinguish explicit and implicit compo-nents of EI	Most research has focused on declarative knowledge and self-beliefs.	Definition of theoretically and psychometrically sound implicit constructs is more difficult and time-consuming than operationalizing explicit knowledge.
Explore the cultural dependence of EI; is there a universal EI for all cultures?	Research on EI has yet to build on cross-cultural perspectives on emotion.	Challenges include detaching emotional adaptation from its cultural context, specifying the role of social conformity in EI, and specifying how EI relates to culture-bound morals and values.
Investigate the adaptive signifi-cance of EI by exploring the benefits and costs of its various facets	EI is generally assumed to be straightforwardly adaptive (except in some trait EI work).	Progress requires a closer look at how variation in EI plays out in specific real-life contexts. Key, but neglected, issues here include exploring management of emotion over extended time periods, accommodating dynamic interaction between person and situation, and evaluating multiple possible outcomes of real-life encounters.
Investigate the processing bases for the facets of EI	A few studies have aimed to relate EI to neural or cognitive processes, with mixed outcomes.	It is unlikely that any single "master process" controls EI. Instead, EI is likely to be distributed over multiple processes at different levels of abstraction from the neural substrate (e.g., sensitivity of brain emotion systems vs. finding personal meaning in events).

Several developments suggest that it may be time to move on from the dichotomy between mixed and ability models of EI (Mayer et al. 2000a, b), at least in some respects. First, some questionnaire researchers (e.g., Petrides and Furnham 2003) claim that self-report inventories belong to the domain of personality ("trait EI") and do not measure abilities, even of the "mixed" kind. Second, questions remain about whether Mayer et al.'s (e.g., 2002) tests measure abilities akin to those assessed by conventional intelligence tests (e.g., Brody 2004). Some fresh thinking on how to measure social-emotional abilities or competencies seems to be needed. Third, conceptual analyses of the kind discussed in the previous section imply that the current range of tests for EI may not adequately sample the full range of constructs that may be labeled as "EI." Thus a review of assessment methods needs not only to evaluate extant tests against standard psychometric criteria but to examine the fundamental principles being used to sample the domain of emotional competence as a basis for test development.

Assessment: Knowns

As demonstrated in chapter 2, the discipline of psychometrics provides relatively uncontroversial principles for determining what constitutes sound assessment practices. Thus the *Test Standards* (AERA/APA/ NCME, 1999) lay out a framework for interpreting reliability and validity; in essence, how the corpus of research should confirm the status of the instrument. Issues of consequential validity (i.e., demonstrating that the construct assessed by the test has meaningful societal consequences), fairness (i.e., showing that items are not biased against a particular subpopulation for inappropriate reasons), and how to appropriately document test development are also critical components of developing an EI measure. All these various processes are ongoing; feeding back to guide theoretical refinements, test development, and future cycles of research. Each piece of evidence is also equally important to establish.

EI Assessments Need to Demonstrate Adequate Reliability It is not incidental that many EI subscales have marginal (i.e., less than 0.60) reliabilities both for self-report and performance-based measures, although superordinate constructs such as experiential EI and general EI have high reliability coefficients (i.e., in excess of 0.90). Strategies for improving the reliability of subscales, such as increasing the number of test items, have curiously been neglected. By way of further illustration, the MSCEIT actually has fewer items than its predecessor the MEIS for several common subscales; and their reliabilities were marginal. There are also relatively few studies of the test-retest reliability of any measure. Moreover, although those that have been conducted are suggestive, they generally come from studies with fairly small sample sizes (e.g., Tett et al. 2005). The jury is still out on whether many existing tests have high enough reliability coefficients for use in applied settings.

EI Assessments Require Various Forms of Validity Evidence   Regrettably, not all forms of validity evidence have been the subject of empirical research on EI. In the quest for construct validity evidence, research has tended instead to focus on factorial validity, convergent and discriminant validity evidence, and test-criterion relationships (Matthews et al. 2007). Next we briefly discuss some of the validity evidence for EI measures.

Factorial Validity   Overall, the data attesting to the factorial validity of virtually every single extant measure of EI are equivocal. For example, Schutte et al. (1998) postulated a single, general factor, for the self-report inventory that they developed (see chapter 4). However, Petrides and Furnham (2000) provide evidence instead for a four factor solution, while still other commentators have not been entirely successful in replicating this, or other, factor solutions for this measure (e.g., see Gignac et al. 2005; Saklofske et al. 2003). Similarly Matthews et al. (2002) reanalyzed data from Bar-On (1995) to reveal inconsistencies in the hypothetical structure purportedly underlying this instrument (see also Livingstone and Day 2005; Palmer et al. 2003). Given the high degree of overlap between questionnaire assessments of EI and standard personality traits, the onus is on researchers working within a mixed- or trait-EI framework to develop factor models that specify the relationship between EI and standard personality traits as latent constructs. However, little progress has been made in this direction. Petrides and Furnham (2001) claim that trait EI is a lower-order construct within the Five Factor Model, but their factor analytic data actually show that different facets of trait EI load on different factors. Some facets attach to the standard Big Five, whereas others define a separate factor.

Performance-based measures fare no better when it comes to showing theoretically defensible factor structure. For example, there are several studies that allege the MSCEIT has four recoverable branches (Mayer et al. 2003). However, no published study has been able to find evidence for an independent emotional facilitation (i.e., using emotions to facilitate thought) construct (see chapter 3). Problems in factor structure also hold true for the MSCEIT's predecessor, the MEIS. Furthermore research is sorely needed to test for factorial invariance of current measures of EI across different sociocultural groups.

Convergent and Discriminant Validity Evidence   Performance-based tests show convergent validity against ability measures, correlating positively with verbal, knowledge-based tests (i.e., crystallized intelligence), particularly for understanding emotion (branch 3). At the same time these measures are relatively weakly related to tests of reasoning ability (fluid intelligence; see chapter 3). Generally, the evidence suggests that ability-based EI measures emotional knowledge, which is related to crystallized intelligence. By contrast, self-report measures of EI have shown poor convergent validity: Thus far they show low (i.e., around zero) correlations with traditional forms of intelligence (see chapter 4).

There is a growing body of evidence that self-report assessments of EI assess dispositional traits rather than a form of intelligence. Hence the magnitude of correlation between the vast majority of self-report assessments of EI and (a lack of) Neuroticism (particularly, anxiety) is strong, with moderate to high correlations also evident between the self-report assessments and agreeableness, conscientiousness, and extraversion, for a good deal of the available scales (see MacCann et al. 2003; Matthews et al. 2002). Given correlations with several personality variables it seems possible that once the variance associated with personality is controlled for statistically, EI-related variance would be minimal. Collectively these findings suggest that self-report measures of EI, whether based on mixed or trait models, have questionable discriminant validity.

A final piece of convergent validity evidence is the relations between different EI assessments. EI measures do not fare well in this respect. The correlation between performance-based and self-report assessments is surprisingly low, ranging somewhere between 0.20 and 0.30 across a slew of studies. More problematic, opposite conclusions can be reached on the basis of these two different assessment approaches when one looks also at external variables like intelligence or at group differences (Zeidner, Shani-Zinovich, et al. 2005).

Test-Criterion Relations   The test-criterion relation, as noted in chapter 2, refers to what was formerly known as predictive validity. For both self-report and ability scales, evidence is often mixed. For example, Brackett and Mayer (2003) tested both kinds of measures as predictors of criteria for emotional competence, controlling for the FFM and cognitive ability. In each case EI predicted only one out of six criteria, with small effect sizes. By contrast, other studies have demonstrated modest test-criterion relations. For ability measures, several studies (see Lopes et al. 2004; Rivers et al. 2007) have shown that the managing emotions branch of the MSCEIT predicts social functioning with personality and ability controlled. Likewise studies have shown that self-report scales for EI can add modestly to prediction of well-being criteria, with the Big Five controlled (e.g., Saklofske et al. 2003). Although uncorrected validity coefficients for questionnaire assessments of EI tend to be higher than for the MSCEIT, most of their predictive validity derives from overlap with personality. (Recall that self-report scales are also vulnerable to criterion contamination, in that they include items referring to well-being or social success.) It is telling that with personality and ability controlled, both types of measure provide only modest incremental validity at best, typically adding 5 percent or so to the variance explained.

EI Assessments Need to Be Premised on Justifiable Scoring Rubrics There is little doubt that investigating self-reported EI can be justified as a research tactic simply by virtue of the fact that self-report methods are used widely across psychology. However, by contrast, compared to more traditional intelligence tests (e.g., vocabulary, matrices), the scoring of performance-based EI tests is difficult, as there is no algorithm for determining the correct answer (see chapters 2 and 3). Objectivity, or "the problem of the correct answer," has proved to be hugely problematic in investigations of social intelligence, and has thus far proved to be an equally difficult issue to traverse in EI research (Zeidner et al. 2001). To elucidate this point, consider the following ability test item: $2^3 = ?$ The response "8" would be veridically correct across the globe. By contrast, the response to the item "What is the best way of appeasing the anger of another person whom you have slighted or wronged?" has no one correct response across cultures or perhaps social settings.

As discussed in chapters 2 and 3, the MSCEIT (and the earlier MEIS) deal with this problem in one of three ways:

1. Assuming emotion experts know the answer (expert scoring).

2. Assuming that the stimulus creators know the answer (target scoring).

3. Assuming that the correct answer is what people generally agree is correct (consensus scoring).

Each of these scoring techniques, as we have shown throughout this book (and especially in chapter 3), has problems.

Assessment: Unknowns

Is the Proposed Dichotomy between Ability and Mixed Models Useful? The current trend toward relating self-reports of EI to the personality domain (Petrides and Furnham 2003) leaves the earlier mixed models of EI (e.g., Bar-On 2000) in limbo. Should we abandon Bar-On's idea that question-naires may be used to assess abilities, or does the notion still have cre-dence? Again, it may be useful to explore differentiation of constructs within the self-report domain. Thus, although the split between perfor-mance and questionnaire tests looms large in the present context, other uncertainties over the optimal choice of assessment methods are appear-ing as the field develops.

For example, assessing one's geographic knowledge by asking a series of question along the lines of "what is the capital city of Denmark" seems more cost-effective and valid than asking a person to "rate how good you are in geography on a seven-point scale from awful to brilliant" (the an-swer to which might suddenly change if you were offered a decent sum of money). Given the choice to assess intelligence with a question that is fac-tually verifiable or a subjective rating, even the staunchest advocate of the latter approach is forced to concede that this is a no-brainer. Besides hav-ing a good deal more face and ecological validity, veridical items are less impervious to faking, coaching, or self-deception biases.

Notwithstanding, self-estimates of intelligence (or related constructs, stressing in particular cognitive engagement) have been used in research settings to generate a variety of theoretically meaningful findings (e.g., Ackerman and Goff 1994; Furnham and Rawles 1999; Rammstedt and Rammasayer 2000). That is, there are some uses for self-reports of intelli-gence, for some types of constructs. Thus it is important not to dismiss self-report approaches of EI out of hand despite their obvious limitations.

How May Ability Testing Be Extended? Most researchers agree that ability tests are more promising than questionnaires for locating a genuinely novel EI construct. However, to date the bulk of ability research has fo-cused on the MEIS and MSCEIT tests. As Brody (2004) points out, these tests are limited in that they assess explicit knowledge of *how* to deal with emotive situations, rather than testing skills and competencies. A variety of techniques are available for assessing emotional competencies rather more directly (see chapter 3), but much needs to be done in order to translate these approaches into reliable and valid tests. Furthermore some potential facets of EI, including identification, communication, and knowledge, appear to be easier to operationalize as objective tests than those that refer to internal regulation of emotion and coping (see Roberts et al. 2007; Scherer 2007). It may be that the future of EI hinges on developing a wider range of objective tests; but, equally, it may transpire that there is no overarching ability supporting individual differences on qualitatively different dimensions.

Are the Stakes at Which EI Assessment Is Targeted Defensible?   Basic research aside, psychological testing is generally conducted for some practical purpose, with varying implications. In general, practitioners and policy makers talk of the tests falling into one of three categories, corresponding to the "fidelity" of the instrument in question for decision-making purposes: (1) high-stakes, (2) medium-stakes, or (3) low-stakes (described in chapter 2). Currently there is considerable push to bring EI measures into the high stakes testing arena. Clearly, in the absence of more carefully documented validity evidence, such usage is questionable. A job applicant rejected on the basis of a low score on a test for EI, and without other mitigating circumstances, might have a reasonable basis to appeal or otherwise consider legal action.

Advanced Psychometric Analyses Are Needed   As alluded to in chapter 2 and 3, a good deal of EI research has been conducted without particularly advanced psychometrics. We are aware, for example, of no published study using item response theory (Embertson and Reise 2000) or differential item functioning (Holland and Wainer 1993), to name but a few of the statistical procedures commonly employed in cognitive assessment today. The key issue (Brody 2004) is to assess EI as a *latent* construct that can be discriminated from the particular test used for measurement. It may be that much of what current tests measure is specific to the assessment method employed. Advanced procedures are important for high-stakes assessment. Their neglect fuels concerns that contemporary EI assessments are suitable only for low-stakes applications.

Recommendations

Mirroring a previous passage, table 12.3 includes a list of recommendations that we would like to make based on our review of assessment issues undertaken throughout this book and culminating in this final chapter.

Table 12.3
Recommendations and challenges for assessment-related research and development that may move the field of EI forward

Recommendation	Current status	Challenges in implementing
Hold a moratorium on the development of self-report assessments	A new self-report springs up almost every month	For early career researchers, in particular, this method is attractive; one can make a "name" and the approach is much less time-consuming and difficult than developing objective assessments.
Study "trait" emotional intelligence as a personality construct	Suggested, but not really implemented; most research in this tradition pays lip-service to the idea	Will require a refocusing of the field; for example, having trait EI measures published in personality—and not intelligence—journals. In addition the term itself is misleading; others need to be vetted (e.g., emotional self-efficacy).
Develop a comprehensive taxonomy of performance-based emotional intelligence measures	Suggested, but few studies combine paradigms from emotions and emotional intelligence research	Major challenges are cost and time; studies of this nature will require large sample sizes and sophisticated statistical analyses. Scoring of performance-based measures also remains a complex issue, but there are some positive inroads (e.g., standards-based protocols).
Develop further performance-based assessments	A few alternatives to the MSCEIT and MEIS (e.g., SJTs assessing emotion management) are emerging	This approach can be time-consuming, especially if one wishes to obtain suitable validity evidence before releasing the instrument to the scientific community. Also it can prove a costly activity, so funding is often required.
Collect more compelling validity evidence for assessments	More studies now capturing personality and intelligence data and expanding criteria space	Experimental designs are needed, but are costly and time-consuming. The criteria for validation are also not well specified, and there needs to be a consensus in the community on what outcomes are valuable.
Educate public and decision makers about assessment	Trade texts dominate and suggest this is "easy stuff"	Did you read chapters 2 through 4 very carefully? ☺

As in those earlier passages, these recommendations serve as possible research topics for interested students and researchers alike; answers to which would appear requisite if the field is to move forward.

Applications of Emotional Intelligence

As noted throughout, a major force fuelling both popular and scientific interest in EI is its potential contributions to well-being of the individual as well as society. EI has been claimed to play an important role in such diverse domains as close personal relationships (see chapter 6), educational attainments (see chapter 8), occupational performance (see chapters 9 and 10), and clinical disorders (see chapter 11). This section will address applications of EI to these various domains of human endeavor.

As already demonstrated, empirical research has not always supported many of the validity claims surrounding this concept, especially in industrial-organizational settings. Nevertheless, there is sufficient evidence for incremental validity of some of the better EI measures to suggest that a focus on EI may enhance personal, social, and organizational functioning and adaptation (Mayer et al. 2003). There are also well-validated intervention programs that are designed to improve emotional functioning, particularly in the domain of education (chapter 8). Such programs lend weight to the notion that training EI may be a valuable practical strategy in many real-life settings.

In education, EI skills and competencies cultivated and trained in social and emotional learning programs, are commonly believed to be able to help motivate students to reach higher levels of achievement, become more socially and emotionally competent, and to become more responsible and productive members of society. It is thought that elevating EI will impact both overt academic goals, such as better grades, and the student's broader personal development. Reviews of the evidence on programs for social-emotional learning, including those using meta-analysis to demonstrate change in outcome criteria, support their efficacy in improving mental health, academic performance, and remediation of various behavior problems (see chapter 8).

EI has also been claimed to be predictive of individual task performance at the workplace, especially in settings requiring creative and transformational leadership, teamwork, or effective communication, as well as contextual or tacit performance (e.g., Abraham 2005; Daus and Ashkanasy 2005). EI may also relate to citizenship behavior, integrity, and effective personal relationships in organizational settings. An assortment of the problems of the modern workplace, including stress and violence, may be attributed to low EI, suggesting a need to improve social-emotional competence in organizations (see chapter 10).

EI may also have considerable potential for applications in clinical settings. Assuming EI is related to disordered affect and dysfunctional affect regulation (which in turn is related to psychopathology) EI might play a pivotal role in clinical diagnosis and treatment (Parker 2005). The growing corpus of research on alexithymia highlights how difficulties in understanding and communicating emotion may be important in affective disorders (Taylor and Bagby 2004). However, whereas many mental disorders are related to emotional dysfunctions and the experience and expression of negative affect, the diversity of these disorders may mitigate against an unambiguous relationship with low EI (see also chapter 11).

Applications: Knowns

There Has Been Irrational Enthusiasm Surrounding the Practical Value of EI   There appears to have been an initial, irrational exuberance regarding the practical utility of EI in applied settings (see chapter 1). Much of the existing evidence is impressionistic, anecdotal, or assembled by private companies and generally not published in the peer-reviewed literature (Murphy 2006a). Further Zeidner et al. (2002) have pointed out that despite popular claims, most of the programs touted as effective EI programs lack clear conceptual frameworks, implementation analyses and checks, and sound evaluation designs. Hence some EI programs are being implemented in applied settings without sufficient theoretical grounding, intervention hypotheses, or rigorous evaluation studies. Nevertheless, the failings of current applied work and training programs do not negate the possibility that more modest practical gains may be attainable in the future.

EI Appears to Be Modestly Related to Performance Outcomes in a Variety of Applied Settings   Research suggests that EI weakly predicts outcomes in a variety of real-life contexts, with evidence available mainly for occupational (chapter 9) and educational settings (chapter 8). Thus, in occupational contexts, the unique contribution of EI to prediction, over and above personality and ability, is typically limited (Day 2004). A concern with the occupational studies reviewed in, for example, chapter 9 is that many use supervisor ratings that may be influenced by the likeability of the employee, rather than their job competence. At the same time there seems to be growing confidence among practitioners that EI measures predict job performance to an extent that is practically useful (Daus and Ashkanasy 2005). From our perspective, while the scope and importance of the validity coefficients for EI remains open for debate, the proponents of EI have made considerable progress in demonstrating that the better EI scales presently available to organizational psychologists have sufficient criterion validity to be taken seriously.

EI has also been claimed to be predictive of occupational performance and job satisfaction, proactive social behaviors and organizational citizenship, and absence or truancy at the worksite. As some evidence suggests, in jobs that appear to require a high level of EI relationships (e.g., police work) job performance and satisfaction are higher than in jobs where emotional demands are low (Daus and Ashkanasy 2005). Specific problems organizational psychologists need to rectify before applying EI effectively in occupational settings include:

1. failure of practitioners to provide an adequate theoretical rationale for their use in a particular occupational setting;

2. lack of occupational-specificity of the EI measure;

3. absence of normative data for EI when used in different occupational groups; and

4. failure to provide evidence for predictive and discriminate validity for EI (both within and across occupational clusters).

In education, EI appears a somewhat weak predictor of academic performance per se. At present, the best estimate of the true validity coefficient for the relationship between EI and academic performance (i.e., grades) is small (around 0.10), albeit based on a limited number of studies. Furthermore the EI-performance relationship appears to be both measure dependent, found to be higher for self-report than ability measures, as well as criterion-dependent. A more compelling argument, though, may be that EI indirectly mediates success by protecting students from salient barriers to classroom learning such as mental distress, teen pregnancy, substance abuse, truancy, delinquency, and violence (Hawkins et al. 2004). Equally the criterion space for studying academic success has so far been rather narrow in that there is more to academic success than grades. Thus school retention, prosocial behavior and citizenship, and psychological well-being and mental health all appear important outcome variables to consider in the educational sector (Roberts, Schulze, et al. 2005, Roberts et al. 2007).

It has also been claimed that EI has merit and practical utility in predicting a broad set of outcomes in one's social life, including quality of interpersonal relationships, marital success, prosocial behaviors, and delinquency. However, compared to academic performance and occupational criteria, these outcomes have often been difficult to measure and operationalize (chapter 7). The theoretical rationale for why EI should be predictive of criteria in a given domain, such as the social realm, needs to be more fully delineated. Thus a broadside approach should not be adopted whenever EI is used in predicting social outcomes without specifying how and why these outcomes are important.

Systematic Approaches Are Required to Match EI Constructs to Applications

In occupational contexts there is currently no empirically validated taxonomy of job types corresponding to separate components of EI. We cannot ascertain what particular facets or components of EI (e.g., regulation of emotions in self/others) are requisite for any given job cluster. Generally, the level of EI critical for occupational success should be positively related to how central EI may be to the work activities under consideration. Thus EI may be more important in some organizations (e.g., social services) than others—although tests of such plausible notions have met with mixed success. Furthermore EI may be more important for those occupying lower positions in the occupational hierarchy relative to those much higher up in the organizational ladder (chapter 9).

Alternatively, the types or facets of EI relevant to a particular job may vary with the type of job and position at the workplace. For example, executive positions require more assertive (even Machiavellian) forms of EI, whereas unskilled workers may require more agreeableness toward supervisors and acceptance of limited rewards. Thus a more systematic approach to matching emotional competencies to career components is needed. For example, a fine-grained analysis of the emotional demands imposed on police officers might support development of a measure of emotional regulation that could be used to assess, select, and place police officers. This measure, in turn, could be validated against job-specific behavioral criteria, such as frequency of physically aggressive behaviors during encounters with the public. Thus there appears a need for "emotional task analysis" to ascertain the affective requirements of different occupations (see chapter 9) much as traditional job analysis is increasingly being supplemented by cognitive task analysis. Practitioners may presently need to rely on a relatively superficial dissection of emotional requirements for specific occupations. However, more theory-driven analysis of emotional tasks at work may become possible as theories of emotional competence become more fully articulated.

Applications: Unknowns

Are Current Research Designs Adequate?   A most basic task for EI validation research is to demonstrate that EI measures reliably differentiate between low- and high-performing groups on particular criteria of importance. To date, the majority of studies have used simple cross-sectional designs allowing EI to be correlated with, typically, some global rating of job performance—often based on ratings of employees or their direct supervisors. There are several ways in which research designs might be improved.

Performance measures against which EI predictors in occupational selection and placement are validated should be valid, reliable, and uncontaminated. However, self- and supervisor ratings are vulnerable to various biases: objective performance assessments uncontaminated by rater bias are preferred. Another approach is to use more sophisticated modeling approaches to discriminate performance as a latent factor from other, potentially confounding factors such as self-confidence, likeability, and impression management. A further basic step is to ensure that EI remains predictive with general intelligence and personality factors statistically controlled.

A greater focus on moderator and mediator factors in EI research is also needed. *Moderators* are variables, such as the emotional demands of the job, that influence how strongly EI relates to outcome criteria. Thus it is important to continue with research that aims to identify the occupations for which EI is more and less important (e.g., social workers vs. financial analysts). Additional moderators include the various dimensions and facets of EI, and general contextual factors such as level of external demands. The facets of EI that might be helpful (or harmful) during periods of intense organizational change may be different to those important during more stable times. *Mediators* are those variables that transmit effects of EI onto performance and behavior. Understanding mediators is important for identifying mechanisms and processes. If we find that EI influences performance, various mediating processes might be distinguished: greater perseverance and application of effort, higher level of objective skill or a better understanding of the critical job requirements. Uncovering the key mechanisms for EI is central to understanding its relevance in organizational and other applied contexts.

A final recommendation is that researchers should design longitudinal studies. Current designs do not tell us whether EI directly affects performance, or performance affects EI, or both variables are influenced by some third factor. Tracking changes in EI and performance across time is necessary to address issues of causality.

To What Degree Can We Develop and Train EI? Programs for helping managers and would-be leaders, as well as students, to become more emotionally intelligent and socially effective have mushroomed. Although many of these programs are promising, not all have systematically been based upon EI theory. Furthermore intervention programs that seek to cultivate EI sometimes lack a clear theoretical and methodological rationale, and employ a miscellany of techniques, whose psychological bases are not always clear (Zeidner et al. 2002). EI, and the competencies linked to it, are based on temperament, learning experiences, and reflective goal-oriented experiences. One-day seminars or workshops can be valuable in educating people and raising awareness, but they may not by themselves lead to the kind of reprogramming that is required for significant improvement (chapters 9 and 10). The limited success of attempts to alleviate stress at work through programs that target individuals also sounds a cautionary note (chapter 10).

Which Components of EI Are the Most Malleable or Susceptible to Intervention(s)? At present, it remains uncertain which of the types or components of EI are most malleable and responsive to training; what the threshold level of EI is for training; or what age level are EI components most responsive to intervention and training. Equally little is known of the following key facets of EI training: specific EI intervention goals, specific EI components most responsive to training, most effective interventions to use for low EI clients, most effective interventions to use for different age levels, and the minimal level of EI that a client needs to benefit from therapy. It is also unclear whether EI can be fostered through one-on-one interventions, or whether competence in group interaction should be trained. In addition to developing standards for program implementation, there is also a need for assessing the return for costs associated with delivering EI programs.

As noted elsewhere (Roberts et al. 2007), in order to develop efficacious assessments and interventions of EI in applied settings, the following preconditions are required:

1. Derivation of a context-specific and relevant theoretical framework.

2. Clear definitional framework for the universe of discourse surrounding EI.

3. Identification of key facets and components relevant to different applied settings.

4. Developing sound context-relevant assessment, scoring, and analytic procedures.

5. Developing sound training techniques tailored to specific contexts.

6. Adapting EI applications congenial to the affordances and constraints of the specific occupational, cultural, and social context.

7. Consideration of developmental age, social background, and cultural norms and values of the target users.

These seven suggestions reflect the need to assure a close partnership between theory, assessment, and application in EI practice. Currently it could be argued that both theory and measurement of EI has not especially "helped the cause" of successfully advancing applications of EI so that they become valuable tools in the practitioner's arsenal. Alternatively, history teaches us that advances in science are often made because of an applied issue that society deems as important—but it takes time to match the theory to the problem.

Recommendations

Recommendations for applications of emotional intelligence are given in table 12.4. Two general points should be added. First, the quality of existing applied research varies enormously. In the relevant chapters we have seen examples of excellent practice together with poor-quality work that fails to meet even minimal standards. Second, the limitations in theory and assessment discussed in previous sections constrain applied efforts. Better models and measures of EI are needed for translation into real-world practice.

Conclusion

In a perfect world we could at this point present a summary of the scientific accomplishments of work on EI. In reality, it is difficult to provide

Table 12.4
Recommendations for applied research that may move the field of emotional intelligence forward

Recommendation	Current status	Challenges in implementing
Adopt realistic goals for applied research, and design studies and interventions accordingly	Initial overenthusiasm for EI is slowly being replaced by more realistic expectations	Some practitioners have a vested interest in overselling the merits of EI, and products and services geared toward EI. Organizations may be more open to enthusiasm than to the more nuanced picture of EI provided by research.
Base practical interventions on adequate theory	Theoretical bases for practical intervention are often tenuous	The principal challenge is the limitations of existing theory. In particular, "broadbrush" theories of EI fail to engage with key features of specific real-life problems.
Choose appropriate metrics for EI; if an intervention targets EI, then EI should be measured directly	Programs that purport to elevate EI often use proxy metrics, whose relevance is questionable	Often the target for intervention is not EI per se but some narrower area of functioning such as teamwork, or prosocial behavior. Practitioners should make explicit choices about when to target EI in a generic sense, as opposed to specific skills.
Use rigorous, experimental designs for evaluating interventions	Need for rigorous program evaluation is becoming more apparent; studies vary in rigor	Resources for creating good control groups for interventions may be lacking. Practitioners may be more geared to finding a short-term fix for problems than toward long-term evaluation. Problems exist both in conceptualization and assessment that limit applied methodologies.
Incorporate contextual factors into interventions and assessments	Awareness of contextual factors is very mixed	It may be difficult to identify the key contextual factors, given the many candidates: for example (in occupational settings), type of work, training of employee, specific EI facets of relevance.
Investigate mediator and moderator factors	Better studies focus on mediators and/or moderators; many do not	Limitations of theory make it difficult to predict the key mediators and moderators for a specific context.

any definitive account of the scientific status of EI, in part because we are dealing with a new and rapidly developing field of inquiry (Matthews, Zeidner, et al. 2002). The best we can do is to summarize some interim conclusions, and to identify some of the major uncertainties that future research will need to address. We will refer to the three key domains covered in the main body of this review—concepts, assessments, and applications—in the passages that follow. Throughout this book we have adopted a critical stance, and delineated shortcomings of existing research where appropriate. However, we also believe that many of the "unknowns" of EI represent tractable research issues, and so these passages also contain suggestions for future research directions.

Conceptualization

Currently, there is no agreed-upon definition of the EI construct. Factors labeled as "EI" may refer to a variety of quite different constructs, at least some of which are reinventions of existing dimensions, or trivial in their real-life relevance. We have suggested that it may be better to use EI as a broad umbrella term for a multiplicity of different constructs that may be only loosely related to one another. At the same time various researchers have identified specific constructs that are conceptually coherent and may add to understanding of emotional functioning (see chapters 3 and 4). Even if none of these different brands of EI turns out to be as important in life as general cognitive intelligence (g), research on EI may prove to usefully extend our understanding of personality, mood-regulation, coping, and even cognitive ability.

A precondition for any large-scale applications of EI in applied settings is the development of well-defined theoretical frameworks and assessment tools. We believe that resolving uncertainties over the conceptualization and theory of EI requires better structural models than presently available (or being employed) in EI research. The analysis represented in table 12.1 suggests that there may be quite different "EI" constructs to be found in different research domains. Various accounts of the key components of EI exist, but these models are in need of systematic comparison and integration. We also see a need for weeding out those constructs that are not well-supported by research or lack a sound theoretical base. Conversely, the stronger constructs in the field need to be related more closely to the process-based models provided by contemporary neuroscience and cognitive and social psychology. Building better conceptual models of EI also requires better psychometric models that specify both the overlaps and the uniqueness of EI constructs in relation to personality and ability.

Assessments

Presently, it is uncertain how EI may be best measured. Various tests of the construct fail to converge and these diverse measures may be assessing different constructs. There is less consensus regarding appropriate vehicles and methods for assessing EI than there appears to be for even the rather underdeveloped conceptual models that saturate the field. Arguably, this is an unsatisfactory state of affairs, one that may be conceived as inhibitory to the development of a science of EI. Certain points of consensus are virtually dictated by the scientific community, most especially with respect to standards set for psychological and educational measurement.

The two different approaches taken by researchers to the assessment of EI has led to two separate scientific literatures emerging on the topic. Often the findings coming out of these two emerging research traditions do not converge. Thus it is perhaps an important undertaking of future research to provide a synthesis of these approaches, should this be possible. Conversely, perhaps it is best to adopt one approach over another according to a cogent set of arguments. It remains to be seen what direction the research community will eventually take. Regardless, the sheer number of self-report measures so far developed in this field, without attendant concerns for the procurement of compelling validity evidence, suggests that it may be time to call for a moratorium on the development of still further instruments of this type. By contrast, the number of performance measures is surprisingly small (though clearly some of those used by emotions researchers could be reconceptualized as measures of specific EI constructs). Developing further objective measures of EI would appear an important future research endeavor.

Applications

The social problems described by Goleman (1995) and others are still with us. There is no doubt that applied psychologists are sorely in need of practical techniques for enhancing emotional regulation in schools, workplaces, and psychiatric clinics. Especially in the educational and organizational domains, interventions directed toward social-emotional competencies have produced sufficient benefits to justify further applied work. Unfortunately, as alluded to above, the practical utility of EI measures is limited by the conceptual and psychometric deficiencies described throughout, despite the appeal of EI to practitioners. Thus available measures of EI generally have questionable validity evidence for current assessment to be used with confidence in making real-world decisions. Moreover intervention programs targeted to enhance EI in applied contexts sometimes appear to lack clearly articulated theoretical and methodological rationales.

Arguably, the theoretical foundations of EI need to be secured before EI can be effectively used in applied settings; otherwise EI will remain a fuzzy and slippery construct, with little practical value. It is also critical that definitional issues are settled before proceeding to operationalize and apply the construct in real-life settings. Of note, research has yet to demonstrate the added value of using EI measures in applied settings relative to narrower measures of individual differences. It also remains to be seen whether training EI, in some global sense, is any more effective than training specific social-emotional skills relevant to the client.

Final Remarks

The noted philosopher of science, Thomas Kuhn (1962), proposed that science advances through qualitative paradigm-shifts. Goleman (1995) saw the psychology of EI as providing a new paradigm for understanding human intelligence and well-being. Within the Kuhnian model, we might expect EI to emerge as a self-contained field of scientific inquiry capable of supplanting some existing approaches and theories, especially the dominance of conventional intelligence. To date, we have seen little sign of a paradigm shift; the authors' view is that work on EI is adding to understanding of intelligence and personality, but there is no evidence so compelling that it requires a radical change in perspective (e.g., Roberts et al. 2007). Of course, it is hard to predict the future; perhaps some of the work we have reviewed contains the seeds of a more far-reaching revision of intelligence theory. Figure 12.1 expresses two possible futures: that

Figure 12.1
Two futures for the heart and the head: separate ways or a partnership?

heart and head will continue to follow separate paths in psychology, or, alternatively, that work on EI will broker a happy marriage between emotions and intellect.

Currently there are grounds for both pessimism and optimism about the future of this new concept. To be pessimistic, there is a danger that EI may be no more than a fad of the type common in business and education (Murphy and Sideman 2006). Indeed, the explosive growth of EI matches the three defining characteristics of such fads identified by these authors: (1) a fast growth trajectory, (2) promise of a great deal more than can be delivered, and (3) evocation of intense reactions, both positive and negative. Such fads, Murphy and Sideman (2006) go on to argue, generally follow a natural life cycle. Interest tends to plateau, followed by a precipitous decline, although the fad may re-emerge years or decades later. While the optimist believes EI is here to stay, the pessimist may believe that EI will burn out before too long.

Research surrounding EI is still new, and the optimist may take the diversity of concepts and measures as a sign of the vitality of the field. As research addresses the controversies we have highlighted here, we can expect to see a shakeout of misconceptions, the maturing of the science, and greater consensus between advocates for EI and skeptics. Progress depends on greater rigor in conceptualization and measurement, and in validation of scales against objective criteria for social-emotional functioning. In applied fields the focus should be on evidence-based studies that show how interventions specifically directed toward EI improve over other, well-attested techniques for improving social functioning. The spirit of "letting a hundred flowers bloom" should not be used as an excuse for poor science or for practical interventions that promise more than they deliver. Will EI stay or will it go? Only time will tell.

Summary Points: Chapter 12

• EI is a promising new construct that may provide important insights into how individuals regulate emotion, in the laboratory and in real life. However, progress has been limited by difficulties in conceptualizing EI, in developing valid measures and tests of EI, and in applying basic research on EI to real-world settings.

• A degree of consensus on the key issues for conceptualizing and defining EI is beginning to appear. It is agreed that EI is a multifaceted construct that may cover a variety of disparate facets or components. The wide scope of EI makes it imperative to differentiate it from related ability and personality dimensions. The potential importance of EI is signaled by the relationships established between various scales for EI and external criteria for well-being and social competence. In addition, exceptional individuals may possess unusually high or low EI, and EI appears to follow a well-defined developmental trajectory. These "knowns" of EI research must be set against various "unknowns" or points of contention.

• The multiplicity of constructs described as "EI" raises problems. It is unclear whether some general, overarching factor of EI actually exists or whether EI corresponds to several distinct, multiple intelligences (or is a label casually affixed to an incoherent set of qualities). There is uncertainty over the specific real-life outcomes to which EI is relevant, and confusion about whether EI necessarily entails ethical behavior. Theory building has been limited by a neglect of the basic neurological, cognitive and emotional processes that confer emotional competency, compounded by neglect of their adaptive significance and the role of the environment in modulating the individual's emotional aptitudes and skills. It cannot be assumed that a high score on an EI test indicates superior adaptation; research and theory development is needed in order to identify the benefits and costs that attach to high EI.

• There is a consensus that valid measurement of EI is essential. In addition there are agreed criteria for establishing that measurement practices are sound. These include demonstrating that measurement is reliable, gathering multiple lines of evidence in support of validity (e.g., convergent and discriminant validity), and providing explicit justification for methods used to score tests of EI. Consensus over psychometric standards has not been mirrored by consensus over the optimal testing of EI. From its inception the field has been driven by choice of measurement strategy, namely whether to use objective tests or questionnaires based on self-report. Both methods are open to criticism, and the two kinds of assessment fail to converge. The utility of the corresponding distinction between (1) ability models and (2) mixed and trait models remains debatable. Further issues relate to the utility of novel ability tests, to the suitability of existing measures for high-stakes testing, and to the benefits that may result from using modern psychometric techniques. For the present EI remains a construct that lacks a universally accepted 'gold standard' test.

• In applied settings, work on EI may be valuable both for identifying emotional geniuses (and the emotionally challenged) and for supporting interventions and training programs for enhancing EI. Some points of agreement have emerged from the applied literature. Much of the early exuberance over EI has proved to be irrational; among serious researchers, even EI optimists typically offer measured and nuanced accounts of the real-life advantages of high EI. A case in point is that EI appears at best to be a modest predictor of job performance. Further progress may require a more systematic matching of EI facets with specific emotional challenges, requiring a more careful analysis of the emotional demands of different jobs and educational contexts.

• It remains controversial how EI in real life should be investigated, and how best to identify potential moderator factors. Although guidelines for developing effective training programs are emerging, unknowns attach to intervention methods also. In addition to general uncertainty about the most effective practical methods for specific contexts, it is also unclear what facets of EI are most open to adaptive change, and how EI should be assessed by the practitioner. Practical interventions for emotional problems in organizational, educational and clinical settings have an established history that long predates interest in EI; it is an open question what work on EI can add to existing practice.

• Research on the new concept of EI is in a state of flux; no definitive judgment on its significance for psychology can be provided. Optimists may point to the diversity and vitality of the field as an omen of future progress; pessimists may be inclined to dismiss EI as no more than a passing fad. We are confident that increasing rigor in basic and applied research will, in time, arrive at a consensus on the value of EI.

Glossary of Terms

Ability model of emotional intelligence   A definition of EI as an orthodox mental ability, implying that EI is reflected in objective performance levels on tasks requiring processing of emotion (compare **mixed models of emotional intelligence, four branch model**).

Achievement tests   Tests designed to measure acquired knowledge in a particular domain. Often the distinction is made that achievement tests emphasize ability acquired through formal learning or training, whereas aptitude tests emphasize innate potential. In addition to their use in academic areas, achievement tests are employed for a variety of vocational, professional, and diagnostic purposes.

Adaptation   In psychology, the set of characteristics and processes that support the person's attempts to fulfill the goals necessary for survival, social functioning, and personal ambitions, within a changing environment. Behaviors may be evaluated in terms of those goals they advance (benefits) and those goals they delay or jeopardize (costs). Biologists use the term more narrowly to refer to the characteristics of an organism that makes it better able to survive and reproduce in its environment, in line with Darwinian theory.

Affect   Umbrella term for feeling states that includes emotions and moods. Affect is broadly divided into positive affect (e.g., happiness) and negative affect (e.g., anxiety, unhappiness, or anger).

Agreeableness   A major personality factor associated with the **five factor model**, referring to the tendency to act in a cooperative, friendly, collegial, unselfish, and nonhostile manner.

Alexithymia   A clinical disorder expressed as difficulty in experiencing, understanding, describing, communicating, or distinguishing among emotions.

Alpha coefficient   *See* **Cronbach alpha coefficient**.

Amygdala   Two almond shaped structures located in the medial temporal lobes of the brain; this area of the brain is believed to be responsible for emotional learning.

Analysis of variance (ANOVA)   Statistical technique for comparing multiple *means,* typically within an experimental design (see also **F-test**).

Antisocial personality disorder   Personality disorder expressed as disregard for others, lack of **empathy, impulsive behaviors**, failure to conform to social norms, and aggression against others.

Anxiety disorders   A group of disorders that are characterized by a number of both mental and physical symptoms, such as extreme nervousness, fear of losing control, dizziness, nausea, and increased heart rate.

Appraisal   Evaluation of the personal significance of a stimulus or event including its potential for harm or benefit.

Aptitude tests   Assessment instruments designed to measure (1) individual concrete abilities such as visual acuity and clerical performance; (2) abilities of candidates for professional training, such as in medicine, engineering, or pharmacy; or (3) a wide range of basic abilities required for academic or vocational success, such as verbal comprehension, numerical ability, mechanical knowledge, and reasoning.

Asperger's syndrome   A pervasive developmental disorder associated with varying degrees of deficits in social and conversational skills, preference for sameness or predictability of events, and difficulty in environmental changes and transitions. It overlaps with **autism**, but there is little delay in the development of language skills and cognitive competencies.

Attachment   Tendency to become emotionally close to certain individuals, and be calm and comfortable in their presence, particularly in infants.

Attention-deficit/hyperactivity disorder   Developmental disorder often expressed as a persistent pattern of inattention and/or hyperactivity-impulsivity, forgetfulness, and distractibility.

Authoritative parenting   A child-centered approach to parenting that is based on the expectations of compliance to parental rules and directions and encourages an open dialogue about those rules in a warm, positive manner.

Autism   A developmental disability diagnosed before the age of three that is characterized by specific impairments to social interaction, communication, interests, imagination, and activities.

Avoidance coping   The case where the individual employs strategies that are designed to circumvent or avoid the stressful situation, either through the use of person-oriented strategies or task-oriented strategies.

Axis I disorders   Disorders, such as anxiety and mood disorders, that designate sets of specific symptoms or syndromes representing a distinct mental disorder.

Axis II disorders   Stable traits, such as abnormalities of personality and mental retardation, that do not necessarily cause severe disruption in living.

Basic emotions   A set of emotions such as anger, fear and happiness that are believed to be fundamental, universal and supported by specific brain circuits. Each has a characteristic facial expression.

Behavior genetics   The study of the inheritance of traits in a population, typically using data from family members (*see also* **nature vs. nurture**).

Behavioral modification   A system of therapy that changes behavior through the use of positive and negative reinforcement.

Bias   Tendency of an assessment device to make systematic errors in prediction for a particular social group (e.g., racial, ethnic, or cultural).

Biodata   Information about an individual's background that can be used to predict future performance.

Bipolar disorder   A mood disorder characterized by one manic episode along with a major depressive episode.

Buffering effect   The protection against stressful experiences that is afforded by an individual's personal characteristics, such as **social support**, positive affect, and sense of coherence (*see also* **moderator**).

Case study   An in depth and detailed analysis of a single individual (often in a clinical context) or of a single rare event.

Causality   Determining the cause of a relationship or an effect.

Chronometric measures   Indexes of behavior based on reaction times, typically obtained in controlled laboratory studies of simple tasks.

Classical conditioning   A form of Pavlovian learning (conditioning) in which an initially neutral stimulus (conditioned stimulus) that is paired repeatedly with a stimulus that elicits an automatic response (unconditioned stimulus) results in a learned or conditioned response whenever the conditioned stimulus is presented. For example, a social situation, when frequently associated with aversive experiences (e.g., humiliation), may elicit an aversive emotion (anxiety), although initially social situations were not associated with negative feelings.

Clinical assessment   Integrated information from multiple procedures used by a clinician to arrive at an assessment/diagnosis of an individual (*see also* **case study**).

Coefficient of correlation   A statistical measure of the degree of linear association between two variables, designated by r. It ranges from $+1.00$ (perfect positive relationship) to -1.00 (perfect inverse relationship). The statistic gives an *effect size* for the strength of the association; it may also be tested for **statistical significance**.

Cognitive abilities   Aptitudes or competencies for processing information, including perception, learning, memory, understanding, awareness, reasoning, judgment, intuition, and language.

Cognitive behavioral programs   A type of intervention program designed to achieve behaviorally defined goals, using techniques and methods of a popular form of therapy (i.e., cognitive behavior therapy), such as relaxation training, communication skill training, and modeling.

Cognitive-behavioral therapy   A form of psychotherapy based on modifying ingrained thoughts and behaviors related to social-emotional dysfunction.

Cognitive-motivational theory   Richard Lazarus's extension of the cognitive appraisal theory that puts equal emphasis on three processes involved in the generation of an emotion: appraisal (the cognitive process), the central role of the individual's striving, intentions, and goals (the motivational process), and the relevance of external events to these striving (the relational process).

Cognitive neuroscience   The branch of psychology that is concerned with understanding how the functioning of nerve cells (neurons) supports cognitive processes, including perception, attention, memory, and choice of action.

Cognitive retrieval mechanisms   Strategies used to recall and bring forth information stored in long-term memory to **working memory**.

Compassion fatigue   A form of burnout and traumatization experienced by caretakers, and other helping professionals, in reaction to working with traumatized persons (e.g., victims of war) over an extended period of time.

Concurrent validity evidence   A form of test validity demonstrated by the relationship between a test and another related criterion measured at the same time.

Conduct disorder   A pattern of behavior in children and adolescence (before the age of 18) that involves violating the rights of others and social norms; including: bullying, physical aggression, cruel behavior toward people and pets, lying, and stealing.

Confirmatory factor analyses   A set of procedures used in the technique of data condensation, called "factor analysis," intended to demonstrate that a group of variables possess a theoretically expected structure (*see also* **structural equation modeling**).

Confounding variable   An extraneous variable that covaries with the independent variable and leads to an alternative explanation of the results.

Conscientiousness   A factor of the **five factor model** that reflects the individual's achievement striving, orderliness, organization, and related behaviors.

Consensus scoring   A system of scoring where the correct answer for an item is the response most frequently selected by the group (i.e., the wisdom of the crowd).

Consequential validity   Both the unintended and intended consequences associated with the use of a psychological or educational test.

Construct   A hypothetical factor that cannot be observed directly but can be inferred from behavioral regularities that follow certain circumstances.

Content validity evidence   Determination of how well a test covers the content it sets out to cover.

Contingent reinforcement   A behaviorist technique in which the delivery of positive events or reinforcements (e.g., social or material reward) is dependent (contingent) on the performance of a desired behavior.

Convergent validity evidence   Evidence demonstrating that performance on a test correlates with other measures of the same construct.

Control group   A group of participants in an experiment that are in the conditions of the experiment in which participants are not exposed to the treatment.

Coping   Strategies employed to mitigate the impact of challenging or harmful events on the person. Major types of coping include **problem-focused, emotion-focused**, and **avoidance coping**.

Correlation   *See* **coefficient of correlation**.

Criterion   An external measure or outcome against which performance on a test is often compared.

Criterion contamination   An instance when the test being used as a predictor contains items that inflate its observed relationship to the criterion being predicted.

Criterion-referenced tests   Tests in which the individual is scored in relation to a specific standard, instead of having their performance compared to the performance of other examinees.

Criterion validity evidence   An index of how well a test correlates with a criterion, that is, an established standard of comparison. The criterion can be measured before, after, or at the same time as the test being validated (*see also* **predictive validity**).

Cronbach alpha coefficient   A **reliability** statistic that, analogous to a **coefficient of correlation**, varies from 0–1.0. It assesses **internal consistency reliability**.

Cross-sectional study   A study in which a sample of participants is tested on a single occasion only (compare **longitudinal study**).

Crystallized intelligence   A broad cluster of **primary mental abilities** acquired via acculturation, reflecting the acquired store of factual knowledge (compare **fluid intelligence**).

Declarative knowledge Memory that can be consciously recalled in response to a request to remember (e.g., name of first president of the United States), as opposed to **procedural knowledge** supporting the actual execution of skills.

Delay of gratification Forgoing an immediate reward (e.g., partying) in order to obtain a more desired reward (college scholarship) in the future.

Diathesis Susceptibility to mental disorders, stemming from biological factors, such as genes or personality, that makes a person vulnerable to stressful events.

Differential psychology The branch of psychology that studies the nature, magnitude, causes, and consequences of psychological differences between individuals and groups, as well as the methods for assessing these differences.

Dimensional model A model of traits or other constructs that assumes that they vary in a continuous fashion rather than as distinct types or categories. For example, rather than assume that people are either extraverts or introverts (types), it is supposed that extraversion-introversion is a spectrum along which people show varying degrees of extraverted and introverted qualities.

Discriminant validity evidence A form of "construct validity" demonstrated by showing that measures of constructs that are conceptually unrelated do not correlate in the data.

DSM-IV (TR) A handbook used by mental health professionals that lists different categories of mental disorders, along with the criteria for diagnosis (TR refers to text revision).

Dyadic communication Communication, including emotional signals, among two people (e.g., husband and wife) in an interpersonal situation.

Ecological validity The degree to which results obtained from research or experiment is representative of conditions in the wider world. For example, psychological research carried out exclusively among first-year psychology college students might have low ecological validity when applied to the population as a whole.

Effect size The quantitative strength of a statistical relationship between variables. A relationship or effect may attain **statistical significance** but remain trivial if the effect size is very small.

Emotion-focused coping The case where the person regulates, reduces, channels, or eliminates the aversive emotions associated with a stressful encounter.

Emotional disclosure Disclosing one's emotions by talking about the emotions or affects to others, writing about the emotional experience, and so forth.

Emotional facilitation Using emotion to facilitate thought and action, including weighing emotions against one another and against other sensations and thoughts, and allowing emotions to direct attention.

Emotional leakage Expression of emotions, mostly negative, that people often attempt to hide. Emotions tend to unintentionally leak out in social situations through nonverbal channels (e.g., voice intonation or pitch, facial expression, posturing).

Emotional management *See* **emotional regulation**.

Emotional regulation The ability to successfully maintain, change, or modify emotions, both in self and others.

Emotional stability A calm, resilient temperament; the opposite of **neuroticism**.

Emotional understanding The ability to comprehend the meanings of emotions, and to reason with emotional material.

Emotion perception   The ability to register, identify, and encode emotional displays and emotional messages.

Empathy   The ability to perceive, identify, and directly feel the emotion(s) of another.

Endorphin   A class of chemicals found mainly in the pituitary gland that function as internal painkillers or opoids ("endogenous morphines"), often during intense physical activity ("runner's high").

Error   The difference between the obtained and true score on a test.

Experimental group   A group of participants exposed to a particular level of the treatment variable ("independent variable") in an experiment. The responses of the experimental group are compared to the responses of the control group, other experimental groups, or both.

Exploratory factor analyses   A set of data-analytical techniques, applied to a covariance or correlation matrix, that may reveal the fundamental dimensions underlying the set of correlation coefficients.

Externalizing behaviors   A broad classification of behaviors observed in reaction to **stress** or tension; these behaviors are characterized primarily by acting out, aggression, and antisocial behavior (contrasted with **externalizing behaviors**).

Extraversion   A broad personality trait of the **five factor model** characterized by open, outgoing, social, and gregarious behavior (*see also* **introversion**).

Evocative interaction   The types of behaviors and emotions one provokes in others.

Expert scoring   A form of scoring that uses judgments by experts to determine correct responses and provide a score for a test.

Extrinsic motivation   Motivation to engage in an activity that comes from an external incentive (contrasted with **intrinsic motivation**).

***F*-Test**   Statistic used to test the **statistical significance** of differences among multiple means, often used with **analysis of variance**.

Face validity   Extent to which a test (on face value) appears to provide a reasonable and acceptable measure.

Factor analysis   A statistical technique that is used to analyze patterns of relationship among (many) different psychological variables. *See also* **confirmatory factor analyses** and **exploratory factor analyses**.

Five factor model (FFM)   A leading personality model that proposes there are five major, universal personality dimensions, known as the Big Five. See also **extraversion, neuroticism, agreeableness, conscientiousness,** and **openness**.

Flow   A state of optimal experience arising from intense involvement in an activity that is enjoyable, such as playing a sport, engaging in an art form, or reading a good book.

Fluid intelligence   A broad cluster of **primary mental abilities** acquired via incidental learning experiences, reflecting the ability to reason and actively process complex information (compare **crystallized intelligence**).

Four branch model   An influential **ability model of emotional intelligence** proposed by Jack Mayer and Peter Salovey that differentiates four facets of EI: **emotional perception, emotional facilitation, emotional understanding,** and **emotional management**.

Frontal lobes   Area of the cerebral cortex of the brain implicated in judgment, decision-making and integration of cognition and emotion. Different sub-areas correspond to different functions of these kinds.

Generalized anxiety disorder Form of **anxiety disorder** characterized by free-floating anxiety and excessive levels of worry.

General mental ability A general cognitive ability (g) that underlies performance on a wide range of tests and cognitively demanding tasks; some critics of the construct attribute g to statistical artifact.

Goodness of fit A statistical measure that establishes whether or not an observed frequency distribution differs from a theoretical (expected) distribution.

Histrionic personality disorder A personality disorder that is primarily characterized by exaggerated displays of emotional reactions in everyday behavior; emotions are expressed with extreme and often inappropriate exaggeration and tend to suddenly shift emotion expression.

Impression management The act of presenting oneself in the way they want themselves to be seen and evaluated by other people.

Impulse control The ability to wait until a later time to obtain something that you want (delay of gratification).

Impulsive behavior When an individual does something careless without regard to the effect their behavior may have on themselves or others.

Incremental validity The extent to which a test adds to the predictive validity already provided by other measures when multiple tests are used to predict some independent criterion.

Information-processing models Models of behavior and performance that seek to specify precisely how information is encoded, represented, and transformed by the mind, similar to the operations of a digital computer. **Chronometric measures** are often used to test these models.

Informed consent The principle that individuals participating in psychological research or assessment should be informed beforehand about the nature of the task and the potential risks and threats inherent in the activity.

Internal consistency reliability A measure of **reliability** that involves assessing consistency in performance across test items (*see* **Cronbach alpha coefficient**).

Internal working model (of attachment) A cognitive construction or set of assumptions about the working relationships, such as expectations of support or affection. The earliest relationship may form the template of this internal model or **schema**, which may be positive or negative.

Internalizing behaviors A broad classification of behaviors observed in reaction to **stress** or tension; these behaviors are characterized primarily by internal responses such as elevated anxiety and depression (contrasted with **externalizing behaviors**).

Intervention A generic term for a systematic program that aims to improve behavioral competence and/or well-being in some specific context. Examples are school programs for enhancing learning, training courses at work, and psychotherapies.

Intrinsic motivation When the motivation to engage in an activity comes from a source other than an external incentive (contrasted with **extrinsic motivation**).

Introversion A broad personality trait involving orientation toward the internal private world of one's self and one's inner thoughts and feelings rather than toward the outer world of people and things. Introverts tend to be relatively reserved, quiet, withdrawn, and deliberate, in relation to their extroverted counterparts.

Investment models   Models of cognitive and emotional intelligence development in which biologically determined dispositions are invested and shaped over time, leading to the development of social competencies through socialization and personal experiences in negotiating social transactions.

Item analysis   A set of statistical techniques for analyzing responses to individual test items and the relationship between item and total test characteristics.

Item response theory   A modern psychometric theory of measurement that assumes the probability of a correct response on an ability test to be a function of the person's underlying latent trait, as well as other parameters such as item difficulty and guessing.

Kleptomania   A disorder conceptualized by the inability of persons to control their strong impulse to steal.

Linear transformation   A method of transforming a psychological test score in order to produce a more useful scale of measurement without changing the essential characteristics of that score.

Longitudinal study   A study where the same sample of people are tested on two or more occasions at different ages, sometimes over many years (compare **cross-sectional study**).

Machiavellianism   A trait or attribute marked by a calculating attitude toward interpersonal relationships and a belief that ends justify the means—however ruthless. Machiavellian individuals tend to view others as objects to be manipulated in pursuit of their goals, even if it involves deliberate deception.

Mean   The sum of all the scores divided by the number of scores (average).

Measurement   Concerned with the assignment of numerals to objects according to a set of rules.

Mediator   A variable that transmits the effect of an independent variable on a dependent variable; the mediator may indicate an intervening mechanism that explains the effect of the independent variable. For example, maladaptive coping may mediate the effect of neuroticism on emotional distress (distinguish from **moderator**).

Meta-analysis   A statistical technique that aggregates and then summarizes the findings from a large pool of related studies in terms of **effect sizes**.

Metacognition   Higher order thinking that involves active control over the thinking processes and learning, involving decisions that help to identify the task on which one is currently working, to evaluate that progress, and predict outcomes of that progress.

Meta-emotion   An awareness of one's current emotional state along with past and current emotional tendencies.

Mindfulness   Awareness of one's thoughts, feelings, and other present-moment experiences.

Mirror neurons   A type of brain cell that responds the same way to a given action or behavior (reaching out to grasp an object, smile, showing compassion, etc.) whether it is performed by the person herself or whether the person has observed another person perform the action.

Mixed models of emotional intelligence   A definition of EI as an array of qualities, including both orthodox mental abilities and personality traits, that may support application of abilities. Such models are sometimes used to justify self-report assessment of EI (compare **ability models of emotional intelligence**).

Mobbing   Bullying in the workplace that may cause severe psychosocial distress.

Moderator A factor or variable that controls the strength and direction of the association between two other variables. For example, social support *moderates* the association between life events and **stress** symptoms (distinguish from **mediator**).

Mood disorder A clinical disorder in which the main symptom is disturbance in mood, ranging from depression to manic behaviors.

Modeling A developmental learning process in which one or more individuals (parents, peers, teachers) serve as examples (models) that the child will emulate.

Multiple intelligence theory Howard Gardner's theory that there are many independent types of intelligence, including musical intelligence, spatial intelligence, and interpersonal intelligence as well as cognitive intelligence.

Multiple regression Statistical technique used to predict a *criterion* variable from multiple independent measures. The multiple **correlation coefficient** is designated as R, and indicates the **effect size** $(0–1.0)$. It may also be tested for **statistical significance**.

Multi-stratum models Models of ability or personality dimensions that discriminate multiple strata or levels of **constructs**, differing in how broadly defined the dimensions are. Upper level constructs are far-reaching in scope (e.g., **general mental ability, crystallized intelligence**, and **fluid intelligence**), whereas lower strata are narrowly defined (e.g., **primary mental abilities**).

Narcissism A personality trait typified by inflated self-esteem, grandiosity, and selfishness; at the extreme, it is a personality disorder.

Nature vs. nurture Dispute over the relative contributions of hereditary and constitutional factors (nature) and environmental factors (nurture) to the development of major traits of the individual. It is addressed by using evidence from **behavior genetics**.

Neuroticism A broad personality factor included in the five factor model, which is characterized by a chronic level of emotional instability, proneness to psychological **stress**, and difficulty in coping with life's challenges (see also **emotional stability**).

Negative correlation A relationship where as one dimension increases, the other decreases.

Nomological net (work) A conceptual network, often comprising inferences about a variable. The construct validity of a test is ascertained through a nomological network reflecting research findings and other experience with the test.

Norepinephrine A brain chemical (hormone and neurotransmitter) produced mainly by nuclei in the brain stem, playing a pivotal role in the activation of the autonomic nervous system in times of **stress**.

Norms (in testing) A detailed record of test performance in a normative group, used to generate an assessment of relative performance levels.

Norms (social) Standards for attitudes, behaviors, and morals generally accepted by a social or cultural group against which the individual's behaviors may be evaluated.

Objective test A test that can be scored in a simple, concise, clerical manner against some independent standard of accuracy; such as multiple choice or true–false questions that have explicit correct and incorrect answers.

Obsessive compulsive disorder Disorder where reoccurring intrusive (obsessive) thoughts and/or images can only be alleviated by patterns of rigid behavior (compulsions).

Openness A major personality factor associated with the **five factor model** relating to qualities including intellectual and artistic interest, curiosity, and, in some accounts, emotional sensitivity.

Operant conditioning   Process in which behavioral change (learning) occurs as a function of rewards or punishments for consequences of behavior (e.g., praising child for nonaggressive handling of anger).

Organizational citizenship   The attitudes and actions at the workplace that benefit the organization and help to create a positive emotional and social milieu.

Organizational psychology   The branch of psychology that studies human behavior in the work environment and applies general psychological principles to work-related issues and problems, notably in such areas as personnel selection, personnel training, employee evaluation, working conditions, accident prevention, job analysis, job satisfaction, leadership, team effectiveness, and work motivation.

Panic disorder   **Anxiety disorder** characterized by an experience of sporadic, intense, and often reoccurring panic attacks.

Partial correlation   The **correlation** between two variables that remains after controlling for one or more other variables; a process described as "partialling out." Partial correlations may be used to control for **confounding variables**; for example, we might calculate a correlation to test whether intelligence predicts job proficiency with social class "partialled out."

Pearson correlation   *See* **coefficient of correlation**.

Peer-reports   Assessment of a target person by peers (classmates, work associates, etc.).

Peer review   The process of having an author's scholarly work be evaluated by others who are experts in the respective field before being published in an academic journal.

Performance-based emotional intelligence   *See* **ability model of emotional intelligence**.

Permissive parenting   A parental style where few behavioral expectations are placed on the child; parents are nurturing and accepting, but nondemanding.

Phobia   **Anxiety disorder** characterized by fear of a specific object, class of objects, or setting (e.g., spiders, open spaces).

Positive psychology   A recently minted field of psychological theory and research that focuses on the psychological states (e.g., contentment, joy, optimism), individual traits, or character strengths (e.g., intimacy, integrity, altruism, wisdom), and social institutions that make life most worth living.

Posttraumatic stress disorder (PTSD)   The result of a traumatic experience where the victim presents reoccurring anxiety disorder symptoms, such as nightmares and flashbacks about the experience, as well as diminished responsiveness and symptoms of fear and arousal.

Post-test   Testing done after a treatment or intervention has ended; post-test scores are compared to **pre-test** scores in order to see if change has occurred.

Predictive validity   An index of how well a test correlates with a variable that is measured in the future, at some point after the test has been administered (e.g., relationship between high school achievement test scores and future college first year GPA).

Pre-test   Testing done before treatment has occurred in-order to establish a baseline score.

Primary mental abilities   Constructs revealed by factor analysis to be essential components of intelligence. The psychometrician Louis Thurstone proposed that there are seven primary abilities: verbal ability (V), word fluency (WF), numerical ability (N), spatial intelligence (S), memory (M), perceptual speed (P), and reasoning (R).

Primary prevention   Way of reducing **stress** by modifying environmental stressors such as the use of direct action to eliminate negative impact on the individual.

Proactive aggression   Hostile behavior or use of force to achieve strategic advantage, committed with the calculated intention of causing harm or injury to others.

Proactive interaction   The way we choose and shape social environments.

Problem-focused coping   Where the individual manages or solves the problem by removing or circumventing the stressor.

Procedural knowledge   Long-term memory for the skills involved in particular tasks. Procedural memory is demonstrated by skilled performance and is often separate from the ability to verbalize this knowledge (**declarative knowledge**). Knowing how to type or skate, for example, requires procedural memory.

Projective test   A measure of personality that involves analyzing an individual's responses to abstract or unstructured stimuli (e.g., inkblots, ambiguous pictures).

Prosocial behaviors   Behaviors that actively help other people or support the goals, values and **social norms** of a group of people.

Psychodynamic approach   A theoretical and therapeutic system in where the primary focus is to reveal the unconscious content of a client's psyche in an effort to alleviate psychic tension.

Psychological mindedness   A personality trait referring to a person's interest in understanding his or her experiences and behaviors.

Psychological test   Measurement instrument that consists of a sample of behavior obtained under standardized conditions and employing established scoring rules. The test provides quantitative scores for some psychological **constructs**.

Psychometrics   The science of applying measurement principles to psychological qualities, leading to development and formal evaluation of **psychological tests**.

Psychosomatic disorders   Also known as somatoform disorders where physical symptoms have no medical cause, although they seem to be part of a general medical condition.

Quasi-experimental design   A type of study, often comparing different groups in the real world, that may be analyzed as though it were an experiment. Such designs cannot yield causal conclusions about the effect of an independent variable because there is incomplete control over all the variables.

Reactive aggression   Emotional reactions to frustration or aversive conditions, often in retaliation. This form of aggression tends to be targeted to the perceived source of the **stress** or misplaced to other objects and people in the environment.

Reactive interaction   How people filter and interpret the social world around them.

Reciprocal determinism   The view that behavior influences and is influenced by the environment.

Regression analysis   Any of several statistical techniques that are designed to allow the prediction of the score on one variable, the dependent variable, from the scores on one or more other variables, the independent variables.

Reliability   The accuracy with which a test measures whatever underlying quality or **construct** it assesses; technically, the correlation between observed test scores and the underlying "true scores" on the measured construct. Statistics for quantifying reliability include **Cronbach alpha**, which assesses **internal consistency reliability**, and **test–retest reliability coefficients**, which assess **stability**.

Response style   A general tendency by participants to agree or disagree with statements, independent of test content.

Schemas   Mental techniques used to organize and understand our world.

Schizoid personality   A personality disorder primarily characterized by a very limited range of emotion, in both expressing and experiencing emotion, and social detachment.

Schizotypal personality disorder   A personality disorder primarily characterized by discomfort in close relationships, distortions in thinking, and eccentric behaviors.

Secondary prevention   Stress reduction by means of **stress** management, developing adaptive coping skills for those who are at high risk for **stress** to better deal with the daily demands of work.

Self-concept   One's mental knowledge and understanding of one's self.

Self-efficacy   Individual's belief in their capacity to act effectively in order to bring about results perceived as favorable or desirable (e.g., belief in ability to control food intake during a ten-week diet program).

Self-reports   A statement or series of answers to questions provided by an individual as to his or her mental state, feelings, beliefs, and so forth. Self-report methods may be impacted by the honesty and self-awareness of the participant.

Significance   See **statistical significance**.

Situational judgment test (SJT)   A test that presents complex work or social situations in a written or video format, and requires the respondents to assess the desirability of various action alternatives.

Social adjustment   A term that loosely describes the person's capacity to form productive, cooperative social relationships with others. It implies also that the person does not typically withdraw or avoid social interaction, and does not violate norms for social interaction.

Social anxiety   An intense fear, apprehension, or worry of social situations and being evaluated with others; this anxiety often involves a physiological, cognitive, and behavioral component.

Social competency   A term similar to **social intelligence** and **social adjustment**, signifying that the person is capable of managing social interactions effectively.

Social emotional learning (SEL)   The process through which students learn to recognize and manage emotions, care about others, make good decisions, behave ethically and responsibly, develop positive relationships, and avoid negative behaviors.

Social intelligence   The set of abilities and competencies hypothesized to support effective social interaction with other people, including social awareness and insight, and the capacity to influence others adaptively.

Social support   The availability of assistance from others in dealing with demanding, potentially stressful events, including both practical help and sympathy.

Socialization   The process of learning the norms, values, and rules of one's culture in order to live in it.

Specific factors (s)   Abilities unique to specific ability tests, over and above **general mental ability**, in the early intelligence theory of Charles Spearman.

Stability   The consistency of test scores over a specified time period, assessed by a **test–retest reliability coefficient**.

Standard error of measurement   A measure of the variability in scores expected as a result of measurement error.

Stanford-Binet Intelligence Scale   A standardized test assessing intelligence and cognitive abilities for individuals aged 2 to 89 years. It currently includes five verbal subtests and five nonverbal subtests that yield verbal, nonverbal, and full scale IQs (with a mean of 100 and a standard deviation of 15) as well as fluid reasoning, knowledge, quantitative reasoning, visual-spatial processing, and working memory index score.

Statistical significance   Loosely, a statistical test is said to be significant when it can be demonstrated that the probability of obtaining a given effect by chance is low. More precisely, significance indicates that the probability of the null hypothesis (that there is actually no effect) is sufficiently low (typically under 5 percent) that we can reject the null hypothesis. That is, the data are compatible with there being a real effect (*see also* **effect size**).

Stress   Loosely, symptoms of distress including negative emotions, disruption of behavior and actual or perceived ill-health. Stress is defined more precisely in the **transactional model of stress** as a state of being taxed or overloaded by external demands for which the person's **coping** capabilities are inadequate. Thus stress reflects both external events ("stressors") and the individual's psychological vulnerabilities.

Structural equation modeling   A statistical technique for modeling causal relationships between multiple variables that are typically latent variables (not measured directly). The adequacy of the model is assessed using a **goodness of fit** statistic.

Suppression   The conscious process of intentionally trying to stop thinking about certain thoughts, which may be counterproductive.

t-**Test**   Statistical test of whether the **means** of two variables differ from one another significantly (*see* **statistical significance**).

Target scoring   Form of scoring that assumes that the stimulus creators can provide a correct answer (e.g., emotional content of a piece of music).

Task-focused coping   *See* **problem-focused coping**.

Temperament   The basic foundation of personality, usually assumed to be biologically determined and present early in life. Temperament includes such characteristics as energy level, emotional responsiveness, impulsiveness, response tempo, and willingness to explore.

Tertiary prevention   The use of programs that target employees who have suffered from high degrees of disabling **stress**, such as "employee assistance programs" focusing on dealing with the outcomes or consequences of the stressful situation.

Test fairness   A test should be reliable and valid in all cultural, racial, and other demographic groups that may take it. In addition test items should not be offensive, irrelevant, or meaningless to individuals belonging to specific groups.

Test-retest reliability coefficient   The correlation between scores on the same test taken on two occasions separated by a designated time interval, providing an index of **stability**. If the test measures a stable **trait**, the coefficient may be used as an index of **reliability**.

Trait   A consistent pattern of behavior in a particular psychological domain (e.g., anxiety, hostility) that shows **stability** over time. Traits are often treated as latent **constructs** that may be measured using **psychological tests**.

Trait emotional intelligence   A model of EI that conceptualizes it as a set of personality dimensions specifically related to social-emotional functioning.

Transactional theory of stress   Influential theory of **stress** and emotion developed by Richard Lazarus, that attributes stress to the dynamic interplay between the individual and a challenging environment (*see also* **coping**).

Transformational leadership   A charismatic, inspiring style of leading others that usually involves heightening followers' motivation, confidence, and satisfaction, uniting them in the pursuit of shared, challenging goals, and changing their beliefs, values, and needs.

True score   The expected value of a test score if measured with perfect **reliability** (i.e., the average value expected over many, many measurements).

Validity   The ability of a test to measure the underlying *construct* that it purports to measure. High **reliability** is a necessary condition for validity, but the converse is not true. Evidence for validity may be provided by **concurrent validity, consequential validity, content validity, convergent validity, criterion validity, discriminant validity, ecological validity, face validity, incremental validity, and predictive validity**).

Wechsler Intelligence Scales   An intelligence test for individuals aged 16 years to 89 years. A modification and replacement of the initial Wechsler-Bellevue Intelligence Scale, the WAIS currently includes seven verbal subsets and seven performance subsets, yielding a verbal IQ, a performance IQ, and a full scale IQ with a mean of 100 and a standard deviation of 15; or both index scores and IQs.

Working memory   A memory system used for the immediate processing of information, requiring both short-term storage and executive control of processing. It may contribute to **general mental ability**.

References

Aber, J. L., Jones, S. M., Brown, J. L., Chaudry, N., and Samples, F. 1998. Resolving conflict creatively: Evaluating the developmental effects of a school-based violence prevention program in neighbourhood and classroom context. *Development and Psychopathology* 10: 187–213.

Abraham, R. 2005. Emotional intelligence in the workplace: A review and synthesis. In R. Schulze and R. D. Roberts, eds., *Emotional Intelligence: An International Handbook*. Cambridge, MA: Hogrefe and Huber, pp. 255–70.

Ackerman, P. L. 1996. A theory of adult intellectual development: Process, personality, interests, and knowledge. *Intelligence* 22: 227–57.

Ackerman, P. L., Beier, M. E., and Bowen, K. R. 2002. What we really know about our abilities and our knowledge. *Personality and Individual Differences* 33: 587–605.

Ackerman, P. L., and Goff, M. 1994. Typical intellectual engagement and personality: Reply to Rocklin. *Journal of Educational Psychology* 86: 150–53.

Akiskal, H. G., Kilzieh, N., Maser, J. D., Clayton, P. J., Schettler, P. J., Shea, M., Endicott, J., Scheftner, W., Hirschfeld, R., and Keller, M. B. 2006. The distinct temperament profiles of bipolar I, bipolar II, and unipolar patients. *Journal of Affective Disorders* 92: 19–33.

Alden, L. E., and Taylor, C. T. 2004. Interpersonal processes in social phobia. *Clinical Psychology Review* 24: 857–82.

Alloy, L. B., and Abramson, L. Y. 1988. Depressive realism: Four theoretical perspectives. In L. B. Alloy, ed., *Cognitive Processes in Depression*. New York: Guilford Press, pp. 223–65.

Alloy, L. B., and Riskind, J. H., eds. 2006. *Cognitive Vulnerability to Emotional Disorders*. Hillsdale, NJ: Erlbaum.

Ambady, N., and Gray, H. M. 2002. On being sad and mistaken: Mood effects on the accuracy of thin-slice judgments. *Journal of Personality and Social Psychology* 83: 947–61.

Amelang, M., and Steinmayr, R. 2006. Is there a validity increment for tests of emotional intelligence in explaining the variance of performance criteria? *Intelligence* 34: 459–68.

American Educational Research Association, American Psychological Association, National Council on Measurement in Education. 1999. *Standards for Educational and Psychological Tests*. Washington, DC: American Educational Research Association.

American Institute of Stress. 2002. *Job Stress*. New York: American Institute of Stress.

Amiot, C. E., Terry, D. J., Jimmieson, N. L., and Callan, V. J. 2006. A longitudinal investigation of coping processes during a merger: Implications for job satisfaction and organizational identification. *Journal of Management* 32: 552–74.

Anastasi, A., and Urbina, S. 1997. *Psychological Testing*, 7th ed. Upper Saddle River, NJ: Prentice Hall.

Anderson, J. R. 1996. ACT: A simple theory of complex cognition. *American Psychologist* 51: 355–65.

Antonakis, J. 2003. Why "emotional intelligence" does not predict leadership effectiveness: A comment on Prati, Douglas, Ferris, Ammeter, and Buckley. *International Journal of Organizational Analysis* 11: 355–61.

Antonakis, J. 2004. On why "emotional intelligence" will not predict leadership effectiveness beyond IQ or the "big five": An extension and rejoinder. *Organizational Analysis* 12: 171–82.

Aquino, K. 2000. Structural and individual determinants of workplace victimization: The effects of hierarchical status and conflict management style. *Journal of Management* 26: 171–93.

Aquino, K., and Bommer, W. H. 2003. Preferential mistreatment: How victim status moderates the relationship between organizational citizenship behavior and workplace victimization. *Organization Science* 4: 274–85.

Argyle, M. 2001. *The Psychology of Happiness*, 2nd ed. New York: Routledge.

Aronson, E. 2000. *Nobody Left to Hate*. New York: Freeman.

Arsenio, W. F., and Lover, A. 1997. Emotions, conflicts, and aggression during preschoolers' free play. *British Journal of Developmental Psychology* 15: 531–42.

Ashforth, B. E., and Humphrey, R. H. 1995. Emotion in the workplace: A reappraisal. *Human Relations* 48: 97–125.

Ashkanasy, N. M., Hartel, C. E. J., and Daus, C. S. 2002. Diversity and emotion: The new frontiers in organizational behavior research. *Journal of Management* 28: 307–38.

Ashkanasy, N. M., Hartel, C. E. J., and Zerbe, W. J. 2000. Commentary: Emerging research agendas. In N. M. Ashkanasy, C. E. J. Hartel, and W. J. Zerbe, eds., *Emotions in the Workplace: Research, Theory, and Practice*. Westport: Quorum Books, pp. 272–74.

Ashkanasy, N. M., and Tse, B. 2000. Transformational leadership as management of emotions: A conceptual review. In N. M. Ashkanasy, C. E. J. Hartel, and W. J. Zerbe, eds., *Emotions in the Workplace: Research, Theory, and Practice*. Westport: Quorum Books/Greenwood Publishers Group, pp. 221–35.

Austin, E. J. 2005a. Emotional intelligence and emotional information processing. *Personality and Individual Differences* 39: 403–14.

Austin, E. J. 2005b. Personality correlates of the broader autism phenotype as assessed by the Autism Spectrum Quotient (AQ). *Personality and Individual Differences* 38: 451–60.

Austin, E. J., and Saklofske, D. H. 2005. Far too many intelligences? On the communalities and differences between social, practical, and emotional intelligences. In R. Schulze and R. D. Roberts, eds., *International Handbook of Emotional Intelligence*. Cambridge, MA: Hogrefe and Huber, pp. 107–28.

Austin, E. J., Saklofske, D. H., and Egan, V. 2005. Personality, well-being, and health correlates of trait emotional intelligence. *Personality and Individual Differences* 38: 547–58.

Averill, J. R., and Nunley, E. P. 1992. *Voyages of the Heart: Living an Emotionally Creative Life*. New York: Free Press.

Averill, J. R., and Thomas-Knowles, C. 1991. Emotional creativity. In K. T. Strongman, ed., *International Review of Studies on Emotion*, vol. 1. London: Wiley, pp. 269–99.

Bachman, J., Stein, S., Campbell, K., and Sitarenios, G. 2000. Emotional intelligence in the collection of debt. *International Journal of Selection and Assessment* 8: 176–82.

Baldwin, M. W., and Fergusson, P. 2001. Relational schemas: The activation of interpersonal knowledge structures in social anxiety. In W. R. Crozier and L. E. Alden, eds., *International Handbook of Social Anxiety: Concepts, Research, and Interventions Relating to the Self and Shyness*. New York: Wiley, pp. 235–57.

Bandura, A. 1965. Behavioral modification through modeling procedures. In L. Krasner and L. P. Ullmann, eds., *Research in Behavior Modification: New Developments and Implications*. New York: Holt, Rinehart, and Winston, pp. 310–40.

Bandura, A. 1997. *Self-Efficacy: The Exercise of Control.* New York: Freeman.

Barchard, K. A. 2003. Does emotional intelligence assist in the prediction of academic success? *Educational and Psychological Measurement* 63: 840–58.

Barchard, K. A., and Hakstian, R. A. 2004. The nature of emotional intelligence abilities: Basic dimensions and their relationships with other cognitive-ability and personality variables. *Educational and Psychological Measurement* 64: 437–62.

Bargh, J. A., and Williams, E. L. 2006. The automaticity of social life. *Current Directions in Psychological Science* 15: 1–4.

Barling, J., Slater, F., and Kelloway, E. K. 2000. Transformational leadership and emotional intelligence: An exploratory study. *Leadership and Organization Development Journal* 21: 157–61.

Barnett, P. A., and Gotlib, I. H. 1988. Dysfunctional attitudes and psychosocial stress: The differential prediction of future psychological symptomatology. *Motivation and Emotion* 12: 251–70.

Bar-On, R. 1995. *EQ-i: The Emotional Quotient Inventory Manual. A Test of Emotional Intelligence.* New York: Multi-Health Systems.

Bar-On, R. 1997. *The Emotional Intelligence Inventory (EQ-i): Technical Manual.* Toronto: Multi-Health Systems.

Bar-On, R. 2000. Emotional and social intelligence: Insights from the Emotional Quotient Inventory. In R. Bar-On and J. D. A. Parker, eds., *The Handbook of Emotional Intelligence.* San Francisco: Jossey-Bass, pp. 363–88.

Bar-On, R. 2004. The Bar-On Emotional Quotient Inventory (EQ-i): Rationale, description, and summary of psychometric properties. In Glenn Geher, ed., *Measuring Emotional Intelligence: Common Ground and Controversy.* Hauppauge, NY: Nova Science, pp. 111–42.

Bar-On, R., and Parker, J. D. A., eds. 2000. *The Handbook of Emotional Intelligence.* San Francisco: Jossey-Bass.

Baron, R. A., and Neuman, J. H. 1996. Workplace violence and workplace aggression: Evidence on their relative frequency and potential causes. *Aggressive Behavior* 22: 161–78.

Baron-Cohen, S. 1995. *Mindblindness: An Essay on Autism and Theory of Mind.* Cambridge: MIT Press.

Barrett, L. F., Gross, J., Christensen, T. C., and Benvenuto, M. 2001. Knowing what you're feeling and knowing what to do about it: Mapping the relation between emotion differentiation and emotion regulation. *Cognition and Emotion* 15: 713–24.

Barrick, M. R., and Mount, M. K. 1991. The Big-Five personality dimensions and job performance: A meta-analysis. *Personnel Psychology* 44: 1–26.

Barrick, M. R., Mount, M. K., and Judge, T. A. 2001. Personality and performance at the beginning of the new millennium: What do we know and where do we go next? *International Journal of Selection and Assessment* 9: 9–30.

Bass, B. M. 1996. A new paradigm of leadership: An inquiry into transformational leadership. *US Army Research Institute for the Behavioral and Social Sciences.* Alexandria, VA: Sciences.

Bass, B. M. 2002. Cognitive, social, and emotional intelligence of transformational leaders. In R. E. Riggio and S. E. Murphy, eds., *Multiple Intelligences and Leadership.* Hillsdale, NJ: Erlbaum, pp. 105–18.

Bastian, V. A., Burns, N. R., and Nettelbeck, T. 2005. Emotional intelligence predicts life skills, but not as well as personality and cognitive abilities. *Personality and Individual Differences* 39: 1135–45.

Batson, C. D., Ahmad, N., Yin, J., Bedell, S. J., Johnson, J. W., Templin, C. M., and Whiteside, A. 1999. Two threats to the common good: Self-interested egoism and empathy-induced altruism. *Personality and Social Psychology Bulletin* 25: 3–16.

Baum, K. M., and Nowicki, S. 1998. Perception of emotion: Measuring decoding accuracy of adult prosodic cues varying in intensity. *Journal of Nonverbal Behavior* 22: 89–108.

Baumeister, R. F., Campbell, J. D., Krueger, J. I., and Vohs, K. D. 2005. Exploding the self-esteem myth. *Scientific American* 292: 84–91.

Baumeister, R. F., Smart, L., and Boden, J. M. 1996. Relation of threatened egotism to violence and aggression: The dark side of high self-esteem. *Psychological Review* 103: 5–33.

Bechara, A., Damasio, H., and Damasio, A. R. 2000. Emotion, decision making, and the orbitofrontal cortex. *Cerebral Cortex* 10: 295–307.

Beck, A. T. 1967. *Depression: Causes and Treatment*. Philadelphia: University of Pennsylvania Press.

Beehr, T. A., and Newman, J. E. 1978. Job stress, employee health, and organizational effectiveness: A facet analysis, model, and literature review. *Personnel Psychology* 31: 665–99.

Bekker, M. H. J., Nijssen, A., and Hens, G. 2001. Stress prevention training: Sex differences in types of stressors, coping, and training effects. *Stress and Health: Journal of the International Society for the Investigation of Stress* 17: 207–18.

Ben Ze'ev, A. 1997. The affective realm. *New Ideas in Psychology* 15: 247–59.

Bentler, P. M. 1980. Multivariate analysis with latent variables. *Annual Review of Psychology* 31: 419–56.

Berenbaum, H., Boden, M. T., Baker, J. P., Dizen, M., Thompson, R. J., and Abramowitz, A. 2006. Emotional correlates of the different dimensions of schizotypal personality disorder. *Journal of Abnormal Psychology* 115: 359–68.

Berry, D. S., and Sherman-Hansen, J. 2000. Personality, nonverbal behavior, and interaction quality in female dyads. *Personality and Social Psychology Bulletin* 26: 278–92.

Bjöerkqvist, K., Oesterman, K., and Kaukiainen, A. 2000. Social intelligence – empathy = aggression?: Erratum. *Aggression and Violent Behavior* 5: 429.

Blair, R. J. 2003. Facial expressions, their communicatory functions and neuro-cognitive substrates. *Philosophical Transactions of the Royal Society of London, B, Biological Sciences* 358: 561–72.

Blair, R. J., and Coles, M. 2000. Expression recognition and behavioral problems in early adolescence. *Cognitive Development* 15: 421–34.

Blair, R. J., Mitchell, D. G., Peschardt, K. S., Colledge, E., Leonard, R. A., Shine, J. H., Murray, L. K., and Perrett, D. I. 2004. Reduced sensitivity to others' fearful expressions in psychopathic individuals. *Personality and Individual Differences* 37: 1111–22.

Bolger, N. 1990. Coping as a personality process: A prospective study. *Journal of Personality and Social Psychology* 59: 525–37.

Bonanno, G. A. 2004. Loss, trauma, and human resilience: Have we underestimated the human capacity to thrive after extremely aversive events? *American Psychologist* 59: 20–28.

Bowman, D. B., Markham, P. M., and Roberts, R. D. 2001. Expanding the frontier of human cognitive abilities: So much more than (plain) *g*! *Learning and Individual Differences* 13: 127–58.

Boyatzis, R. 1982. *The Competent Manager: A Model for Effective Performance*. New York: Wiley.

Boyatzis, R., Goleman, D., and Rhee, K. 2000. Clustering competence in Emotional Intelligence: Insights from the emotional competence inventory. In R. Bar-On and J. D. A. Parker, eds., *The Handbook of Emotional Intelligence*. San Francisco: Jossey-Bass, pp. 343–62.

Brackett, M. A., and Katulak, N. A. 2007. Emotional intelligence in the classroom: Skill-based training for teachers and students. In J. Ciarrochi and J. D. Mayer, eds., *Applying Emotional Intelligence: A Practitioner's Guide*. New York: Psychology Press, pp. 1–27.

Brackett, M. A., and Mayer, J. D. 2003. Convergent, discriminant, and incremental validity of competing measures of emotional intelligence. *Personality and Social Psychology Bulletin* 29: 1147–58.

Brackett, M. A., Mayer, J. D., and Warner, R. M. 2004. Emotional intelligence and its relation to everyday behavior. *Personality and Individual Differences* 36: 1387–1402.

Bracket, M. A., Rivers, S. E., Shiffman, S., Lerner, N., and Salovey, P. 2006. Relating emotional abilities to social functioning: A comparison of self-report and performance measures of emotional intelligence. *Journal of Personality and Social Psychology* 91: 780–95

Brackett, M. A., Warner, R. M., and Bosco, J. S. 2005. Emotional intelligence and relationship quality among couples. *Personal Relationships* 12: 197–212.

Bradlee, P. M., and Emmons, R. A. 1992. Locating narcissism within the interpersonal circumplex and the five-factor model. *Personality and Individual Differences* 13: 821–30.

Brenner, E. M., and Salovey, P. 1997. Emotion regulation during childhood: Developmental, interpersonal, and individual considerations. In P. Salovey and D. J. Sluyter, eds., *Emotional Development and Emotional Intelligence: Educational Implications*. New York: Basic Books, pp. 168–95.

Brody, N. 2004. What cognitive intelligence is and what emotional intelligence is not. *Psychological Inquiry* 15: 234–38.

Bruch, M. A. 2002. Shyness and toughness: Unique and moderated relations with men's emotional inexpression. *Journal of Counseling Psychology* 49: 28–34.

Buck, R. 1984. *The Communication of Emotion*. New York: Guilford Press.

Bulatao, E. Q., and VandenBos, G. R. 1996. Workplace violence: Its scope and the issues. In G. R. VandenBos and E. Q. Bulatao, eds., *Violence on the Job: Identifying Risks and Developing Solutions*. Washington, DC: American Psychological Association, pp. 1–23.

Burke, M. J., and Day, R. R. 1986. A cumulative study of the effectiveness of managerial training. *Journal of Applied Psychology* 71: 232–45.

Burke, R. J., and Cooper, L. 2006. The new world of work and organizations: Implications for human resource management. *Human Resource Management Review* 16: 83–85.

Burns, N. R., Bastian, V. A., and Nettelbeck, T. 2007. Emotional intelligence: More than personality and cognitive ability? In G. Matthews, M. Zeidner, and R. D. Roberts, eds., *The Science of Emotional Intelligence: Knowns and Unknowns*. New York: Oxford University Press, pp. 167–96.

Burrowes, B. D., and Halberstadt, A. G. 1987. Self- and family-expressiveness styles in the experience and expression of anger. *Journal of Nonverbal Behavior* 11: 254–68.

Buss, A. H., and Plomin, R. A. 1984. *Temperament: Early Developing Personality Traits*. Hillsdale, NJ: Erlbaum.

Campbell, K. W., Reeder, G. D., Sedikides, C., and Elliot, A. J. 2000. Narcissism and comparative self-enhancement strategies. *Journal of Research in Personality* 34: 329–47.

Campos, J. J., and Barrett, K. C. 1984. Toward a new understanding of emotions and their development. In C. E. Izard, J. Kagan, and R. B. Zajonc, eds., *Emotions, Cognition, and Behavior*. Cambridge: Cambridge University Press, pp. 229–63.

Caprara, G. V., Barbaranelli, C., Pastorelli, C., Bandura, A., and Zimbardo, P. G. 2000. Prosocial foundations of children's academic achievement. *Psychological Science* 11: 302–306.

Caprara, G. V., Barbaranelli, C., and Zimbardo, P. G. 1996. Understanding the complexity of human aggression: Affective, cognitive, and social dimensions of individual differences in propensity toward aggression. *European Journal of Personality* 10: 133–55.

Caprara, G. V., and Cervone, D. 2000. *Personality, Determinants, Dynamics, and Potentials*. Cambridge: Cambridge University Press.

Carmeli, A. 2003. The relationship between emotional intelligence and work attitudes, behavior, and outcomes: An examination among senior managers. *Journal of Managerial Psychology* 18: 788–813.

Carmeli, A., and Josman, E. 2006. The relationship among emotional intelligence, task performance, and organizational citizenship behaviors. *Human Performance* 19: 403–19.

Carroll, J. B. 1993. *Human Cognitive Abilities: A Survey of Factor-Analytic Studies.* New York: Cambridge University Press.

Carstensen, L. L., Gottman, M. J., and Levenson, R. W. 1995. Emotional behavior in long-term marriage. *Psychology and Aging* 10: 140–49.

Carstensen, L. L., Graff, J., Levenson, R. W., and Gottman, M. J. 1996. Affect in intimate relationships: The development course of marriage. In C. Magai and S. H. McFadden, eds., *Handbook of Emotion, Adult Development and Aging.* San Diego: Academic Press, pp. 227–47.

Cartwright, S., and Cooper, C. L. 1996. Coping in occupational settings. In M. Zeidner and N. S. Endler, eds., *Handbook of Coping.* New York: Wiley, pp. 202–20.

Cartwright, S., and Cooper, C. 2005. Individually targeted interventions. In J. Barling, E. K. Kelloway, and M. R. Frone, eds., *Handbook of Work Stress.* Thousand Oaks, CA: Sage, pp. 607–22.

Caruso, D. R., Bienn, B., and Kornacki, S. A. 2006. Emotional intelligence in the workplace. In J. Ciarrochi, J. P. Forgas, and J. D. Mayer, eds., *Emotional intelligence in everyday life*, 2nd ed. Hove, UK: Psychology Press, pp. 187–205.

Caruso, D. R., and Wolfe, C. J. 2004. Emotional intelligence and leadership development. In D. V. Day, S. J. Zaccaro, and S. M. Halpin, eds., *Leader Development for Transforming Organizations: Growing Leaders for Tomorrow.* Mahwah, NJ: Erlbaum, pp. 237–63.

Caspi, A., and Bem, D. 1990. Personality continuity and change across the life course. In L. A. Pervin, ed., *Handbook of Personality Theory and Research.* New York: Guilford Press, pp. 549–75.

Cattell, R. B. 1971. *Abilities: Their Structure, Growth, and Action.* Boston: Houghton Mifflin.

Cervone, D. 2000. Thinking about self-efficacy. *Behavior Modification* 24: 30–56.

Chamorro-Premuzic, T., Moutafi, J., and Furnham, A. 2005. The relationship between personality traits, subjectively-assessed, and fluid intelligence. *Personality and Individual Differences* 38: 1517–28.

Cherniss, C. 2000a. Leadership and emotional intelligence. In R. Burke and C. Cooper, eds., *Inspiring Leaders.* London: Routledge, pp. 132–48.

Cherniss, C. 2000b. Social and emotional competence in the workplace. In R. Bar-On and J. D. A. Parker, eds., *The Handbook of Emotional Intelligence.* San Francisco: Jossey-Bass, pp. 433–58.

Cherniss, C., and Adler, M. 2000. *Promoting Emotional Intelligence in Organizations.* Alexandria, VA: American Society for Training and Development.

Cherniss, C., and Goleman, D. 2001. Training for emotional intelligence: A model. In C. Cherniss and D. Goleman, eds., *The Emotionally Intelligent Workplace.* San Francisco: Jossey-Bass, pp. 209–33.

Cherniss, C., Goleman, D., Emmerling, R., Cowan, K., and Adler, M. 1998. *Bringing Emotional Intelligence in Organizations.* New Brunswick, NJ: Consortium for Research on Emotional Intelligence in Organizations, Rutgers University.

Cherry, N. M., Chen, Y., and McDonald, J. C. 2006. Reported incidence and precipitating factors of work-related stress and mental ill-health in the United Kingdom (1996–2001). *Occupational Medicine* 56: 414–21.

Christensen, A., and Shenk, J. L. 1991. Communication, conflict and psychological distance in nondistressed, clinic, and divorcing couples. *Journal of Consulting and Clinical Psychology* 59: 458–63.

Ciarrochi, J., and Blackledge, J. 2006. Mindfulness-based emotional intelligence training: A new approach to reducing human suffering and promoting effectiveness. In J. Ciarrochi, J. Forgas, and J. Mayer, eds., *Emotional Intelligence in Everyday Life: A Scientific Inquiry*, 2nd ed. New York: Psychology Press/Taylor and Francis, pp. 206–208.

Ciarrochi, J., Caputi, P., and Mayer, J. D. 2003. The distinctiveness and utility of a measure of trait emotional awareness. *Personality and Individual Differences* 34: 1477–90.

Ciarrochi, J., Chan, A. Y. C., and Bajgar, J. 2001. Measuring emotional intelligence in adolescents. *Personality and Individual Differences* 31: 1105–19.

Ciarrochi, J., Chan, A. Y. C., and Caputi, P. 2000. A critical evaluation of the emotional intelligence construct. *Personality and Individual Differences* 28: 539–61.

Ciarrochi, J., Deane, F. P., and Anderson, S. 2002. Emotional intelligence moderates the relationship between stress and mental health. *Personality and Individual Differences* 32: 197–209.

Ciarrochi, J., Wilson, C. J., Deane, F. P., and Rickwood, D. 2003. Do difficulties with emotions inhibit help-seeking in adolescence? The role of age and emotional competence in predicting help-seeking intentions. *Counselling Psychology Quarterly* 16: 103–20.

Clark, D. A., Beck, A. T., and Alford, B. A. 1999. *Scientific Foundations of Cognitive Theory and Therapy of Depression*. New York: Wiley.

Clore, G. L., Ortony, A., and Foss, M. A. 1987. The psychological foundations of the affective lexicon. *Journal of Personality and Social Psychology* 53: 751–66.

Cohen, J. 1988. *Statistical Power Analysis for the Behavioral Sciences*, 2nd ed. Hillsdale, NJ: Erlbaum.

Cohen, J., ed. 1999a. *Educating Minds and Hearts: Social Emotional Learning and the Passage into Adolescence*. New York: Teachers College Press.

Cohen, J. 1999b. Learning about social and emotional learning: Current themes and future directions. In J. Cohen, ed., *Educating Minds and Hearts*. New York: Teacher's College Press, pp. 184–91.

Cohen, J. 1999c. Social and emotional learning: Past and present. In J. Cohen, ed., *Educating Minds and Hearts*. New York: Teachers College Press, pp. 3–23.

Coie, J. D., and Dodge, K. A. (1998). Aggression and antisocial behavior. In N. Eisenberg, ed., *Handbook of Child Psychology: Social, Emotional, and Personality Development*. New York: Wiley, pp. 779–862.

Cooper, C. L., Liukkonen, P., and Cartwright, S. 1996. *Stress Prevention in the Workplace*. Dublin, Ireland: European Foundation for the Improvement of Living and Working Conditions; Lanham, MD: UNIPUB.

Cooper, C. L., Dewe, P. J., and O'Driscoll, M. P. 2001. *Organisational Stress: A Review and Critique of Theory, Research, and Applications*. Thousand Oaks, CA: Sage.

Cooper, C. L., and Marshall, J. 1978. Sources of managerial and white collar stress. In C. L. Cooper and R. Payne, eds., *Stress at Work*. Chichester, UK: Wiley, pp. 81–105.

Cooper, C. L., and Payne, R., eds. 1978. *Stress at Work*. Chichester, UK: Wiley.

Cooper, M. L., Wood, P. K., Orcutt, H. K., and Albino, A. 2003. Personality and the predisposition to engage in risky or problem behaviors during adolescence. *Journal of Personality and Social Psychology* 84: 390–410.

Cooper, R. K., and Sawaf, A. 1997. *Executive EQ: Emotional Intelligence in Leaders and Organizations*. New York: Grosset/Putnam.

Corno, L., Cronbach, L. J., Kupermintz, H., Lohman, D. F., Mandinach, E. B., Porteus, A. W., and Talbert, J. E., eds. 2002. *Remaking the Concept of Aptitude: Extending the Legacy of R. E. Snow*. Mahwah, NJ: Erlbaum.

Corr, P. J. 2004. Reinforcement sensitivity theory and personality. *Neuroscience and Biobehavioral Reviews* 28: 317–32.

Costa, P. T., Jr., Bagby, R. M., Herbst, J. H., and McCrae, R. R. 2005. Personality self-reports are concurrently reliable and valid during acute depressive episodes. *Journal of Affective Disorders* 89: 45–55.

Costa, P. T., Jr., and McCrae, R. R. 1992a. *NEO PI-R Professional Manual*. Odessa, FL: Psychological Assessment Resources.

Costa, P. T., Jr., and McCrae, R. R. 1992b. Four ways five factors are basic. *Personality and Individual Differences* 13: 653–65.

Costa, P. T., Jr., and McCrae, R. R. 2000. NEO Personality Inventory. In A. E. Kazdin, ed., *Encyclopedia of Psychology*, vol. 5. Washington, DC: American Psychological Association, pp. 407–409.

Costa, P. T., Jr., Terraciano, A., and McCrae, R. R. 2001. Gender differences in personality traits across cultures: Robust and surprising findings. *Journal of Personality and Social Psychology* 81: 322–31.

Côté, S., and Miners, H. 2006. Emotional intelligence, cognitive intelligence, and job performance. *Administrative Science Quarterly* 51: 1–28.

Crick, N. R., and Dodge, K. A. 1996. Social information-processing mechanisms in reactive and proactive aggression. *Child Development* 67: 993–1002.

Crocker, L., and Algina, J. 1986. *Introduction to Classical and Modern Test Theory*. New York: CBS College Publishing.

Cronbach, L. J. 1990. *Essential of Psychological Testing*, 5th ed. New York: Harper and Row.

Cummings, G., Hayduk, L., and Estabrooks, C. 2005. Mitigating the impact of hospital restructuring on nurses: The responsibility of emotionally intelligent leadership. *Nursing Research* 54: 2–12.

Cusack, J., Deane, F. P., Wilson, C. J., and Ciarrochi, J. 2006. Emotional expression, perceptions of therapy, and help-seeking intentions in men attending therapy services. *Psychology of Men and Masculinity* 7: 69–82.

Damasio, A. R. 1994. *Descartes' error: Emotion, Reason, and the Human Brain*. New York: Avon Books.

Darwin, C. 1872. *The Expression of the Emotions in Man and Animals*. Chicago: University of Chicago Press.

Daus, C. S. 2006. The case for an ability-based model of emotional intelligence. In K. R. Murphy, ed., *A Critique of Emotional Intelligence: What Are the Problems and How Can They Be Fixed?* Mahwah, NJ: Erlbaum, pp. 301–24.

Daus, C. S., and Ashkanasy, N. M. 2005. The case for the ability-based model of emotional intelligence in organizational behavior. *Journal of Organizational Behavior* 26: 453–66.

David, C. F., and Kistner, J. A. 2000. Do positive self-perceptions have a "dark side"? Examination of the link between perceptual bias and aggression. *Journal of Abnormal Child Psychology* 28: 327–37.

Davies, M., Stankov, L., and Roberts, R. D. 1998. Emotional intelligence: In search of an elusive construct. *Journal of Personality and Social Psychology* 75: 989–1015.

Davis, M. H., and Kraus, L. A. 1997. Personality and empathic accuracy. In W. Ickes, ed., *Empathic Accuracy*. New York: Guilford Press, pp. 144–68.

Dawda, D., and Hart, S. D. 2000. Assessing emotional intelligence: Reliability and validity of the Bar-On Emotional Quotient Inventory (EQ-i) in university students. *Personality and Individual Differences* 28: 797–812.

Dawson, G., Webb, S. J., Carver, L., Panagiotides, H., and McPartland, J. 2004. Young children with autism show atypical brain responses to fearful versus neutral facial expressions of emotion. *Developmental Science* 7: 340–59.

Day, A. L. 2004. The measurement of emotional intelligence: The good, the bad, and the ugly. In G. Geher, ed., *Measuring Emotional Intelligence: Common Ground and Controversy*. New York: Nova Science Publishers, pp. 245–70.

Day, A. L., Therrien, D. L., and Carroll, S. A. 2005. Predicting psychological health: Assessing the incremental validity of emotional intelligence beyond personality, type A behaviour, and daily hassles. *European Journal of Personality* 19: 519–36.

De Raad, B. 2000. *The Big Five Personality Factors: The Psycholexical Approach to Personality*. Kirkland, WA: Hogrefe and Huber Publishers.

De Raad, B. 2005. The trait-coverage of emotional intelligence. *Personality and Individual Differences* 38: 673–87.

Deffenbacher, J. L., Oetting, E. R., and Lynch, R. S. 1994. Development of a driving anger scale. *Psychological Reports* 74: 83–91.

Denham, S. A. 1998. *Emotional Development in Young Children*. New York: Guilford Press.

Denham, S. A. 2006. The emotional basis of learning and development in early childhood education. In B. Spodek and O. N. Saracho, eds., *Handbook of Research on the Education of Young Children*, 2nd ed. Mahwah, NJ: Erlbaum, pp. 85–103.

Denham, S. A., Blair, K. A., DeMulder, E., Levitas, J., Sawyer, K., Auerbach-Major, S., and Queenan, P. 2003. Preschool emotional competence: Pathway to social competence. *Child Development* 74: 238–56.

Derksen, J., Kramer, I., and Katzko, M. 2002. Does a self-report measure for emotional intelligence assess something different than general intelligence? *Personality and Individual Differences* 32: 37–48.

Derryberry, D., Reed, M. A., and Pilkenton-Taylor, C. 2003. Temperament and coping: Advantages of an individual perspective. *Development and Psychopathology* 15: 1049–66.

Dewe, P. 2003. A closer examination of the patterns when coping with work-related stress: Implications for measurement. *Journal of Occupational and Organizational Psychology* 76: 517–24.

Dewey, J. 1909. *Moral Principles in Education*. Boston: Houghton Mifflin.

Dodge, K. A., and Coie, J. D. 1987. Social-information processing factors in reactive and proactive aggression in children's peer groups. *Journal of Personality and Social Psychology* 53: 1146–58.

Douglas, S. C., and Martinko, M. J. 2001. Exploring the role of individual differences in the prediction of workplace aggression. *Journal of Applied Psychology* 86: 547–59.

Duckworth, A. L., and Seligman, M. E. P. 2005. Self-discipline outdoes IQ predicting academic performance in adolescents. *Psychological Science* 16: 939–44.

Dunn, J., Brown, J., and Beardsall, L. 1991. Family talk about feeling states and children's later understanding of others' emotions. *Developmental Psychology* 27: 448–55.

Dunning, D., Heath, C., and Suls, J. M. 2004. Flawed self-assessment: Implications for health, education, and business. *Psychological Science in the Public Interest* 5: 69–106.

Duran, A., Extremera, N., and Rey, L. 2004. Self-reported emotional intelligence, burnout and engagement among staff in services for people with intellectual disabilities. *Psychological Reports* 95: 386–90

Durlak, J. A., Taylor, R. D., Kawashima, K., Pachan, M. K., DuPre, E. P., Celio, C. I., Berger, S. R., Dymnicki, A. B., and Weissberg, R. P. 2007. Effects of positive youth development programs on school, family, and community systems. *American Journal of Community Psychology* 39: 269–86.

Durlak, J. A., and Weissberg, R. P. 2005. A major meta-analysis of positive youth development programs. Presentation at the Annual Meeting of the American Psychological Association, August 2005. Washington, DC.

Duyckinick, E. 1873. *Portrait Gallery of Eminent Men and Women in Europe and America*. New York: Johnson, Wilson.

Eagleton, T. 2004. Too clever by half: Even the Left now despises intellectuals.... *New Statesman*, September 13. Available at http://www.newstatesman.com/.

Eccles, J. S. 1999. The development of children ages 6 to 14. *The Future of Children* 9: 30–44.

Edwards, J. A., and Weary, G. 1993. Depression and the impression-formation continuum: Piecemeal processing despite the availability of category information. *Journal of Personality and Social Psychology* 64: 636–45.

Eisenberg, N., Cumberland, A., and Spinrad, T. L. 1998. Parental socialization of emotion. *Psychological Inquiry* 9: 241–73.

Eisenberg, N., Cumberland, A., Spinrad, T. L., Fabes, R. A., Shepard, S. A., Reiser, M., Murphy, B. C., Losoya, S. H., and Guthrie, I. K. 2001. The relations of regulation and emotionality to children's externalizing and internalizing problem behavior. *Child Development* 72: 1112–34.

Eisenberg, N., and Fabes, R. A. 1990. Empathy: Conceptualization, assessment, and relation to prosocial behavior. *Motivation and Emotion* 14: 131–49.

Eisenberg, N., Fabes, R. A., Guthrie, I. K., and Reiser, M. 2000. Dispositional emotionality and regulation: Their role in predicting quality of social function. *Journal of Personality and Social Psychology* 78: 136–57.

Eisenberg, N., Fabes, R. A., and Losoya, S. H. 1997. Emotional responding: Regulation, social correlates, and socialization. In P. Salovey and D. J. Sluyter, eds., *Emotional Development and Emotional Intelligence: Educational Implications*. New York: Basic Books, 129–67.

Eisenberg, N., Fabes, R. A., Murphy, B. C., Shepard, S. A., Guthrie, I. K., Mazsk, P., Poulin, R., and Jones, S. 1999. Prediction of elementary school children's socially appropriate and problem behavior from anger reactions at age 4–6 years. *Journal of Applied Developmental Psychology* 20: 119–42.

Eisenberg, N., Fabes, R. A., Schaller, M., Carlo, G., and Miller, P. A. 1991. The relations of parental characteristics and practices to children's vicarious emotional responding. *Child Development* 62: 1393–1408.

Eisenberg, N., Valiente, C., Morris, A. S., Fabes, R. A., Cumberland, A., Reiser, M., Gershoff, E. T., Shepard, S. A., and Losoya, S. 2003. Longitudinal relations among parental emotional expressivity, children's regulation, and quality of socioemotional functioning. *Developmental Psychology* 39: 2–19.

Ekman, P. 1999. Basic emotions. In T. Dalgleish and M. J. Power, eds., *Handbook of Cognition and Emotion*. Chichester, UK: Wiley, pp. 45–60.

Elfenbein, H. A., and Ambady, N. 2002. Predicting workplace outcome from the ability to eavesdrop on feeling. *Journal of Applied Psychology* 87: 963–71.

Elfenbein, H. A., Der-Foo, M., Boldry, J. G., and Tan, H. H. 2006. Dyadic effects in nonverbal communication: A variance partitioning analysis. *Cognition and Emotion* 20: 149–59.

Elias, M. J., and Clabby, J. 1992. *Building Social Problem Solving Skills: Guidelines from a School-based Program*. San Francisco: Jossey-Bass.

Elias, M. J., Hunter, L., and Kress, J. S. 2001. Emotional intelligence and education. In J. Ciarrochi, J. P. Forgas, and J. D. Mayer, eds., *Emotional Intelligence in Everyday Life*. Philadelphia: Psychology Press, pp. 133–49.

Elias, M. J., Zins, J. E., Weissberg, R. P., Frey, K. S., Greenberg, M. T., Haynes, N. M., Kessler, R., Schwab-Stone, M. E., and Shriver, T. P. 1997. *Promoting Social and Emotional Learning: Guidelines for Educators*. Alexandria, VA: Association for Supervision and Curriculum Development.

Elkin, A. J., and Rosch, P. J. 1990. Promoting mental health at the workplace: The prevention side of stress management. *Occupational Medicine: State of the Art Review* 5: 739–54.

Ellis, A. 1962. *Reason and Emotion in Psychotherapy*. New York: Lyle Stuart.

Embretson, S., and Reise, S. 2000. *Item Response Theory for Psychologists*. Mahwah, NJ: Erlbaum.

Endler, N. S., and Parker, J. D. A. 1990. Multi-dimensional assessment of coping: A critical review. *Journal of Personality and Social Psychology* 58: 844–54.

Engelberg, E., and Sjoberg, L. 2004. Emotional intelligence, affect intensity, and social adjustment. *Personality and Individual Differences* 37: 533–42.

Epstein, S. 1998. *Constructive Thinking: The Key to Emotional Intelligence.* Westport, CT: Praeger/Greenwood.

Espelage, D. L., and Swearer, S. M. 2003. Research on school bullying and victimization: What have we learned and where do we go from here? *School Psychology Review* 32: 365–83.

Extremera, N., and Fernandez-Berrocal, P. 2005. Perceived emotional intelligence and life satisfaction: Predictive and incremental validity using the Trait Meta-Mood Scale. *Personality and Individual Differences* 39: 937–48.

Eysenck, H. J. 1976. *Sex and Personality.* London: Open Books.

Eysenck, H. J. 1995. Creativity as a product of intelligence and personality. In D. H. Saklofske and M. Zeidner, eds., *International Handbook of Personality and Intelligence.* New York: Plenum Press, pp. 231–48.

Eysenck, M. W. 1992. *Anxiety: The Cognitive Perspective.* Hove, UK: Erlbaum.

Fellner, A. N., Matthews, G., Funke, G., Emo, A., Perez, J. C., Zeidner, M., and Roberts, R. D. 2007. The effects of emotional intelligence on visual search of emotional stimuli and emotion identification. *Proceedings of the Human Factors and Ergonomics Society 51st Annual Meeting.* Santa Monica, CA: Human Factors and Ergonomics Society, pp. 845–49.

Fellner, A. N., Matthews, G., Warm, J. S., Zeidner, M., and Roberts, R. D. 2006. Learning to discriminate terrorists: The effects of emotional intelligence and emotive cues. In *Proceedings of the Human Factors and Ergonomics Society 50th Annual Meeting.* Santa Monica, CA: Human Factors and Ergonomics Society, pp. 1249–53.

Fellner, A. N., Perez, J. C., Emo, A., and Matthews, G. 2006. How is trait emotional intelligence related to personality and to mood states? Ninety-seventh Annual Meeting of the Southern Society for Philosophy and Psychology, Durham, NC, April 2005

Fernandez-Berrocal, P., Alcaide, R., Extremera, N., and Pizarro, D. 2006. The role of emotional intelligence in anxiety and depression among adolescents. *Individual Differences Research* 4: 16–27.

Feshbach, N. D. 1978. Studies on empathic behavior in children. In B. A. Maher, ed., *Progress in Experimental Personality Research*, vol. 8. New York: Academic Press, pp. 1–47.

Feshbach, N. D., and Cohen, S. 1988. Training affects comprehension in young children: An experimental evaluation. *Journal of Applied Developmental Psychology* 9: 2201–10

Feshbach, N. D., and Feshbach, S. 1987. Affective processes and academic achievement. *Child Development* 58: 1335–47.

Figley, C. R. 1995. Systemic traumatization: Secondary traumatic stress disorder in family therapists. In R. H. Mikesell, D. D. Lusterman, and S. H. McDaniel, eds., *Integrating Family Therapy: Handbook of Family Psychology and Systems Theory.* Washington, DC: American Psychological Association, pp. 571–81.

First, M. B., Pincus, H. A., Levine, J. B., Williams, J. B. W., Ustun, B., and Peele, R. 2004. Clinical utility as a criterion for revising psychiatric diagnoses. *American Journal of Psychiatry* 161: 946–54.

Fitness, J. 2001. Emotional intelligence in intimate relationships. In J. Ciarrochi, J. P. Forgas, and J. D. Mayer, eds., *Emotional Intelligence in Everyday Life.* Philadelphia: Psychology Press, pp. 98–112.

Fitzgerald, M., and Bellgrove, M. A. 2006. The overlap between alexithymia and Aspergers' syndrome. *Journal of Autism and Developmental Disorders* 36: 573–76.

Flanagan, D. P., McGrew, K. S., and Ortiz, S. O. 2000. *The Wechsler Intelligence Scales and Gf-Gc Theory: A Contemporary Approach to Interpretation.* Needham Heights, MA: Allyn and Bacon.

Flavell, J. H., Green, F. L., and Flavell, E. R. 1995. Young children's knowledge about thinking. *Monographs of the Society for Research in Child Development* 60, Serial No. 243. Chicago: University of Chicago Press.

Flury, J., and Ickes, W. 2001. Emotional intelligence and empathic accuracy. In J. Ciarrochi, J. P. Forgas, and J. D. Mayer, eds., *Emotional Intelligence in Everyday Life*. Philadelphia: Psychology Press, pp. 113–32.

Folkman, S. 1984. Personal control and stress and coping processes: A theoretical analysis. *Journal of Personality and Social Psychology* 46: 839–52.

Folkman, S. 1991. Coping across the lifespan: Theoretical issues. In E. M. Cummings, A. L. Greene, and K. H. Karraker, eds., *Life-span Developmental Psychology: Perspectives on Stress and Coping*. Hillsdale, NJ: Erlbaum, pp. 3–19.

Foo, M. D., Elfenbein, H. A., Tan, H. H., and Aik, V. C. 2004. Emotional intelligence and negotiation: The tension between creating and claiming value. *International Journal of Conflict Management* 15: 411–29.

Forgas, J. P. 2001. Affective intelligence: The role of affect in social thinking and behavior. In J. Ciarrochi, J. P. Forgas, and J. D. Mayer, eds., *Emotional Intelligence in Everyday Life*. Philadelphia: Psychology Press, pp. 46–63.

Fredrickson, B. L., and Losada, M. F. 2005. Positive affect and the complex dynamics of human flourishing. *American Psychologist* 60: 678–86.

Freedy, J. R., and Donkervoet, J. C. 1995. Traumatic stress: An overview of the field. In J. R. Freedy and S. E. Hobfoll, eds., *Traumatic Stress: From Theory to Practice*. New York: Plenum Press, pp. 3–28.

French, J. R. P., and Caplan, R. D. 1973. Organizational stress and individual strain. In A. J. Marrow, ed., *The Failure of Success*. New York: AMACOM, pp. 30–36.

Freudenthaler, H. H., and Neubauer, A. C. 2007. Measuring emotional management abilities: Further evidence of the importance to distinguish between typical and maximum performance. *Personality and Individual Differences* 42: 1561–72.

Frey, J. 2003 *A Million Little Pieces*. New York: Nan A. Talese/Doubleday.

Frick, P. J., and Morris, A. S. 2004. Temperament and developmental pathways to conduct problems. *Journal of Clinical Child and Adolescent Psychology* 33: 54–68.

Frith, U. 2004. Emanuel Miller lecture: Confusions and controversies about Asperger syndrome. *Journal of Child Psychology and Psychiatry* 45: 672–86.

Furedi, F. 2004. *Therapy Culture: Cultivating Vulnerability in an Uncertain Age*. Philadelphia: Routledge/Taylor and Francis Group.

Furedi, F. 2006. *Where Have All the Intellectuals Gone? Confronting 21st Century Philistinism*, 2nd ed. London: Continuum Press.

Furnham, A. 1986. Response bias, social desirability, and dissimulation. *Personality and Individual Differences* 7: 385–400.

Furnham, A., and Heaven, P. 1999. *Personality and Social Behaviour*. London: Hodder Arnold.

Furnham, A., and Rawles, R. 1999. Correlations between self-estimated and psychometrically measured IQ. *Journal of Social Psychology* 139: 405–10.

Furr, R. M., and Funder, D. C. 1998. A multimodal analysis of personal negativity. *Journal of Personality and Social Psychology* 74: 1580–91.

Furr, R. M., and Funder, D. C. 1999. Personal negativity and the accuracy of interpersonal perception. Paper presented at the 79th Annual Convention of the Western Psychological Association, May, Irvine, CA.

Gable, S., and Isabella, R. A. 1992. Maternal contributions to infant regulation of arousal. *Infant Behavior and Development* 15: 95–107.

Galea, S., Ahern, J., Resnick, H., Kilpatrick, D., Bucuvalas, M., Gold, J., and Vlahov, D. 2002. Psychological sequelae of the September 11 terrorist attacks in New York City. *New England Journal of Medicine* 346: 982–87.

Gardner, H. 1983. *Frames of Mind: The Theory of Multiple Intelligences.* New York: Basic Books.

Gardner, H. 1999. Foreward. In J. Cohen, ed., *Educating Minds and Hearts.* New York: Teacher's College Press

Garner, P. W., Jones, D. C., and Miner, J. L. 1994. Social competence among low-income preschoolers: Emotion socialization practices and social cognitive correlates. *Child Development* 65: 622–37.

Garner, P. W. 1995. Toddlers' emotion regulation behaviors: The roles of social context and family expressiveness. *Journal of Genetic Psychology* 156: 417–30.

Geher, G., Warner, R. M., and Brown, A. S. 2001. Predictive validity of emotional accuracy research scale. *Intelligence* 29: 373–88.

George, J. M. 2000. Emotions and leadership: The role of emotional intelligence. *Human Relations* 53: 1027–55.

Ghaziuddin, M., and Mountain-Kimchi, K. 2004. Defining the intellectual profile of Asperger Syndrome: Comparison with high-functioning Autism. *Journal of Autism and Developmental Disorders* 34: 279–84.

Gibbs, N. 1995. What's your EQ? *Time*, October 2, pp. 60–68.

Gignac, G. E., Palmer, B. R., Manocha, R., and Stough, C. 2005. An examination of the factor structure of the Schutte self-report emotional intelligence (SSREI) scale via confirmatory factor analysis. *Personality and Individual Differences* 39: 1029–42.

Glass, S., and Newman, J. 2006. Recognition of facial affect in psychopathic offenders. *Journal of Abnormal Psychology* 115: 815–20.

Goetz, T., Frenzel, C. A., Pekrun, R., and Hall, N. 2005. Emotional intelligence in the context of learning and achievement. In R. Schulze and R. D. Roberts, eds., *Emotional Intelligence: An International Handbook.* Cambridge, MA: Hogrefe and Huber, pp. 233–53.

Gohm, C. L., and Clore, G. L. 2002a. Four latent traits of emotional experience and their involvement in well-being, coping, and attributional style. *Cognition and Emotion* 16: 495–518.

Gohm, C. L., and Clore, G. L. 2002b. Affect as information: An individual difference approach. In L. Feldman-Barrett and P. Salovey, eds., *The Wisdom in Feeling: Psychological Processes in Emotional Intelligence.* New York: Guilford Press, pp. 89–113.

Goldberg, L. R. 1993. The structure of phenotypic personality traits. *American Psychologist* 48: 26–34.

Goldenberg, I., Matheson, K., and Mantler, J. 2006. The assessment of emotional intelligence: A comparison of performance-based and self-report methodologies. *Journal of Personality Assessment* 86: 33–45.

Goleman, D. 1995a. *Emotional Intelligence: Why It Can Matter More Than IQ.* New York: Bantam Books.

Goleman, D. 1995b. EQ: What's your emotional intelligence quotient? *The Utne Reader*, 72.

Goleman, D. 1998. *Working with Emotional Intelligence.* New York: Bantam Books.

Goleman, D. 2001. Emotional intelligence: Issues in paradigm building. In C. Cherniss and D. Goleman, eds., *The Emotionally Intelligent Workplace.* San Francisco: Jossey-Bass, pp. 13–26.

Goleman, D., Boyatzis, R., and McKee, A. 2002. *Primal Leadership: Realizing the Power of Emotional Intelligence.* Boston: Harvard Business School Press.

Gooding, D., and Tallent, K. 2003. Spatial, object, and affective working memory in social anhedonia: An exploratory study. *Schizophrenia Research* 63: 247–60.

Goodwin, R. D., and Friedman, H. S. 2006. Health status and the five-factor personality traits in a nationally representative sample. *Journal of Health Psychology* 11: 643–54.

Gottman, J. M. 1994. *What Predicts Divorce: The Relationship between Marital Processes and Marital Outcomes*. Hillsdale, NJ: Erlbaum.

Gottman, J. M. 1997. *Meta-Emotion: How Families Communicate Emotionally*. Mahwah, NJ: Erlbaum.

Gottman, J. M., Guralnick, M. J., Wilson, B., and Swanson, C. C. 1997. What should the focus of emotion regulation in children? A nonlinear dynamic mathematical model of children's peer interaction in groups. *Development and Psychopathology* 9: 421–52.

Gottman, J. M., Katz, L. F., and Hooven, C. 1996. Parental meta-emotion philosophy and the emotional life of families: Theoretical models and preliminary data. *Journal of Family Psychology* 10: 243–68.

Gottman, J. M., Natarius, C., Markman, H., Banks, D., Yoppi, B., and Rubin, M. E. 1976. Behavior exchange theory and marital decision-making. *Journal of Personality and Social Psychology* 34: 14–23.

Gowing, M. K. 2001. Measures of individual emotional competencies. In C. Cherniss and D. Goleman, eds., *The Emotionally Intelligent Workplace*. San Francisco: Jossey-Bass, pp. 83–131

Graves, K. D., Schmidt, J. E., and Andrykowski, M. A. 2005. Writing about September 11, 2001: Exploration of emotional intelligence and the social environment. *Journal of Language and Social Psychology* 24: 285–99.

Greenberg, L. S. 2006. Emotion-focused therapy: A synopsis. *Journal of Contemporary Psychotherapy* 36: 87–93.

Greenberg, L. S., and Pascual-Leone, A. 2006. Emotion in psychotherapy: A practice-friendly research review. *Journal of Clinical Psychology* 62: 611–30.

Greenberg, M. T., Domitrovich, C. B., and Bumbarger, B. 2001. The prevention of mental disorders in school-aged children: Current state of the field. *Prevention and Treatment*, 4.

Greenberg, M. T., Kusche, C. A., and Riggs, N. 2004. The PATHS curriculum: Theory and research on neurocognitive development and school success. In J. E. Zins, M. R. Bloodworth, R. P. Weissberg, and H. J. Walberg, eds., *Building Academic Success on Social and Emotional Learning: What Does the Research Say?* New York: Teachers College Press, pp. 170–88.

Greenberg, M. T., Weissberg, R. P., O'Brien, M. U., and Zins, J. E. 2003. Enhancing school based prevention and youth development through coordinated social, emotional, and academic learning. *American Psychologist* 58: 466–74.

Grolnick, W. S., and Ryan, R. M. 1989. Parent styles associated with children's self-regulation and competence in school. *Journal of Educational Psychology* 81: 143–54.

Gross, J. J. 1998. The emerging field of emotion regulation: An integrative review. *Review of General Psychology* 2: 271–99.

Gross, J. J., and John, O. P. 2002. Wise emotion regulation. In L. F. Barrett and P. Salovey, eds., *The Wisdom in Feeling: Psychological Processes in Emotional Intelligence*. New York: Guilford Press, pp. 297–319.

Gross, J. J., and John, O. P. 2003. Individual differences in two emotion regulation processes: Implications for affect, relationships, and well-being. *Journal of Personality and Social Psychology* 85: 348–62.

Grubb, W. L., and McDaniel, M. A. 2007. The fakability of Bar-On's Emotional Quotient Inventory Short Form: Catch me if you can? *Human Performance* 20: 43–59.

Guilford, J. P. 1967. *The Nature of Human Intelligence*. New York: McGraw-Hill.

Guilford, J. P. 1988. Some changes in the structure-of-intellect model. *Educational and Psychological Measurement* 48: 1–4.

Gullone, E., and Moore, S. 2000. Adolescent risk-taking and the five-factor model of personality. *Journal of Adolescence* 23: 393–407.

Halberstadt, A. G., Denham, S. A., and Dunsmore, J. C. 2001. Affective social competence. *Social Development* 10: 79–119.

Halberstadt, A. G., and Eaton, K. L. 2003. A meta-analysis of family expressiveness and children's emotion expressiveness and understanding. *Marriage and Family Review* 34: 35–62.

Halberstadt, A. G., and Hall, J. A. 1980. Who's getting the message? Children's nonverbal skill and their evaluation by teachers. *Developmental Psychology* 16: 564–73.

Hamner, C., and Tosi, D. 1974. Relationship of role conflict and role ambiguity to job involvement measures. *Journal of Applied Psychology* 4: 497–99.

Hare, R. D. 1999. *Without Conscience: The Disturbing World of the Psychopaths among Us.* Guilford Press, New York.

Harkness, K. L., Bagby, R. L., Joffe, R. T., and Levitt, A. 2002. Major depression, chronic minor depression, and the Five-Factor Model of Personality. *European Journal of Personality* 16: 271–81.

Harpur, T. J., Hart, S. D., and Hare, R. D. 2002. Personality of the psychopath. In P. T. Costa Jr., and T. A. Widiger, eds., *Personality Disorders and the Five-Factor Model of Personality*, 2nd ed. Washington, DC: American Psychological Association, pp. 299–324.

Harris, M., and Schaubroeck, J. 1988. A meta-analysis of super-supervisor, self-peer, and peer-supervisor ratings. *Personnel Psychology* 41: 43–62.

Haviland, M., Sonne, J., and Kowert, P. A. 2004. Alexithymia and psychopathy: Comparison and application of California Q-set prototypes. *Journal of Personality Assessment* 82: 306–16.

Hawkins, J. D., Smith, B. H., and Catalano, R. F. 2004. Social development and social and emotional learning. In: J. E. Zins, R. P. Weissberg, M. C. Wang, and H. J. Walberg, eds., *Building Academic Success on Social and Emotional Learning. What Does the Research Say?* New York: Teachers College Press, pp. 135–150.

Hay Group 2000. Emotional intelligence: A "soft" skill with a hard edge. ⟨http://ei .haygroup.com/about_ei/⟩

Head, J., Kivimaki, M., Martikainen, P., Vahtera, J., Ferrie, J. E., and Marmot, M. G. 2006. Influence of change in psychosocial work characteristics on sickness absence: The Whitehall II study. *Journal of Epidemiology and Community Health* 60: 55–61.

Hedlund, J., and Sternberg, R. J. 2000. Too many intelligences? Integrating social, emotional, and practical intelligence. In R. Bar-On and J. D. A. Parker, eds., *The Handbook of Emotional Intelligence*. San Francisco: Jossey-Bass, pp. 171–91.

Herrnstein, R. J., and Murray, C. 1994. *The Bell Curve: Intelligence and Class Structure in American Life.* New York: Free Press.

Hochschild, A. 1983. Comment on Kemper's "Social constructionist and positivist approaches to the sociology of emotions." *American Journal of Sociology* 89: 432–34.

Hoel, H., and Cooper, C. L. 2000. Destructive conflict and bullying at work. Unpublished report: University of Manchester, Institute of Science and Technology.

Hogan, R., Curphy, G. J., and Hogan, J. 1994. What we know about leadership: Effectiveness and personality. *American Psychologist* 49: 493–504.

Hogan, R., and Stokes, L. W. 2006. Business susceptibility to consulting fads: The case of emotional intelligence. In K. R. Murphy, ed., *A Critique of Emotional Intelligence: What Are the Problems and How Can They Be Fixed?* Mahwah, NJ: Erlbaum, pp. 263–80.

Holland, P. W., and Wainer, H., eds. 1993. *Differential Item Functioning.* Hillsdale, NJ: Erlbaum.

Holt, R. R. 1993. Occupational stress. In L. Goldberger and S. Breznitz, eds., *Handbook of Stress: Theoretical and Clinical Aspects.* New York: Free Press, pp. 342–67.

Hooven, C., Gottman, J. M., and Katz, L. F. 1995. Parental meta-emotion structure predicts family and child outcomes. *Cognition and Emotion* 9: 229–64.

Horn, J. L., and Hofer, S. M. 1992. Major abilities and development in the adult period. In R. J. Sternberg and C. Berg, eds., *Intellectual Development*. New York: Cambridge University Press, pp. 44–99.

House, J. S. 1981. *Work Stress and Social Support*. Reading, MA: Addison-Wesley.

Howard, A., and Bray, D. W. 1988. *Managerial Lives in Transition*. New York: Guilford Press.

Howlin, P. 2004. *Autism and Asperger Syndrome: Preparing for Adulthood*, 2nd ed. London: Routledge.

Humphrey, N., Curran, A., Morris, E., Farrell, P., and Woods, K. 2007. Emotional intelligence and education: A critical review. *Educational Psychology* 27: 235–54.

Hunter, J. E., and Hunter, R. F. 1984. Validity and utility of alternative predictors of job performance. *Psychological Bulletin* 96: 72–98

Hunter, J. E., and Schmidt, F. L. 1998. The validity and utility of selection methods in personnel psychology: Practical and theoretical implications of 85 years of research findings. *Psychological Bulletin* 124: 262–74.

Hurrell, J. J., Jr. 2005. Organizational stress intervention. In J. Barling, E. K. Kelloway, and M. R. Frone, eds., *Handbook of Work Stress*. Thousand Oaks, CA: Sage, pp. 623–45.

Innes, K. A., and Niedenthal, P. M. 2002. Emotion concepts and emotional states in social judgment and categorization. *Journal of Personality and Social Psychology* 83: 804–16.

Isen, A. M. 1987. Positive affect, cognitive processes, and social behavior. *Advances in Experimental Social Psychology* 20: 203–53.

Isen, A. M. 2001. An influence of positive affect on decision making in complex situations: Theoretical issues with practical implications. *Journal of Consumer Psychology* 11: 75–85.

Ivancevich, J. M., and Matteson, M. T. 1987. Organizational level stress management interventions: A review and recommendations. In J. M. Ivancevich and D. C. Ganster, eds., *Job Stress: From Theory to Suggestion*. New York: Wiley, pp. 229–48.

Izard, C. E. 2001. Emotional intelligence or adaptive emotions? *Emotion* 1: 249–57.

Izard, C. E., Fine, S. E., Schultz, D., Mostow, A. J., Ackerman, B. P., and Youngstrom, E. A. 2001. Emotion knowledge as a predictor of social behavior and academic competence in children at risk. *Psychological Science* 12: 18–23.

Izard, C. E., Trentacosta, C. J., King, K. A., and Mostow, A. J. 2004. An emotion-based prevention program for head start children. *Early Education and Development* 15: 407–22.

Izard, C. E., Trentacosta, C., King, K., Morgan, J., and Diaz, M. 2007. Emotions, emotionality, and intelligence in the development of adaptive behavior. In G. Matthews, M. Zeidner, and R. D. Roberts, eds., *The Science of Emotional Intelligence: Knowns and Unknowns*. New York: Oxford University Press, pp. 127–50.

Jensen, A. R. 1998. *The g Factor: The Science of Mental Ability*. Westport, CT: Praeger/Greenwood Publishing.

Jensen-Campbell, L. A., and Graziano, W. G. 2001. Agreeableness as a moderator of interpersonal conflict. *Journal of Personality* 69: 323–62.

Jenson, W. R., Olympia, D., Farley, M., and Clark, E. 2004. Positive psychology and externalizing students in a sea of negativity. *Psychology in the Schools* 41: 67–79.

Johnson-Laird, P. N., and Oatley, K. 1992. Basic emotions, rationality, and folk theory. *Cognition and Emotion* 6: 201–23.

Jones, F., and Bright, J. 2007. Stress, health, and illness In A. Monat, R. S. Lazarus, and G. Reevy, eds., *The Praeger Handbook on Stress and Coping*, vol. 1. Westport, CT: Praeger, pp. 141–68.

Jones, S., Eisenberg, N., Fabes, R. A., and MacKinnon, D. P. 2002. Parents' reactions to elementary school children's negative emotions: Relations to social and emotional functioning at school. *Merrill-Palmer Quarterly* 48: 133–59.

Joormann, J., and Gotlib, I. H. 2006. Is this happiness I see? Biases in the identification of emotional facial expressions in depression and social phobia. *Journal of Abnormal Psychology* 115: 705–14.

Jordan, P. J., Ashkanasy, N. M., and Ascough, K. 2007. Emotional intelligence in organizational behavior and industrial-organizational psychology. In G. Matthews, M. Zeidner, and R. D. Roberts, eds., *Emotional Intelligence: Knowns and Unknowns*. New York: Oxford University Press, pp. 356–75.

Jordan, P. J., Ashkanasy, N. M., and Hartel, C. E. J. 2002. Emotional intelligence as a moderator of emotional and behavioral reactions to job insecurity. *Academy of Management Review* 27: 361–72.

Jordan, P. J., and Troth, A. C. 2002. Emotional intelligence and conflict resolution: Implications for human resource development. *Advances in Developing Human Resources* 4: 62–79.

Judge, T. A., Erez, A., Bono, J. E., and Thoresen, C. 2002. Are measures of self-esteem, neuroticism, locus of control, and generalized self-efficacy indicators of a common core construct? *Journal of Personality and Social Psychology* 83: 693–710.

Judge, T. A., Colbert, A. E., and Ilies, R. 2004. Intelligence and leadership: A quantitative review and test of theoretical propositions. *Journal of Applied Psychology* 89: 542–52.

Judge, T. A., Van Vianen, A. E. M., and De Pater, I. E. 2004. Emotional stability, core self-evaluations, and job outcomes: A review of the evidence and an agenda for future research. *Human Performance* 17: 325–46.

Kafetsios, K. 2004. Attachment and emotional intelligence abilities across the life course. *Personality and Individual Differences* 37: 129–45.

Kafetsios, K., and Zampetakis, L. A. 2008. Emotional intelligence and job satisfaction: Testing the mediatory role of positive and negative affect at work. *Personality and Individual Differences* 44: 712–22.

Kagan, J. 1994. *Galen's Prophecy*. New York: Basic Books.

Kahn, R. L., Wolfe, D. M., Quinn, R., Snoek, J. D., and Rosenthal, R. A. 1964. *Organizational Stress: Studies in Role Conflict and Ambiguity*. New York: Wiley.

Karasek, R., and Theorell, T. 1990. *Healthy Work: Stress Productivity and the Reconstruction of Working Life*. New York: Wiley.

Keashly, L., and Jagatic, K. 2000. The nature and extent of emotional abuse at work: Results of a statewide survey. Paper presented at the symposium on persistent patterns of aggressive behavior at work, Academy of Management annual meeting, August, Toronto.

Keltner, D., and Haidt, J. 2001. Social functions of emotions. In T. J. Mayne and G. A. Bonanno, eds., *Emotions: Current Issues and Future Directions*. New York: Guilford Press, pp. 192–213.

Keltner, D., and Kring, A. M. 1998. Emotion, social function, and psychopathology. *Review of General Psychology, 2*, 320–342.

Kennedy-Moore, E., and Watson, J. C. 1999. *Expressing Emotion: Myths, Realities, and Therapeutic Strategies*. New York: Guilford Press.

Kerlinger, F. N. 1973. *Foundations of Behavioral Research*, 2nd ed. New York: Holt, Rinehart, and Winston.

Kerns, J. G. 2006. Schizotypy facets, cognitive control, and emotion. *Journal of Abnormal Psychology* 115: 418–27.

Kerr, R., Garvin, J., and Heaton, N. 2006. Emotional intelligence and leadership effectiveness. *Leadership and Organizational Development Journal* 27: 265–79.

Kihlstrom, J. F., and Cantor, N. 2000. Social intelligence. In R. J. Sternberg, ed., *Handbook of Intelligence*. New York: Cambridge University Press, pp. 359–79.

Kliewer, W., Fearnow, M. D., and Miller, P. A. 1996. Coping socialization in middle childhood: Tests of maternal and paternal influences. *Child Development* 67: 2339–57.

Klin, A., Jones, W., Schultz, R., Volkmar, F., and Cohen, D. 2002. Visual fixation patterns during viewing of naturalistic social situations as predictors of social competence in individuals with autism. *Archives of General Psychiatry* 59: 809–16.

Kochanska, G., and Coy, K. C. 2002. Child emotionality and maternal responsiveness as predictors of reunion behaviors in the Strange Situation: Links mediated and unmediated by separation distress. *Child Development* 73: 228–40.

Kochanska, G., Coy, K. C., and Murray, K. T. 2001. The development of self-regulation in the first four years of life. *Child Development* 72: 1091–1111.

Kohler, J. M., Munz, D. C., and Grawitch, M. J. 2006. Test of a dynamic stress model for organisational change: Do males and females require different models? *Applied Psychology: An International Review* 55: 168–91.

Kolen, M. J., and Brennan, R. L. 2004. *Test Equating: Methods and Practices*, 2nd ed. New York: Springer-Verlag.

Kopp, C. B. 1989. Regulation of distress and negative emotions: A developmental view. *Developmental Psychology* 25: 343–54.

Kosson, D. S., Suchy, Y., Mayer, A. R., and Libby, J. 2002. Facial affect recognition in criminal psychopaths. *Emotion* 2: 398–411.

Kottkamp, R. B., and Travlos, A. L. 1986. Selected job stressors, emotional exhaustion, job satisfaction, and thrust behavior of the high school principal. *Alberta Journal of Educational Research* (September): 234–48.

Kracke, W. H. 1988. Kagwahiv mourning. II: Ghosts, grief, and reminiscences. *Ethos* 16: 209–22.

Kristja'nsson, K. 2006. "Emotional intelligence" in the classroom? An Aristotelian critique. *Educational Theory* 56: 39–56.

Krystal, H. 1979. Alexithymia and psychotherapy. *American Journal of Psychotherapy* 33: 17–31.

Krystal, H. 1988. *Integration and Self-Healing: Affect, Trauma, Alexithymia*. Hillsdale, NJ: Analytic Press.

Kuhn, T. S. 1962. *The Structure of Scientific Revolutions*. Chicago: University of Chicago Press.

La Rocco, J. M., and Jones, A. P. 1978. Co-worker and leader support as moderators of stress-strain relationships in work situations. *Journal of Applied Psychology* 63: 629–34.

Lainhart, J. E. 1999. Psychiatric problems in individuals with autism, their parents, and siblings. *International Review of Psychiatry* 11: 278–98.

Landy, F. J. 2005. Some historical and scientific issues related to research on emotional intelligence. *Journal of Organizational Behavior* 26: 411–24.

Landy, F. J. 2006. The long, frustrating, and fruitless search for social intelligence: A cautionary tale. In K. R. Murphy, ed., *A Critique of Emotional Intelligence: What Are the Problems and How Can They Be Fixed?* Mahwah, NJ: Erlbaum, pp. 81–123.

Lane, R. D. 2000. Levels of emotional awareness: Neurological, psychological, and social perspectives. In R. Bar-On and J. D. A. Parker, eds., *The Handbook of Emotional Intelligence: Theory, Development, Assessment, and Application at Home, School, and in the Workplace*. San Francisco: Jossey-Bass, pp. 171–91.

Lane, R. D., Quinlan, D. M., Schwartz, G. E., Walker, P. A., and Zeitlin, S. B. 1990. The Levels of Emotional Awareness Scale: A cognitive-development measure of emotion. *Journal of Personality Assessment* 55: 124–34.

Lane, R. D., Sechrest, L., Reidel, R., Weldon, V., Kaszniak, A. W., and Schwartz, G. 1996. Impaired verbal and nonverbal emotion recognition in alexithymia. *Psychosomatic Medicine* 58: 203–10.

Langdon, R., and Coltheart, M. 1999. Mentalising, schizotypy, and schizophrenia. *Cognition: International Journal of Cognitive Science* 71: 43–71.

Lantieri, L., and Patti, J. 1996. *Waging Peace in Our Schools*. Boston: Beacon Press.

Larsen, R. J., and Ketelaar, T. 1989. Extraversion, neuroticism, and susceptibility to positive and negative mood induction procedures. *Personality and Individual Differences* 10: 1221–28.

Larstone, R. M., Jang, K. L., Livesley, W. J., Vernon, P. A., and Wolf, H. 2002. The relationship between Eysenck's P-E-N model of personality, the five-factor model of personality, and traits delineating personality dysfunction. *Personality and Individual Differences* 33: 25–37.

Law, K. S., Wong, C. S., and Song, L. J. 2004. The construct and criterion validity of emotional intelligence and its potential utility for management studies. *Journal of Applied Psychology* 89: 483–96.

Lawson, W. 1998. *Life behind Glass: A Personal Account of Autism Spectrum Disorder*. Lismore, NSW: Southern Cross University Press. London: Jessica Kingsley.

Lazarus, R. S. 1990. Theory-based stress measurement. *Psychological Inquiry* 1: 3–13.

Lazarus, R. S. 1991. *Emotion and Adaptation*. New York: Oxford University Press.

Lazarus, R. S. 2003. Does the positive psychology movement have legs? *Psychological Inquiry* 14: 93–109.

Lazarus, R. S. 1999. *Stress and Emotion: A New Synthesis*. New York: Springer.

Lazarus, R. S., and Folkman, S. 1984. *Stress, Appraisal, and Coping*. New York: Springer.

Ledley, D. R., Fresco, D. M., and Heimberg, R. G. 2006. Cognitive vulnerability to social anxiety disorder. In L. B. Alloy and J. H. Riskind, eds., *Cognitive Vulnerability to Emotional Disorders*. Mahwah, NJ: Erlbaum, pp. 251–83.

Legree, P. J. 1995. Evidence for an oblique social intelligence factor established with a Likert-based testing procedure. *Intelligence* 21: 241–47.

Leible, T. L., and Snell, W. E. 2004. Borderline personality disorder and multiple aspects of emotional intelligence. *Personality and Individual Differences* 37: 393–404.

Lengua, L. J., West, S. G., and Sandler, I. N. 1998. Temperament as a predictor of symptomatology in children: Addressing contamination of measures. *Child Development* 69: 164–81.

Lennon, M. C., Dohrenwend, B. P., Zautra, A. J., and Marbach, J. J. 1990. Coping and adaptation to facial pain in contrast to other stressful life events. *Journal of Personality and Social Psychology* 59: 1040–50.

Lewis, M., and Saarni, C. 1985. Culture and emotions. In M. Lewis and C. Saarni, eds., *The Socialization of Emotions*. New York: Plenum Press, pp. 1–17.

Lieberman, M. D., and Rosenthal, R. 2001. Why introverts can't always tell who likes them: Multitasking and nonverbal decoding. *Journal of Personality and Social Psychology* 80: 294–310.

Lippa, R. A., and Dietz, J. K. 2000. The relation of gender, personality, and intelligence to judges' accuracy in judging strangers' personality from brief video segments. *Journal of Nonverbal Behavior* 24: 25–43.

Livingstone, H. A., and Day, A. L. 2005. Comparing the construct and criterion-related validity of ability-based and mixed-model measures of emotional intelligence. *Educational and Psychological Measurement* 65: 757–79.

Lochman, J. E., and Dodge, K. A. 1994. Social-cognitive processes of severely violent, moderately aggressive, and non-aggressive boys. *Journal of Consulting and Clinical Psychology* 62: 366–74.

Lochman, J. E., and Lenhart, L. A. 1993. Anger coping intervention for aggressive children: Conceptual models and outcome effects. *Clinical Psychology Review* 13: 785–805.

Locke, E. A. 2005. Why emotional intelligence is an invalid concept. *Journal of Organizational Behavior* 26: 425–31.

Loney, B. R., Frick, P. J., Clements, C. B., Ellis, M. L., and Kerlin, K. 2003. Callous unemotional traits, impulsivity, and emotional processing in adolescents with antisocial behavior problems. *Journal of Clinical Child and Adolescent Psychology* 32: 66–80.

Lopes, P. N., Brackett, M. A., Nezlek, J. B., Schutz, A., Sellin, I., and Salovey, P. 2004. Emotional intelligence and social interaction. *Personality and Social Psychology Bulletin* 30: 1018–34.

Lopes, P. N., Grewal, D., Kadis, J., Gall, M., and Salovey, P. 2006. Evidence that emotional intelligence is related to job performance and affect and attitudes at work. *Psicothema* 18 (suppl): 132–38.

Lopes, P. N., and Salovey, P. 2004. Toward a broader education: Social, emotional, and practical skills. In J. E. Zins, M. R. Bloodworth, R. P. Weissberg, and H. J. Walberg, eds., *Building Academic Success on Social and Emotional Learning: What Does the Research Say?* New York: Teachers College Press, pp. 76–93.

Lopes, P. N., Salovey, P., Côté, S., and Beers, M. 2005. Emotion regulation abilities and the quality of social interaction. *Emotion* 5: 113–18

Lopes, P. N., Salovey, P., and Straus, R. 2003. Emotional intelligence, personality, and the perceived quality of social relationships. *Personality and Individual Differences* 35: 641–58.

Louth, S. M., Hare, R. D., and Linden, W. 1998. Psychopathy and alexithymia in female offenders. *Canadian Journal of Behavioural Science* 30: 91–98.

Luminet, O., Vermeulen, N., Demaret, C., Taylor, G. J., and Bagby, R. M. 2006. Alexithymia and levels of processing: Evidence for an overall deficit in remembering emotion words. *Journal of Research in Personality* 40: 713–33.

Lumley, M. A., Gustavson, B. J., Partridge, R. T., and Labouvie-Vief, G. 2005. Assessing alexithymia and related emotional ability constructs using multiple methods: Interrelationships among measures. *Emotion* 5: 329–42.

Lyons, J. B., and Schneider, T. R. 2005. The influence of emotional intelligence on performance. *Personality and Individual Differences* 39: 693–703.

Mabe, P., and West, S. 1982. Validity of self-evaluation of ability: A review and meta-analysis. *Journal of Applied Psychology* 67: 280–86.

MacCann, C. 2006. New approaches to measuring emotional intelligence: Exploring methodological issues with two new assessment tools. PhD dissertation. University of Sydney, Australia.

MacCann, C., Matthews, G., Zeidner, M, and Roberts, R. D. 2003. Psychological assessment of emotional intelligence: A review of self-report and performance-based testing. *International Journal of Organizational Analysis* 11: 247–74.

MacCann, C., Matthews, G., Zeidner, M., and Roberts, R. D. 2004. The assessment of Emotional Intelligence: On frameworks, fissures, and the future. In G. Geher ed., *Measuring Emotional Intelligence: Common Ground and Controversy.* Hauppauge, NY: Nova Science, pp. 21–52.

MacCann, C., Roberts, R. D., Matthews, G., and Zeidner, M. 2004. Consensus scoring and empirical option weighting of performance-based emotional intelligence (EI) tests. *Personality and Individual Differences* 36: 645–62.

Mack, D. A., Nelson, D. L., and Quick, J. C. 1998. The stress of organisational change: A dynamic process model. *Applied Psychology: An International Review* 47: 219–32.

Magai, C., and McFadden, S. H. 1995. *The Role of Emotions in Social and Personality Development: History, Theory, and Research.* New York: Plenum Press.

Magnus, K., Diener, E., Fujita, F., and Pavot, W. 1993. Extraversion and neuroticism as predictors of objective life events: A longitudinal analysis. *Journal of Personality and Social Psychology* 65: 1046–53.

Magnusson, D. 1976. The person and the situation in an interactional model of behavior. *Scandinavian Journal of Psychology* 17: 253–71.

Malecki, C. K., and Elliot, S. N. 2002. Children's social behaviors as predictors of academic achievement: A longitudinal analysis. *School Psychology Quarterly* 17: 1–23.

Malterer, M. B., Glass, S. J., and Newman, J. P. 2008. Psychopathy and trait emotional intelligence. *Personality and Individual Differences* 44: 735–45.

Mandler, G. 1975. *Mind and Emotion*. New York: Wiley.

Martinez-Pons, M. 1997. The relation of emotional intelligence with selected areas of personal functioning. *Imagination, Cognition, and Personality* 17: 3–13.

Martinez-Pons, M. 1998. Parental inducement of emotional intelligence. *Imagination, Cognition, and Personality* 18: 3–24.

Masia, C. L., McNeil, D. W., Cohn, L. G., and Hope, D. A. 1999. Exposure to social anxiety words: Treatment for social phobia based on the Stroop paradigm. *Cognitive and Behavioral Practice* 6: 248–58.

Mason, O., and Claridge, G. 2006. The Oxford-Liverpool Inventory of Feelings and Experiences (O-LIFE): Further description and extended norms. *Schizophrenia Research* 82: 203–11.

Mathews, A. 2004. On the malleability of emotional encoding. *Behaviour Research and Therapy* 42: 1019–36.

Matsumoto, D., LeRoux, J. A., Bernhard, R., and Gray, H. 2004. Unraveling the psychological correlates of intercultural adjustment potential. *International Journal of Intercultural Relations* 28: 281–309.

Matsumoto, D., LeRoux, J., Wilson, C., Raroque, J., Ekman, P., Yrizarry, N., Loewinger, S., Uchida, H. Y. A., Amo, L., and Goh, A. 2000. A new test to measure emotion recognition ability: Matsumoto and Ekman's Japanese and Caucasian Brief Affect Recognition Test (JACBART). *Journal of Nonverbal-Behavior* 24: 179–209.

Matthews, G. 1997. Extraversion, emotion, and performance: A cognitive-adaptive model. In G. Matthews, ed., *Cognitive science perspectives on personality and emotion*. Amsterdam: Elsevier, pp. 339–442.

Matthews, G. 2002. Towards a transactional ergonomics for driver stress and fatigue. *Theoretical Issues in Ergonomics Science* 3: 195–211.

Matthews, G., Campbell, S. E., Falconer, S., Joyner, L., Huggins, J., Gilliland, K., Grier, R., and Warm, J. S. 2002. Fundamental dimensions of subjective state in performance settings: Task engagement, distress, and worry. *Emotion* 2: 315–40.

Matthews, G., Deary, I. J., and Whiteman, M. C. 2003. *Personality Traits*, 2nd ed. Cambridge: Cambridge University Press.

Matthews, G., Derryberry, D., and Siegle, G. J. 2000. Personality and emotion: Cognitive science perspectives. In S. E. Hampson, ed., *Advances in Personality Psychology*, vol. 1. Philadelphia: Psychology Press/Taylor and Francis, pp. 199–237.

Matthews, G., Emo, A. K., Funke, G. J., Zeidner, M., Roberts, R. D., Costa, P. T., Jr., and Schulze, R. 2006. Emotional intelligence, personality, and task-induced stress. *Journal of Experimental Psychology Applied* 12: 96–107.

Matthews, G., Emo, A. K., Roberts, R. D., and Zeidner, M. 2006. What is this thing called emotional intelligence? In K. R. Murphy, ed., *A Critique of Emotional Intelligence: What Are the Problems and How Can They Be Fixed?* Mahwah, NJ: Erlbaum, pp. 3–6.

Matthews, G., and Funke, G. J. 2006. Worry and information-processing. In G. C. L. Davey and A. Wells, eds., *Worry and Psychological Disorders: Theory, Assessment and Treatment*. Chichester, UK: Wiley, pp. 51–68.

Matthews, G., Roberts, R. D., and Zeidner, M. 2004. Seven myths about emotional intelligence. *Psychological Inquiry* 15: 179–96.

Matthews, G., Schwean, V. L., Campbell, S. E., Saklofske, D. H., and Mohamed, A. A. R. 2000. Personality, self-regulation, and adaptation: A cognitive-social framework. In M. Boekaerts, P. R. Pintrich, and M. Zeidner, eds., *Handbook of Self-Regulation*. New York: Academic Press, pp. 171–207.

Matthews, G., and Wells, A. 2000. Attention, automaticity, and affective disorder. *Behavior Modification* 24: 69–93.

Matthews, G., and Zeidner, M. 2000. Emotional intelligence, adaptation to stressful encounters, and health outcomes. In R. Bar-On and J. D. A. Parker, eds., *The Handbook of Emotional Intelligence*. San Francisco: Jossey-Bass, pp. 459–89.

Matthews, G., and Zeidner, M. 2003. Negative appraisals of positive psychology: A mixed-valence endorsement of Lazarus. *Psychological Inquiry* 14: 137–43.

Matthews, G., Zeidner, M., and Roberts, R. D. 2002. *Emotional Intelligence: Science and Myth*. Cambridge: Bradford Book/MIT Press.

Matthews, G., Zeidner, M., and Roberts, R. D. 2005. Emotional intelligence: An elusive ability? In O. Wilhelm and Randall Engle, eds., *Handbook of Understanding and Measuring Intelligence*. Beverly Hills: Sage, pp. 79–100.

Matthews, G., Zeidner, M., and Roberts, R. D. 2006a. Measuring emotional intelligence: Promises, pitfalls, solutions? In A. D. Ong and M. H. Van Dulmen, eds., *Oxford Handbook of Methods in Positive Psychology*. Oxford: Oxford University Press, pp. 189–204.

Matthews, G., Zeidner, M., and Roberts, R. D. 2006b. Models of personality and affect for education: A review and synthesis. In P. A. Alexander and P. H. Winne, eds., *Handbook in Educational Psychology*, 2nd ed. Mahwah, NJ: Erlbaum, pp. 163–86.

Matthews, G., Zeidner, M., and Roberts, R. D., eds. 2007. *The Science of Emotional Intelligence: Knowns and Unknowns*. New York: Oxford University Press.

Mayer, J. D., Caruso, D. R., and Salovey, P. 1999. Emotional intelligence meets traditional standards for an intelligence. *Intelligence* 27: 267–98.

Mayer, J. D., Caruso, D. R., and Salovey, P. 2000. Selecting a measure of emotional intelligence: The case for ability scales. In R. Bar-On and J. D. A. Parker, eds., *The Handbook of Emotional Intelligence: Theory, Development, Assessment, and Application at Home, School, and in the Workplace*. San Francisco, CA: Jossey-Bass, pp. 320–42.

Mayer, J. D., Caruso, D. R., and Salovey, P. 2002. *The Mayer-Caruso-Salovey Emotional Intelligence Test (MSCEIT)*, Version 2.0. Toronto, Canada: Multi-Health Systems.

Mayer, J. D., and Geher, G. 1996. Emotional intelligence and the identification of emotion. *Intelligence* 22: 89–113.

Mayer, J. D., Goleman, D., Barrett, C., Gutstein, S., Boyatzis, R., Goldberg, E., Jung, A., Book, H., Goffee, R., Gergen, D., Harman, S., Lalich, J., George, W., Thomas, M. T., Bartz, C., Takeuchi, H., Stone, L., and Heifetz, R. 2004. Leading by feeling. *Harvard Business Review* 82: 27.

Mayer, J. D., Panter, A. T., Salovey, P., Caruso, D. R., and Sitarenios, G. A. 2005. Discrepancy in analyses of the MSCEIT—Resolving the mystery and understanding its implications: A reply to Gignac. *Emotion* 5: 236–37.

Mayer, J. D., Roberts, R. D., and Barsade, S. G. 2008. Human abilities: Emotional intelligence. *Annual Review of Psychology* 59: 507–536.

Mayer, J. D., and Salovey, P. 1993. The intelligence of emotional intelligence. *Intelligence* 17: 433–42.

Mayer, J. D., and Salovey, P. 1997. What is emotional intelligence? In P. Salovey and D. J. Sluyter, eds., *Emotional Development and Emotional Intelligence: Educational Implications*. New York: Basic Books, pp. 3–31.

Mayer, J. D., Salovey, P., and Caruso, D. R. 2000a. Emotional intelligence as zeitgeist, as personality, and as a mental ability. In R. Bar-On and J. D. A. Parker, eds., *The Handbook of Emotional Intelligence*. New York: Jossey-Bass.

Mayer, J. D., Salovey, P., and Caruso, D. R. 2000b. Competing models of emotional intelligence. In R. J. Sternberg, ed., *Handbook of Human Intelligence*, 2nd ed. New York: Cambridge University Press, pp. 396–420.

Mayer, J. D., Salovey, P., and Caruso, D. R. 2004. Emotional intelligence: Theory, findings, and implications. *Psychological Inquiry* 15: 197–215.

Mayer, J. D., Salovey, P., Caruso, D. R., and Sitarenios, G. 2003. Measuring emotional intelligence with the MSCEIT V2.0. *Emotion* 3: 97–105.

Mayne, T. J. 1999. Negative affect and health: The importance of being earnest. *Cognition and Emotion* 13: 601–35.

McCallum, M., and Piper, W. E. 2000. Psychological mindedness and emotional intelligence. In R. Bar-On and J. D. A. Parker, eds., *The Handbook of Emotional Intelligence*. San Francisco: Jossey-Bass, pp. 118–35.

McCombs, B. L. 2004. The learner-centered psychological principles: A framework for balancing academic achievement and social-emotional learning outcomes. In J. E. Zins, M. R. Weissberg, M. C. Wang, and H. J. Walberg, eds., *Building Academic Success on Social and Emotional Learning: What Does the Research Say?* New York: Teachers College Press, pp. 23–39.

McCrae, R. R. 2000. Emotional intelligence from the perspective of the big-five model of personality. In R. Bar-On and J. D. A. Parker, eds., *The Handbook of Emotional Intelligence*. San Francisco: Jossey-Bass, pp. 263–76.

McCrae, R. R., Costa, P. T., Jr., de Lima, M. P., Simoes, A., Ostendorf, F., Angleitner, A., Marusic, I., Bratko, D., Caprara, G. V., Barbaranelli, C., Chae, J. H., and Piedmont, R. L. 1999. Age differences in personality across the adult life span: Parallels in five cultures. *Developmental Psychology* 35: 466–77.

McCullough, M. E., Worthington, E. L. J., and Rachal, K. C. 1997. Interpersonal forgiving in close relationships. *Journal of Personality and Social Psychology* 73: 321–36.

McEnrue, M. P., and Groves, K. 2006. Choosing among tests of emotional intelligence: What is the evidence? *Human Resource Development Quarterly* 17: 9–42.

McEwen, B., and Lasley, E. N. 2007. Allostatic load: When protection gives way to damage. In A. Monat, R. S. Lazarus, and G. Reevy, eds., *The Praeger Handbook on Stress and Coping*, vol. 1. Westport, CT: Praeger, pp. 99–109.

McIsaac, H. K., and Eich, E. 2004. Vantage point in traumatic memory. *Psychological Science* 15: 248–53.

Messick, S. 1988. The once and future issues of validity: Assessing the meaning and consequences of measurement. In H. Wainer and H. Braun, eds., *Test Validity*. Hillsdale, NJ: Erlbaum, pp. 33–48.

Michielsen, H. J., Croon, M. A., Willemsen, T. M., De Vries, J., and Van Heck, G. L. 2007. Which constructs can predict emotional exhaustion in a working population? A study into its determinants. *Stress and Health: Journal of the International Society for the Investigation of Stress* 23: 121–30.

Mikolajczak, M., Menil, C., and Luminet, O. 2007. Explaining the protective effect of trait emotional intelligence regarding occupational stress: Exploration of emotional labour processes. *Journal of Research in Personality* 41: 1107–17.

Miller, J. D., and Lynam, D. R. 2006. Reactive and proactive aggression: Similarities and differences. *Personality and Individual Differences* 41: 1469–80.

Montagne, B., Schutters, S., Westenberg, H. G., van Honk, J., Kessels, R. P., and de Haan, E. H. 2006. Reduced sensitivity in the recognition of anger and disgust in social anxiety disorder. *Cognitive Neuropsychiatry* 11: 389–401.

Murphy, K. R., ed. 2006a. *A Critique of Emotional Intelligence: What Are the Problems and How Can They Be Fixed?* Mahwah, NJ: Erlbaum.

Murphy, K. R. 2006b. Four conclusions about emotional intelligence. In K. R. Murphy, ed., *A Critique of Emotional Intelligence: What Are the Problems and How Can They Be Fixed?* Mahwah, NJ: Erlbaum, pp. 345–54.

Murphy, K. R., and Sideman, L. 2006. The fadification of emotional intelligence. In K. R. Murphy, ed., *A Critique of Emotional Intelligence: What Are the Problems and How Can They Be Fixed?* Mahwah, NJ: Erlbaum, pp. 283–99.

Nation, M., Crusto, C., Wandersman, A., Kumpfer, K. L., Seybolt, D., Morrissey-Kane, E., and Davino, K. 2003. What works in prevention: Principles of effective prevention programs. *American Psychologist* 58: 449–556.

Nettle, D. 2006. Schizotypy and mental health amongst poets, visual artists, and mathematicians. *Journal of Research in Personality* 40: 876–90.

Newman, J. D., and Beehr, R. 1979. Personal and organizational strategies for handling job stress: A review of research and opinion. *Personnel Psychology* 32: 1–43.

Newsome, S., Day, A. L., and Catano, V. M. 2000. Assessing the predictive validity of emotional intelligence. *Personality and Individual Differences* 29: 1005–16.

NIOSH 1999. *Stress at Work*. Publication 99-101. Cincinnati, OH: DHHS.

Nolen-Hoeksema, S. 2001. Ruminative coping and adjustment to bereavement. In M. S. Stroebe, R. O. Hansson, W. Stroebe, and H. Schut, eds., *Handbook of Bereavement Research: Consequences, Coping, and Care*. Washington, DC: American Psychological Association, pp. 545–62.

Norton, P. J., and Hope, D. A. 2001. Kernels of truth or self-distorted perceptions: Self and observer ratings of social anxiety and performance. *Behavior Therapy* 32: 765–86.

Nowicki, S., and Carton, J. 1993. The measurement of emotional intensity from facial expressions. *Journal of Social Psychology* 133: 749–50.

Nowicki, S., and Duke, M. P. 1994. Individual differences in the nonverbal communication of affect: The Diagnostic Analysis of Nonverbal Accuracy Scale. *Journal of Nonverbal Behavior* 18: 9–35.

Nunnally, J. C. 1978. *Psychometric Theory*, 2nd ed. New York: McGraw-Hill.

Nykliček, I., Vingerhoets, A., and Denollet, J. 2002. Emotional (non-)expression and health: Data, questions, and challenges. *Psychology and Health* 17: 517–28.

O'Connor, R. M., and Little, I. S. 2003. Revising the predictive validity of emotional intelligence: Self-report versus ability-based measures. *Personality and Individual Differences* 35: 1893–1902.

O'Neil, R., and Parke, R. D. 2000. Family-peer relationships: The role of emotion regulation, cognitive understanding, and attentional processes as mediating processes. In K. A. Kerns, J. M. Contreras, and A. M. Neal-Barnett, eds., *Family and Peers: Linking Two Social Worlds*. New York: Praeger, pp. 195–225.

Oatley, K. 2004. Emotional intelligence and the intelligence of emotions. *Psychological Inquiry* 15: 216–38.

Oatley, K., and Johnson-Laird, P. N. 1995. The communicative theory of emotion: empirical tests, mental models, and implications for social interaction. In L. L. Martin and A. Tesser, eds., *Goals and Affect*. Hillsdale, NJ: Erlbaum, pp. 363–93.

O'Connor, R. M., and Little, I. S. 2003. Revisiting the predictive validity of emotional intelligence: Self-report versus ability-based measures. *Personality and Individual Differences* 35: 1893–1902.

O'Driscoll, M. P., and Cooper, C. L. 1994. Coping with work-related stress: A critique of existing measures and proposal for an alternative methodology. *Journal of Occupational and Organizational Psychology* 67: 343–54.

Oginska-Bulic, N. 2005. Emotional intelligence in the workplace: Exploring its effects on occupational stress and health outcomes in human service workers. *International Journal of Occupational Medicine and Environmental Health* 18: 167–75.

Olweus, D. 2001. Peer harassment: A critical analysis and some important issues. In J. Juvonen and S. Graham, eds., *Peer Harassment in School: The Plight of the Vulnerable and Victimized.* New York: Guilford Press, pp. 3–20.

Ones, D. S., Viswesvaran, C., and Schmidt, F. L. 1993. Comprehensive meta-analysis of integrity test validities: Findings and implications for personnel selection and theories of job performance. *Journal of Applied Psychology* 78: 679–703.

Ormel, J., and Wohlfardh, T. 1991 How neuroticism, long-term difficulties, and life situation change influence psychological distress: A longitudinal model. *Journal of Personality and Social Psychology* 60: 744–55.

O'Sullivan, M. 2007. Trolling for trout, trawling for tuna: The methodological morass in measuring emotional intelligence. In G. Matthews, M. Zeidner, and R. D. Roberts, eds., *The Science of Emotional Intelligence.* New York: Oxford University Press, pp. 283–87.

O'Sullivan, M., Guilford, J. P., and deMille, R. 1965. The measurement of social intelligence. Report 34. Psychological Laboratory, University of Southern California, Los Angeles.

Palmer, B. R., Donaldson, C., and Stough, C. 2002. Emotional intelligence and life satisfaction. *Personality and Individual Differences* 33: 1091–1100.

Palmer, B. R., Gignac, G., Manocha, R., and Stough, C. 2005. A psychometric evaluation of the Mayer-Salovey-Caruso Emotional Intelligence Test Version 2.0. *Intelligence* 33: 285–305.

Palmer, B. R., Manocha, R., Gignac, G., and Stough, C. 2003. Examining the factor structure of the Bar-On Emotional Quotient Inventory with an Australian general population sample. *Personality and Individual Differences* 35: 1191–1210.

Palmer, B. R., Walls, M., Burgess, Z., and Stough, C. 2001. Emotional intelligence and effective leadership. *Leadership and Organisational Development Journal* 22: 5–10.

Panksepp, J. 1998. *Affective Neuroscience: The Foundations of Human and Animal Emotions.* New York: Oxford University Press.

Papageorgiou, C., and Wells, A. 2003. An empirical test of a clinical metacognitive model of rumination and depression. *Cognitive Therapy and Research* 27: 261–73.

Parker, J. D. A. 2000. Emotional intelligence: Clinical and therapeutic implications. In R. Bar-On and J. D. A. Parker, eds., *The Handbook of Emotional Intelligence: Theory, Development, Assessment, and Application at Home, School, and in the Workplace.* San Francisco: Jossey-Bass, pp. 490–504.

Parker, J. D. A. 2005. The relevance of emotional intelligence for clinical psychology. In R. Schulze and R. D. Roberts, eds., *International Handbook of Emotional Intelligence.* Cambridge, MA: Hogrefe and Huber, pp. 271–88.

Parker, J. D. A., Creque Sr., R. E., Barnhart, D. L., Harris, J. I., Majeski, S. A., Wood, L. M., Bond, B. J., and Hogan, M. J. 2004. Academic achievement in high school: Does emotional intelligence matter? *Personality and Individual Differences* 37: 1321–30.

Parker, J. D. A., Hogan, M. J., Eastabrook, J. M., Oke, A., and Wood, L. M. 2006. Emotional intelligence and student retention: Predicting the successful transition from high school to university. *Personality and Individual Differences* 41: 1329–36.

Parker, J. D. A., Summerfeldt, L. J., Hogan, M. J., and Majeski, S. A. 2004. Emotional intelligence and academic success: Examining the transition from high school to university. *Personality and Individual Differences* 36: 163–72.

Parker, J. D. A., Taylor, G. J., and Bagby, R. M. 2001. The relationship between emotional intelligence and alexithymia. *Personality and Individual Differences* 30: 107–15.

Parkinson, B. 1996. Emotions are social. *British Journal of Psychology* 87: 663–83.

Parkinson, B., Fischer, A. H., and Manstead, A. S. R. 2005. *Emotions in Social Relations: Cultural, Group, and Interpersonal Processes.* New York: Psychology Press.

Parrott, W. G. 2002. The functional utility of negative emotions. In L. Feldman-Barrett and P. Salovey, eds., *The Wisdom in Feeling: Psychological Processes in Emotional Intelligence.* New York: Guilford Press, pp. 341–59.

Patti, J., and Lantieri, L. 1999. Waging peace in our schools: Social and emotional learning through conflict resolution. In J. Cohen, ed., *Educating Minds and Hearts: Social Emotional Learning and the Passage into Adolescence.* New York: Columbia University Press, pp. 126–36.

Paulhus, D. L. 1998. Interpersonal and intrapsychic adaptiveness of trait self-enhancement: A mixed blessing? *Journal of Personality and Social Psychology* 74: 1197–1208.

Paulhus, D. L., and John, O. P. 1998. Egoistic and moralistic biases in self-perception: The interplay of self-deceptive styles with basic traits and motives. *Journal of Personality* 66: 1025–60.

Paulhus, D. L., Lysy, D. C., and Yik, M. S. M. 1998. Self-report measures of intelligence: Are they useful proxies as IQ tests? *Journal of Personality* 66: 525–54.

Payne, W. L. 1986. A study of emotion: Developing emotional intelligence; self integration; relating to fear, pain and desire. *Dissertation Abstracts International* 47: 203A.

Pearlin, L. I., and Schooler, C. 1978. The structure of coping. *Journal of Health and Social Behavior* 19: 2–21.

Pekrun, R., and Frese, M. 1992. Emotions in work and achievement. *International Review of Industrial and Organizational Psychology* 7: 154–200.

Pennebaker, J. W. 1992. Inhibition as the linchpin of health. In H. S. Friedman, ed., Hostility, coping, and health. Washington, DC: American Psychological Association, pp. 127–39.

Pennebaker, J. W. 1997. Writing about emotional experiences as a therapeutic process. *Psychological Science* 8: 162–66.

Pennebaker, J. W., Kiecold-Glaser, J., and Glaser, R. 1988. Confronting traumatic experience and immunocompetence: A reply to Neale, Cox, Valdimarsdottir, and Stone. *Journal of Consulting and Clinical Psychology* 56: 638–39.

Perez, J. C., Petrides, K. V., and Furnham, A. 2005. Measuring trait emotional intelligence. In R. Schulze and R. D. Roberts, eds., *Emotional Intelligence: An International Handbook* (pp. 181–201). Cambridge, MA: Hogrefe and Huber, pp. 181–201.

Pervin, L. A., Cervone, D., and John, O. P. 2005. *Personality: Theory and Research.* New York: Wiley.

Petrides, K. V., Fredrickson, N., and Furnham, A. 2004. The role of trait emotional intelligence in academic performance and deviant behavior at school. *Personality and Individual Differences* 36: 277–93.

Petrides, K. V., and Furnham, A. 2000. On the dimensional structure of emotional intelligence. *Personality and Individual Differences* 29: 313–20.

Petrides, K. V., and Furnham, A. 2001. Trait emotional intelligence: Psychometric investigation with reference to established trait taxonomies. *European Journal of Personality* 15: 425–48.

Petrides, K. V., and Furnham, A. 2003. Trait emotional intelligence: Behavioural validation in two studies of emotion recognition and reactivity to mood induction. *European Journal of Personality* 17: 39–57.

Petrides, K. V., and Furnham, A. 2006. The role of trait emotional intelligence in a gender-specific model of organizational variables. *Journal of Applied Social Psychology* 36: 552–69

Petrides, K. V., Furnham, A., and Mavroveli, S. 2007. Trait emotional intelligence: Moving forward in the field of EI. In G. Matthews, M. Zeidner, and R. D. Roberts, eds., *The Science of Emotional Intelligence: Knowns and Unknowns.* New York: Oxford University Press, pp. 151–66.

Petrides, K. V., Pérez-González, J. C., and Furnham, A. 2007. On the criterion and incremental validity of trait emotional intelligence. *Cognition and Emotion* 21: 26–55.

Philippot, P., and Douilliez, C. 2005. Social phobics do not misinterpret facial expression of emotion. *Behaviour Research and Therapy* 43: 639–52.

Pierloot, R., and Vinck, J. 1977. A pragmatic approach to the concept of alexithymia. *Psychotherapy and Psychosomatics* 28: 156–66.

Pitterman, H., and Nowicki, S. J. 2004. A test of the ability to identify emotion in human standing and sitting postures: The Diagnostic Analysis of Nonverbal Accuracy-2 Posture Test (DANVA2-POS). *Genetic, Social, and General Psychology Monographs* 130: 146–62.

Pizzino, A. 2002. Dealing with violence in the workplace: The experience of Canadian unions. In M. Gill, B. Fisher, and V. Bowie, eds., *Violence at Work: Causes, Patterns, and Prevention.* Cullompton, UK: Willan, pp. 165–79.

Prati, M., Douglas, C., Ferris, G. R., Ammeter, A. P., and Buckley, M. R. 2003. The role of emotional intelligence in team leadership: Reply to the critique by Antonakis. *The International Journal of Organizational Analysis* 11: 361–67.

Purdon, C. 2004. Empirical investigations of thought suppression in OCD. *Journal of Behavior Therapy and Experimental Psychiatry* 35: 121–36.

Rafaeli, A., and Sutton, R. I. 1989. The expression of emotion in organizational life. *Research in Organizational Behavior* 11: 1–42.

Ramos, N. S., Fernandez-Berrocal, P., and Extremera, N. 2007. Perceived emotional intelligence facilitates cognitive-emotional processes of adaptation to an acute stressor. *Cognition and Emotion* 21: 758–72.

Raine, A. 2002. The role of prefrontal deficits, low autonomic arousal, and early health factors in the development of antisocial and aggressive behavior in children. *Journal of Child Psychology and Psychiatry* 43: 417–34.

Repetti, R. L. 1993. The effects of workload and the social environment at work on health. In L. Goldberger and S. Breznitz, eds., *Handbook of Stress: Theoretical and Clinical Aspects.* New York: Free Press, pp. 368–85.

Reis, D. L., Brackett, M. A., Shamosh, N. A., Kiehl, K. A., Salovey, P., and Gray, J. R. 2007. Emotional intelligence predicts individual differences in social exchange reasoning. *NeuroImage* 35: 1385–91.

Rammstedt, B., and Rammsayer, E. 2000. Sex differences in self-estimates of different aspects of intelligence. *Personality and Individual Difference* 20: 869–80.

Renneberg, B., Heyn, K., Gebhard, R., and Bachmann, S. 2005. Facial expression of emotions in borderline personality disorder and depression. *Journal of Behavior Therapy and Experimental Psychiatry* 36: 183–96.

Riley, H., and Schutte, N. S. 2003. Low emotional intelligence as a predictor of substance-use problems. *Journal of Drug Education* 33: 391–98.

Rivers, S. E., Brackett, M. A., Salovey, P., and Mayer, J. D. 2007. Measuring emotional intelligence as a set of mental abilities. In G. Matthews, M. Zeidner, and R. D. Roberts, eds., *The Science of Emotional Intelligence: Knowns and Unknowns.* New York: Oxford University Press, pp. 230–57.

Roberts, R. D., Beh, H. C., and Stankov, L. 1988. Hick's law, competing-task performance, and intelligence. *Intelligence* 12: 111–30.

Roberts, R. D., Markham, P. M., Matthews, G., and Zeidner, M. 2005. Assessing intelligence: Past, present, and future. In O. Wilhelm and Randall Engle, eds., *Handbook of Understanding and Measuring Intelligence.* Thousand Oaks, CA: Sage, pp. 333–60.

Roberts, R. D., Schulze, R., and MacCann, C. 2008. The measurement of emotional intelligence: A decade of progress? In G. Boyle, G. Matthews, and D. Saklofske, eds., *The Sage Handbook of Personality Theory and Assessment. Vol. 1. Personality Theories and Models.* Thousand Oaks, CA: Sage, pp. 461–69.

Roberts, R. D., Schulze, R., O'Brien, K., MacCann, C., Reid, J., and Maul, A. 2006. Exploring the validity of the Mayer-Salovey-Caruso Emotional Intelligence Test (MSCEIT) with established emotions measures. *Emotion* 6: 663–69.

Roberts, R. D., Schulze, R., Zeidner, M., and Matthews, G. 2005. Understanding, measuring, and applying emotional intelligence: What have we learned? What have we missed? In R. Schulze and R. D. Roberts, eds., *International Handbook of Emotional Intelligence*. Cambridge, MA: Hogrefe and Huber, pp. 311–41.

Roberts, R. D., and Stankov, L. 1999. Individual differences in speed of mental processing and human cognitive abilities: Towards a taxonomic model. *Learning and Individual Differences* 11: 1–120.

Roberts, R. D., Stankov, L., Schulze, R., and Kyllonen, P. C. 2007. Extending intelligence: Conclusions and future directions. In P. C. Kyllonen, R. D. Roberts, and L. Stankov, eds., *Extending Intelligence: Enhancement and New Constructs*. Mahwah, NJ: Erlbaum, pp. 433–452.

Roberts, R. D., Zeidner, M., and Matthews, G. 2001. Does emotional intelligence meet traditional standards for an intelligence? Some new data and conclusion. *Emotion* 1: 196–231.

Roberts, R. D., Zeidner, M., and Matthews, G. 2007. Emotional intelligence: Knowns and unknowns. In G. Matthews, M. Zeidner, and R. D. Roberts, eds., *The Science of Emotional Intelligence: Knowns and Unknowns*. New York: Oxford University Press, pp. 419–74.

Roberts, W., and Strayer, J. 1996. Empathy, emotional expressiveness, and prosocial behavior. *Child Development* 67: 449–70.

Rogge, R. D., Bradbury, T. N., Hahlweg, K., Engl, J., and Thurmaier, F. 2006. Prediction of marital satisfaction and dissolution over 5 years: Refining the two-factor hypothesis. *Journal of Family Psychology* 20: 156–59.

Rolls, E. T. 1999. *The Brain and Emotion*. New York: Oxford University Press.

Rolls, E. T. 2007. A neurobiological approach to emotional intelligence. In G. Matthews, M. Zeidner, and R. D. Roberts, eds., *The Science of Emotional Intelligence: Knowns and Unknowns*. New York: Oxford University Press, pp. 72–100.

Romasz, T. E., Kantor, J. H., and Elias, M. J. 2004. Implementation and evaluation of urban school-wide social-emotional learning programs. *Evaluation and Program Planning* 27: 89–103.

Roseman, I. J. 1984. Cognitive determinants of emotion: A structural theory. *Review of Personality and Social Psychology* 5: 11–36.

Rosenthal, R., Archer, D., Hall, J. A., DiMatteo, M. R., and Rogers, P. L. 1979. Measuring sensitivity to nonverbal communication: The PONS test. In A. Wolfgang, ed., *Nonverbal Behavior: Applications and Cultural Implications*. New York: Academic Press.

Rosete, D., and Ciarrochi, J. 2005. Emotional intelligence and its relationship to workplace performance outcomes of leadership effectiveness. *Leadership and Organization Development Journal* 26: 388–99.

Rothbart, M. K., and Derryberry, D. 1981. Development of individual differences in temperament. In M. E. Lamb and A. L. Brown, eds., *Advances in Developmental Psychology*. Hillsdale, NJ: Erlbaum, pp. 37–86.

Rozell, E. J., Pettijohn, C. E., and Parker, R. S. 2004. Customer-oriented selling: Exploring the roles of emotional intelligence and organizational commitment. *Psychology and Marketing* 21: 405–24.

Rubin, K. H., and Clark, M. L. 1983. Preschool teachers' ratings of behavioral problems: Observational, sociometric, and social-cognitive correlates. *Journal of Abnormal Child Psychology* 11: 273–86.

Rude, S. S., and McCarthy, C. J. 2003. Emotion regulation in depressed and depression vulnerable college students. *Cognition and Emotion* 17: 799–806.

Rufer, M., Ziegler, A., Alsleben, H., Fricke, S., Ortmann, J., Bruckner, E., Hand, I., and Peter, H. 2006. A prospective long-term follow-up study of alexithymia in obsessive-compulsive disorder. *Comprehensive Psychiatry* 47: 394–98.

Saarni, C. 1999. *The Development of Emotional Competence*. New York: Guilford Press.

Saarni, C. 2000a. Emotional competence: A developmental perspective. In R. Bar-On and J. D. A. Parker, eds., *The Handbook of Emotional Intelligence*. San-Francisco: Jossey-Bass, pp. 68–91.

Saarni, C. 2000b. The social context of emotional development. In M. Lewis and J. Haviland, eds., *The Handbook of Emotion*, 2nd ed. New York: Guilford Press, pp. 306–22.

Sabin, F. R., and Turpin, G. 2003. Vicarious traumatization: Implications for the mental health of health workers? *Clinical Psychology Review* 23: 449–80.

Sacks, O. 1995. *An Anthropologist on Mars*. New York: Vintage Books.

Saklofske, D. H., Austin, E. J., Galloway, J., and Davidson, K. 2007. Individual difference correlates of health-related behaviours: Preliminary evidence for links between emotional intelligence and coping. *Personality and Individual Differences* 42: 491–502.

Saklofske, D. H., Austin, E. J., and Minski, P. S. 2003. Factor structure and validity of a trait emotional intelligence measure. *Personality and Individual Differences* 34: 707–21.

Sala, F. 2002. *Emotional Competence Inventory (ECI): Technical Manual*. Boston: Hay/McBer Group.

Salin, D. 2003. Ways of explaining workplace bullying: A review of enabling, motivating, and precipitating structures and processes in the work environment. *Human Relations* 56: 1213–32.

Salkovskis, P. M. 1999. Understanding and treating obsessive-compulsive disorder. *Behaviour Research and Therapy* 37(suppl. 1): S29–S52.

Salovey, P., Bedell, B. T., Detweiler, J. B., and Mayer, J. D. 1999. Coping intelligently: Emotional intelligence and the coping process. In C. R. Snyder, ed., *Coping: The Psychology of What Works*. New York: Oxford University Press, pp. 141–64.

Salovey, P., Bedell, B. T., Detweiler, J. B., and Mayer, J. D. (2000). Current directions in emotional intelligence research. In M. Lewis and J. M. Haviland-Jones, eds., *Handbook of Emotions*. New York: Guilford Press, pp. 504–20.

Salovey, P., Hsee, C. K., and Mayer, J. D. 1993. Emotional intelligence and the self-regulation of affect. In D. M. Wegner and J. W. Pennebaker, eds., *Handbook of Mental Control*. Englewood, NJ: Prentice-Hall, pp. 258–77.

Salovey, P., and Mayer, J. D. 1990. Emotional intelligence. *Imagination, Cognition, and Personality* 9: 185–211.

Salovey, P., Mayer, J. D., Goldman, S., Turvey, C., and Palfai, T. 1995. Emotional attention, clarity, and repair: Exploring emotional intelligence using the Trait Meta-mood Scale. In J. W. Pennebaker, ed., *Emotion, Disclosure, and Health*. Washington, DC: American Psychological Association, pp. 125–54.

Salovey, P., Stroud, L. R., Woolery, A., and Epel, E. S. 2002. Perceived emotional intelligence, stress reactivity, and symptom reports: Further explorations using the trait meta-mood scale. *Psychology and Health* 17: 611–27.

Schabracq, M. J. 2003. Organisational culture, stress, and change. In M. J. Schabracq, J. A. M. Winnubst, and C. L. Cooper, eds., *The Handbook of Work and Health Psychology*. New York: Wiley, pp. 37–62.

Schat, A. C. H., and Kelloway, E. K. 2005a. Workplace aggression. In J. Barling, E. K. Kelloway, and M. R. Frone, eds., *Handbook of Work Stress*. Thousand Oaks, CA: Sage, pp. 189–218.

Schat, A. C. H., and Kelloway, E. K. 2005b. Training as a workplace aggression intervention strategy. In E. K. Kelloway, J. Barling, and J. J. Hurrell Jr. eds., *Handbook of Workplace Violence*. Thousand Oaks, CA: Sage, pp. 579–605.

Schaubroeck, J., and Jones, J. R. 2000. Antecedents of workplace emotional labor dimensions and moderators of their effects on physical symptoms. *Journal of Organizational Behavior* 21: 163–83.

Scherer, K. R. 2007. Componential emotion theory can inform models of emotional competence. In G. Matthews, M. Zeidner, and R. D. Roberts, eds., *The Science of Emotional Intelligence: Knowns and Unknowns.* New York: Oxford University Press, pp. 101–26.

Scherer, K. R., Banse, R., and Wallbott, H. G. 2001. Emotion inferences from vocal expression correlate across languages and cultures. *Journal of Cross-cultural Psychology* 32: 76–92.

Scherer, K. R., Schorr, A., and Johnstone, T., eds. 2001. *Appraisal Processes in Emotion.* New York: Oxford University Press.

Schmidt, F. L., and Hunter, J. E. 1998. The validity and utility of selection methods in personnel psychology: Practical and theoretical implications of 85 years of research findings. *Psychological Bulletin* 124: 262–74.

Schnall, P. L., Landsbergis, P. A., and Baker, D. 1994. Job strain and cardiovascular health. *Annual Review of Public Health* 15: 381–411.

Schneider, S. L. 2001. In search of realistic optimism: Meaning, knowledge, and warm fuzzies. *American Psychologist* 56: 250–63.

Schore, A. N. 2001. The effects of early relationship trauma on right brain development, affect regulation, and infant mental health. *Infant Mental Health Journal* 22: 201–69.

Schuler, R. S. 1980. Definition and conceptualization of stress in organizations. *Organizational Behavior and Human Performance* 25: 184–215.

Schutte, N. S., Malouff, J. M., Bobik, C., Coston, T. D., Greeson, C., Jedlicka, C., and Rhodes, E. W. G. 2001. Emotional intelligence and interpersonal relations. *Journal of Social Psychology* 141: 523–36.

Schutte, N. S., Malouff, J. M., Hall, L. E., Haggerty, D. J., Cooper, J. T., Golden, C. J., and Dornheim, L. 1998. Development and validation of a measure of emotional intelligence. *Personality and Individual Differences* 25: 167–77.

Schutte, N. S., Malouff, J. M., Simunek, M., McKenlye, J., and Hollander, S. 2002. Characteristic emotional intelligence and emotional well-being. *Cognition and Emotion* 16: 769–85.

Schutte, N. S., Malouff, J. M., Thorsteinsson, E. B., Bhullar, N., and Rooke, S. E. 2007. A meta-analytic investigation of the relationship between emotional intelligence and health. *Personality and Individual Differences* 42: 921–33.

Seligman, M., and Csikszentmihalyi, M. 2000. Positive psychology: An introduction. *American Psychologist* 55: 5–14.

Shenk, J. W. 2005. *Lincoln's Melancholy.* Boston: Houghton Mifflin.

Shinn, M., Rosario, M., Morch, H., and Chesnut, D. E. 1984. Coping with job stress and burnout in the human services. *Journal of Personality and Social Psychology* 46: 864–76.

Shirom, A. 2003. The effects of work stress on health. In M. J. Schabracq, J. A. M. Winnubst, and C. L. Cooper, eds., *The Handbook of Work and Health Psychology.* New York: Wiley, pp. 63–82.

Shoda, Y., Mischel, W., and Peake, P. K. 1990. Predicting adolescent cognitive and self-regulatory competencies from preschool delay of gratification: Identifying diagnostic conditions. *Developmental Psychology* 26: 978–86.

Shriver, T. P., Schwab-Stone, M., and DeFalco, K. 1999. Why SEL is the better way: The New Haven Social Development Program. In J. Cohen, ed., *Educating Minds and Hearts: Social Emotional Learning and the Passage into Adolescence.* New York: Teachers College Press, pp. 43–60.

Sidanius, J., and Pratto, F. 1999. *Social Dominance: An Intergroup Theory of Social Hierarchy and Oppression.* Cambridge: Cambridge University Press.

Sifneos, P. E. 1972. *Short-term Psychotherapy and Emotional Crisis.* Cambridge: Harvard University Press.

Simpson, J. A., Ickes, W., and Blackstone, T. 1995. When the head protects the heart: Empathic accuracy in dating relationships. *Journal of Personality and Social Psychology* 69: 629–41.

Sinclair, R. C., and Mark, M. M. 1995. The effects of mood state on judgmental accuracy: Processing strategy as a mechanism. *Cognition and Emotion* 9: 417–38.

Skinner, C., and Spurgeon, P. 2005. Valuing empathy and emotional intelligence in health leadership: A study of empathy, leadership behavior, and outcome effectiveness. *Health Services Management Research* 18: 1–12.

Slaski, M. 2001. An investigation into emotional intelligence, managerial stress, and performance in a UK supermarket chain. Unpublished manuscript.

Slaski, M., and Cartwright, S. 2002. Health, performance, and emotional intelligence: An exploratory study of retail managers. *Stress and Health* 18: 63–68.

Smillie, L. D., Yeo, G. B., Furnham, A., and Jackson, C. J. 2006. Benefits of all work and no play: The relationship between neuroticism and performance as a function of resource allocation. *Journal of Applied Psychology* 91: 139–55.

Smith, M., and Walden, T. 1999. Understanding feelings and coping with emotional situations: A comparison of maltreated and nonmaltreated preschoolers. *Social Development* 8: 93–116.

Spearman, C. E. 1923. *The Nature of Intelligence and the Principles of Cognition.* London: Macmillan.

Spielberger, C. D., and Reheiser, E. C. 2005. Occupational stress and health. In A. G. Antoniou and C. L. Cooper, eds., *New Perspectives in Occupational Health Psychology.* Cheltenham, Great Britain: Edward Elgar, pp. 441–54.

Spitzer, C., Siebel-Jurges, U., Barnow, S., Grabe, H. J., and Freyberger, H. J. 2005. Alexithymia and interpersonal problems. *Psychotherapy and Psychosomatics* 74: 240–46.

Sternberg, R. J. 1985. *Beyond IQ: A Triarchic Theory of Human Intelligence.* Cambridge, UK: Cambridge University Press.

Sternberg, R. J. 2002. *Why Smart People Can Be So Stupid.* New Haven, CT: Yale University Press.

Stevens, D., Charman, T., and Blair, R. J. R. 2001. Recognition of emotion in facial expressions and vocal tones in children with psychopathic tendencies. *Journal of Genetic Psychology* 16: 201–11.

Stone, S. V., and Costa, P. T., Jr. 1990. Disease-prone personality or distress-prone personality. In H. S. Friedman, ed., *Personality and Disease.* New York: Wiley, pp. 178–200.

Stout, M. 2000. *The Feel-Good Curriculum: The Dumbing down of America's Kids in the Name of Self-Esteem.* Cambridge, MA: Perseus Books.

Strahan, E. Y. 2003. The effects of social anxiety and social skills on academic performance. *Personality and Individual Differences* 38: 187–201.

Suls, J. 2001. Affect, stress, and personality. In J. P. Forgas, ed., *Handbook of Affect and Social Cognition.* Mahwah, NJ: Erlbaum, pp. 392–409.

Summerfeldt, L. J., Kloosterman, P. H., Antony, M., and Parker, J. D. A. 2006. Social anxiety, emotional intelligence, and interpersonal adjustment. *Journal of Psychopathology and Behavioral Assessment* 28: 57–68.

Surguladze, S. A., Young, A. W., Senior, C., Brebion, G., Travis, M. J., and Phillips, M. L. 2004. Recognition accuracy and response bias to happy and sad facial expressions in patients with major depression. *Neuropsychology* 18: 212–18.

Surtees, P. G., and Wainwright, N. W. J. 1996. Fragile states of mind: Neuroticism, vulnerability, and the long-term outcome of depression. *British Journal of Psychiatry* 169: 338–47.

Sutton, J., and Keogh, E. 2000. Social competition in school: Relationships with bullying, Machiavellianism, and personality. *British Journal of Educational Psychology* 70: 443–56.

Swiller, H. 1988. Alexithymia: Treatment utilizing combined individual and group psychotherapy. *International Journal of Group Psychotherapy* 38: 47–61.

Sy, T., Tram, S., and O'Hara, L. A. 2006. Relation of employee and manager emotional intelligence to job satisfaction and performance. *Journal of Vocational Behavior* 68: 461–73.

Sykes, C. J. 1995. *Dumbing down Our Kids: Why America's Children Feel Good about Themselves but Can't Read, Write, or Add*. New York: St. Martin's Griffin.

Taylor, G. J. 2000. Recent developments in alexithymia theory and research. *Canadian Journal of Psychiatry* 45: 134–42.

Taylor, G. J., and Bagby, R. M. 2000. An overview of the alexithymia construct. In R. Bar-On and J. D. A. Parker, eds., *The Handbook of Emotional Intelligence*. San Francisco: Jossey-Bass, pp. 40–67.

Taylor, G. J., and Bagby, R. M. 2004. New trends in alexithymia research. *Psychotherapy and Psychosomatics* 63: 68–77.

Taylor, G. J., Parker, J. D. A., and Bagby, R. M. 1999. Emotional intelligence and the emotional brain: Points of convergence and implications for psychoanalysis. *Journal of the American Academy of Psychoanalysis* 27: 339–54.

Teasdale, J. D., Segal, Z. V., Williams, J. M., Ridgeway, V. A., Soulsby, J. M., and Lau, M. A. 2000. Prevention of relapse/recurrence in major depression by mindfulness-based cognitive therapy. *Journal of Consulting Clinical Psychology* 68: 615–23.

Terracciano, A., McCrae, R. R., Brant, L., and Costa, P. T., Jr. 2005. Hierarchical linear modeling analyses of the NEO-PI-R Scales in the Baltimore Longitudinal Study of Aging. *Psychology and Aging* 20: 493–506.

Tett, R. P., Fox, K. E., and Wang, A. 2005. Development and validation of a self-report measure of emotional intelligence as a multidimensional trait domain. *Personality and Social Psychology Bulletin* 31: 859–88.

Thayer, R. E. 1996. *The Origin of Everyday Moods: Managing Energy, Tension, and Stress*. New York: Oxford University Press.

Thomas, B. J. 1952. *Abraham Lincoln: A Biography*. New York: Knopf.

Thompson, R. A. 1998. Emotional competence and the development of self. *Psychological Inquiry* 9: 308–309.

Thorndike, E. L. 1920. Intelligence and its uses. *Harper's Magazine* 140: 227–35.

Thurstone, L. L. 1931. Multiple factor analysis. *Psychological Review* 38: 406–27.

Thurstone, L. L. 1938. *Primary Mental Abilities*. Chicago: University of Chicago Press.

Topping, K. J., Holmes, E. A., and Bremner, W. G. 2000. The effectiveness of school-based programs: For the promotion of social competence. In R. Bar-On and J. D. A. Parker, eds., *The Handbook of Emotional Intelligence*. San Francisco: Jossey-Bass, pp. 411–32.

Trapnell, P. D., and Wiggins, J. S. 1990. Extension of the interpersonal adjective scales to include the big five dimensions of personality. *Journal of Personality and Social Psychology* 59: 781–90.

Trentacosta, C. J., Izard, C. E., Mostow, A. J., and Fine, S. E. 2006. Children's emotional competence and attentional competence in early elementary school. *School Psychology Quarterly* 21: 148–70.

Trinidad, D. R., and Johnson, C. A. 2002. The association between emotional intelligence and early adolescent tobacco and alcohol use. *Personality and Individual Differences* 32: 95–105.

Trinidad, D. R., Unger, J. B., Chou, C., Azen, S. P., and Johnson, C. A. 2004a. Emotional intelligence and smoking risk factors in adolescents: Interactions on smoking intentions. *Journal of Adolescent Health* 34: 46–55.

Trinidad, D. R., Unger, J. B., Chou, C. P., and Johnson, C. A. 2004b. The protective association of emotional intelligence with psychosocial smoking risk factors for adolescents. *Personality and Individual Differences* 36: 945–54.

Tripp, T. M., and Bies, R. J. 1997. What's good about revenge? The avenger's perspective. In R. J. Lewicki, R. J. Bies, and B. H. Sheppard, eds., *Research on Negotiation in Organizations*, vol. 6. Greenwich, CT: JAI Press, pp. 145–60.

Trull, T. J., and Sher, K. J. 1994. Relationship between the five-factor model of personality and axis I disorders in a nonclinical sample. *Journal of Abnormal Psychology* 103: 350–60.

Twenge, J. M. 2000. The age of anxiety? The birth cohort change in anxiety and neuroticism, 1952–1993. *Journal of Personality and Social Psychology* 79: 1007–21

Twenge, J. M. 2006. *Generation Me: Why Today's Young Americans Are More Confident, Assertive, Entitled—and More Miserable Than Ever Before*. New York: Free Press

Twenge, J. M., and Im, C. 2007. Changes in the need for social approval, 1958–2001. *Journal of Research in Personality* 41: 171–89.

Vachon, D., and Bagby, R. M. 2007. The clinical utility of emotional intelligence: Association with related constructs, treatment, and psychopathology. In G. Matthews, M. Zeidner, and R. D. Roberts, eds., *The Science of Emotional Intelligence: Knowns and Unknowns*. New York: Oxford University Press, pp. 339–55.

Vakola, M., Tsaousis, I., and Nikolaou, I. 2004. The role of emotional intelligence and personality variables on attitudes toward organizational change. *Journal of Managerial Psychology* 19: 88–110.

Van der Kolk, B. A., and McFarlane, A. C. 1996. The black hole of trauma. In B. A. van der Kolk, A. C. McFarlane, and L. Weisaeth, eds., *Traumatic Stress: The Effects of Overwhelming Experience on Mind, Body, and Society*. New York: Guilford Press, pp. 3–23.

Van der Linden, W. J. 1996. Assembling tests for the measurement of multiple traits. *Applied Psychological Measurement* 20: 373–88.

Van der Zee, K., and Wabeke, R. 2004. Is trait emotional intelligence simply or more than just a trait? *European Journal of Personality* 18: 243–63.

Van Ghent, D. 1953. *The English Novel: Form and Function*. New York: Harper and Row.

Van Rooy, D. L., Dilchert, S., Viswesvaran, C., and Ones, D. S. 2006. Multiplying intelligences: Are general, emotional, and practical intelligence equal? In K. R. Murphy, ed., *A Critique of Emotional Intelligence: What Are the Problems and How Can They Be Fixed?* Mahwah, NJ: Erlbaum, pp. 235–62.

Van Rooy, D. L., and Viswesvaran, C. 2004. Emotional intelligence: A meta-analytic investigation of predictive validity and nomological net. *Journal of Vocational Behavior* 65: 71–95.

Vermeulen, N., Luminet, O., and Corneille, O. 2006. Alexithymia and the automatic processing of affective information: Evidence from the affective priming paradigm. *Cognition and Emotion* 20: 64–91.

Vitale, J. E., Newman, J. P., Bates, J. E., Goodnight, J., Dodge, K. A., and Pettit, G. 2005. Deficient behavioral inhibition and anomalous selective attention in a community sample of adolescents with psychopathic traits and low-anxiety traits. *Journal of Abnormal Child Psychology* 33: 461–70.

Vitaro, F., Gendreau, P. L., Tremblay, R. E., and Oligny, P. 1998. Reactive and proactive aggression differentially predict later conduct problems. *Journal of Child Psychiatry and Psychology* 39: 377–85.

Wagner, R. J. 2000. Practical intelligence. In R. J. Sternberg, ed., *Handbook of Human Intelligence*, 2nd ed. New York: Cambridge University Press, pp. 380–95.

Wakabayashi, A., Baron-Cohen, S., and Wheelwright, S. 2006. Are autistic traits an independent personality dimension? A study of the Autism-Spectrum Quotient (AQ) and the NEO-PI-R. *Personality and Individual Differences* 41: 873–83.

Waldeck, T. L., and Miller, L. S. 2000. Social skill deficit in schizotypal personality disorder. *Psychiatry Research* 93: 237–46.

Wallace, J. F., and Newman, J. P. 2004. A theory-based treatment model for psychopathy. *Cognitive and Behavioral Practice* 11: 178–89.

Warwick, J., and Nettelbeck, T. 2004. Emotional intelligence is …? *Personality and Individual Differences* 37: 1091–1100.

Waterhouse, L. 2006. Inadequate evidence for multiple intelligences, Mozart effect, and emotional intelligence theories. *Educational Psychologist* 41: 247–55.

Watson, D., and Clark, L. A. 1988. Development and validation of brief measures of positive and negative affect: The PANAS scales. *Journal of Personality and Social Psychology* 54: 1063–70.

Wedeck, J. 1947. The relationship between personality and "psychological ability." *British Journal of Psychology* 37: 133–51.

Weis, S., and Suess, H.-M. 2005. Social intelligence: A review and critical discussion of measurement concepts. In R. Schulze and R. D. Roberts, eds., *International Handbook of Emotional Intelligence*. Cambridge, MA: Hogrefe and Huber, pp. 203–30.

Weisinger, H. 1998. *Emotional Intelligence at Work: The Untapped edge for Success*. San Francisco: Jossey-Bass.

Weissberg, R. P., and Greenberg, M. T. 1998. School and community competence-enhancement and prevention programs. In I. E. Siegel and K. A. Renninger, eds., *Handbook of Child Psychology*, vol. 4. *Child Psychology in Practice*, 5th ed. New York: Wiley, pp. 877–954.

Weissberg, R. P., Kumpfer, K., and Seligman, M. E. P. 2003. Prevention that works for children and youth: An introduction. *American Psychologist* 58: 425–32.

Welbourne, J. L., Eggerth, D., Hartley, T. A., Andrew, M. E., and Sanchez, F. 2007. Coping strategies in the workplace: Relationships with attributional style and job satisfaction. *Journal of Vocational Behavior* 70: 312–25

Wells, A. 1997. *Cognitive Therapy of Anxiety Disorders: A Practice Manual and Conceptual Guide*. Chichester, UK: John Wiley.

Wells, A. 2000. *Emotional Disorders and Metacognition: Innovative Cognitive Therapy*. Chichester, UK: Wiley.

Wells, A., and Matthews, G. 1994. *Attention and Emotion: A Clinical Perspective*. Hove, UK: Erlbaum.

Wells, A., and Matthews, G. 2006. Cognitive vulnerability to anxiety disorders: An integration. In L. B. Alloy and J. H. Riskind, eds., *Cognitive vulnerability to emotional disorders*. Mahwah, NJ: Erlbaum, pp. 303–25.

Welsh, M., Park, R. D., Widaman, K., and O'Neil, R. 2001. Linkages between children's social and academic competence: A longitudinal analysis. *Journal of School Psychology* 39: 463–81.

Wentzel, K. R. 1994. Relations of social goal pursuit to social acceptance, classroom behavior and perceived social support. *Journal of Educational Psychology* 86: 173–82.

Widiger, T., and Shea, T. 1991. Differentiation of axis I and axis II disorders. *Journal of Abnormal Psychology* 100: 399–406.

Widiger, T. A., Costa, P. T., Jr., and McCrae, R. 2002. A proposal for Axis II: Diagnosing personality disorders using the five-factor model. In P. T. Costa Jr. and T. A. Widiger, eds., *Personality Disorders and the Five-Factor Model of Personality*. Washington, DC: American Psychological Association, pp. 431–56.

Wilson, D. B., Gottfredson, D. C., and Najaka, S. S. 2001. School-based prevention of problem behaviors: A meta-analysis. *Journal of Quantitative Criminology* 17: 247–72.

Wolff, S. 2000. Schizoid personality in childhood and Asperger syndrome. In A. Klin, F. R. Volkmar, and S. S. Sparrow, eds., *Asperger Syndrome*. New York: Guilford Press, pp. 278–305.

Wong, C. S., and Law, K. S. 2002. Development of an emotional intelligence instrument and an investigation of its relationship with leader and follower performance and attitudes. *Leadership Quarterly* 13: 243–74.

Yammarino, F. J., and Bass, B. M. 1990. Long-term forecasting of transformational leadership and its effects among naval officers: some preliminary findings. In K. E. Clark and M. B. Clark, eds., *Measures of Leadership*. West Orange, NJ: Leadership Library of America, Inc., pp. 151–69.

Yousfi, S., Matthews, G., Amelang, M., and Schmidt-Rathjens, C. 2004. Personality and disease: Correlations with multiple trait scores with various illnesses. *Journal of Health Psychology* 9: 627–47.

Yukl, G. 1997. Developing leaders. In D. Druckman, J. Singer, and H. Van Cott, eds., *Enhancing Organizational Performance*. Washington DC: National Academy Press.

Zahn-Waxler, Cummings, E. M., McKnew, D., and Radke-Yarrow, M. 1984. Affective arousal and social interactions in young children of manic depressive parents. *Child Development* 55: 112–22.

Zahn-Waxler, C., Radke-Yarrow, M., and King, R. A. 1979. Child rearing and children's prosocial initiations toward victims of distress. *Child Development* 50: 319–30.

Zapf, D., Knorz, C., and Kulla, M. 1996. On the relationship between mobbing factors, and job content, the social work environment and health outcomes. *European Journal of Work and Organisational Psychology* 5: 215–37.

Zapf, M. K. 1999. Location and knowledge-building: Exploring the fit of western social work with traditional knowledge. *Native Social Work Journal* 2: 139–53.

Zeidner, M. 1998. *Test Anxiety: The State of the Art*. New York: Plenum Press.

Zeidner, M. 2005. Emotional intelligence and coping with occupational stress. In A. G. Antoniou and C. L. Cooper, ed., *New Perspectives in Occupational Health Psychology*. Cheltenham, UK: Edward Elgar, pp. 218–39.

Zeidner, M., and Kaluda, I. (2008). Romantic love: What's emotional intelligence (EI) got to do with it? *Personality and Individual Differences* 44: 1684–1695.

Zeidner, M., Kaluda, I., Olnick, D., Matthews, G., and Roberts, R. D. (under preparation). Emotional intelligence and coping with stress.

Zeidner, M., and Matthews, G. 2000. Personality and intelligence. In R. J. Sternberg, ed., *Handbook of Human Intelligence*, 2nd ed. New York: Cambridge University Press, pp. 359–79.

Zeidner, M., and Matthews, G. 2005. Evaluation anxiety: Current theory and research. In A. J. Elliot and C. S. Dweck, eds., *Handbook of Competence and Motivation*. New York: Guilford Press, pp. 141–63.

Zeidner, M., Matthews, G., and Roberts, R. D. 2001. Slow down, you move too fast: Emotional intelligence remains an "elusive" intelligence. *Emotion* 1: 265–75.

Zeidner, M., Matthews, G., and Roberts, R. D. 2004. Emotional intelligence in the workplace: A critical review. *Applied Psychology: An International Review* 53: 371–99.

Zeidner, M., Matthews, G., and Roberts, R. D. 2006. Emotional intelligence, coping, and adaptation. In J. Ciarrochi, J. Forgas, and J. D. Mayer, eds., *Emotional Intelligence in Everyday Life: A Scientific Inquiry*, 2nd ed. Philadelphia, PA: Psychology Press, pp. 100–25.

Zeidner, M., Matthews, G., Roberts, R. D., and MacCann, C. 2003. Development of emotional intelligence: Towards a multi-level investment model. *Human Development* 46: 69–96.

Zeidner, M., Roberts, R. D., and Matthews, G. 2002. Can emotional intelligence be schooled? A critical review. *Educational Psychologist* 37: 215–31.

Zeidner, M., and Saklofske, D. S. 1996. Adaptive and maladaptive coping. In M. Zeidner and N. S. Endler, eds., *Handbook of Coping*. New York: Wiley, pp. 505–31.

Zeidner, M., Shani-Zinovich, I., Matthews, G., and Roberts, R. D. 2005. Assessing emotional intelligence in gifted and non-gifted high school students: Outcomes depend on the measure. *Intelligence* 33: 369–91.

Zhou, Q., Eisenberg, N., Losoya, S. H., Fabes, R. A., Reiser, M., Guthrie, I. K., Murphy, B. C., Cumberland, A. J., and Shepard, S. A. 2002. The relations of parental warmth and positive expressiveness to children's empathy-related responding and social functioning: A longitudinal study. *Child Development* 73: 893–915.

Zins, J. E., Bloodworth, M. R., Weissberg, R. P., and Walberg, H. 2004. The scientific base linking social and emotional learning to school success. In J. E. Zins, R. P. Weissberg, M. C. Wang, and H. J. Walberg, eds., *Building Academic Success on Social and Emotional Learning: What Does the Research Say?* New York: Teachers College Press, pp. 3–22.

Zins, J. E., Elias, M. J., Greenberg, M. T., and Weissberg, R. P. 2000. Promoting social and emotional competence in children. In K. M. Minke and G. C. Bear, eds., *Preventing School Problems—Promoting School Success: Strategies and Programs That Work*. Washington, DC: National Association of School Psychologists, pp. 71–99.

Zins, J. E., Payton, J. W., Weissberg, R. P., and O'Brien, M. U. 2007. Social and emotional learning for successful school performance. In G. Matthews, M. Zeidner, and R. D. Roberts, eds., *Emotional Intelligence: Knowns and Unknowns*. New York: Oxford University Press, pp. 376–95.

Zins, J., Travis F., III, and Freppan, P. A. 1997. Linking research and educational programming to promote social and emotional learning. In P. Salovey and D. J. Sluyter, eds., *Emotional Development and Emotional Intelligence*. New York: Basic Books, pp. 168–92.

Zins, J. E., Weissberg, R. P., Wang, M. C., and Walberg, H. J., eds. 2004. *Building Academic Success on Social and Emotional Learning: What Does the Research Say?* New York: Teachers College Press.

Zuckerman, M. 2005. *Psychobiology of Personality*, 2nd ed. New York: Cambridge University Press.

Illustration Credits

Index